Martha Vicinus is professor of English literature and women's studies at the University of Michigan. She is the editor of *Suffer and Be Still: Women in the Victorian Age* and *A Widening Sphere: Changing Roles of Victorian Women*. For twelve years the editor of *Victorian Studies*, she has also published in *Feminist Studies*, *Signs*, and many other journals.

Jacket illustration, "Westfield College, June 1889," courtesy of Westfield College, University of London.

Cameron Poulter Design

Printed in U.S.A.

Independent Women

Women in Culture

and

Society

A S E R I E S E D I T E D B Y

Catharine R. Stimpson

Independent Women

WORK AND COMMUNITY FOR SINGLE WOMEN

1850–1920

MARTHA VICINUS

The
University of
Chicago
Press

CHICAGO AND

LONDON

MARTHA VICINUS is professor of English literature
and women's studies at the University of Michigan.
She is the editor of *Suffer and Be Still: Women in the Victorian Age*
and *A Widening Sphere: Changing Roles of Victorian Women*.
For twelve years the editor of *Victorian Studies*,
she has also published in *Feminist Studies, Signs,*
and many other journals.

The University of Chicago Press, Chicago 60637
The University of Chicago Press, Ltd., London

94 93 92 91 90 89 88 87 86 85   54321

Library of Congress Cataloging in Publication Data

Vicinus, Martha.
  Independent women.

  (Women in culture and society)
  Bibliography: p.
  Includes index.
    1. Single women—England—Social conditions.   2. Middle
classes—England—History—19th century.   3. Single
women—Employment—England—History—19th century.
4. Community life. I. Title. II. Series.
HQ800.2.V53   1985   305.4'890652   84-16158
ISBN 0-226-85567-8

For Bea Nergaard

Contents

Contents

Series Editor's Foreword

Studying modern women often demands taking on the historically novel and the new. Martha Vicinus's subject is the middle-
class English woman, the first of her sex who could afford to live
on her own earnings "outside heterosexual domesticity or church
governance." She wanted and needed to work. Meticulous, resonant, original, triumphant, *Independent Women* tells of the efforts and endurance of this Victorian woman; of her courage and
the constraints that she rejected, accepted, and created.

The pivot of *Independent Women* is two generations of women:
those born in the 1840s and 1850s and those born in the 1870s and
1880s. Their precursors were the formidable pioneers—like Florence Nightingale—born before 1830. They built women's communities and spaces: boarding schools, colleges, convents, nursing corps. The second generation was more apt than the first to
demand social and political change. After 1920 those institutions
and demands seemed obsolete, a decline that Vicinus maps with
control and sensitivity. Yet the independent women are the "foremothers" of any woman today who seeks significant work, emotionally satisfying friendships, and a morally charged freedom.

Independent Women has the lucidity that a scholar achieves
only at the end of deep immersion in a question or a period. Vicinus
adroitly balances material and psychic realities. She respects our
foremothers and their energetic wrestling with their moment. She
realizes, for example, that their mazelike homoerotic friendships
were not "immature" but were "an effort to balance three problematic areas: sexuality, spirituality, and power."

Equally, Vicinus respects complexity. She knows that we balk
and stumble as we struggle with, and for, change. She incisively
analyzes the tensions among overwhelming Victorian ideologies,
women's needs, and actual practices. She is alert to the fact that
the institutions her independent women created were at once

"powerful and peripheral"; that class divisions riddled their lives; that their expressions of friendship were often passionate, valuable, and naive; and that the myth of women's difference in which genteel Victorian women believed, and which they manipulated, has insidious dangers. Yet Vicinus's capacity for complexity permits her to balance irony with tact, judgment with grace.

I hope that the historian of independent women and their institutions in the middle and late twentieth century will have the compassionate, realistic, bountiful intelligence of the author of *Independent Women*.

Catharine R. Stimpson

Acknowledgments

This book could not have been written but for the women's movement of the past fifteen years. The very idea of a book about work and communities of women is a product of this generation's search for its roots in the first modern women's movement of the nineteenth century. Moreover, I have been encouraged and sustained throughout the research and writing by women's groups, conferences, and publications. Without this essential intellectual exchange I would never have experienced the necessary testing and refining of ideas so important to scholarly growth. My debt, therefore, is not simply to those whom I thank, but in a larger sense to the women's movement as a whole, through which I have learned and shared so much.

Throughout my work I have been supported by scholarly institutions. I am grateful to Indiana University for a summer faculty research grant and for a sabbatical leave during the early stages of my research. A timely small grant from the University of Michigan during the final stages enabled me to hire a typist and an assistant for statistical work. I also received a most generous American Council of Learned Societies summer grant-in-aid of research in 1979, and a John Simon Guggenheim fellowship in 1980–81. These two grants enabled me to complete my research and to write most of the book without the distraction of other responsibilities.

The far-ranging nature of my research has introduced me to new libraries and new scholars; I owe a great debt to those who so readily responded to my requests for information, research materials, and manuscript readings. Scholars I had never met generously shared their specialties with me, exchanging unpublished articles and hard-won research information and critiquing my work with a keenness that has substantially improved the quality of each chapter. I can affirm that I have found a community of working scholars equal to any I describe here. Friends responded with unfailing generosity and goodwill, even when my research and think-ing veered far from their own specialties. Gail Malmgreen read each chapter in an early version, sensing my overall purpose amid the often unwieldy and inchoate pages I sent her. I also owe her a special debt for helping me find appropriate photographs. Judith R. Walkowitz read the final version, offering acute and helpful criti-cism while reminding me of the general historical debate within which my own subject lives. Donna Wessel Walker read the entire book with a keen eye, pointing out the differences between En-glish and American readers; her comments and encouragement were most timely. Bea Nergaard assisted in uncounted ways, from tracking down remote references to checking notes; she read each chapter more than once, with a fine sense of the major issues and the interplay of the personal and the public. But most important, she reminded me of the larger purpose of the book itself. Margaret Maison, with great generosity, wrote to me from Oxford offering to read each chapter and to check the quotations and notes. One of the unforeseen pleasures of writing this book has been her as-sistance. As a link with the generations I have written about, I hope that she has found the book worthy of them, and of her own pioneering research. Suzanne Burr was the ideal research assis-tant, cheerfully hunting down sources, ordering interlibrary loans and providing photocopies on short notice. Nancy Horn researched the census returns for the tables in chapter 1; I am grateful for her thorough work. Tish O'Dowd Ezekiel took countless photographs of murky Victorian pictures; unless otherwise credited, all illus-trations were photographed by her, and I am grateful for her pa-tience and skill. Warren Olin-Ammentorp typed the manuscript with enviable speed and efficiency on a word processor new to him and to me; my thanks for his careful work.

Individual chapters were read and criticized by friends and fel-low scholars. Barbara Sicherman offered extremely useful com-ments on chapters 1 and 5 at a time when I was struggling with too much material. Brian Heeney, Michael Hill, and the Deacon-ess Community of St. Andrew critiqued chapter 2. Celia Davies and Christopher Maggs not only read chapter 3, but also put me in touch with the growing number of historians interested in nurs-ing. Sheldon Rothblatt, Ann Philips, and Gillian Sutherland read chapter 4; Gillian Sutherland sent me difficult-to-obtain refer-ences as well as her own work in progress, which is quoted here with her permission. Joyce Senders Pedersen brought her unique

Acknowledgments

xiii

knowledge of girls' education to her reading of chapter 5. Chapter 6 was read with the keen eye of a participant by Gladys Barrett. Chapter 7 was fully and most generously read by my study group, as well as by members of the international conference on "The New Woman and the New Family." Last, a special note of thanks to Ellen Ross and Ann Summers for their fine critiques of the book. Ellen Ross generously offered to reread a revised version of the introduction and first chapter during the final stages of writing; her detailed suggestions were invaluable.

No foreigner working in England can do without the assistance of librarians who know and love their collections. Often without sufficient time to spend taking detailed notes, I have had to rely upon a librarian to find an item, photocopy it, and send it to me. I owe a special debt to not only the speciality libraries, but also the British Library, whose facilities remain one of the greatest gifts to a scholar. Every scholar who works on Victorian women knows the value of the Fawcett Library, City of London Polytechnic; the tireless enthusiasm of David Doughan often cheered me during long days of work. Thanks also to the Greater London Record Office, which now holds the records of the Nightingale Training School; permission to quote material from these archives has been granted by St. Thomas' Hospital. My thanks also to the Royal College of Nursing and the Boston University Nursing Archives. I spent four rainy days at the Pusey House Library, Oxford, happily re-creating the early days of Anglican sisterhoods. Special thanks are due to the Society of St. Margaret's, East Grinstead, the Deaconess Community of St. Andrew's, and the Community of St. John Baptist, Clewer. All three communities welcomed me into their midst, sharing not only their archives but also their daily lives. I consider it a rare privilege to have been introduced to Victorian sisterhoods by those who carry on, yet alter, their traditions. At Cheltenham Ladies' College, I examined both the archives and the famous stained glass windows of feminine heroines. Victoria Moger, Special Collections, the Museum of London, shared her knowledge of the suffrage movement with me, as well as expeditiously providing me with materials from their rich collection of unpublished materials, memorabilia, photographs, and prison records. The settlement house movement has been much less careful about preserving its archives than has the militant suffrage movement. I have had to depend upon published records deposited in the London Borough of Hackney Library, Southwark Borough Library, and the Tower Hamlets Local History Library. The Women's University Settlement is the happy exception; I have been guided through its archives by Gladys Barrett, who is writing a history of the settlement, now called the Blackfriars Settlement. The women's colleges of Newnham, Girton, Lady Margaret Hall, Somerville, and Westfield all welcomed me. I am most grateful for the assistance of S. M. G. Reynolds of Lady Margaret Hall, Margaret Gaskell of Girton, and Lady Anne de Villiers of Somerville. Ann Phillips and Jane Heal introduced me to Newnham's archives and traditions, and when I had finished my research they sent me off with an Ordanance Survey map for a day of cycling in Cambridgeshire. Janet Sondheimer of Westfield College shared her enthusiasm for Constance Maynard, the founder of Westfield College, as well as giving me incomparable facilities for studying the college archives. Finally, I was very dependent upon the services of the interlibrary loan departments at the University of California, Berkeley, the University of British Columbia, Indiana University, and the University of Michigan; without their aid I could never have followed up countless references. I am most grateful to the librarians of these universities for their assistance.

During my years of research I called upon the expertise of many friends and scholars, including not only those that I have mentioned above, but also Rosemary Auchmuty, who lent me her doctoral thesis on Victorian spinsters just as I was beginning my own work, Janet Murray, who shared the bibliographic information and files for her fine anthology *Strong-Minded Women*, Jane Marcus, who generously shared her knowledge and love of early twentieth-century feminism and literature, and Harry C. Payne, who sent me his forthcoming chapter on Jane Harrison and shared with me his research and understanding of her and her circle. Emily Abel, Joan Burstyn, Ruth C. Claus, Alan Deacon, Carol Dyhouse, Edward Ellsworth, Patricia Otto Klaus, Catherine Nelson, David Rubinstein, Ann Scott, Elaine Showalter, Louise Tilly, Thea Thompson, and others mentioned in the appropriate notes all answered my queries about their areas of research and shared their work with me. Leonore Davidoff and Anna Davin deserve special mention for their constant encouragement over the years; each has provided both support and references, never forgetting the work of her friends, even in the midst of her own responsibilities.

I shall close with an anecdote that captures some of the concerns of this book as well as the supportive environment within which I researched and wrote it. At a gathering in England we were discussing the change to coeducation at Oxford and Cambridge and its possible effect upon both women and men, students and staff. One friend mentioned that the former women's colleges were now making an effort to hire more men, so that their new male undergraduates would have appropriate role models. Another mentioned the defeat of an effort to open All Soul's, Oxford, to women. Then, as if by inspiration, one person lifted her glass in a toast to the first woman principal of Balliol College, Oxford. As the premier intellectual college of Oxford, how long will it be before it recognizes the talents and capabilities of a woman in such fashion? This question can mark, perhaps, how far we have yet to travel on the road to equality of opportunity and recognition. Only a little over a hundred years ago, women were tentatively permitted to attend separate lectures and to take portions of the examinations at Oxford and Cambridge. Now, with coeducation, will women go forward or backward?

Portions of chapters 1, 4, 5, and 7 have appeared previously in a different form in *Feminist Studies*, *Signs*, and *A Century of Change: Women in Culture and Politics*, edited by Judith Friedlander, Blanche Wiesen Cook, Alice Kessler-Harris, and Carroll Smith Rosenberg (Bloomington: Indiana University Press, 1985). I am grateful for permission to reprint this material.

Introduction

Harken, O Eve, Mother of us all, greatest and grandest of women: you who have been maligned all down the ages, know at
least that one of your daughters blesses you, and proclaims
your choice good. To you, oh Eve, we owe it that we are as
gods, and not as children playing in the garden—that we know
the good and evil and are not lapt in ignorance and lust. Man
had stayed ever in uninquiring peace, but to you was given
strength to grasp the apple, to proclaim that woman at least
prefers wisdom and the wilderness to idle lasciviousness in
Eden.[1]

At the end of the nineteenth century when Honnor Morten ex-
ultantly rewrote the fall of Eve, women seemed on the edge of revolutionary change. Half a century of agitation, work, and education had radically changed conditions for them, so that the more
daring hoped women might be the leaders in forming a new society. Morten saw her generation as part of a phalanx of women
who individually and collectively had escaped the confining "garden" of homelife into freedom and adventure. During the 1890s
Morten went to Bedford College, trained at a London hospital,
served on the London School Board, and started a settlement in
the East End before she became a Tolstoyan and opened a home in
the country for sick children. She seized the opportunities pioneered by an earlier generation of women, but she never forgot the
importance of further change. Morten believed passionately that,
in order to help others, unmarried women of the middle class had
a right and duty to train for and seek out paid work. This passion
for meaningful work, so often underestimated and misunderstood,
was the sacred center of nineteenth-century single women's lives
and communities. It was the means out of the garden, out of idleness, out of ignorance, and into wisdom, service, and adventure.

Morton's enthusiasm came in the midst of the struggle of

middle-class single women to gain public respect for their work. The distance women had traveled in little over fifty years can be measured by the bitter comments of an earlier generation, who paced narrow gardens, locked out of wider experience and the opportunity to serve themselves or others. Florence Nightingale, born in 1820, despaired of finding work to meet her talents and energies. After dragging through her twenties, at thirty-two she cried out, "Why have women passion, intellect, moral activity—these three—and a place in society where no one of the three can be exercised? . . . Give us back our suffering, we cry to Heaven in our hearts—suffering rather than indifferentism; for out of nothing comes nothing."[2] Nightingale's secret agony was felt by countless women of her generation. Many must have found a solution of sorts in daydreaming, an activity that occupied Nightingale as she listened to her father read snippets of the newspaper and her mother chatter about social engagements.[3] Elaborate fantasies of heroic action seemed almost essential for an intelligent and ambitious woman desiring a public—and therefore male—role at midcentury.

Since the middle of the eighteenth century the doctrine of separate spheres—he for the public, she for the private—had been gaining strength. Society had been marked by a progressive isolation of different classes and sexes; the economic and social upheaval of the times was controlled by erecting clear boundaries. Rigid social rules ensured the safety of the bourgeois family; within the home women were assigned a special position as caretakers of morality and religion, for their unique sensibility made them alone capable of child care and domestic responsibilities. Their influence, however, was based upon preconceived ideas of female characteristics.[4] As a wife and mother, a woman could have power, but only within a carefully delimited sphere. An ideal of domesticity masked the exclusion of middle-class women from political, economic, and social power.

The higher standard of living made possible by industrialization carried a major drawback: middle- and upper-class men and women were unwilling to marry until they could support a family in a suitable style. After a generation of advising the rising middle class on the proper age, circumstances, income, and style for marrying, the authors of advice books did an about-face in the 1850s and 1860s and began warning men and women against expecting excessive luxury and waiting too long before marrying.[5] Men's reluctance to marry was blamed on women for being "fast" or too expensive. Metaphors of industry and commerce dominated the debate. Eliza Lynn Linton attacked "the Girl of the Period," "whose sole idea of life [was] plenty of fun and luxury" and who married for "his house, his carriage, his balance at the banker's, his title."[6] The *Saturday Review*, antifeminist throughout the century, suggested that women should not be offered a viable economic alternative, lest they never marry. A woman who failed to find a husband or lost him after marriage was dismissed with the comment, "she has failed in business, and no social reform can prevent such failures."[7]

By the mid-nineteenth century middle-class spinsters appeared to have no larger purpose in life. Single women had held key positions in preindustrial society, including the management of large convents in the Middle Ages, the administration of vast estates during the Renaissance, and the running of countless shops, small businesses, and inns throughout the early modern period in English history. But increased wealth and the consolidation of bourgeois social values in the early nineteenth century condemned spinsters to unremitting idleness and to marginal positions in the home, church, and workplace. The genteel poor woman had a choice of three underpaid and overcrowded occupations—governess, companion, or seamstress. Voluntary work among the poor and needy was severely circumscribed by social custom and organized religion. Yet the numbers of "redundant women" appeared to be rising dramatically as their status fell. How could these women be made to fit into the rigid social pattern decreed by their culture and class?

For middle-class social commentators the plight of the single woman was symbolic of the larger social disorder brought about by industrialization and urbanization. One of the best-known solutions to "the woman question" was proposed by the influential journalist W. R. Greg in 1862, under the title "Why Are Women Redundant?" He lamented the unnatural number of single women living in industrial England:

> there is an enormous and increasing number of single women
> in the nation, a number quite disproportionate and quite ab-
> normal; a number which, positively and relatively, is indica-
> tive of an unwholesome social state, and is both productive
> and prognostic of much wretchedness and wrong. There are

hundreds of thousands of women—not to speak more largely still—scattered through all ranks, but proportionally most numerous in the middle and upper classes,—who have to earn their own living, instead of spending and husbanding the earnings of men; who, not having the natural duties and labours of wives and mothers, have to carve out artificial and painfully-sought occupations for themselves; who, in place of completing, sweetening, and embellishing the existence of others, are compelled to lead an independent and incomplete existence of their own.[8]

For Greg and his peers, woman's only true place was "embellishing the existence of others." In his calculations of the number of redundant women in England, he eliminated domestic servants because "they fulfill both essentials of woman's being; *they are supported by and they minister to, men.*"[9] Greg's solution was twofold: first, the bulk of the estimated 750,000 single women over thirty should be sent to Canada, Australia, and the United States, where men were in the majority by some 440,000. While admitting the difficulty of getting enough ships to Liverpool, Greg believed that emigration to a better marriage market was the best solution for single women. Second, he advised those who stayed at home to learn from upper-class courtesans. Women should make themselves so agreeable that men would prefer marriage to their mistresses and clubs. Moreover, both men and women should give up the prevailing love of luxury and aim for a more modest style of life that would make earlier marriage possible. The "artificial" state of the remaining 310,000 unmarried women would be solved by coquetry and common sense.

Greg's solutions drew fire from the small number of feminists of the day, but his underlying assumptions remained popular throughout the century.[10] The very stridency with which Greg and other commentators insisted upon pushing spinsters into their "natural" sphere is a clue to the discomfort Victorians felt about the position of women. Both women and men were trapped by an ideology that proclaimed roles for each sex that were often at odds with the realities of daily life. The family, moreover, could not remain isolated from the larger social forces of the day. Victorian society encouraged both physical and social mobility, individual development, and hard work. These liberal values were antithetical to the ideal of female behavior—namely, the submission of self, voluntary labor, and a minimum of mobility outside the family circle. An idle wife or daughter might increase a man's status, but society provided a countervailing pressure by rewarding self-improvement and the conscientious performance of philanthropic duties. Contradictions within and outside the family created an environment that made change possible.

Single woman could be successful and independent, however, yet still be labeled "superfluous" by social commentators. A major task was the reworking of so pervasive an ideology. Victorian England had created a symbolic triad, binding a woman to extremes: she was either the ideal mother/wife or a celibate spinster or a promiscuous prostitute. Greg's recommendation that the unmarried learn from courtesans in order to catch a man simply underscores this triangle of mythic possibilities. Much has been written about the Victorian prostitute as a mirror image of the ideal Victorian lady, but scholars have neglected the division between the single woman and the mother (the role of wife was clearly subordinate in this mythology). Since genteel single women could be neither mothers nor prostitutes, they were forced to redefine themselves in terms beyond those of the nuclear family. If the prostitute symbolized the extremes of unbridled passion and evil in woman, the spinster had thrust upon her absolute purity and goodness. She was supposed to remain virginal and utterly self-sacrificing for all who needed her. Single women transformed this passive role into one of active spirituality and passionate social service. Celibacy, within the context of loving friendships, became a vital and empowering ideal. Women did not reject the Victorian myths but reinterpreted them.

The ideology of spiritual leadership went hand in hand with changing economic and social conditions. Victorian England needed cheap skilled labor for the multiplying bureaucracies of business and government; education was growing rapidly; and the level of health care was rising. Educated single women were direct beneficiaries of this expansion.[11] The percentage of the total working population holding such positions as teacher, nurse, shop assistant, clerk, and civil servant increased from 7.6 percent in 1861 to 14.1 percent in 1911; the percentage of women workers in these occupations rose from 5.0 percent to 16.4 percent[12] Although salaries remained meager and working conditions often poor, educated women workers found an increasing number and variety of jobs opening throughout the second half of the century. No matter how contradictory family life might have been during this time, without the commensurate growth in suitable work for women middle-class single women would not have been able to survive outside the nuclear family.

For the first time in history a small group of middle-class women could afford to live, however poorly, on their own earnings outside heterosexual domesticity or church governance. This book analyzes their new opportunities and the ways they used them. Once labeled anomalous, these better-off women reacted against this status; they led in the creation of an active women's movement, seeking not only political change and education, but also jobs and ultimately, as Morton implied, a whole new way of structuring their lives. Middle-class single women had the education, economic opportunities, and personal confidence to take advantage of larger social changes. Perhaps most important of all, like their male counterparts, they believed passionately in the morally redeeming power of work; paid public work would give them dignity and independence. These women pioneered new occupations, new living conditions, and new public roles that have all had important implications for the twentieth-century woman, single or married.

I have excluded widows from my study, although they were clearly an important part of the life of every social class. B. L. Hutchins, the Fabian sociologist, estimated that in 1901 one out of every eight women was a widow.[13] Historically and to the present day, they have suffered from economic and social invisibility, but no one could claim that widows, beset with the problems of raising children and working, were redundant. Their unique economic and social status deserves a separate study. So too, I neglect the experiences and circumstances of working-class single women; their very different opportunities and constraints should also be explored separately. I am concerned here with the expanding middle class, including not only the more prominent upper middle class, edging into the aristocracy, but also the middle middle and the lower middle class. The fathers of single women from these classes ranged from the wealthy merchants who benefited so spectacularly from England's increase in foreign trade to the anonymous clerks who worked for the empire builders. Many of the most publicly visible single women had fathers who lived by their professional skills, such as clergymen, doctors, lawyers, military officers, and middle managers in the burgeoning industries. These daughters could expect little in the way of an income after the death of their fathers, and so had the most to gain from the new educational and job opportunities.

This book brings together very different movements and occupations affecting women and argues for their unity of purpose. I believe that women are never passive participants in the larger culture but actively transform and redefine their external constraints.[14] My focus is upon single women as leaders in the ideological battle for women's rights, and as the persons most affected by the opening of respectable alternatives to marriage. The heroic pioneers—Anna Jameson, Florence Nightingale, Barbara Bodichon, and Frances Power Cobbe—were all born before 1830. They laid the foundation for a generation who built institutions that then grew in directions well beyond their original conception. I concentrate upon the women who built and sustained separate women's communities—those largely born in the 1840s and 1850s, and then a second generation, born in the 1870s and 1880s, who took the cause one step further, demanding political and social changes. I am especially interested in the ways in which single women effectively altered the negative connotations of "redundancy," creating new models for women's public roles. How and when single women fought for public recognition, what they gained, and what they lost are all important aspects of building a woman's world.

My focus upon residential institutions is a means of examining the ways women ordered their space and time when given the opportunity.[15] A woman-controlled space became an experiment in the operation of what today would be described as women's culture. Since even women who lived outside an institution frequently worked with and through one in order to participate in the benefits of a women's community, I believe that examining work-based institutions is essential to understanding the Victorian single woman. Formal institutions were alternatives to the nuclear family. Within them we can see the development of leadership skills, friendship networks, and a power base for public work. Earlier scholars have already described the process of institution building; I am concerned with the daily lives of women within these cherished new "homes." The ways women organized their time, their work priorities, and their leisure activities are analyzed. Friendships, rituals, and customs are examined closely, for they cemented bonds of loyalty and affection. My central focus is the emotional, spiritual, and social significance of women's separate institutions.

The two generations discussed here combined the personal and political, the private and public, in a way that has attracted our own generation. But their institutions and lives differed in many ways from our own. The women's movement of the 1970s and 1980s has also built new institutions, but these have most often been in opposition, rather than complementary, to existing male-dominated institutions. Thus we have built alternative health centers, whereas in the nineteenth century women started nurses' schools in order to work in hospitals. Some of us have deliberately chosen separatism from men, while the pioneers were separatists by necessity. They were labeled deviant because they did not marry; in our generation deviancy has been applied to lesbians far more than to single women as a category. Active sexuality always meant heterosexuality in the past, so that intense friendships flourished in a supportive, yet often claustrophobic, environment. The impetus for public reform was based upon a sense of moral superiority. As the *Woman's Signal* insisted, the "woman's revolt" was a revolt "that is Puritan and not Bohemian. It is an uprising against the tyranny of organized intemperance, impurity, mammonism, and selfish motives."[16] Such puritanism has by and large been rejected in the twentieth century.

Yet both women's movements share many beliefs and hopes. Women today have continued the tradition of their predecessors in public service, fighting to maintain and extend help to the powerless and needy. Struggles for equal pay, child care, abortion rights, health care, and countless other issues all have their roots in the nineteenth century. The very longevity and persistence of our foremothers provides an increasingly important model for activists today. The specifically religious basis upon which so many pioneers argued for greater freedom lives on, transformed into a more general belief in women's spirituality. Many women have begun to reclaim celibacy as a valid alternative to the sexual demands of our times. Under the impact of the modern-day women's movement, issues previously thought to have been settled during the early years of the twentieth century have come under fresh scrutiny. For example, early twentieth-century psychologists and anthropologists effectively overturned the Victorian belief in the innate "natural" differences between maternal women and aggressive men. Present-day psychologists Nancy Chodorow and Carol

Gilligan have now again argued that there are profound psychological and even moral differences between men and women.[17] The
strengths and weaknesses of the nineteenth century live on, even
when changed beyond immediate recognition.

About 1849 the brilliant unmarried Geraldine Jewsbury wrote
her friend, the married Jane Carlyle, a poignant letter describing
the current position of women. They were poised on the edge of
great changes, she ardently hoped:

> I believe we are touching on better days, when women will
> have a genuine, normal life of their own to lead. There, per-
> haps, will not be so many marriages, and women will be
> taught not to feel their destiny *manqué* if they remain single.
> They will be able to be friends and companions in a way that
> they cannot be now. . . . I regard myself as a mere faint indica-
> tion, a rudiment of the idea, of certain higher qualities and
> possibilities that lie in women, and all the eccentricities and
> mistakes and miseries and absurdities I have made are only
> the consequences of an imperfect formation, an immature
> growth.[18]

Jewsbury self-consciously concluded, "but I can see there is a
precious mine of a species of womanhood yet undreamed of by the
professors and essayists on female education, and I believe also
that we belong to it. So there is a modest climax!"[19] But hers was
not a modest climax. Single women did go on to create a new
"species of womanhood." Indeed, Jewsbury herself lived long
enough to disapprove of the early feminists. The higher qualities
and possibilities, longed for by these two intellectual friends, became realities for the next two generations.

As we celebrate the achievements of this group of women, we
need to evaluate them in terms of a larger historical context.
A close examination of the personal lives and public careers of
single women reveals no simple picture of either passive suffering
or steady improvement; rather, the women and their institutions
appear simultaneously powerful and peripheral. The seven chapters of this book explore this paradox of power and marginality, of
enormous strength within narrow limits, of unity and support
linked with division and doubt. Over a period of sixty-odd years
independent women and their institutions changed and developed
under the constraints of their own weaknesses and the power of
established traditions, social opinion, and economic weakness.

I

The Revolt against Redundancy

At midcentury virtually all commentators agreed that a single woman from the middle class should remain at home throughout her adulthood and fulfill her duties as daughter and sister. But the murmur of private complaints and criticism against this narrow interpretation of a spinster's duties was rising; all was not well in a world where so many young women longed for action in a wider sphere than their own families. Conservative spokespersons redoubled their efforts to demonstrate the attractiveness of staying at home. One of the most popular explorations of the life of the unmarried daughter was Charlotte Yonge's *The Daisy Chain; or, Aspirations* (1856). The young heroine, Ethel May, at first tries to keep up with her brother's Greek lessons and rushes heedlessly into reforming the local poor. Over nearly seven hundred pages she learns to subdue her pride and folly and finally comes to accept her true role in life as the family's surrogate mother. She resigns herself at twenty-three to a useful spinsterhood serving her widowed father and numerous brothers and sisters. Her thoughtful acceptance of this role prepares her to face a life of loneliness and thankless toil:

> she had begun to understand that the unmarried woman must not seek undivided return of affection, and must not set her love, with exclusive eagerness, on aught below, but must be ready to cease in turn to be first with any. . . . She felt that this was the probable course, and that she might look to becoming comparatively solitary in the course of years—then tried to realize what her lonely life might be, but broke off smiling at herself, "What is that to me? What will it be when it is over? My course and aim are straight on, and He will direct my paths. . . . Some one there must be to be loved and helped, and the poor for certain."[1]

11

Yonge reassures her readers that although Ethel feels forgotten, "her kind heart, upright intention, and force of character, had influence far beyond her own perception. Indeed, she knew not that she had personal influence at all, but went on in her own straightforward humility."[2] In spite of her dislike of such tasks as sewing and nursing, Ethel's womanly heart ties her to her family, who reward her with love and respect. But Yonge especially praises Ethel's complete selflessness; she and many others severely castigated any self-consciousness or self-assertion on the part of a single woman.

Much of *The Daisy Chain's* popularity among readers of the mid-Victorian period must have come from its comforting portrayal of a large and happy middle-class family, composed of good but faulty boys and girls. But Ethel May touched a chord in the hearts of many aspiring young girls who wanted to follow their brothers into the active, hardworking world of industrial England and its empire. In 1856 all of England was ringing with the achievements of Florence Nightingale and her small band of nurses who had just returned from the Crimea. As early as 1840 the Quaker Elizabeth Fry (safely married) had started the Institution for Nursing Sisters, and throughout the 1840s and early 1850s numerous high-church residential sisterhoods were founded to work with the poor. Louisa Twining and her friends had already begun visiting workhouses to read the Bible and give comfort to inmates; in 1858 she started the Workhouse Visiting Society in order to fight overseers who forbade women to visit. These early organizations were all founded upon the principle that women had a natural aptitude for helping the poor, and a right to do so.

Yonge, as a conservative high-church spinster, was writing in a combative rather than a complacent spirit. Familiar herself with the temptations of joining a sisterhood, she felt the tensions and urgency of the issue of women's work. She made Ethel's decision to suppress her ambitions palatable by showing how powerful she was within the domestic sphere; her father cannot do without her, even though one son is preparing to go into partnership with him, another is a curate nearby, and his best friend lives next door. Womanly influence is essential for the happiness of the May household. But Ethel's power is limited to the humble round of home duties; should she look further abroad than teaching in the local church school, she would be punished by failure or social ostracism. Single women in fiction were not permitted to be single and happy outside a carefully defined set of family duties.

12

Charlotte Yonge's unmarried heroine was a sign of the historical times. Behind the literary portrayal of the good daughter lies the question why middle-class single women were seen as a problem during the Victorian period. All available historical evidence points to a large number of unmarried women and men throughout European history. Like so many other social causes discovered by the Victorians to be problems—sanitation, slums, and slavery come to mind—single women of the middle class had survived for centuries unnoticed. Women who could not or would not follow Ethel May's example had somehow to be made to fit. Yet many a young woman found herself seeking outside work by choice or necessity.

Discontent with women's lot, already expressed among Owenite and antislavery women, was slowly spreading throughout middle-class society in the 1850s and 1860s.[3] The single woman necessarily took a leadership position in the effort to redefine woman's role in society. Her very lack of an ascribed role in private—she was not a mother or a wife—and in public—she was not part of the male political and social spheres—was to prove both drastically limiting and immensely liberating. Single women had to tackle their marginal position ideologically, economically, and socially. First a rationale had to be found to justify creating a new role for women in which they could be both public, that is, paid workers, and feminine, that is, domestic. Second, the economic position of women who had to work, or wanted to, had to be improved through better training, increased job opportunities, and adequate pay. Third, alternatives to the nuclear family had to be created so that single women could live respectably away from home; surrogate families would turn an unpleasant necessity—work—into a happier existence. These areas clearly overlap; a perceived need for better jobs went hand in hand with a rationale for raising the single woman's status and, in many occupations, so did residential living quarters. Nevertheless, the solution to the "problem" of the single woman can best be understood through a separate consideration of each area.

The Mid-Victorian Debate

Ethel May was fortunate in having her life's duties set before her. But in reality many middle-class single women were not needed at home; their time hung heavily day after day. Alternatively, a young woman might find herself fighting an unequal battle for sufficient work at reasonable pay to support herself and dependent relatives. Between these two extremes were many women who could not count on any home or income after the death of their parents, or who had to start contributing as soon as they were able to do so. They needed marketable skills and they knew it. Nevertheless, all of these women, whatever their personal circumstances, were warned against working for pay and advised to follow Ethel's path. The discrepancy between the ideal and the reality gave reformers their principal weapon in the struggle to improve the status and opportunities of single women. But it was uphill work: young women and their families assumed they would marry until it was too late to seek skilled training; it was widely believed that any marriage was better than being an old maid; and women themselves were isolated from each other and almost wholly lacking in positive role models. Counterbalancing these factors were the Victorian British economy's obvious need for trained women, the frustration of a number of brilliant and well-to-do women willing to become leaders, and the demands of the needy women themselves.

In spite of the substantial numbers of middle-class women who sought work, conservative upper-class commentators wrote exclusively about the spinster at home. The 1850s and 1860s saw a spate of advice books for such women, all recommending religion and restraint. The married author of *The Afternoon of Unmarried Life* (1858) condescendingly advised,

> On the ground of self-preservation, it behoves every unmarried woman to find some harmless mode of doing active service; for, if she is without it, she inevitably becomes the prey of her own egotism, especially if she is exposed to the pernicious influence of a very secluded life, as certainly dangerous to spiritual health, as the miasma of standing water to health of the body.[4]

She recommended gardening as an innocuous antidote to "that state of unbalanced religious excitement" to which many older spinsters were prone.[5] Women were to subdue all emotions in silence, isolated from both fellow sufferers and the consolations of an extreme enthusiasm.

Fiction, advice books, and memoirs present a vivid picture of time hanging heavily upon a woman confined to a tiny space in the corner of her family's home. This was, indeed, often the situation in reality. The well-to-do Constance Maynard (1849–1935), who went on to pioneer in higher education, spent the years between fifteen and twenty-three at home with her three older sisters caring for her invalid mother. Each sister willingly spent several hours daily at her mother's bedside, but time hung heavily and was filled with projects that seemed to go nowhere. Maynard could find privacy only by fleeing to the far end of the orchard, where she studied Greek, theology, and history; she was not permitted to leave the family estate unescorted. Later in life she felt that she and her sisters had been shut up "like eagles in a hen house."[6] Maynard finally left for college, and one other sister escaped into nursing, but two sisters spent their lives dispensing charity and meeting trivial responsibilities. Less self-disciplined daughters than the Maynards took to novel reading or psychosomatic illnesses; the foolishly flirtatious or mysteriously ill maiden sister reflected in fiction what had often become a reality.

Maynard's spatial limitations and lack of privacy were characteristic of the situation of the genteel single woman. After she had escaped, Maynard was dismayed at the childlike, stunted lives of her two sisters at home, even though she admired their saintly selflessness. As they aged, she felt, they had lost the ability to think and act for themselves. Single women could not be given a place of their own within the family because they were ancillary to their mother or married sisters, and because their state was considered temporary. To give them space—and independence— was to admit not only their failure in the marriage market, but also their family's. Unmarried daughters were therefore expected to be invisible, doing good without thanks, forbearing to give advice, yet always available when needed. At times it seemed as if the only space freely allotted to a spinster was the grave. In the words of Dinah Mulock Craik, she could look forward to death as the culmination of

> A finished life—a life which has made the best of all the materials granted to it, and through which, be its web dark or bright, its pattern clear or clouded, can now be traced plainly the hand of the Great Designer; surely this is worth living for? And though at its end it may be somewhat lonely; though a servant's and not a daughter's arm may guide the failing step; though most likely it will be strangers only who come about the dying bed, close the eyes that no husband ever kissed, and

draw the shroud kindly over the poor withered breast where
no child's head has ever lain; still, such a life is not to be
pitied, for it is a completed life.[7]

The single woman at mid-century knew her marginality but was
actively forbidden to look outside her home for a remedy.

The problem of the single woman could be solved only by altering the divisions between men and women, between the public
and the private; yet any radical change was unthinkable for the
middle class. The question then became: What changes could be
made that would improve the lot of spinsters without disturbing
the ascribed areas and roles of each sex? The answer lay in carrying the domestic world into the public or, in the words of an early
feminist, Anna Jameson, "that the *maternal* as well as the *pater-
nal* element should be made available, on the principal which I
believe is now generally acknowledged, that the more you can
carry out the family law, the 'communion of labour,' into all social institutions, the more harmonious and the more perfect they
will be."[8] English feminists responded to the plight of the idle and
unhappy spinster by arguing for woman's unique contribution to
the public world. The principle of complementarity gave single
women a means of entering into new work; they could make a
maternal contribution to "all social institutions." Reformers at
first appear to have accepted marginal roles and subsidiary spheres
for women as an unreflective adaptation to what seemed possible;
only later in the century did they turn their argument for "special
spheres" into a conscious strategy. Over the long run an ideology
based upon woman's innate nature had benefits and liabilities that
could not be foreseen during the early struggles to gain respect for
single women's work.

At first women did not claim arenas already controlled by men,
such as politics; rather, they captured unclaimed areas and pushed
out from there. The public debate about conditions among the urban poor gave reformers the opening they needed. Surely, they argued, women should carry the virtues of the home into the wider
world, to raise the moral tone of the workhouse, hospital, school,
or other public institution. In the words of the moderate feminist
Frances Power Cobbe:

The private and home duties of *such women as have them*
are, beyond all doubt, their first concern, and one which,
when fully met, must often engross all their time and ener-

gies. But it is an absurdity, peculiar to the treatment of women, to go on assuming that all of them *have* home duties, and tacitly treating those who have none as if they were wrongly placed on God's earth, and had nothing whatever to do in it. There must needs be a purpose for the lives of single women in the social order of Providence . . . she has *not* fewer duties than others, but more extended and perhaps laborious ones. Not selfishness—gross to a proverb—but self-sacrifice more entire than belongs to the double life of marriage, is the true law of celibacy.[9]

Cobbe was one of the best-known promulgators of a freely chosen celibacy. She was among the first feminists to carve out a satisfying and happy life as a journalist and public lecturer on such favorite topics as suffrage, education, antivivisection, homeopathy, and child welfare.[10] But part of her success was surely due to her willingness to work within the traditional definitions of women's duties; Cobbe was an effective spokesperson for self-sacrifice rather than self-development.

Very few feminists fought for women as human beings who were potentially equal to men in intellect, instincts, and morals— a radical message unacceptable until the early years of the twentieth century.[11] The ideas of the eighteenth-century radicals and the Owenite socialists of the first half of the nineteenth century were forgotten in the quest for respectability.[12] A single woman was trapped in a paradox: the price of independence was the reinforcement of sexual stereotyping. Her personal ambition had to be hidden from herself and society under the cloak of self-sacrifice. Women who often had turned down offers of marriage and had no interest in children spent their lives strengthening the nuclear family among the poor and needy. As long as they were not too obviously happy with their situation or too assertive about their demands for themselves, independent women could be accepted.[13] Both they and society emphasized duties, not rights, social service, not political action.

Girls were repeatedly reminded that to fulfill their "natural" destiny they must marry. But so much weight was put upon the decision to marry that a sensitive woman with an alternative— either her father's home or a woman's community—might well have hesitated. As the feminist Mary Taylor succinctly argued, given the pitfalls of marriage and the possibilities of no offer, "the first duty in the matter is for every woman to protect herself from the danger of being forced to marry."[14] Behind arguments in favor of economic self-protection were more personal fears. Women who had been brought up in virtual ignorance of their own sexuality knew even less of men's. By reputation men were insatiable and virtually uncontrollable and women were without sexual feeling. Such extremes were difficult to negotiate, even for the sake of children. Well-publicized divorce and separation cases after the Divorce Act of 1857 shocked many into recognizing the degree of violence and adultery found in upper-class homes, and not just in the aristocracy. Frances Power Cobbe warned against the "lottery" of marriage, which might bring "either an unfaithful or cruel husband."[15] Even less serious consequences could be intimidating in a world where married women had virtually no legal recourse.[16] Mary Cadbury, who came from a happy Quaker family, could still write to her favorite sister, "I reckon I shall soon be at 50, now happily there are blessings [that] come with getting old and we are able to keep up a great measure of our spirit of our youth[;] we haven't had it crushed and trampled down by overbearing or warring or exacting husbands."[17]

By necessity and choice single women strengthened their friendships with each other and minimized their heterosexuality. It was convenient for them that some leading doctors claimed women had no sexual feelings until after experiencing intercourse. Unmarried women often portrayed themselves either as asexual saints, a role the religious found particularly attractive, or as strong women whose sexuality was sublimated into a wider sphere of action. Celibate women united with their married sisters in campaigns against rampant male sexuality, like the anti-Contagious Diseases Act movement. Feminists frequently drew comparisons between the virtue of spinsters and the profligate behavior of bachelors. Cobbe praised women's friendships and castigated her male readers in terms that were typical throughout the nineteenth century:

> Nor does the "old maid" contemplate a solitary age as the bachelor must usually do. It will go hard but she will find a *woman* ready to share it. . . . She thinks to *die*, if without having given or shared some of the highest joys of human nature, yet at least without having caused one fellow-being to regret she was born to tempt to sin and shame. We ask it in all solemn sadness—Do the *men* who resolve on an unmarried life, fixedly purpose to die with as spotless a conscience?[18]

Single women writers protected the ethic of sexual purity by fostering ties with other women, and by distancing men emotionally and physically. As long as close relationships with men were socially difficult, women had much to gain by keeping their distance and strengthening their connections with each other. Such distancing, however, reinforced the belief that men and women were diametrically opposite to each other in their sexual needs and personal characteristics.

Given all the perceived perils involved in marriage, it is not surprising that some social commentators argued against providing any alternatives, lest women refuse men entirely.[19] They were convinced that feminism actively encouraged women to spurn good offers. The feminist writers, on the other hand, were strong advocates of a higher marital standard, based upon love and mutual interests rather than on male sexual desire and female economic necessity. The *Englishwoman's Review* insisted that "the higher a woman's nature is, the more likely it is that she will prefer rather to forego marriage altogether, than surrender herself to a union that would sink her below her own ideal."[20] Both sides of the debate kept within carefully defined parameters, with neither side admitting that women might have much to lose in a marriage or that marriage might interfere with ambition.

Only when we examine the private papers of single women do we find women admitting their growing sense of self-worth and independence. Celibacy could be a means to self-development, not self-repression. Florence Nightingale turned down the rising young journalist Richard Monckton Milnes because of her own sense of destiny, although at the time she had no definite future course of action. She was agonizingly lonely afterward, but she told herself,

> I know I could not bear his life . . . that to be nailed to a continuation, an exaggeration of my present life without hope of another would be intolerable to me—that voluntarily to put it out of my power ever to be able to seize the chance of forming for myself a true and rich life would seem to me like suicide.[21]

Constance Maynard, after she had begun her teaching career, refused a highly eligible Scots minister. She wrote in her diary at the time,

> if he mentioned me, it was with reference to himself. There was not one word about giving *me* a fine, full, rounded life, not a word of scope and freedom, or even of things we would

enjoy together, but he seemed to be on the lookout to see what effect I had on him.[22]

She did occasionally regret her decision, under the stress of administering a woman's college, but she never felt that her career was inferior to that of her sister who gave up nursing to marry. The conservatives were correct in assuming that ambition and public work would make some women reluctant to marry.

Advocates of greater opportunities for women called for a more purified form of marriage, idealizing a relationship between equals while simultaneously they created a model of the heroic, pioneering single woman. Feminist journals of the 1850s, 1860s, and 1870s were filled with success stories, tales of heroines from the past, and "first woman to . . ." accounts. These narratives encouraged single women and reminded them of their heritage, but they also placed a burden upon the less strong or committed. The average woman, without an overriding cause to inspire her to overwork and struggle in isolation, had to find consolation in religion, family, and friends. High-minded self-sacrifice, with little humor or relaxation, characterized the first generation of pioneers that the ordinary worker was to emulate. Heroic individualism, of course, fit the dominant ethos of the times, which idealized the individual man who made his way in politics, business, or the jungle. The female version was more religiously inclined, but she too was expected to overcome opposition for the sake of her vision; victory was assumed to go to the hardworking and committed. Her triumph was respectability and status for women's new careers.

The most important model for single women was Florence Nightingale, whose adventures in the Crimea still thrill girls seeking a more exciting role than is usually permitted women. She was both like and unlike many Victorian single women who sought public service. In a society that fostered weak egos in women and encouraged them to remain childlike and dependent, those rare individuals who broke away from the female stereotype possessed enormous vitality and self-confidence. Yet they were also often forced to pay a very high price. Most women managed to resolve the conflict between family duties and their own personal calling by winning over some family members to their special project. But Nightingale's family was especially adept at tying her down. Everyone, including Florence, had attacks of psychosomatic illnesses at convenient times. In 1844 Florence's plan to study nursing at Salisbury hospital had been vetoed, but by 1847 she was ill enough to win a trip to Rome with sympathetic friends. On the edge of a nervous breakdown, in 1849 she took an even longer trip abroad, including a brief visit to the German nursing institute at Kaiserswerth.

Nightingale's illnesses were both a means to escape and an escape in themselves. Illness permitted a retreat into the self in order to gain the courage and ego strength to break out permanently. In a later generation Jane Addams underwent the same pattern of initial freedom through study and travel, personal irresolution and family opposition, a mysterious protracted illness, and then a long life of incredible productivity and focus. Individual single women had to come to terms first with their ambitions and their denied heterosexuality before forging a public career. Some women of intelligence and ambition broke down under the combined pressures of family opposition, social expectations, and a lack of clear personal goals. Often a family urged a beloved daughter to return home rather than pursue a lonely course of action. Few women had the determination of Florence Nightingale, whose self-confidence was unassailable once she had broken away. She established her own living quarters and used illness with the same ruthlessness and creativity as her sister and mother in order to keep all distractions at bay.

After her return from the Crimea Nightingale spent the remainder of her long life fighting behind the scenes for reforms in military and hospital administration. But she remained a symbol of feminine achievement for her two years' work at the war front in 1854–56. Nightingale was exceptional in many ways—her class connections, iron determination, and brilliant analytic skills would have placed her in the forefront of any age—but her highly publicized work in military camps gave her an incomparable public image. Ladies had never before been active workers in an army field hospital, and under the eyes of the entire nation (through the *Times* correspondent) they rose to the occasion.[23] Nightingale's Crimea expedition was a public triumph for single women that echoed over the next half-century, liberating, shaping, and confining ambitious women. Like Joan of Arc, she proved what an exceptional woman could do given the opportunity—but could the ordinary single woman rise to the dreary mundaneness of daily labor?

Work Opportunities

Countless popular biographies enshrined Florence Nightingale as someone who completely fulfilled woman's self-sacrificing role, overcoming barriers of class and circumstance to succour wounded soldiers. Her ambitiousness and her ruthlessness were never included, as these characteristics did not fit public assumptions about women. "The Lady with the Lamp" inspired a good many women to enter the field of nursing, as chapter 3 shows, but she could not and would not help the average poorly educated and uncommitted spinster. For such women the study of foreign languages or art and philanthropy were thought to be suitable recreations.[24] Neither occupation removed one from the home. Even Nightingale's family had encouraged her enthusiasm for things Italian, but positively forbade unladylike mathematics lessons; they permitted dabbling in nursing the local poor, but not formal training. Single women were to pursue the arts and to help the poor, not become professionals.

Since women had been assigned the task of elevating the moral tone of the family, some learning, if kept private, was often approved. Ethel May's mother agreed to her Greek studies as long as they did not interfere with her normal round of duties, because she could then read the New Testament and tutor her youngest brother. The well-to-do educationist Emily Shirreff hoped to improve the lives of upper-class single women through study, rather than through competition with men in the public domain:

> What society wants from women is not labour, but refinement, elevation of mind, knowledge, making its power felt through moral influence and sound opinions. It wants civilizers of men, and educators of young. And society will suffer in proportion as women are either driven by necessity or tempted by seeming advantages to leave this their natural vocation, and to join the noisy throng in the busy markets of the world.[25]

Shirreff's recommendations bore little relation to reality but were influential during the beginning stages of the struggle to improve girls' and women's education. Even that determined feminist Emily Davies urged men to consider what better wives educated girls would make.

But unmarried women who attempted to follow an organized

program of study met many roadblocks from family and friends. Mary Taylor had little faith in informal intellectual efforts. When she tried to talk to her friends about her reading, Taylor found that they "all had the impression that it was wrong; not morally wrong, perhaps, but a sort of solecism in manner like putting your knife in your mouth. Not anything that would prevent you from getting to Heaven, but fatal to your acceptability on earth."[26] With public opinion against them, only the most committed pursued their schoolgirl vows to continue their studies. As a result, women who either had to work or wanted to often found themselves poorly equipped to do so and without the necessary foundation to learn new skills. An early group of feminists found that they had to teach ladies elementary arithmetic before they could apply for jobs as shop clerks.[27] Men were always willing to admit that a few exceptional women, such as George Eliot or Florence Nightingale, were their intellectual equals, but well into the twentieth century doctors and academics were claiming that women were incapable of meeting male standards of work and that if they tried to do so they would risk damage to their reproductive organs.[28] Even Shirreff's mild recommendations met with opposition.

Philanthropy, however, offered more opportunities for women to take initiative and further the "maternal influence" in their parish or town. Probably the greatest achievements of Victorian women were in the area of philanthropy, yet even here we find them encouraged to remain amateurs. All religious denominations depended heavily upon women volunteers for parish visiting, but they were admonished against upstaging the clergy. Authors of advice books, such as Sarah Stickney Ellis, regularly warned restless daughters that charity began at home and that an excessive zeal for visiting the poor meant a neglect of home duties. Nevertheless, religious belief gave many women courage to move beyond conformity to social norms.[29] Most of the pioneering generation of single women first gained experience and leadership skills in some charity organization; some spent their entire lives promoting important social reforms under the aegis of philanthropy. Although men usually controlled the governing boards and finances of such organizations, they did not have the same amount of time, devotion, or experience as single women. Indeed, many charities preferred using women to visit the poor because they alone could advise other women on housewifery, nursing, and child care. Enormous numbers of women volunteered regu-

larly for various charities; by the end of the century, as chapter 6
documents, they were the largely unpaid foundation of the social
service system. Women were remarkably successful in carving out
a special sphere for themselves that chimed with growing social
needs.

At the root of many fears about the superfluous woman was
economic instability. The desperate efforts of the Brontë sisters to
find remunerative employment were being duplicated by less brilliant daughters throughout England. Whatever discontent the
wealthy Florence Nightingale might feel was nothing compared
with the situation facing her local curate's daughter. Fathers were
repeatedly warned to make plans for their daughters after their
deaths. Presumably the fictional Dr. May was wise enough to invest in a good insurance policy for Ethel, unlike another fictional
doctor, Dr. Madden in *The Odd Women* (1893), who left five
daughters virtually penniless and without job training. Only the
most confident and ambitious woman could have applauded Harriet Martineau's sense of liberation after her family's loss of
fortune.[30]

Spinsters had been eking out an existence for centuries on the
edge of respectable social circles, but middle-class journalists
were still shocked to discover how many and how poor they were.
The overwork and destitution of gentlewomen was defined as a social problem, while far worse conditions among poor women were
ignored. The long hours and physically exhausting work of so
many working-class women, especially servants, did not arouse
much interest because they were fulfilling their accepted social
destiny. But gentlewomen slaving away over ill-paid sewing or
painfully trying to bring order into a schoolroom pressed all too
visibly upon upper-class consciences. Particularly pitiable were
women in their forties and fifties looking for work for the first
time after the death of their parents. Although charitable organizations rebuked the working class for failing to save for old age,
elderly middle-class women were extended much sympathy and
sometimes a little money. The annual reports of the Governesses'
Benevolent Institution (GBI, founded in 1841) starkly documented
the large numbers of gentlewomen willing to work for inadequate
pay for fear of being totally unemployed. Jobs offering as little as
£5 and £10 per year with room and board would be flooded with
applicants. One GBI annuity of £20 drew 150 applicants over fifty
years old, of whom 83 had not one penny in the world.[31]

Nevertheless, reformers saw work as the key to the single woman's liberation. At a time when the height of male ambition was to earn enough money to stop working and buy an estate, women thirsted after work. The first step for them was improved job opportunities and better education. The GBI, under the leadership of the Christian Socialist F. D. Maurice, opened Queen's College for Women in 1848 to provide better education for governesses, who might then command better salaries. A few years later a small group of feminists was quietly helping single women. The "ladies of Langham Place"—Barbara Leigh Smith Bodichon, Bessie Rayner Parkes, Adelaide Procter, and Jessie Boucherett—started the first women's periodical devoted to women's issues, the *English Woman's Journal*. They also organized the first petition to Parliament for women's suffrage, published pamphlets on women's legal position and work opportunities, and used their rented rooms at Langham Place as a combination informal employment agency and drop-in center for women.[32] Through the pages of the *Journal* and its successor, the *Englishwoman's Review*, readers were alerted to every new opening for women. The progress of women's suffrage in Parliament, the efforts of Emily Davies to open public examinations to girls and to found a women's college, the establishment of women's clubs and model housing, and every unusual job were all faithfully described. The *Review* was refreshingly free of the morbid sermonizing that characterized so many tracts on single women; the editors were vigorous and confident in their assertion that women should be given a fairer share of life's work.

The distrust of formal training and paid work for ladies was combined with a belief in woman's innate abilities to teach and to nurse; special education for either occupation was considered unnecessary. Anna Jameson pointed out that no one suspected a trained soldier of being less brave than an untrained one, so why distrust the training of woman's instinctive feelings?[33] But the edict against professionalism laid a heavy hand upon all efforts to educate and train girls. Mary Taylor was an exception in her hearty dismissal of status; she had gone to New Zealand with her brother and had successfully managed a store. But she had an acute sense of why girls preferred to wait for a suitor rather than work:

No one dare say of the few women who maintain themselves that their industry makes them inferior. It is not found that they deteriorate, or become unfit for the class they belong to. But so long as living in the expectation of being provided for is thought more worthy of respect, the majority, of course, will endeavour to do so. Respect is more to them than money. Competence, friends, the happiness of marriage, all are involved in the choice between working and waiting—only waiting; nothing worse than that. . . . So the years that should be passed in active work, or in learning how, are spent in waiting, and the untaught woman is made incapable for life.[34]

Moreover, unless driven by dire distress, middle-class girls were repeatedly admonished that if they worked they took away the job of someone who needed it more.

In spite of the recommendations of Mary Taylor and a few other isolated voices that women should enter unconventional and therefore less crowded fields of employment, women stuck to the familiar and growing occupations of teaching, nursing, clerical work, shop work, and organized philanthropy. Alternative jobs in business and industry were difficult for most women to prepare for and then to find. From the beginning of the reform of middle-class employment to the present day, women have clustered in the service occupations, all of which were and largely remain low paying and overcrowded. Generally speaking women received one-third to one-half of a man's earnings for similar work; at the top of her profession a woman could earn only about two-thirds of a man's salary.[35] In 1904 Ada Moore pointed out that a beginning house surgeon earned as much as a hospital head matron who "has reached the height of her profession." As she succinctly summarized women's work, "a woman leaves off where a man considers he is only beginning."[36]

A more serious problem for many was the pressure placed upon nurses and teachers to retire in their mid-fifties. Very few institutions made any provisions for retirement, as employees were expected to save for their own pensions, investing in the many small insurance companies that sprang up to meet the growing need for some old-age insurance. A good many nurses after their retirement from a hospital opened small nursing homes or boardinghouses for private nurses between jobs. Teachers could choose between private tutoring or descending to a less prestigious school. Despite the pressures of early retirement, Clara Collet recommended that young teachers should not save if they earned less than £100 per year because they would risk losing their health and go into debt or lose their position.[37] If promotion did not come by the age of thirty-five, a professional woman could expect to earn no more and gain no better position than she held, a fate that hardly made middle age an attractive prospect. The culmination of many years of work could be survival on a minute pension, made possible by "years of self-restraint and life-long traditions."[38] The files of the GBI sixty years after its foundation were still overflowing with petitions from elderly ladies on the verge of starvation.

Grim as conditions could be for working women from the middle class, their poverty must be kept in its social context. During the second half of the nineteenth century skilled laborers supported themselves and their families upon an average of £1 per week, supplemented by the small earnings of their wives and children. Working-class women rarely earned more than a shilling a day, and sometimes less, for the lowest forms of outwork.[39] But a middle-class woman who earned less than a pound a week could not maintain her social status, according to her peers. Difficulties arose because everyone knew that many ladies *did* earn less than £52 a year, even when room and board were taken into consideration for such jobs as nursing or boarding-school teaching. The dire financial straits of some older single women from the upper classes were not exaggerated, but their numbers were small in comparison with the vast population of working-class women and men who lived below any reasonable standard of living. Once again, as with the perceived problem of single women, upper-class women in poverty received a disproportionate amount of attention and sympathy among social commentators in the middle-class press.[40]

A closer look at the statistics in regard to spinsters shows that fathers were correct in assuming that their daughters had a good chance of marrying and that they would be better off financially. Although the age at which men and women of all classes married slowly increased until 1911, the proportion who married remained virtually unchanged.[41] Approximately seven out of every eight women could expect to marry. If we take forty-five as the age after which few women married, the total number of spinsters increased steadily, but their percentage of all women over forty-five increased only slightly (table 1). Throughout the period under consideration the aristocracy and the middle class remained roughly 15 percent of the population, although the number of so-

TABLE I
Unmarried Women over Forty-five

Year	Total Number of Unmarried Women 45+	Unmarried Women 45+ as Percentage of All Women 45+	Total Number of Middle-Class Women Unmarried and 45 +
1851	204,650	11.7	30,698
1861	225,183	11.2	33,777
1871	260,404	11.2	39,061
1881	292,147	11.2	43,822
1891	342,072	11.6	51,311
1901	421,549	12.4	63,232
1911	579,026	14.1	86,854
1921	788,800[a]	15.4	118,320

Note: For total population of men and women, of women between twenty and forty-five and over forty-five, and population divided according to marital status, see Appendix A.
[a] rounded to nearest 100.

called white-collar middle-class jobs was increasing at a higher rate than unskilled work.[42] Fifteen percent of the figures above, as shown in the final column, gives us a much smaller number of single middle-class women than was generally assumed by contemporaries. Even if we assume that many women, like Ethel May, knew well before age forty-five that they would not marry, the total number of middle-class women who remained unmarried and in need of work was very small in comparison with their working-class sisters. Whether the middle class married less frequently than the working class is difficult to calculate, but available evidence suggests that they did not.[43] The conviction shared by all middle-class commentators that the number of unmarried middle-class women was steadily increasing was due to their increase in absolute numbers and their increased visibility, brought about in part by their acceptance of paid work and in part by the public discussion of their plight.

In spite of the large increase in professional jobs for women during the second half of the nineteenth century, the numbers of women employed in such work remained small. As late as 1901 only 45.5 percent of spinsters over forty-five were occupied in some form of paid employment; 54.5 percent were listed as retired or unoccupied.[44] How many of this 54.5 percent wanted to work or worked without pay for their families or worked part time is impossible to calculate. Obviously some were over sixty or sixty-five and retired, but some may have been prematurely retired. In contrast, 70.8 percent of unmarried women between the ages of twenty and forty-five worked in paid employment. A breakdown of the major occupations in 1901 for what might be called "career women," those over forty-five, reveals that slightly over 12 percent of them were in middle-class jobs (tables 2 and 3).[45] If we add government positions and commerce to the professions, we have a figure of 12.3 percent of unmarried women over forty-five in jobs requiring special training. Some nurses and board school teachers would have come from the working class, but some middle-class women would have been engaged in the categories of industry, dress, and other. Limiting our figures to the three occupations requiring some formal education still provides a reasonably accurate account of the percentage of actively employed middle-class single women.

The percentage of unmarried women between the ages of twenty and forty-five in the government, professions, and commerce for 1901 and 1911 is very close to the figures for unmarried women over forty-five in these three occupations (table 4). In 1901 the total number of women over twenty employed in these three occupations was 238,510, or 12.1 percent of employed single women over twenty. In 1911 the total of employed single women in these occupations had risen to 373,420 and was 15.6 percent of employed single women over twenty. As table 5 shows, the number of unmarried women who did not work remained high, although it was never as high as that of married women and widows. In 1901 there were 9,880,194 women over twenty; 15 percent of this population is 1,482,029 women in the upper classes. Unmarried working women over twenty in the three occupations of government, commerce, and the professions constituted 6.2 percent of this latter figure. In these circumstances the continued refusal of upper-class parents to train their daughters for a life other than marriage is understandable.

Even though job opportunities and salaries had not improved as much as reformers may have hoped, by the end of the nineteenth century public opinion had begun to support middle-class women's work. Women had been in positions of public leadership for over half a century and had proved their abilities in philanthropy, teaching, and nursing. However limited their successes may seem

TABLE 2
Occupations of Unmarried Women over Forty-five

Occupation	1901		1911	
	Number	%	Number	%
Government	1,336	0.7	2,769	1.0
Professions[a]	21,193	11.0	37,159	13.7
Commerce	1,128	0.6	2,576	0.9
Domestic service	88,364	46.1	112,107	41.3
Agriculture	3,879	2.0	6,537	2.4
Industry	23,153	12.1	35,147	12.9
Dress	32,429	16.9	41,879	15.4
Food, tobacco, drink, lodging	17,639	9.2	29,499	10.9
Other	2,597	1.4	4,138	1.5
Total	191,718	100.0	271,811	100.0

[a]See table 3 for breakdown.

TABLE 3
Unmarried Women over Forty-five Engaged in Professions

Occupation	1901		1911	
	Number	%	Number	%
Clerical				
Nuns, sisters of charity	3,159	1.6	4,852	1.8
Legal				
Law clerks	13		35	
Medical				
Physicians	20		60	
Midwives	90		245	0.1
Sick nurses	5,231	2.7	8,937	3.3
Other	133	0.1	348	0.1
Teaching				
Teachers	9,668	5.0	17,045	6.3
Other	301	0.2	742	0.3
Literary, scientific, political				
Authors, journalists	179	0.1	385	0.1
Scientists, other	64		453	0.2
Art, music, drama				
Artists	445	0.2	854	0.3
Photographers	84		153	
Musicians	1,725	0.9	2,768	1.0
Actresses	43		64	
Other	38		218	0.1
Total	21,193	11.0	37,159	13.7

TABLE 4
Women over Twenty Engaged in Selected Occupations and Percentage
of All Unmarried Working Women in Each Age Category

| | 1901 | | | | 1911 | | | |
| | 20–45 | | 45+ | | 20–45 | | 45+ | |
Occupation	Number	%	Number	%	Number	%	Number	%
Government	15,272	0.9	1,336	0.7	31,334	1.5	2,769	1.0
Professions	164,492	9.2	21,193	11.0	223,602	10.5	37,159	13.7
Commerce	35,089	2.0	1,128	0.6	75,980	3.6	2,576	0.9
Total	214,853	12.1	23,657	12.3	330,916	15.6	42,504	15.6

TABLE 5
Female Population over Twenty, England and Wales

| | 1901 | | 1911 | |
Age	Unmarried	Married or Widowed	Unmarried	Married or Widowed
	Retired or Unemployed			
20–45	735,368	3,509,252	738,305	3,869,349
45+	229,831	2,514,743	307,215	3,017,071
Total	965,199	6,023,995	1,045,520	6,886,420
	Engaged in Occupations			
20–45	1,784,816	452,790	2,131,111	568,254
45+	191,718	461,676	271,811	520,214
Total	1,976,534	914,466	2,402,922	1,088,468

in retrospect, they laid the foundations for women's political activism during the years before the First World War. Not only Florence Nightingale, but also Mary Carpenter, Louisa Twining, Sister Dora Pattison, Octavia Hill, Emily Davies, Frances Power Cobbe, and Ellice Hopkins, among many others, were household names for the middle class. But their public gains would never have been possible without the support of other single women. For this early generation the tradition of female self-sacrifice was transformed into sacrifice for the betterment of women, for a community of sisters. A network of women's organizations and institutions supported each single woman entering the newly developing professions for women.

New Work, New Communities

Single women were often simply redundant in middle-class homes. Even Ethel May has to recognize that her younger brothers and sisters will grow up, leaving her with no immediate family responsibilities. A natural reaction to the isolation of so many spinsters was to form their own communities, united by their own tasks, fulfilling social needs that could not be met by married women or by men. Independent women wanted their own space, apart from the domestic world of their married sisters and from the male world in which they often moved. A community was a refuge, a foothold from which to launch into the wider world, but most of all, it was a home.

The very success of these institutions—schools, colleges, sisterhoods, settlement houses, and many others—has obscured their difficulties and strengths. Fear of women is deep seated in European culture. In Greek mythology the Amazons are repeatedly defeated, and women's organizations have been a target of mockery or amusement for almost as long. The Victorians repeated these attitudes in their writings with an increasing vehemence as the demand for and number of women's separate institutions grew. Ethel May's mission school almost flounders when a ladies' committee takes it up; only the timely intervention of her father's best friend saves it. Women would quarrel with each other if they lived and worked together, argued Charlotte Yonge and many less conservative commentators. Unlike men, they had not spent long years in single-sex institutions such as schools, colleges, the military services, clubs or pubs, so they could not be expected to know how to behave in a corporate environment. But neither should they learn how, lest they lose their devotion to their families.

The very idea of an effective women's community was frightening. It implied that women could be self-sufficient and that men were dispensable. Attacks upon single women and their communities generally focused on the threatened loss of a woman's mothering and her denial of family duties; only rarely did critics openly denounce the sexual independence of women implied by celibacy. Yet this sexual self-sufficiency was an important subtext, most obviously expressed in the portrayal of old maids in literature and in medical texts. For nineteenth-century novelists, the fatuous flirtations or prurient prudery of unmarried women were naturally antithetical to youth, love, and marriage. The pantomime and burlesque "dame," played by a male comic, invariably accentuated the ugliness of a middle-aged spinster; her absurd trust in makeup and wigs gave ample room for visual as well as verbal assaults upon the old maid's character and person. In fiction these foolish maiden aunts were confined by comedy with remarkable ease, but in real life they could be frightening portents of a world turned upside down.

The terms of the medical debate changed over a half-century, shifting from pity for the celibate woman's failed motherhood to accusations about her misguided influence and questionable friendships. It is hard to estimate how seriously the general middle-class public took the frequent medical diatribes about women's health, the dangers of overexertion, the possible shrinking of a woman's sexual organs from disuse, and the general decline of the species. For some, such opinions fed fears about any change in women's roles, while others considered them simple exaggerations on the part of a profession consolidating its prestige and power.[46] But feminists invariably felt called upon to respond to all medical experts, whose scientific language veiled an underlying sexual antagonism that hardened as women became more publicly visible.[47] Although the single woman's sexuality—active, failed, or denied—was most frequently discussed in code, it was always an issue for the opponents of women's single-sex communities and institutions. Against this background of fear, distrust, and ridicule, women had to forge their new organizations.

In a society as strictly divided by sex and class as nineteenth-century England, middle-class women had their own separate customs and rituals that brought them together.[48] An elaborate round of domestic and social duties, both private and voluntary, united them against men and outsiders. They came together in times of crisis and to assist in and celebrate the primary acts of life—marriage, childbirth, and death. But after the wedding, the birth, or the burial, they left the principal actor to face her husband, father, or male God alone. The occasions that brought women together were deeply important to the family, but in male terms they were never part of its public responsibilities. Although women presided over the continuance of the family, they remained irrelevant to the larger political and economic worlds at the very time when the middle class was gaining power in both. Moreover, no matter how self-sufficient the domestic women's world, their communities were only ancillary; women without men were incomplete. Whatever power they had excluded single women. Many single women disliked and distrusted the confining domestic world of married women and sought either individual independence or a new style of community.

The pioneering single women had more conflict with their parents than was common in the nineteenth century. While still young they had questioned the casual assumption that they would live the life of Ethel May if a proper suitor did not come along. Although very few had as much difficulty with their families as Florence Nightingale, they did not maintain as close ties with their relatives as sisters who remained at home or married. Many women lamented their estrangement from their families but did relatively little to change the situation. Constance Maynard worked hard to stay in touch with her two sisters at home, but she was utterly bored with their village charity and never ceased to regret the waste of their talents. On the other hand, women with younger sisters were very likely to bring them into their own orbit. Jane Frances Dove, headmistress of St. Leonards School and founder of Wycombe Abbey School, earned enough to send one sister through college and another through medical school.[49] Some young women were fortunate in receiving every possible encouragement from their families; Elizabeth Garrett Anderson never won her mother over, but she was financially and emotionally supported by her father during her struggle to become the first British woman doctor.[50]

Exceptional Victorian women generally prided themselves on their independence both from the narrow community of domesticated women and from the newly vocal feminists. They had made their way in the world by hard work, perseverance, and determination, and they were convinced that others could do as well, if only they would try. They were utterly scathing about weak-minded women who depended constantly upon the opinions of others or expected special favors simply because they were ladies. In 1861 Florence Nightingale wrote her friend Clarkey a damning indictment of women's ineffectiveness:

Women crave *for being loved*, not for loving. They scream out at you for sympathy all day long, they are incapable of giving *any* in return, for they cannot remember your affairs long enough to do so. . . . They cannot state a fact accurately to another, nor can that other attend to it accurately enough for it to become information.[51]

Without peers, the "heroic" generation had little patience for the tedious work of encouraging individual women and building a new identity based on shared strengths. For them such notions as "community" and "unity" smacked of mediocrity and the pulling down of individual talents, rather than self-development and support. Like the heroes in self-help tracts, Nightingale and other outspoken pioneers preferred the power to be won by individual effort to any cooperation, no matter how beneficial to women as a whole.

Conservative women, such as novelist Charlotte Yonge and Sarah Stickney Ellis, a writer of etiquette books, exalted a kind of community they hoped would be a bulwark against both the self-sufficiency praised by Nightingale and the collectivity championed by feminists. Ellis, a purveyor of saccharine advice reminding women always to dissemble their true feelings, lavishly praised the sympathy and affection women had for each other. She wrote, "[Unlike men], women *do* know what their sex is formed to suffer; and for this very reason, there is sometimes a bond existing between sisters, the most endearing, the most pure and disinterested of any description of affection which this world affords. . . . [This bond] arises chiefly out of their mutual knowledge of each other's capacity of receiving pain."[52] She recommended that young women prepare for the pain of marriage by forming communities of "disinterested kindness . . . where they should be accustomed to consider their time not as their own but lent them solely for the purpose of benefiting their fellow creatures."[53] The belief in woman's special sensitivity, her willing sacrifice of self for others, sustained many women through injustice and powerlessness.

Young women were, in fact, developing a very different kind of sisterhood from the one Ellis imagined. During the eighteenth century middle-class families had begun to send their daughters away to finishing school for a year or two. This custom continued into the nineteenth century, enabling young women to form close friendships with women of their same age and social class. Such relations often lasted a lifetime, although the friends rarely lived together and after marriage met infrequently.[54] "Romantic friendship" with another woman was an accepted prelude, even preparation for, marriage, but it was also a subversive outlet for ambitions and hopes that went beyond familiar domestic subjects. Charlotte Brontë confided some of her most intimate fears and plans to Ellen Nussey; Florence Nightingale to her friend in Paris, Clarkey. Geraldine Jewsbury urged her friend Jane Carlyle to ignore the demands and discouragement of her famous husband and "to set to work upon a story or a book." She recommended that "You must respect your own work and your own motives; if people only did what others thought good and useful, half the work in the world would be left undone."[55] Jane Carlyle never found the time or energy to write a book, but she and Jewsbury remained friends for twenty-five years, until her death. Similar examples of lifelong friendships abound.

These friendships between girls and young women were strongly encouraged by advisors such as Sarah Stickney Ellis, who saw them as excellent training in sincerity, devotion, and service. But families were also warned about the excessive affections of their daughters. From the very beginning a tension surfaced between the desirability of forming close friendships and fears of their superseding family claims. The conservative educationist Elizabeth Sewell warned, "when romantic friendship puts itself forward as having a claim above those ties which God has formed by nature, it becomes the source of untold misery to all who are connected with it."[56] Indeed, she was convinced that "the home history of half the families in England" was one in which friendships led to "jealousies, suspicions, unwarrantable influence, neglect of home duties, perhaps ultimate estrangement from home relations."[57] Sewell's fears were couched in the exaggerated language of so many Victorian etiquette books, but they point to a deep-seated distrust of uncontrolled emotions. Daughters were expected to remain emotionally tied to their families, and especially their mothers, until marriage. As a result, friendships were frequently the arena in which young women first fought for their independence from family demands. Nightingale depended upon her beloved friend Selina Bracebridge to help her convince her family that she should have an independent life.[58] The careful mother of Constance Maynard stopped her correspondence with a favorite school friend at about the same time she checked an older sister from "hanging over the pillow" of a gardener boy dying of consumption.[59] Rebellion festered in Maynard's heart, though she obeyed. She was the most dutiful of daughters, but she disliked

the artificial manner she and her sisters cultivated in order to protect themselves from their mother's intrusions.

Even though intense friendships were encouraged, especially for
their spirituality (Maynard felt that her mother did not understand how important religion was for her and her friend), they
were still to be kept within carefully regulated bounds. As Dinah
Mulock Craik pointed out, the ideal romantic friendship was supportive, loyal, and yet limited. She especially disliked the extremes of sentimentality single women fell into "for want of natural domestic ties," but she had nothing but praise for the ideal
friendship:

> For two women, past earliest girlhood, to be completely ab-
> sorbed in one another, and make public demonstration of the
> fact, by caresses or quarrels, is so repugnant to common
> sense, that where it ceases to be silly it becomes actually
> wrong. But to see two women, whom Providence has denied
> nearer ties, by a wise substitution making the best of fate,
> loving, sustaining, and comforting one another, with a tender-
> ness often closer than that of sisters, because it has all the
> novelty of election which belongs to the conjugal tie itself—
> this, I say, is an honourable and lovely sight.[60]

The new generation of professional women, many of whom were
deeply involved with a special friend, agreed with Craik and
wished to avoid the excessive displays of affection that seemed to
mark so many women's friendships. But they also did not wish to
think of their choice—celibacy with a special friend—as a "wise
substitution" or second best. Although they controlled their feelings publicly, they found in romantic friendships an essential emotional underpinning to difficult and often discouraging work.[61]
Throughout the second half of the nineteenth century single
women were labeled "deviant" not because of their friendships,
but because of their refusal to marry. Ultimately women's friendships were a threat simply because they were an alternative to
marriage. Behind Elizabeth Sewell's exaggerated language was a
fear of independent women.

Few women could live apart from their families, no matter how
much they might long to join a special friend, unless they had
full-time work. For the sake of respectability and safety, hospitals,
schools, shops, and charities frequently supplied room and board
as part of the salary. Few women who worked could afford a flat or
house, and communal living was cheaper and pleasanter than

a boardinghouse. The provision of room and board lowered a woman's wages, but for most women its compensations were greater than the loss of earning power. Furnished lodgings might lead to a loss of status, whereas at work one lived with one's peers, indeed, friends, and not whoever a landlady might let in. As so often happens with women, a necessity, living with others, was turned into an advantage, companionship and support.[62]

One of the chief attractions of the new women's communities was their gift of privacy and time for self-development. Community life validated individuality in a culture that assumed women never needed time alone and would always be at the beck and call of others. In spite of the bourgeois family's keen sense of privacy, a woman could expect none of her own at home. Jane Austen concealed her scribbling whenever anyone came into the drawing room, lest she interfere with the sociability of her family. Florence Nightingale arose before dawn in order to have time for thorough study of government reports and statistics. But not every woman was so determined or so capable. As Caroline Emilia Stephen warned the women at Newnham College,

> One thing which all who live alone certainly need is the power—mainly I believe imaginative—to outline their own lives. And by this I mean the power of marking out distinctly the channels into which one's energies should flow, and for which they should be reserved. People are but too ready to make demands on time and strength not obviously appropriated; and without a distinct outline in one's own mind it is doubly hard not to yield to such demands.[63]

But the privileges of time and space would not alone make a community. Underpinning all women's work was a sense of religious commitment. Single women of vastly different convictions felt consecrated in their work to a sacred cause. This devotion to others' welfare was the highest expression of and validation for the idea of women's self-sacrificing nature. The stigma of paid labor for many middle-class women was thus removed. The rather negative notion of doing one's duty was changed into a positive hope for the future; work for others was part of God's plan, in which single women played a crucial role. Louisa Hubbard argued in 1875 a theme that was echoed over the decades:

> The fact that so many are appointed to this "second best" woman's lot in life, convinces me that in their case it is *not*

"second best" to them but quite the best; even so, it is *not* new to us to learn that the race rises by the deprivation of the few, and as one great value in professional excellence is the effect it has in raising the quality of amateur work, so I conclude that the special gifts and graces developed by single life among women, will, if it is not treason to say so, strengthen similar faculties in all women, whether married or single.[64]

Reformers hoped to create true communities of service out of the rather heterogeneous mixture of women drawn together by a shared workplace. They constantly spoke of the need to build esprit de corps among women, of turning the duty of work into a shared mission. At midcentury, when reformers first began talking about single women living communally, they had only two models to base their new institutions upon, religious orders and boarding schools. Both aroused deep feelings of hostility and distrust; neither promulgated independence and community. Religious orders appeared to demand the complete surrender of a woman's liberty and to cut her off entirely from her family, issues that will be discussed in greater detail in the next chapter. Traditional boarding schools, on the other hand, suffered from the opposite extreme. They prided themselves on being run as families, offering protection without responsibilities or liberty. The tightly enclosed life of the typical old-fashioned boarding school was suffocating in its emphasis upon superficial knowledge and husband hunting. Cobbe sarcastically recorded her "conviction that a better system than [her school] could scarcely have been devised to attain the maximum of cost and labour and the minimum of solid results."[65]

Without totally discarding these two models, reformers adopted some features of both. The long-established male institutions, such as the famous Oxbridge colleges or men's clubs, were rejected. Rather, women fell back on what they knew best—the family. Their new communities were to be families, but without their complications and disadvantages. The traditional family was a model that did not excite fears or hostility, problems Florence Nightingale faced when she adapted a military model for modern nursing. At its simplest, but most enduring, the model meant mothering the needy, creating homes for the friendless and weak. This sentiment is captured in an epigraph Louisa Hubbard used at the beginning of her 1875 edition of *The Yearbook of Women's Work*:

"I think it is because God means so much in home life, and so deeply means that everybody should have it, that some are left like you and I, Tibbie," said Sarah. "For while the world goes on as it is, some of the threads will slip from their proper place in its pattern, and get into tangles. . . . We cannot make a home for ourselves, but we can make ourselves a home for others, and then by and by we find that their love has built our loving service into a shelter for ourselves, or if their love fails, another love comes in and performs their part—that love that supplements all effort, and saves all failures, and looks after all lost things."[66]

Numbers of single women made middle-class homes for themselves in the slums and happily set about to untangle the lives of overworked mothers, teenage girls, and children.

A philanthropy that imitated the emotional ties and obligations of one's own home was emotionally comfortable and unthreatening. But mothering alone was not sufficient. Firm leadership, steady followers, and a new generation to train were also important ingredients in most women's communities. Women in the new institutions were pioneers who had to devise new models of behavior, public and private. Such traditional roles as dutiful daughter, loving sister, or faithful church helper did not offer many guidelines for public leadership and professional conduct. Living in a "family" that was not a family often exacerbated the deep conflict between the old social expectations of marriage and children and the new opportunities for independence and personal fulfillment. The most common solution to the stresses and strains of living together and building a new institution was to continue the traditional emotional ties of the nuclear family while attempting cool, professional ways of behaving and working in the job and in the world outside. However, since "family" and work were often within the walls of the same institution, many women found it difficult to draw a clear line between appropriate work behavior and personal emotions.

However revolutionary communities of working women were in providing alternative space for single women, they were as socially and economically stratified as the larger society of Victorian England. The status of a community was closely linked to cost, exclusivity, and choice, all elements tied to the social position of one's family. Distinctions were guarded jealously, especially at the upper reaches of the middle class. Ladies were particularly anxious not to lose any of their class privileges; some reformers suggested that they bypass any training requirements for a job and move immediately into positions of authority. Their "training" at home for the previous twenty-odd years was assumed to be sufficient preparation.[67] Others, however, realized that an expensive period of training ensured that the working class was kept out of the occupations middle- and upper-class women wished to enter.

Women's communities were as age-conscious as they were class-conscious. Age was a peculiar matter for a single woman. On the one hand, she was often infantilized, forced to remain childlike well beyond the time when her sisters were married and became heads of households. Charles Dickens satirized the grotesque prolongations of youth in Flora Finching, Volumnia Dedlock, and Miss Tox. Women eager to take up a career sometimes had to wait years before being released by their families. Many single women looked forward with relief to turning thirty, when they could put aside any pretense of being marriageable and concentrate upon their own interests. Women who embarked upon professional work accentuated their age and asexuality to emphasize a professional identity and minimize their youthful eligibility. The gray or navy suit recommended to rising young women executives today had its counterpart in the severe, dark clothing of nineteenth-century high-school teachers and social workers.

Although women found that greater respect was given to age, opportunities slipped by those who were too old. For the first generation, leadership opportunities came at remarkably early ages to the intrepid and determined. With new schools opening, hospitals expanding, and philanthropic organizations professionalizing, in the 1870s and 1880s a woman could often be hired as a head-mistress, matron, or head secretary in her twenties. The sheer dearth of trained women meant that any confident woman with a reasonable modicum of knowledge and connections could find work. Even for a later generation, when opportunities for leadership were far fewer, a woman expected to be promoted early or not at all. For those with no special training or confidence, thirty-five could mark the apex of their career, with the remaining years of work a wasteland of small economies. The worst off were those who entered the job market late, after the death of well-cared-for parents. With no work experience, they had little to offer beyond good manners and a genteel accent.[68]

Freedom was both exhilarating and frightening. There were few role models beyond the older heroic individuals who had worked alone. Perhaps most frightening of all was the definitive nature of committing oneself to a career. Constance Maynard had prayed and waited for nearly ten years before she was able to open her own college in 1882. Despite her success, she wept hearing behind her "the clang of the iron Convent gates, [knowing] my fate was irrevocable."[69] Although she had turned down two marriage offers and knew that her life's ambition had come true, Maynard still felt the pain of closing off all hope of a family. Nineteenth-century women could rarely have both a career and a family; even under such favorable conditions as Maynard's, the choice was not easy. The pioneering women who chose a career would not have broken away from the traditional woman's life if they had not already felt uncomfortable with the prospect of marriage, but the path into the future was unmarked and often lonely. The continuing public distrust of women's communities, the general lack of funds in every area, and simply the wear and tear of long years of work took their toll. Many women resolved their ambivalence about their new roles by forging ahead intellectually and institutionally, disregarding personal life; others intensified their reliance upon a few friends and relatives.

The success of the new colleges and institutions depended upon women's canvassing for money, convincing governing boards about policies, converting parents and young women, and even testifying before government committees. This meant a cool and reasoned approach to work, carefully developed tactics and farsighted strategies—all "male" characteristics. The emotionalism, religiosity, and close domestic ties of traditional women had to be replaced with rationality, scientific knowledge, and corporate loyalties. Women leaders embraced these new modes of behavior, eager to prove to themselves and to men that they were capable of responsibility; indeed, had they not done so, they would have endangered the future of their institutions and thereby the progress of women's emancipation. But the pressures to do and be so much necessarily put a strain on close relationships. Women demanded too much from themselves and their friends, leaning heavily upon those they trusted, insisting upon complete loyalty and dedication. Organizing their lives so as to avoid criticism, they seemed to dissolve under the slightest disapproval from trusted allies. In a sense, they had to protect themselves and their embryo organizations from both public and private criticism during their incubation period, until they were strong enough to emerge fully and survive in a critical world. But later, when that time came, many leaders were understandably suspicious of change and fearful of a loss of their power.[70]

Rituals and rules helped to strengthen the resolve of those within the community to commit themselves to it and to its work. A brief morning prayer service united everyone before the day's work began. May festivals, specially written plays, prize-giving ceremonies, and other special occasions brought newly founded communities together for pleasure. Such formal requirements as changing for dinner or addressing each other by surnames in public places gave women who lived and worked together the necessary distance from each other so that a hard-won personal autonomy was not lost. But the most obvious manifestation of the "New Woman's" life-style was the particular pride felt among Anglican sisters, college teachers, and settlement-house workers in plain living, plain clothes, and plain food. Luxury was saved for the community, in the form of a finer altar, a better library, or a larger girls' club. The wealth of the community expressed itself in its size, numbers, and influence, while the women themselves minimized their personal power and wealth both within and outside the institution.

A clear hierarchy created a sense of permanency and stability and was an effective defense against external criticism. Those who did not trust women working together could see that their regulations and conduct were above reproach. Not surprisingly, strong bodily control, invariably expressed as heterosexual purity, was an especially important part of community life. Indeed, it appears to have gone hand in hand with the careful delineation of roles within each institution. The price for this was, in retrospect, quite high, for successful communities and organizations could be extremely exclusionary. In the early 1880s the Ladies' National Association for the Repeal of the Contagious Diseases Acts did not admit nonbelievers and agnostics into its inner circles.[71] Constance Smedley in 1907 unsuccessfully petitioned the president of the Lyceum Club to admit a remarried divocée; Lady Strachey firmly informed her, "Before playing the great game a woman must naturally have made up her mind that it was worth while to pay the stakes—which after all in this particular matter are not very heavy."[72] Radical or visionary women were often forced to work apart from the support system of "reputable" single women.

While a hierarchy enhanced the stability of a new institution, it also left many leaders isolated. A woman who found herself mothering a class of young girls or a hospital ward but "fathering" the teachers and nurses under her leadership might well wish at times that she had a child who loved her for herself and did not expect her to play all roles for all people. In many cases a spinster aunt virtually adopted a favorite niece or nephew, helping with his or her education and providing a congenial home away from home. But a lonely woman sometimes sought someone of her own, especially if she faced old age or a personal crisis. Mary Carpenter, after some twenty years of work among delinquent children, at fifty-one adopted a child. She delightedly wrote a shocked relative:

> Just think of me with a little girl of *my own*, about five years old! Ready made to hand and nicely trained, without the trouble of marrying, etc. a darling little thing, an orphan. I feel already a *mére de famille*, happy in buying little hats and socks and a little bed to stand in my own room, out of *my own* money. It is a wonderful feeling![73]

Two years later when little Rosanna's mother showed up at the door, Carpenter sent her away, calling her an incompetent mother for having abandoned her daughter.[74] Constance Maynard felt it was the hand of God when a friend in the Salvation Army offered her a six-year-old French girl; whatever doubts she had were swept away by her sense of mission.[75] Charlotte Despard, the militant suffragette, adopted the illegitimate daughter of one of her brother's junior cavalry officers.[76] Although some adoptions were successful, many were not, including these three. Indeed, they illustrate the discrepancy between the familial ideology of single women and the reality of their lives.

"Wider maternal responsibilities" gave single women permission to behave independently. But ambition, administrative skills, and public leadership were qualities they either denied or had to force into narrow acceptable channels. Many found it difficult to recognize within themselves the distance their work had carried them from conventional maternal feelings and behavior. Lives dedicated to public work, to firm leadership, and to fighting opposition were not easily altered to include the qualities necessary for good mothering. Charlotte Despard refused to give up any of her committee work and left the day-to-day care of her child to her secretary. She was astonished and hurt when her best friend criticized her, and she wrote in her diary, "She does not understand—I have my duty to the people."[77] Constance Maynard never understood why the firm religious discipline of her own upbringing turned Effie into a liar. Although she was willing to devote entire vacations to Effie, she usually included a favorite student or friend for adult companionship. As a result Effie either sullenly ignored Maynard or clamored for all her attention.[78] Middle-aged single women simply could not change their life-styles to fit the imperative demands of children. Unfortunately for such women as Maynard, her belief in woman's innate maternal instincts only accentuated a sense of failure. Even when a single woman knew that her married sisters might not have done any better, failure was difficult for eminently successful women to accept. Carpenter, Maynard, and Despard all responded by intensified mothering of their favorite causes, pouring personal frustrations and loves onto reform-school girls, college students, or slum children.

No matter how much single women kept up their family connections or tried adopting children, their primary connections remained with their peers—working women in positions similar to their own. In spite of their ideology, single women were not mothers living in surrogate families. They were hardworking, ambitious, and visionary women setting forth with great courage upon untrodden paths. But they were also intensely conflicted, deeply emotional women, seeking to fulfill themselves in ways society would approve while still moving beyond its limitations. Edith Simcox, looking back on an isolated heroine, Mary Carpenter, noted sadly that she had received so little encouragement in her early days that she appeared "a diffident novice at five-and-forty." But her heroic sacrifices had helped "to provide a modest field for the aspirations of the unheroic many."[79] Simcox, a generation later, reminded her readers that,

> It is evident that if the characters of women vary in this fundamental way, they cannot all be contentedly provided for by a common destiny. Marked individualities must feel their way towards an individual lot, but the health and happiness of the whole nature suffers by the arbitrary repression of the part which happens to have taken a line of development unfore-

seen by our neat generalities concerning the sex. . . . There can be no general rule for single lives, but it is a safe conclusion that whatever society ends by approving or applauding in its members, the said members should be allowed to undertake with unexhausted strength and spirits unbroken by wanton delay, opposition, and discouragement.[80]

A single woman who took up a career during the nineteenth and early twentieth centuries carried the burden of "wanton delay, opposition, and discouragement."

2

Church Communities: Sisterhoods and Deaconnesses' Houses

In 1855 the well-known art critic and feminist Anna Jameson gave a lecture titled "Sisters of Charity," openly advocating the creation of Protestant religious orders to train women in nursing, teaching, social work, and other "womanly" tasks. Speaking to a receptive middle-class public that had followed Nightingale's exploits in the Crimea, she argued that only through organized religious communities could the large number of superfluous single women find the training, discipline, and moral sustenance that would enable them to help the weak, friendless, and sick. These women would help to regenerate society, which desperately needed women "on a larger scale [as] mother, sister, nurse and help."[1] Jameson's lecture brought to the attention of a larger audience what religious women had been doing for years. As far back as 1840 the Quaker Elizabeth Fry had founded the Institution for Nursing Sisters, which trained respectable religious women to nurse the poor. The high-church Oxford Movement leaders John Henry Newman and E. B. Pusey had openly advocated, and then assisted in, the revival of Anglican sisterhoods in the 1840s. Like Charlotte Yonge, Jameson caught an idea that was coming of age and publicized it widely.

Victorian society assumed that religion would be the inspiration for women's work; religious belief kept the high idealism of charity strong, sanctifying both the giver and the receiver. From Roman Catholicism came the model of sisterhoods, and from Protestant Germany came deaconesses; both offered examples of fully trained and educated single women dedicated to nursing, teaching, and good works. They also demonstrated the greater effectiveness of women working in organized groups rather than as isolated individuals doling out soup and poultices. Amateur charity and slovenly nursing were to be replaced by "brave women, whose vocation is fixed and whose faculties of every kind have been trained and disciplined to their work."[2] Amid the rhetoric of Christian obedience and duty, a narrow path of self-fulfillment was created for devout single women.

The revival of the Anglican sisterhoods and diaconate brought together three important strands in Victorian life: the need to respond to poverty and social distress among the mass of people, the widespread religious renaissance involving Nonconformists and both Evangelicals (low church) and Tractarians (high church) within the Church of England, and the problem of redundant women. Reformers of every stripe argued that Christian middle-class women had a right to devote themselves full time to charitable works, though they differed widely on what religious form this should take.[3] In defending the creation of special orders for women, advocates combined lofty idealism with practicality. Dean J. S. Howson, the chief proponent of deaconesses, spoke of the necessity "not simply to utilise, but to relieve aspirations after self-devotion," yet he also pointed out that the formation of a diaconate would be the perfect answer to "the excessive supply of dejected governesses and distressed needlewomen."[4] The Rev. A. P. Forbes, in a pamphlet describing the advantages of sisterhoods, felt that unmarried middle-class women who lacked "the purifying chastisement of toil" might be much happier working for a "noble, heart-stirring, Divine object, to give a life to minister to the poor of Christ."[5]

In spite of their similar rhetoric in regard to single women, high and low churchmen were deeply divided over the nature of women's religious orders. The low-church Evangelicals distrusted anything that smelled of popery and Rome; they insisted upon calling their consecrated women "deaconesses," who were free to leave at any time and were never to take vows.[6] Most deaconesses lived in the parish where they worked, under the direct supervision of the local vicar; even when they returned nightly or weekly to a central home, as did members of the Mildmay Institute, their primary commitment was to their regional mission work. In contrast, the high churchmen emphasized the importance of a separate communal life and long hours of regular prayer and vows. The dominant metaphor for the Evangelicals was the light of God, in which each deaconess carried his light like a sunbeam into the homes of the poor. The dominant image for the sisterhoods was of a consecrated, pure space apart from the world, where seekers could come for relief and succor.

Both men and women had an active role in founding the early religious orders. Evangelical and Dissenting women had originally started simple institutions that trained and coordinated the efforts of unmarried and devout working women, who were paid a small sum for their work. These organizations ranged all the way from small homes for visiting nurses to Ellen Henrietta Raynard's Bible women, who went from door to door in the slums, selling Bibles and offering elementary medical assistance.[7] But sisterhoods such as Jameson recommended, for middle- and upper-class women, were largely founded by the leading clerics of either the high or the low church. These men dominated the public debate for and against religious orders; religious women expected to obey their male mentors in all church matters. Nevertheless, by finding, in Jameson's words, their "*distinct* capacities and responsibilities in the great social commonwealth," deaconesses and sisters carved out an area of expertise and power within their male-dominated churches. Anglican sisterhoods were clearly in the vanguard of women's single-sex organizations, in both their organizational autonomy and their insistence upon women's right to a separate religious life. But Evangelical women were also capable of independent initiative. A thorough examination of the rise, organization, and work of women's religious orders reveals a complicated picture of institutional subordination and self-determination. Religion opened and closed doors for single women.

The Consecrated Religious Life

Religious communities, whether Evangelical or Tractarian, attracted women for two major and very different reasons. For many a community was the logical next step after years of piecemeal philanthropy at home or isolated district visiting.[8] If they had no or few home duties, an organized religious life among like-minded women simply made for more effective service. Moreover, under the protection of the church, women could go out and act in ways that would be forbidden on their own. A uniformed sister or deaconess could more easily be recognized as a nurse, a slum visitor, or a foreign missionary. A sisterhood or mission promised adventure linked with duty. On the other hand, many women sought out a religious community in order to seek perfection, that is, personal satisfaction through a relationship with God. For these

NO REASONABLE OFFER REFUSED

1. "A Sketch from Nature." (Punch,
1884.) Typical middle-class attitude
toward redundant women.

2. *"Adopting an Orphan." (*Our Work,
*1883.) Sister of the Church introduces
an orphan to a girl and her mother,
who will donate money weekly for the
orphan's support.*

3. *Agnes Grahame, deaconess, invites
a waif into the church, out of the rain
and cold. (M. A. M.,* Agnes Grahame,
Deaconess: A Story of Woman's Work
for Christ and His Church, *1879.)*

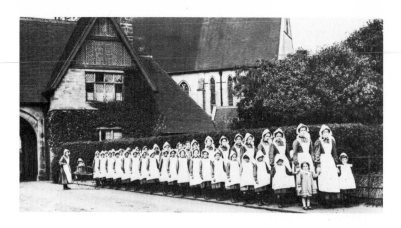

4. "Children of St. Margaret's
Orphanage, ca. 1910." The older girls
escort the younger to church.
Courtesy of the Society of St.
Margaret's, East Grinstead.

5. "A Group of Sisters of the People,
1897." (Samuel Chadwick, The
Church in the City, 1910.) Courtesy
of the City of Manchester Public
Libraries.

6. *Typical ward, St. Thomas'*
Hospital, ca. 1890. Note the carpeting,
easy chairs, and plants, to create a
homelike atmosphere. Courtesy of
St. Thomas' Hospital.

7. *Sister with her nurses, Charing
Cross Hospital, ca. 1890. Courtesy of
Charing Cross Hospital.*

8. *Miss Eva Lückes, matron of the London Hospital, with her office staff, 1914. Courtesy of the London Hospital.*

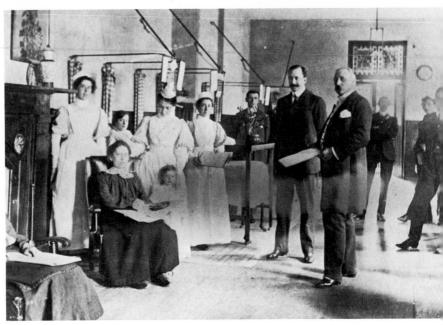

9. *London Hospital patients, nurses,*
doctors, and medical students,
ca. 1900. Note the relative importance
of each as reflected in their postures.
Courtesy of the London Hospital.

women prayer, not works, was central. In the early days of the sisterhoods, this choice was difficult for many to rationalize, and none of the early orders was contemplative. Indeed, throughout the nineteenth century, public charity was declared essential to a woman's religious life. By training and belief the Evangelicals would naturally emphasize more the importance of good works, while the sisterhoods placed more importance on regular services of prayer, Holy Communion, and meditation. But religious women, whatever their initial motivations in joining a community, often found it difficult to balance prayer and charitable work.

In the 1840s, the high-church Tractarians, led by E. B. Pusey, hoped to purify the Church of England, bringing it back to the early church fathers. They sought to revive a sisterhood that would focus upon regular prayer, penance, and retreat from the world. As early as 1841 Pusey professed Marian Hughes of Oxford in her religious vows, but she was not part of a community. This next move came about with the help of laymen who saw sisterhoods as a means of enabling women to do good works under church control. William E. Gladstone, in conjunction with other eminent laymen and clergy, wrote the first proposal for an Anglican sisterhood. Gladstone had already begun his night wandering, seeking out young prostitutes to reform, and was well acquainted with the poor of London's streets. Anxious to attack "the intensity of accumulated misery" of the large cities of England in a more systematic way, his committee proposed the establishment of a religious order that would go to the poor and sick in their homes, visit hospitals, workhouses, and prisons, run an orphanage for destitute children, give shelter to distressed women of good character, and assist in the burial of the dead.[9] In 1845 these high churchmen founded the first Anglican order, called the "Park Village Sisters." In 1848 Lydia Sellon began a sisterhood to work among the poor during a cholera epidemic in the Cornish town of Devonport. In the same year the St. John's sisterhood, a training institute for nurses, began. Others followed in rapid succession. These early orders faced many problems, including how many hours they should pray, what rule they should live under, and what kind of service to the poor was appropriate (their uniforms frightened many, who thought they were Roman Catholics seeking converts). But in spite of setbacks, the sisterhoods grew apace, and by 1860 fourteen orders had been founded with about a hundred sisters. Growth continued to be rapid; by 1900 there were fifty-four sisterhoods in Great Britain with two to three thousand women.[10]

The internal organization and ideology of the Anglican sisters differed from that of the other women's groups studied here. Victorian women's organizations were formed to promote specifically women's issues—education, jobs, legal reform, a social life, or philanthropy. Membership depended largely upon a shared outlook and a fair degree of class homogeneity. Either disagreements were patched up or a breakaway group formed a new organization; unanimity of belief and friendship were almost always projected. Women overwhelmingly agreed that only by effective public actions could they validate claims for changing women's position in the world. All Victorian women's communities depended upon help from male allies, especially in their early days; but the sisterhoods and deaconesses remained uniquely tied to the male hierarchy of their churches. Girls' schools, women's colleges, and even nursing homes could be founded and survive without male assistance, but within formal religion, men were essential to the continued existence of women's organizations. While men disagreed vehemently—and publicly—about women's religious orders, without the backing of powerful male friends in the church establishment, the sisterhoods would never have survived. Born amid so much public controversy, the high-church orders worked especially hard to avoid publicity for their members as individuals or as a group. In the words of Mother Etheldreda of the Sisters of Bethany, sisters should "efface themselves."[11] Entry, training, and full membership were formal, ritualized, and demanding; each was designed to separate a woman from the world psychologically and physically. This loss of self within the order meant far greater strength and unity for the community as a whole, so that on occasion the Anglican sisterhoods could be very powerful spokeswomen for religion and for women in religion. But change for single women was sought in the religious sphere, never the public.

What kind of women did sisterhoods appeal to? As late as the 1880s Dinah Mulock Craik, the popular novelist, praised them for taking in the "waifs and strays" of unmarried women; she bluntly stated that "entering a Sisterhood, almost any sort of Sisterhood where there was work to do, authority to compel the doing of it, and companionship to sweeten the same, would have saved many a woman from a lunatic asylum."[12] Yet such women as Craik had in mind would have wilted under the rigorous regimen of prayer and work undertaken by most sisters. Clearly the pull toward a sisterhood had to be stronger than the push away from a more conventional life with one's family. The rapid growth of sisterhoods points to characteristics within Victorian society that made women of the period well suited to the new religious opportunities. Ingrained in many women's confined lives were a passionate desire to do good works, a belief in guidance from authorities, and a desire to unite the disparate elements of life under one great ideal. If a woman felt a strong religious calling, this combination made the move into a sisterhood a natural choice.

Critics of sisterhoods were convinced that a woman chose to join an order because she was unhappy at home and wished to escape her household duties. Certainly homelife, as Florence Nightingale so eloquently testified, could be stultifying, boring, and unloving. The potential fulfillment of a life of self-sacrifice was obvious when compared with endless hours whiled away with flower arranging, visiting, and tea parties. But equally important was what Michael Hill has called "preliminary socialization."[13] Studies of modern-day nuns have found that a majority come from large, authoritarian families. The weakening of the traditional religious family has led to a substantial decline in vocations. But respectable Victorian girls were almost invariably brought up in patriarchal religious homes. The psychological transference of loyalty and daily habits to a religious community would have been relatively easy, in spite of family opposition. And of course, some high-church families could enthusiastically endorse their daughters' choice, adding further incentive to follow a calling.

For many women entry into a sisterhood meant the fulfillment of a long-cherished ambition to unite more closely with God—a vocation that insisted upon a complete dedication to the religious life. In 1843, after hearing John Henry Newman preach, Jane Ellacombe broke her engagement of three years. She explained that she had thought that marriage "was my path of duty, and my mind was made up to *endure* it (the expression is not stronger than the truth), till I was led to think that feeling as I did, it was my duty to lead a single life . . . little as I could have hoped for it, and unworthy as I felt I was of it." Six months later, when she read an article in the *Christian Remembrancer* recommending sisterhoods, her excitement was unbounded; it was as if someone shared her vision of life and had offered her a way to follow. She wrote her father, "I don't ask your consent [to join], and I don't want you to take too much responsibility," but she begged him to let her "act as a woman":

Do not deprive me of the blessed privilege of working for Christ with my brethren. . . . Do not think I myself should be in danger of running wild and doing all sorts of rash things—I should be then only one of many comrades, and we should all act together in our different parts towards one end, and my rashness and inexperience would be corrected and guided by the deep and earnest yet wise and calm spirits who would influence us.[14]

Her letter concludes with a vow to make further inquiries, for "these are extraordinary times and call for uncommon deeds." Her enthusiasm and commitment were finally rewarded when she became one of the first two women to enter the Park Village sisterhood.

Margaret Goodman went to Plymouth in 1848 to join Lydia Sellon's new Devonport Sisterhood in order to care for the sick and poor. Despite her later disillusionment with Sellon, she spoke of the early days as a time of "hard work, love, and obedience. . . . The household was the happiest, busiest, merriest, least constrained and most united of any I ever was in."[15] She found ample scope for her nursing skills and was honored to be among the sisters chosen to accompany Florence Nightingale to the Crimea. But the gradual enforcement of stricter and stricter regulations and the unbridled authority of Lydia Sellon caused her to leave in 1859; she wrote two books describing her experiences and condemning sisterhoods for giving unchecked power to women. Yet despite her antagonism, Goodman remained impressively positive about the life of active service she had experienced and recommended a more enlightened form of service for single women.

For some, entering a sisterhood was the most natural thing in the world—and a wonderfully fulfilling adventure. A Methodist Sister of the People, in an article on her life in the East End, exclaimed, "Life is a great unexplored country—it is full of beauty and wonder, whose secret has to be won. We mean to go through it on the tramp. We take the staff in the hand, and the burden upon the shoulder, and set out upon the march with a spirit braced to endurance, and a heart ready with reverence, and open to all it may encounter on the road."[16] Her enthusiasm was shared by Mother Kate, who spent a lifetime working at St. Saviour's Priory, Haggerston. Although the daughter of a clergyman, as a child she "loved to run wild about the garden with the dogs, and I cared more for horses than anything in the world." But in 1857, "Something suddenly seemed to come into my heart that put everything in a different light before me."[17] She eagerly joined the growing Society of St. Margaret's and was soon assigned to the new work they were undertaking in the slums of London. In her memoirs she cheerfully describes staving off curious boys, chasing down rats, killing fleas, and giving away her last petticoat to a needy woman. "We were all young, all enthusiastic, all very keen on doing."[18] Everything was an adventure willingly undertaken by these pioneers in bringing the church to the poor. Her infectious pleasure in life and those she helped contrasts sharply with the self-sacrificing nature of Jane Ellacombe's call. For Mother Kate the Society brought untold opportunities for service and worship, unavailable only a few years before she entered.

Although evidence is necessarily scanty, common sense tells us that other women, frustrated with a useless life and oppressed with a sense of their own unworthiness, might join an order from more inchoate motives. The impulsive act of a moment could become the satisfying choice of a lifetime. The low-church Constance Maynard considered her cousin's entry into the Society of All Saints to be a strange fluke. She recorded in her diary the visit of "poor, rebellious Emmie Wheeler," who seemed so "peevish, impetuous, discontented, finding in life nothing to do,—could not draw, hated riding, & above all hated housekeeping & being punctual & tidy." On the last night of her stay with the devout and serious Maynard family, Emmie spoke poignantly to her uncomprehending cousin:

> It was after supper & singing hymns, & she & I stood in the uncarpeted new Schoolroom, looking at the brilliant half-moon, which threw squares of light on the bare floor. She put her arms round me & said something to the effect that she couldn't possibly give up something & be a Christian. It was asking too much, altogether too much, & she couldn't do it. I said, "Oh, Emmie, it *is* worth it! It is a sacrifice, I know, because it is such a tremendous change, such a thorough surrender of our own will, but oh, it is so *really* worth it, Emmie, do try, *do* just try!" She answered, "Oh, but you don't know in the least the blackness & deceitfulness of my heart, I don't *want* to be good, I don't *want* to change. I want to go on &

always have my own way." She seemed relieved to have confessed this, & we stood still a minute looking at the moon,
she turned to me & said gently & affectionately, "You can
pray, Consy, you are so very good, you are safe and happy, but
you mustn't forget poor, straying Emmie."[19]

A few months later she met a nursing sister at another friend's
house and was so impressed that she decided to join an order. Emmie wrote her low-church relatives that she "was convinced that
she was so dreadfully, so utterly bad, that these people who led a
ruled life were the only ones who could help her," and that she
felt "a sense of remorse so deep that it was nearly despair" when
she compared her life with that of her pious cousins. Emmie never
left the order, and to Maynard's knowledge appears to have found
the peace that had so eluded her.

"Poor Emmie" must have been representative of other Victorian
girls, under great pressure from their families to feel a commitment to traditional religion, while facing a life without any purpose other than a society marriage and conspicuous consumption.
The discipline and idealism of the new orders attracted many who
sought a more purposeful life but lacked Nightingale's genius or
Maynard's sense of duty. Yet fears remained that women who entered sisterhoods were neglecting distasteful home duties. The romantic elements of "taking the veil" were encouraged by the art
and literature of the day.[20] The novelty of the sisterhoods, the secret confession, and the delicious sense of disobeying one's parents for a higher cause must have attracted some.[21] Then, too, a
great many women had fought hard for permission to enter an order; they would be reluctant or unable to return home and so were
forced to continue as sisters, taking solace in the work and security.[22] Throughout most of the nineteenth century it was considered somewhat questionable and possibly fanatical to enter an order; nevertheless, a more confident note appears in publications
by the 1880s, calling attention to the possibilities of a life of active service in God's name. The richly rewarding life of the community was contrasted with "those who drag out aimless frivolous lives 'in society,' working hard in the service of the world."[23]
The conflicting demands placed upon an upper-class woman in
late Victorian life, which insisted upon family duties, philanthropy, and socializing, were resolved by the devout when they
made a wholehearted commitment to religious service.

55

Women came from all parts of England to join the sisterhoods, but they appear to have been drawn largely from more traditional rural parishes or marketing towns. Virtually all of the sisterhoods were in London or the South; they had little impact upon the industrial North, which was left to the Evangelicals. Although women without money or with very little were welcome, the new sisterhoods needed the financial and social cachet of the wealthier classes. Poorer women were encouraged to become lay sisters, doing much of the daily drudgery of the community, while the better off became choir sisters (occasionally bringing their maids with them to serve as lay sisters). Very few orders united the educated and uneducated. The choir sisters sang (or chanted) the offices and took a leadership role in running the convent and its many projects. Most orders permitted members to keep their personal property and income, though some insisted that everything be disposed of before entry. Choir sisters were expected though not required to bring a dowry and to contribute between £30 and £50 annually to their expenses.[24] This compares favorably with the normal cost of living for a lady, but the amount was sufficient to discourage those without an independent income who would not wish to be lay sisters.

The sisterhoods from the earliest days attracted daughters of high-church clergy and the leisured class; several titled women joined, to the dismay of their families and opponents of sisterhoods. Before heading the Community of St. John Baptist at Clewer (1852), Harriet Monsell had been well known and popular in high-church circles. Both the Community and All Saints, London (1851), were known as fashionable sisterhoods; the substantial dowries received in turn helped to expand their work. Worried about recruitment into "his" sisterhood, Pusey complained that the fame of Monsell and the Reverend T. T. Carter was such that it had become a matter of course to go to Clewer instead of a smaller order.[25] Certainly Clewer was remarkably successful in recruiting women; twenty-nine years after its founding, in 1881, the order had 180 sisters; at Carter's death in 1901 it had more than 300.[26] Had the sisterhoods drawn from less prominent families, they might have attracted less unfavorable publicity. As with nursing, the class implications disturbed Victorian society. On the one hand, the religious believed that only well-educated, gently born women had the right combination of intelligence, tact, and commitment for the work of helping the destitute and fallen. On the other hand, upper-class ladies were simply not supposed to know about, much less consort with, such people. The upper-class character of sisterhoods was both a liability and an asset. If wealthy ladies had not joined, the movement might have floundered, but by stamping their image upon certain orders, they reinforced class prejudices.

The process of becoming a sister has been described many times before, especially in regard to Roman Catholic orders.[27] Until the more recent revolution within both the Roman Catholic and the Anglican churches, their systems of postulancy, novitiate, and sisterhood were quite similar, though obviously the doctrinal education was different. Although the severity and emphasis of each order varied, the training and daily life were roughly the same for all Anglicans admitted. A woman was first admitted as a postulant for any time up to six months; she then became a novice and underwent a more severe training period, usually lasting from one to three years. Vows were then taken for a limited period of time, to be renewed regularly. A novice was carefully watched for her spiritual devotion, behavior, and relations with others. During this testing period a woman was physically separated from her family and friends, wore a special dress, and was permitted to speak only to the other novices and her novice mistress. Strict division prevented any sister from influencing her. The training was not theological or biblical but involved mastering a complicated schedule of services (for choir sisters) or learning the correct way to clean and pray (for lay sisters). Very little free time was available, and only exceptional circumstances permitted deviation from the regulated times for prayer, work, eating, sleep, and recreation. A sister looking back on her novitiate during World War I laughingly explained, "Oh, I was cheeky in those days. I once told the Sister in charge of novitiates, to succeed here, you just have to remember, 'Speak when you are spoken to, Come when I call, Shut the door after you, That will be all.'"[28] The severe discipline, long periods of silence, and complicated rituals were meant to humble the new entrant and to separate her from the world; isolated and alone, she would then be lifted up into greater spirituality. There the love, community, and security of the sisters enclosed her. One's real mother was left for a spiritual mother, far more demanding but far more rewarding.

Although the amount of time set aside for daily prayer and meditation might vary from three to six hours, the Anglican sisterhoods all followed a strict and ritualized order of prayer and work. The prayer life and rules of the Anglican sisterhoods were a product of much thought, experimentation, and borrowing from the Roman Catholic orders. In the early days supporters worried about how well even the most devout women would respond to long periods of meditation and prayer without special training. Pusey felt that long oral prayers were too Presbyterian and unsuitable for Anglicans; he designed a system of responses for each office of the day to hold the attention of the Park Village sisters.[29] Most orders obeyed the injunction, "Seven times a day will I praise Thee, O Lord." Seven formal offices were said, along with private prayer and self-examination. The day began at 6 : 00 a.m. or earlier with Lauds, followed by meditation, and then Prime and Holy Communion. After breakfast came Terce at 9 : 00 a.m. The time from approximately 9 : 15 to 12 : 00 was spent in work. At 12 : 00 came Sext, followed by dinner and usually an hour's recreation consisting of general conversation, along with knitting and needlework. About three hours were spent in work each afternoon. Vespers came between 5 : 00 and 6 : 00 p.m. A brief supper was followed by another short period of recreation or meditation. Sisters working in missions went to their evening clubs or classes. Compline was at 9 : 00, with private prayers and meditation until 10 : 00. The "greater silence" was from Compline until Terce, with a "lesser silence" practiced during the working hours of the day, varying according to the work undertaken and the strictness of the order.[30]

The most popular alternative to the sisterhoods was the creation of a professional group of women church workers. The lobbying of Dean J. S. Howson and other interested church members revived interest in the ancient order of the diaconate. In late 1861 Elizabeth Ferard started a communal deaconess order; from the beginning she sought closer ties with the church hierarchy than had the sisterhoods. Like Florence Nightingale, she had visited and worked at the German deaconess institution at Kaiserswerth before starting her own order. She disagreed with Pastor Fliedner in feeling that Anglican deaconesses, unlike their German counterparts, should be drawn largely from the middle class and should not undertake the onerous tasks connected with nursing; she also placed more emphasis upon a permanent communal life and distinctive dress. Ferard hoped that by drawing from the upper classes she would attract women with varied skills that would be more useful to parish clergy. But her London Diocesan Deaconess Institution grew slowly; many women sought out the more stringent and independent sisterhoods, while others preferred the non-communal low-church diaconate. The increasing association of the title "deaconess" with the Evangelicals may also have discouraged high-church women from considering the LDDI or a similar diaconate training order. By 1900 there were probably about 180 official deaconesses in the Church of England.[31]

The LDDI and its affiliates followed a life similar to that of the sisterhoods internally, but they did work for parish clergy much like the rapidly expanding numbers of Evangelical and dissenting "deaconesses" and "sisters." (Since the low church did not believe in vows, its women did not officially use such titles.) Trained full-time workers in the large urban parishes of Victorian England were clearly of great assistance to clergymen of all kinds. So popular did the idea of organized churchwomen become that by 1900 almost every Protestant sect had a "sisterhood" by some title. The largest was the Wesleyan Sisters of the People, under Mrs. Hugh Price Hughes. Begun in 1887 so that "devout and educated" women could work more systematically for the Methodists, its sisters undertook teaching, nursing, and mission work.[32] Some six Church of England deaconess organizations, along with many different dissenting sisters, the Salvation Army, and Roman Catholic sisters worked in London alongside thirteen Anglican orders when Charles Booth made his monumental survey, *Life and Labour of the People of London* (1902–3).[33] Except for the Anglican sisterhoods, all of these church workers were under local ministers, wore a uniform (mainly for safety in the slums), and followed some kind of regular prayer life. However controversial the high-church sisterhoods remained, by 1900 trained full-time women workers had been accepted by the churches.

It is impossible to review completely the many Evangelical and Dissenting church organizations for women, but an examination of one of the most important will help to highlight the differences and similarities between these more loosely associated groups and the Anglican sisterhoods. The Reverend William Pennefather founded the Mildmay Institute in 1860 because "it seem[ed] strange that, while training institutions and colleges are deemed essential for men who are to be used either as *medical* missionaries or as preachers of the Gospel, there should not be institutions where women may acquire that knowledge of the bodies and

minds of their fellow-creatures which would render them capable
of fulfilling their high destiny as help-meets to man."[34] The Institute became the largest and best-known training center for
Evangelicals within the Anglican church, with some two hundred
workers at any one time. Unlike Ferard and Howson, the Pennefathers did not intend to revive the early church diaconate, but
simply wished to give training, and recognition, to full-time
women church workers. They provided intensive training and a
permanent home for their deaconesses, many of whom became
nursing missionaries abroad. After completing her training, a
Mildmay deaconess was expected to live in the mission where she
had been assigned, acting as an example of Christian life for the
parishioners. On Friday evenings she returned "home" to Mildmay to share problems, relax with friends, and receive encouragement from all. Somewhat defensively, one admirer claimed that
the Institute refuted those who believed that Evangelicals were
"lax and easygoing" or that fifty women could not live together
without the strict rules of the high-church sisterhoods.[35] Both the
Mildmay and Wesleyan sisters were expected to show initiative
and self-reliance in their work while remaining subservient to
their minister; in reality they probably had a great deal of independence because they would know more about an issue or situation than an overworked minister with competing worries.

The procedures for joining an Evangelical institution were
simpler than those for joining an Anglican sisterhood. So too was
the daily life substantially different, with more emphasis upon
daily prayer and Bible reading as opposed to formal services and
frequent communion. Any woman who wished to become a deaconess at Mildmay would be interviewed by Mrs. Pennefather,
and if she could bring testimonials from her minister, had sound
beliefs on doctrine, and was of good character and strong commitment, she was admitted without further ado. After a trial period
of about a month, she would be asked to leave if she seemed lacking in the necessary maturity and devotion. The period of formal
training was at first one year and later two years. Regulations were
organized for the "thoughtful consideration and kindness" of a
large family; indeed, the Institute was repeatedly called a family,
and the deaconesses were encouraged to look upon it as their home.
The day opened and closed with family prayers. At breakfast
"each member of the family repeats a verse of Scripture, either on
a subject given for the day or selected by herself."[36] A half-hour

service followed breakfast, and for women in training, there was a morning of Bible study with afternoons devoted to mission work. Deaconesses were expected to set aside an hour each day for religious reading and meditation. Mildmay believed that the high-church sisterhoods encouraged "the morbid or visionary" and a "love of novelty or excitement," so their women were specifically discouraged from fanciful idealism in undertaking a life of "self-surrender and of self-abnegation."[37]

The Evangelical diaconate never attracted upper-class women to the same degree as the sisterhoods; wealthy Evangelical women were more likely to take their beliefs into a sphere of public service less limiting than a religious organization. Moreover, unlike the sisterhoods, the Evangelicals anticipated a greater turnover in membership; many deaconesses married clergymen and "retired" to work as wives in a parish. Mildmay, the Sisters of the People, and similar groups had among their ranks many widows, older women, and lifetime workers, but they appealed especially to the young churchgoer. The Methodist leader Katherine Price Hughes specifically envisaged an organization for "the young women of the leisured classes with their youthful idealisms, who in Protestant England were without a chance of finding a vocation and had consequently no scope for their energies or their gifts. . . . each pledged to devote her time and powers to the furtherance of a new idea of human solidarity and brotherhood."[38] Generally speaking, women who became members of an Evangelical or Dissenting group were not paid or were minimally reimbursed for their work. But expenses were not as great as those a woman might be expected to bear as a choir sister. No fees are mentioned in the studies of the Mildmay Institute beyond the cost of room and board, with the proviso that anyone was welcome regardless of income. But most religious women expected to pay a pound a week contribution toward upkeep. The financial barriers were less obvious among low churchmen but were nevertheless sufficiently high to ensure a reasonably homogeneous group of middle-class women workers.

The success of the diaconates and sisterhoods depended greatly upon volunteers. For every full-time worker, at least ten part-timers were required to run the various clubs, classes, and other projects in a mission. Every order had associates who lived at home, often following a modified rule of prayer; they also devoted a set number of hours per week to service and stayed for short intervals at the community. Many of these women had home duties that made it impossible to join until after the death of a parent, or they lacked the physical or emotional stamina to become full-time members.[39] Among the Evangelicals the volunteers were less fully organized, but they too were active participants in prayer groups as well as the usual round of charitable activities. By working as volunteers many more churchwomen participated in the communal life of their unmarried sisters, enjoying the benefits of women's leadership and responsibilities within the church. And without their help the enormous amount of labor done in the East End missions would have shrunk to a few overworked sisters or deaconesses meeting the needs of only a small number of women and children.

Both deaconesses and sisters were sustained in their work by a shared life of prayer and work. However different their daily lives might be, every consecrated woman drew her strength from this combination of prayer and community. As one Mildmay deaconess explained, "it is such a comfort to feel that we are not working alone, with no one to take an interest in what we do, but that we are mutually linked together, and must do all we can to help and comfort, uphold and strengthen, one another."[40] Emmeline Pethick-Lawrence, the militant suffragette leader, worked as a Sister of the People in the 1890s when she was in her twenties. She found that life as a sister gave "that emancipation of mental and practical powers which is to be found by working as a free person in a community of equals . . . [and] the beginning for me of a new life of the spirit."[41] A member of the Sisters of the Church felt that only in a sisterhood could she find "the intimate way in which each member participates in all good done by the rest of the community."[42] A sister or deaconess sacrificed a great deal of personal freedom in return for a community that helped her to overcome her failings and supported her as completely as any family could. Through community work she gained self-development and self-knowledge. Life within a religious community, at its best, was a living example of the Christian paradox that to lose one's life for others was to gain it.

The Growth and Development of the Community

In her review of church work in 1893, Emily Janes had remarked upon how "the stricter the rule the more it attracts," and in spite of grumbling, women thereby learned to "develop *esprit de corps.*"[43] Esprit de corps was essential if a community were to go forward in its work and sustain its workers' enthusiasm and commitment. But the means by which this was developed varied greatly from sisterhood to sisterhood, deaconesses' home to deaconesses' home. As religious women, both high- and low-church women were locked into the Victorian definition of the family as central to the moral life of a woman. Many aspects of the traditional family were embodied in the communities, yet ultimately an order, whatever its doctrinal basis, was antithetical to the family because a woman had to place her church life and responsibilities over any personal claims. Emmeline Pethick-Lawrence was correct in seeing that her entry into a new life commenced with leaving her family and realigning her loyalties to the Sisters of the People. Esprit de corps embraced traditional values, but it also involved reorienting priorities.

Many early leaders, both men and women, were ignorant about how to run a women's religious community and distrustful of women's powers of leadership, initiative, and ability to live together. Having so few guidelines, the new sisterhoods made a good many mistakes; only later did entering an Anglican sisterhood became less of an adventure into the unknown. One of the most common problems was the periodic conversion of members to the Catholic faith. The minister in charge and the first head of the Park Village sisterhood defected. The head and only choir sister of the young Community of St. Mary the Virgin, Wantage, founded in 1848, converted leaving only two lay sisters to begin anew. In reaction to these episodes, sisters were discouraged from getting to know women in other orders; a sister might be poached by a rival or become unsettled in her place. Since each order's rule was in the process of being codified and many sisters received contradictory advice from interested clergy, occasionally erratic and extreme penances were undertaken without adequate supervision. When Jane Ellacombe died at thirty-five, after nine years at Park Village, her sister wrote sadly that her death came from no known cause, but "the cramped mental life and bodily austerities of those nine years. I think many mistakes were made in that sisterhood."[44]

Equally difficult was the lack of experience or traditions about how a sister or deaconess should behave in public. The Evangelicals did much soul-searching over wearing uniforms, which seemed to smack of the high church. Mildmay justified its decision by calling attention to the difficulty of finding plain, unassuming dresses and bonnets; they insisted that their distinctive dress be worn only when "on duty."[45] A constrained and rigid manner often characterized early Anglican sisters, unsure about how to behave and when to relax. The Reverend Henry Daniel Nihill was pleased that his Sisters of the Poor went "forth in the spirit of the seventy disciples, saluting no man by the way, intent upon the one work that they mean to do in His Name, and they would no more think of not praying in silence as they go along, than of walking backwards."[46] Mission work among the poor was weakened, however, if the sisters were unable to speak to people on the streets. The Reverend J. M. Neale was amused to find how shocked the leaders of the Community of St. John Baptist were when he told his order, the Society of St. Margaret, not to withdraw if a family where a member was nursing had guests.[47]

A major problem was convincing Victorian parents that entering a sisterhood was not eccentric, willful, or capricious. Dr. Pusey wrote regularly to the Reverend Mr. Ellacombe, trying to quiet his fears about the step his daughter was so determined to take. Yet at the same time he strongly believed in answering a call from God, even at the price of disobeying one's parents.[48] Pusey was rather too unworldly in his blindness to parental concerns. Virtually all who opposed sisterhoods concentrated their venom on the unnatural breaking of family ties. Pamphlets were filled with anecdotes about women denied permission to return to dying mothers or forced to make over their entire inheritance to an order. Issues of family property, and a single woman's right to dispose of hers as she wished, were often underneath this opposition. A father who had vehemently opposed his twenty- seven-year-old daughter's entry into the Society of St. Margaret published an inflammatory attack when she died and left £400 to the order (the bulk of her property was left to her brother). The ensuing pamphlet war badly damaged the reputation of the Society and led to the withdrawal of the bishop of Chichester as Visitor.[49] The deaconesses also had to be careful not to overstep family boundaries; every applicant to Mildmay was questioned in regard to her home duties before she was admitted.

To some Protestants the attractions of the new sisterhoods seemed fearfully irresistible to vulnerable young girls seeking a more exciting life. The long services, unpleasant physical work, and rigidly ordered day seemed degrading to outsiders, who could not accept the idea that any well-brought-up Victorian lady would agree to such a life unless she had been duped or artificially estranged from her family. One critic inveighed against the "unbounded influence" of the Mother Superior, who could so entirely convert a young woman that after a few visits to a convent she would find her own home "irksome and distasteful" and would beg to join the order.[50] Another sarcastically reminded her readers, "Is it to be supposed that adopting particular habits of dress and daily routine, irksome duty at stated times, and the inflexible, worrying discipline of a female lawgiver, would secure as much variety of self-sacrifice as a home where the most teasing kinds of duty cannot be foreseen, nor self-chosen, nor agreed upon?"[51] Any single woman wanting to practice self-denial, it was suggested, should try a little at home in her own family circle and social class, not in a sisterhood or among the poor. Critics of convent life had to deny or rationalize the unpalatable fact that many women were unhappy at home and were willing to undertake far more arduous duties because they were meaningful and freely chosen.

Partisans of sisterhoods were rather ingenuous in their defense. In justifying them they chose examples of mature women with no parents or financially independent women with supportive parents. Many sisterhoods and deaconesses' homes prided themselves on their family atmosphere. A sister called her head "Mother," a distant and all-powerful father came at stated intervals to administer communion and hear confession, and fellow members were her sisters. Yet this vocabulary masked a very different kind of organization. While the outward forms of family life might continue, postulants were repeatedly reminded that worldly friendships and ties must be abandoned in favor of God. No one could serve both her family and God in a sisterhood. Even the most kindly taught complete detachment and renunciation; T. T. Carter felt that fears of separation from one's family were an indication of God's testing.[52] Moreover, the health of the community depended upon discouraging particular friendships among sisters. As Mother Harriet Monsell advised a sister,

> I do not think you need trouble yourself because you love me. As a fact you do. All efforts to think or feel otherwise will only be unreal and lead to no good. All you need strive for is

to love God more, more singly and simply; to still the human
actings and impulses of your being in Him.[53]

To another sister she recommended inner peace "not by weakening love, but [by] . . . taking the self and the excitement out of
love, making it more pure and real."[54] Sisters had to, at whatever
cost, break their earthly ties in order to achieve more perfect spiritual union with God.

A major difficulty faced by all women entering a sisterhood was
reconciling their expectations with the realities of the community.[55] Romantics seeking novelty and personal thrills would of
course be disappointed, but the issues were more complicated.
Simply entering a convent demanded great strength and self-
assertion for a Victorian woman in the early days of sisterhoods;
even by the end of the century it was not easy. But once within its
walls she was supposed to submit herself to the will of God as expressed in the order's rule. Impetuosity and enthusiasm had to
be curbed and channeled into submission and obedience. The
very characteristics that gave an independent-minded daughter
strength to enter a convent might also bring her into conflict with
the community's requirements. Much emphasis was placed upon
an applicant's unworthiness before God, on the necessity of patience, and on waiting for the right moment to act. Jane Ellacombe's eagerness was rebuked by both John Henry Newman and
Pusey. Yet the early founders were also worried lest sisterhoods attract too many "waifs and strays" among single women. The Reverend William Dodsworth feared that a well-financed and secure
home for life would be too comfortable and would attract the
wrong sort of recruit while inhibiting the religious life of the
devout:

> To live a holy and useful life is one thing, to live a life of self-
> sacrifice is another. It is very aweful [sic] to remember the ser-
> vice with which they are consecrated to God and to a life of
> entire self-renunciation. And yet unless there is something of
> painful labour, theirs is in many respects of worldly comfort a
> life much to be preferred to that of a governess, and which
> many might covet for its comfort: so we might lead them into
> a great snare.[56]

The Governesses' Benevolent Institution's reports document
many cases of grim poverty and isolation among unemployed and

aging women, so Dodsworth's fears were not without foundation. A sisterhood gave security for life and could ill afford to be filled with incompetent or weak women, any more than it could be overwhelmed by romantics and individualists.

The Evangelicals faced rather different problems among their recruits. They did not place so much emphasis upon a lifetime commitment, yet it would obviously damage morale if too many women left after a brief period of work. Sisterhoods founded their own hospitals, orphanages, schools, penitentiaries, and other institutions, which they then controlled. Deaconesses, in contrast, were more likely to be working under a clergyman in a mission or slum church. In such circumstances they might find their opportunities limited or discover that a particular project had burst its boundaries. Sister Grace Kimmins spent many years leading the Guild of the Brave Poor Things, an organization of cripples that she had started; she also successfully launched a campaign to improve their work and training opportunities. Her commitment to cripples, however, outgrew the Methodist mission, and she went on to found and administer the Heritage Craft Schools for training cripples from all over England.[57] Emmeline Pethick-Lawrence and Mary Neal after four or five years' work felt frustrated by their distance from the poor as long as they lived at the Sisters of the People home; when their petition to live among the poor in their own flat was denied, they decided to break away and start their own project.[58] Yet none of these women renounced her religious beliefs or the experience she had gained from working as a Sister of the People. If opportunities were denied a high-church sister, she had few choices beyond submission or resignation. The low-church women had centrifugal tendencies, taking their vision of a better world outward, affecting wider and wider circles. High-church women brought the world into their own space, their circle of holiness. This inward turning could either purify or stultify, just as the breaking away of the most creative talents could advance or limit the low-church deaconesses.

The Victorians combined an enviable optimism about the possibilities of individual and corporate action with a willingness to tackle any problem that lay at hand. Both deaconesses and sisterhoods combined Mary and Martha; hours of prayer invigorated and sustained each woman in her work of winning souls. But sisterhoods still differed markedly from the low-church groups in their wholehearted commitment to a separate life of prayer. Even in the most active sisterhoods, prayer took priority over good works. The Evangelicals could point out with pride that they were always available to the poor, whereas the high-church orders set aside certain hours, keeping sacred times for prayer. The Evangelicals worked on the principle of permeating the lives of the poor; they "enter[ed] darkened lives, knowing that through the opening we may make there will stream in afterwards, sunshine, and fresh air, and a thousand influences to lighten, quicken, and invigorate."[59] For the high-church sisters, a life apart was essential, for "their work for others will be fruitful only in proportion as they advance in the work of conquering themselves."[60] In the words of a Sister of the Church, a sister "makes a holocaust of herself, consecrates to God all she had, keeps nothing back."[61]

This holocaust of self can be seen spatially and temporally. Victorian women upon entering a sisterhood moved from a world where their largely empty time was filled with casual engagements and intermittent family responsibilities to an enclosed community that took all of their time and divided it into minute fractions. Their days were completely at the command of the order and completely filled. For those women whose idleness weighed heavily upon them and who found that they could not escape the deadly round of trivia, the ordered time of the convent must have come as a relief. No less welcome for many was the austerity of the surroundings; the cluttered space of the Victorian wealthy home was exchanged for unadorned and simple rooms. Many women left a life where every whim was catered to by servants and where no one sat down to a table not laid with linen, crystal, silver, and china. The deal tables and earthenware dishes were forcible reminders of the vow of poverty. One novice spoke plaintively about how "in my ideal pictures of holy poverty, I had never realised these practical details, and they appalled me."[62] She felt that she could not face a lifetime of mugs, steel forks, and bare rooms. But others embraced this austerity gladly, finding in it the necessary space to encounter God. And compensation could be had in the lavish beauty of the church and the services. Indeed, Bishop Samuel Wilberforce justified the expense spent on the chapel at the Community of St. John Baptist as sanctifying the pleasures of pure taste for those who had given up the ordinary pleasures of making a home of their own.[63]

Strain and tension necessarily arise among women who are expected to seek perfection and selflessness in communal life while involved in active and intense work outside the walls of the convent. The importance of the mother superior can hardly be overestimated; she was not only the representative of Christ within the convent, but also the chief guide and confessor. The quality of the spiritual life of the community, as well as the smooth and happy running of the order, depended upon her. Firm and wise guidance was essential, yet Victorian women had not been trained for leadership positions, much less for leading a religious order; certainly many nineteenth-century churchmen found nothing more contrary to God and nature.[64] The women themselves called for submission, doubting their own capabilities and fearing that they might be swayed by emotionalism and enthusiasm. Somehow vigorous leadership had to be found that did not contradict the necessary humility.

The Evangelicals continued the church tradition of male leadership, even when a woman might actually have more knowledge and responsibility. Mildmay Institute was in the charge of a very popular minister, while his wife and a trusted assistant ran the deaconesses' home. The Reverend Mr. Pennefather was always available should the deaconesses have any problems, and of course his unimpeachable credentials helped the cause in the face of potential critics within the ranks of the Evangelicals. Mrs. Pennefather could argue that she had only extended the usual role of the clergyman's wife into new areas to meet the demands of a changing society; her married state ensured that she was not a dangerous enthusiast. Moreover, the looser organization of the Home, with the bulk of the trainees and deaconesses serving elsewhere, meant that it was more a home base than a mysterious cloister. Nevertheless, one should not minimize the difficulties of Evangelical and Nonconformist women who wished to become full-time church workers. The Reverend Mr. Pennefather belonged to the radical wing of the low church, as did the Methodist Hugh Price Hughes and his wife. When Mrs. Price Hughes founded the Sisters of the People at the end of the century, "The very ideal that women should leave their homes and live in the comparative freedom of a community, in order to carry out rather subversive principles of social sharing, was a bombshell to the large mass of conservative low-church and Nonconformist opinion."[65] The charismatic leadership of Price Hughes and his assistant Mark Guy Pearse was instrumental in ensuring the success of the Methodist sisters.[66]

Good leadership was more difficult for the London Diocesan Deaconess Institution, an order that seemed a weaker version of the sisterhoods. Elizabeth Ferard unfortunately was a distant and shy person, discouraging applicants by her manner. After Sister Elizabeth's resignation as head because of ill health, the tiny community lost its visitor and second head within months. Louisa M. Hubbard, a lifelong champion of women's causes, had been a firm supporter of the fledgling organization, but even her faith faltered when she saw the small numbers after nearly fifteen years' work. The third chaplain wrote in late 1874, rallying her to the side of the Institution, "The only hope of executing a good idea lies in *confidence.*" He went on to agree with her suggestion that since no one had been trained to replace Ferard, it might be a good idea to hire a man and wife, "but where to find such a man . . . unless *the* man is found it would not be well to think of such an appointment."[67] Funds were available, but no one came forward.

Although the Pennefathers had successfully led the Mildmay deaconesses, the high-church LDDI was reluctant to follow suit, and Louisa Hubbard's suggestion was quietly dropped. No matter how powerful the founding fathers, within the walls of the sisterhood women were in charge. But their sphere of influence was carefully demarcated to include only their own communities. The sisterhoods never challenged men in regard to the running of the Church of England or its dogma; they opposed the move to admit women to the priesthood after World War I.[68] They found the struggle to gain public and church acceptance of female leadership hard enough. Fortunately it was a cardinal belief of the religious that God would give strength to those called to new tasks. Even if women had never nursed soldiers on the battlefield, with God's grace they would do so successfully. Any sister would be equally ready for a responsible position within the convent.

The most controversial of the early superiors was Lydia Sellon, the lady superior of the Devonport Sisterhood and a close friend of Pusey. Even her most charitable biographers now admit that she was given to excesses; contemporaries were more divided.[69] She aroused great loyalty or great hatred among the women under her. One sister told Pusey that she considered Sellon a "maniac," hated by almost everyone in the order. Pusey was horrified and would brook no criticism of "Dearest Mother."[70] When Sellon demanded that a novice lie on the floor in the shape of a cross for hours or remain absolutely silent for a week, he supported her. Sellon herself, from the tone of her replies in the pamphlet war she engendered, appears to have been a domineering and self-righteous woman, and yet someone of considerable personality and intelligence. She was able to hold together a small band of women in the face of continual defections and public criticism, no small feat in the circumstances.

One of the recurrent accusations against Sellon, and later the Sisters of the Church, was the misuse of funds. Charitable organizations are always liable to such allegations, and when combined with inflammatory information about practices behind convent walls, they became powerful weapons. A great deal, for example, was made of the money spent on flowers at Devonport. Lydia Sellon's father repudiated such charges in detail, claiming that on one occasion a friend had spent £3 of her own money on flowers when intending to spend only £1, but that she had never spent the exaggerated amount of £7.[71] Sellon herself argued that

> Women may give their whole heart to God and His poor, to
> labour for them, but *we are women and have women's tastes.*
> We still love flowers and pictures. We have done with gay
> dresses for they are expensive and would be a mockery to the
> poor, but we like the brightness and gaiety of flowers, and
> friends give them to us—why should we not use them as we
> will?[72]

The issue of flowers at the altar or in the superior's room became a symbol of all that was wrong with the new sisterhoods. Their extravagance and femininity seemed to run counter to a true religious life; moreover, to critics they represented women's inability to govern themselves. Indeed, this was the main criticism against the followers of Lydia Sellon. The disaffected Margaret Goodman had high praise for "the mental and moral qualities of Miss Sellon," but she attacked Sellon's encouragement of adulatory flattery from her followers. She hoped that the firm hand of the bishop of Exeter would check such tendencies and return the community to its original conception. But the bishop had withdrawn his sanction of the order in 1852.[73]

Lydia Sellon was, like Florence Nightingale, a pioneer in seizing responsibilities that had not been previously available to women in the nineteenth century. She too found the women under her to be very mixed in their training and self-discipline; both leaders believed their chief task was to drill their probationers in obedience, self-control, and accuracy. Ladies had never been asked to perform tasks promptly and thoroughly without complaining or questioning the order. Needless to say, protests were inevitable when Sellon tried to turn her ladies into servants of God. Accusations that her sisterhood was "unladylike" were true in the sense that sisters were expected to do all the work, from the meanest to the most spiritual. Moreover, she insisted upon total obedience to her personal authority, in the name of the church. The insistence upon obedience and hard work was combined with traditional methods of female control. Nineteenth-century women had been labeled capricious, and certainly Sellon controlled her sisters with the same tactics that might have gone into controlling a drawing room. She kept favorites who spied on others for her. Regulations were constantly changed, so that an individual never knew whether she was obeying the superior correctly. Sellon was also emotionally manipulative, first severely punishing a sister and withdrawing her love, then lavishly praising her and treating her to special favors. In this disturbing state any word of praise, especially when reinforced by long periods of silence, was doubly comforting. Sellon's methods came under fire both from defectors, such as Goodman, and from those who opposed sisterhoods; for many she represented the worst aspects of female leadership. Indeed, the process of developing a new feminine *and* professional style of leadership was slow and difficult.

A more attractive model for women's leadership was the Victorian family, with a strong pater familias and a benevolent but firm mother. This was the path chosen by the Community of St. Mary the Virgin, Wantage, and by the Community of St. John Baptist, Clewer. After the loss of the first mother superior to Rome, the lay sister Harriet Day was elevated to mother superior of St. Mary the Virgin. Lacking in confidence or experience, she relied heavily upon the founder, the Reverend W. J. Butler. Growth was slow but steady under her stewardship. In 1861, thirteen years after the community's founding, Butler published a short description of the sisters' life. Wantage was like a well-ordered family, where "the intercourse with friends and relations is jealously maintained, and every arrangement is made to facilitate it."[74] To this day the convent "has the feeling of being in a family rather than in a community of nuns."[75] Clewer too had its influential male head in T. T. Carter, but it was blessed with the firm and effective leadership of Harriet Monsell. Her rule would have been familiar to the Victorian daughters under her, for she united a motherly concern with a firm sense of duty. One American visitor wrote rapturously about "the perfect understanding and affection that seemed to exist . . . and the total absence of all restraint, save that of affectionate respect towards the older Sister on the part of the Novices." She was especially attracted to the assistant superior, whose cosy room was "ornamented with a number of pretty pictures and knicknacks, & in a cushioned chair nestled a downy ball of a kitten."[76] The long motherly leadership of Harriet Day and Harriet Monsell gave the two orders stability and familiarity. Wantage and Clewer grew to be two of the largest Anglican communities; they did not frighten because they did not go to extremes.

A generation after Harriet Day, Harriet Monsell, Lydia Sellon, and Florence Nightingale, women everywhere were taking up leadership positions in the many different philanthropic and social organizations that sprang up. But the succcessful building of a women's institution still demanded single-minded tenacity and confidence, characteristics the remarkable Emily Ayckbowm brought to her church work. In 1859 at the age of twenty-three, she gathered together friends to collect money to rebuild her father's church. By 1864 she had formed the Church Extension Association to raise money to build churches in poor parishes and to rent pews so the poor could worship freely. Steady growth and planning led to the formation of the Sisters of the Church in 1870. The order grew rapidly in numbers and good works. Unlike leaders of previous orders, Mother Emily was not afraid of publicity, and she made effective use of the press to raise money for her many projects. During a period of sixteen years she read widely in the church fathers, and then completed the community's rule; she carefully placed limitations on the power of the mother superior and established a system of elected delegates. Though she was one of the most ardent advocates of women's rights within the church, she also warned that, "Women as a . . . rule are neither logical nor deep-thinkers, and in consequence are far more liable than men to be led astray by inaccurate and sophistical arguments and the plausible novelties in doctrine, as well as the unrealities of emotional and sentimental religion."[77]

Mother Emily's opinion of women was never as low as that of Florence Nightingale, but she shared with her great contemporary a sense of exceptionalism. She could behave high-handededly when she believed she was right. Humility and submission were all very well, but not when they interfered with doing God's work. In the mid-nineties, when Mother Emily faced widespread criticism, the patron of the Church Extension Association, Archbishop Benson, asked to inspect the conditions and administration of the orphanages and institutions in order to make necessary corrections. Mother Emily flatly refused, saying, "We humbly believe that we have been guided to undertake and carry on our work for the Church, by the guidance of God, and may not lightly go against the experiences of over twenty years."[78] Less tactfully, in the same letter she and the senior sisters announced that all male patrons were being removed from their circulars and would no longer be called upon. Astonished at her reply to so important a person as himself, the archbishop in his diary called Mother Emily "the most comically audacious Mother in the Universe." At first the order made no attempt to justify its move. Later it tartly explained that the patrons had been merely nominal and had had no authority over the Association, whereas the patronesses took "a real personal interest in the work of the C.E.A. They visit our Homes, make themselves acquainted with the details of our management, and help us with advice, contributions and personal assistance as opportunity may offer."[79] It was indeed audacious to admit that famous men were mere window dressing while the women did the real work. Until the end of her life, Mother Emily refused to have an Episcopal Visitor for the community. While Mother Lydia Sellon claimed to her dying day that nothing would give her greater pleasure than the return of the bishop of Exeter as visitor, Mother Emily made no pretence of wanting male interference.

The price Mother Emily paid for independence was high. Contemporary feeling found her injudicious at best, guilty at worst. Difficulties plagued her until her premature death in 1900. Nevertheless, the principle of women ruling women, and of women standing on their experience as equal to any man's cursory knowledge, remained. Anna Jameson's plea half a century earlier that women should care for women was not lightly put aside for any archbishop. As one sister wrote, "We are responsible to God for our children. For twenty years we have worked among them day and night, gaining practical experience, and how could we answer at the Day of Judgement if we gave up this experience blindfold for any human respect or favour."[80] Eventually matters were resolved between the Sisters of the Church and the church hierarchy. Mother Emily had pushed as far as possible within the church; any further separation might have led to expulsion. Women had gone a long way in less than fifty years toward gaining autonomy and power within the church, but within religion obedience necessarily curbed independence.

Good Works among the Destitute and Fallen

The major tasks undertaken by sisters and deaconesses encompassed three areas: outreach to the poor in city parishes, care of the sick and homeless, and reform of fallen women. The Victorians assumed that religious women by their very example would bring out the latent goodness in those they sought to help. A belief in the sinfulness of mankind, including themselves, bridged class differences. But these differences were also supposed to aid the largely middle- and upper-class sisters and deaconesses. As Archdeacon Harris argued in regard to the effectiveness of sisters working with prostitutes, "[T]here is no higher form [of Christianity] than that of a highly educated, devout English woman."[81] Class superiority went hand in hand with moral superiority. Churchwomen were offering the very best that their class could give the poor and needy—themselves. Whether high or low church, they believed profoundly in the importance of bearing witness to Christian values in their daily lives and actions. The very strengths and weaknesses of Victorian philanthropy can be seen in microcosm in the work of the sisterhoods and deaconesses.

A saintly life for an Evangelical woman meant that in her work, "as noiselessly as a sunbeam, she entered every door and left it ajar."[82] The children's story *Agnes Grahame, Deaconess* (1879) presented one ideal of the deaconess's work. Sister Agnes, in a simple but distinctive dress, went "nursing the sick, comforting the mourner, helping to raise the weak and wandering; and fearlessly warning the dissolute of the dread consequences of a sinful life."[83] As the tale progresses, we discover that she had lost her husband and children in the Indian mutiny of 1857; only after the death of those who might have a prior claim on her did she take up nursing as an expression of her religious beliefs. Sister Agnes, working alone under the guidance of a devoted clergyman, successfully converts hardened men and careless women. In time she softens the heart of the local industrialist by showing him that the practice of Christian charity will improve his business. As a fictional deaconess, Sister Agnes's work never fails, she never feels tired, and most of all, she never loses her patience. Yet in actuality, deaconesses were often ineffective with both poor and rich, could be intrusive in their self-righteousness, and rarely worked alone or in complete harmony with the clergy.

In spite of these human realities, low-church women worked steadily among the poor, concentrating on the conversion of individuals, hoping that, like the proverbial leaven, they would influence the mass. The ideal of Agnes Grahame, going from door to door and gently insinuating herself into the lives of those with whom she worked, remained a potent symbol, although most deaconesses found themselves concentrating on the daily toil of running girls' clubs, mothers' groups, and health clinics. Deaconesses were proud of being constantly available, providing both an example of the Christian life and a means of attaining it. Sister Lily, of the Sisters of the People, emphatically states that "The service of the people stands first with all our Sisters, and unless they show during their probation that that is their chief consideration, we cannot ask them to remain with us."[84] Such a policy, however, left little time for privacy, prayer, or planning. The demands of the moment could become so pressing that they overwhelmed whatever Christian sunlight a woman might wish to offer. Indeed, Charles Booth in his study of the religious life of London at the end of the nineteenth century comments on the small part religion appeared to play in the progress reports of the Sisters of the People.[85]

Ideologically Evangelicals did not have any mechanism for admitting failure. A system of counting each individual's conversion helped to sustain faith and legitimize the small numbers reached. A certain shaving of the truth, however, can be detected in the Agnes-Grahame optimism of mission reports.[86] Both for their own morale and to encourage donors, all organizations needed to show progress. The works of churchwomen flourished not simply because material needs of the poor were met, but also because the women themselves derived immense satisfaction from their efforts. The pleasures for the well-to-do women leaders can be seen in the gala accounts of trips to the seaside or country where more staid residents were shocked by the boisterous spirits of their protégés. The mischievous youths of the slums acted out some of the unexpressed dislike for rigid social mores felt by single women. Although the work of saving prostitutes was always presented in its most lugubrious light, clearly some respectable women rather enjoyed roaming the streets at midnight, invading brothels and arguing with sinners.[87] While they took away the freedom of the prostitutes by sending them to penitentiaries, they enhanced their own freedom of movement.

Although the work done by the sisterhoods was quite similar to that of the Evangelicals, their symbolic world was quite different. In spite of the fact that the sisterhoods had many missions in the slums and their full share of "havens" for repentent prostitutes, they placed much more emphasis upon establishing a sacred place apart. While the Evangelical woman was more likely to seek out fallen women night after night, offering temporary food and shelter and then training, a sister emphasized penitentiary work, building Homes of Refuge in which the repentent spent time apart from the world, expiating her sins and learning new habits. The high-church orders also heightened the distinction between sin and purity by emphasizing the need for regular church observances to protect the sinner from the temptations of the world. Their own austere and separate life was offered as an ideal for rescued sinners. If Evangelicals overemphasized the sudden change of heart, the Tractarians exaggerated the benefits of a daily discipline.

The high church continually focused upon the importance of consecrating to religion the simple daily tasks of a sisterhood. The Reverend Mr. Nihill's Sisters of the Poor gloried in their manual work, seeing it as an outward sign of their humility. They scrubbed and cleaned their small mission themselves in order to create a pure space, in contrast to the filth and degradation around them. Nihill boasted in characteristically Victorian fashion of the class advantages of ladies' doing physical labor, "I think you can understand the moral influence of a family of ladies who are not only not above putting their delicate fingers to the very roughest manual work, but who look upon labour and talk about it as (what they really feel it to be) an occupation full of dignity that no woman need be ashamed of."[88] One wonders how long their fingers remained delicate under such conditions, but Nihill assured his readers that the sisters' health had improved after undertaking the order's work. Ladies in these circumstances did not become like the poor; they remained ladies, furnishing a moral example both to their class and to those below them. Class differences mattered, even when on one's knees scrubbing or praying.

The work Nihill's sisters did was of greater importance to them than to the poor, for it upheld a crucial belief that no task was degrading if done in a religious spirit. Society in the nineteenth century had a very strong sense of boundaries for the upper classes; what was right and wrong to do, say, and believe was clearly known to true ladies and gentlemen. Physical labor had been plainly labeled as demeaning for ladies. The revived sisterhoods, however, insisted that no work was unsuitable or degrading, because no lady could lose her innate class status. They did not take the step of St. Francis of Assisi and proclaim their equality with the poor; class distinctions remained both within and outside the convent walls. Yet their achievement should not be underestimated; until all work was validated for women, no women's work would be fully respected. In this sense, sisterhoods were "masculine" and "unladylike," as their accusers claimed.[89] If the early orders had not insisted upon strenuous, unladylike work in areas of great social neglect, they would never have broken through the narrow confines of the Victorian woman's role. Humility was a double-edged sword.

Nothing illustrates the combination of purity and humility within a class context better than the work priorities of the sisterhoods. The orders founded before 1870 almost all undertook nursing or the reform of fallen women, or both. Even Dean Howson, in spite of his preference for deaconesses, admitted that sisters were peculiarly well suited to "the recovery of the fallen and the nursing of the sick."[90] Only the very highest type of religious woman could succor the ill or penitent, according to the new mythology rapidly gaining ground at midcentury. Nursing, the dirtiest and most polluting of occupations in its unreformed state, meant infection, fevers, pus, dirty bandages, and filthy working conditions. But the cool cleanliness of the devoted sisters would wipe away the physical illness and its moral implications. Not surprisingly, then, should sisters—the cleanest and purest of women—seek out as their special responsibility the reform of prostitutes—the vilest and most impure of women. When working with the fallen, the sister's purity was her safeguard against possible pollution, whereas someone less disciplined and devoted might become polluted. In a society fascinated with sexuality as a symbol of man's fallen nature, the picture of highly controlled and pure women caring for prostitutes had a peculiar appeal and reassurance. Only through the conjunction of extreme purity and extreme filth could reform occur. The sisters through their actions would redeem both the penitent and the society that had caused her plight. This comfortable idyll was made secure by cordoning off the penitents with the sisters in isolated refuges. No fundamental change was necessary in the relations of men and women, or upper-class and lower-class women. Moreover, sisters, unlike other women of the time, did not campaign against either the double standard or poor wages. They worked entirely in a private, enclosed space, concentrating on the victim and not the seducer.

Convents by their very nature are total institutions, embracing all members within high walls, separating them from the world. Houses of Mercy were doubly confining, confining both the sisters and the prostitutes, each in carefully defined spheres. Penitents chose to enter a House, but once there they were treated like prisoners. They were never "forgiven," nor expected to forget their sin; they could not go back into society as if they had never fallen. Upon admittance penitents were given a sober uniform and sometimes a short haircut; all personal clothing and belongings were removed. Each woman was watched at all times and never permitted to talk alone with anyone. All contacts with her past life were broken; to speak of it, or of one's family, or of one's children was forbidden. The "sentence," decided upon by the mother superior after a woman had proved herself reasonably docile and amenable to reform was usually fixed at two years. Sometimes an entirely separate and secluded spot was set aside for "lady penitents," who followed the same rules as the others but spent their time in embroidery work. A rigid and strict regimen stripped the women of their former identity and remolded them to a new one. Throughout the process distance was always kept between the penitents and the sisters. Contamination was avoided by strict regulation and physical separation.[91] Penitents were taught to bow low before any sister and to speak only when spoken to. Although the pure helped the fallen, they had to keep their hands metaphorically unstained. Reform was through punishment, through an almost exaggerated rejection of the prostitutes' past behavior, as if the reformers were afraid of its roots in the unacknowledged fantasies of the pure women who cared for them. Unconsciously the prostitute and sister may have shared more than they ever knew.

Perhaps no greater comment can be made on the division between the fallen and the pure than the Reverend T. T. Carter's claim that "modes of discipline and control, very different from those of a family, are absolutely requisite. It is impossible to train penitents in the ways of an ordinary household. They must be dealt with in a body, under special rule."[92] That Victorian idol, the family, had to be discarded to work effectively with such degraded women. The program for reform made no room for maternal feelings among the penitents; just as penitents were not treated as members of a family within the refuge, so too they could not retain their ties with their own children, who were sent into adoption. Neither could they become full members of the religious community. Isolation from each other and the sisters marked their days. Since the entire social system taught the poor how inferior they were to the upper classes, some women readily accepted their humble position in regard to the exalted sisters. For many, the attention they received, however severe, was better than neglect. A combination of kindness and distance made the sisters attractive, and for those completely estranged from their families, the refuge became their home. When the time came to leave, they could not face earning their own living outside and asked to stay permanently. They were enrolled in a special Magdalen order and given positions guarding the newer penitents.

Such "successes," however, were in the minority. Women were not always as docile and repentant as they might have been when they first arrived. At Clewer women working in the large laundry (a major source of income for the order and job training for the penitents) threw the heavy irons at the sisters and each other when they were angry.[93] One penitent at an unnamed House went on a hunger strike in order to get out and rejoin her children. She was punished by being put into solitary confinement, but in time the sister superior agreed to release her.[94] Though penitents had to sign an agreement to live peaceably and obediently, they might rebel by running away, hunger striking, or committing acts of random violence. The Houses seemed most successful with the very young and inexperienced or with the old, who faced an increasingly difficult life on the streets. Among these, usually the more pliant, many fell into an excessive religiosity that left them ill prepared to face ordinary life after their two years were completed.

Critics complained that the exalted religious feeling the sisters encouraged inevitably led to a falling away and to self-hatred from failing to live up to so high an ideal.[95]

The eagerness with which the new sisterhoods took up the unpleasant tasks of society should not be exaggerated. They all rapidly expanded into new areas of work; not all women had a special calling for the care of penitents. Sisters took on missions in the slums, the care of convalescents, working in old people's homes, teaching at every level, church embroidery, and other service-related tasks. The women who joined sisterhoods expected to be obedient to their orders' needs, but it was also in the best interests of an order to offer the widest variety of projects to appeal to all talents. Very few spent a lifetime caring for fever victims or former prostitutes. Women throughout society were seeking greater fulfillment in every area; religion could not remain unaffected. The sisterhoods can be described, as Michael Hill has done, as transitional organizations, providing an acceptable means for women to move out beyond traditional roles,[96] but this explanation best fits the early days of the orders, when they did pioneering work in nursing and social reform. By the 1880s sisterhoods had turned to as many new areas of work as professional women outside the convent walls; growth meant not only prayer and submission, but also thorough training in professional skills. These changes were an adaptation to changing social priorities in Victorian society as a whole, and they signaled a greater integration into that very society. The sisters and deaconesses no longer pioneered in doing work that no one else would undertake, but rather accepted responsibilities that were also being performed by parallel nonreligious institutions. The running of orphanages, schools, soup kitchens, and other social services was recognized as "women's work" that might be best done by the religious but was by no means limited to them. Thus, even as women's religious orders expanded their areas of work, they also became more conventional, more integrated into the mores of the existing society.

This change in emphasis is nowhere better shown than in the work of the fifty-four orders founded between 1870 and the present day. Only three undertook penitentiary work as their prime activity; far greater numbers chose working in poor neighborhoods or with children. By the 1870s social attitudes toward fallen women were changing rapidly, and criticisms were beginning to be voiced against the punitive Houses of Mercy.[97] Work with the fallen continued to grow, but public attention shifted to other social issues. The change to mission work and teaching was in some senses a conservative move. Class distinctions continued, along with the cult of purity and cleanliness. The orphanage of the Community of St. John Baptist had "room for children of every age, also of every condition, for after attempting to classify them according to years or learning, it has been found necessary to separate them according to their station in life—a troublesome and complicated division, but answering much better than the other."[98] The orphanages, like the penitentiaries, were total institutions, but the children were kept innocent and prevented from falling by a rigorous care and discipline that maintained class and family status. Girls were taught housewifery, not job skills. In the missions working-class wives were taught to accept their position, not to change it. Active church membership was the goal, not social change.

Anglican sisterhoods continued to grow throughout the nineteenth century and up through World War I. The Community of St. John Baptist, for example, peaked in size in 1917 with approximately four hundred sisters.[99] The Sisters of the People, founded in 1887, grew steadily until World War I. The largest growth came in the years 1880–1910, when the feminist movement, educational opportunities, and new jobs were all expanding for educated women. These years also saw an increased consciousness about the plight of the poor. A previous generation of sisters and deaconesses had led the way, and now a new generation could take up the work they had started, but with the great advantage of joining a strong community of fellow workers. Idealistic and devout young women up until World War I found a religious community to be a natural outlet for action. Emmeline Pethick-Lawrence described her own work as a sister:

> It was a wonderful thing at that period to be young among young comrades, for the ninth decade of the last century was a time of expansion and vision. In spite of sordidness and insecurity in the lives of the poor, everything was on the upgrade. . . . It was an era of religion and faith, and at the same time of intellectual challenge. We read, discussed, debated and experimented and felt that all life lay before us to be changed and moulded by our vision and desire.[100]

Coinciding with the new sense of power religious women felt in the wider world was an increased secularization of society. Nonconformists and Anglicans both felt on the defensive, fighting not only scientific thought, but also the larger social trends toward material and political solutions to social problems. Previous generations had feared that an unbelieving populace would lead to social anarchy. Now anxieties were voiced that the new agnosticism was attracting large numbers of educated women. Despite the efforts of the early principals, the women's colleges of Girton and Somerville were suspected of nurturing free thought.[101] If women lost touch with religion, society would suffer the loss of their moral leadership within the family. Deeply religious women who were affected by the perceived increase in unbelief reacted by strengthening their religious commitments. This naturally included working either as a volunteer or as a full member of one of the many religious orders for women.

One of the most characteristic sisterhoods of this period was Emily Ayckbowm's Sisters of the Church. Her order's far-flung charities reached out in every direction. In the 1890s it had over six hundred girls in orphanages, in addition to a large home for disabled children, soup kitchens, doss houses, secondhand clothing depots, and numerous other projects to relieve the poor. The income of the Church Extension Association, their parent organization, rose from £503 in 1871 to £17,000 in 1887 to £38,000 in 1895, making it one of the largest charitable organizations in England.[102] The order had about one hundred sisters and forty novices at this time, phenomenal growth in twenty years. Mother Emily was determined that her church schools would provide a better education, as well as religious instruction, than any of the new board schools, so sisters were sent to the new training colleges to learn the most modern methods. Volunteers were encouraged to "adopt" an orphan, taking her out for outings and sending her presents. Journalists were encouraged to visit the doss houses and soup kitchens, and the ensuing publicity was used to garner more donations. Such activism was representative of the larger orders and deaconesses' organizations at the end of the century.

In the midst of its many services to the poor, the Sisters of the Church received two heavy blows. In 1895 the Charity Organization Society accused it of "indiscriminate giving," rather than checking to see if those who asked for help really needed it. Others complained of the misuse of funds and the possible abuse of orphans in its care.[103] These accusations greatly damaged the CEA's standing as a charity and led to a decline in donations. But more serious internally was the defection of nearly twenty sisters and novices in 1894; two different groups, led by old and trusted friends of Mother Emily, left to form new Anglican orders that placed more emphasis upon prayer and less upon good works. Toward the end of the nineteenth century a few voices within the Church of England were raised in protest against the pragmatic and instrumental side of the religious life and in favor of a shared prayer life. By the twentieth century orders slowly began to turn to a more contemplative life; some were even founded with this as their exclusive aim. The many activities of the Sisters of the Church or the Methodist Sisters of the People could only soften the underlying class inequalities of Victorian and Edwardian society. As the state took over the functions of the charity organizations between the wars their work declined, and a life consecrated to prayer and spiritual succor came to the fore.[104]

The Anglican sisterhoods were one of the most important women's communities in the nineteenth century. They were among the first to insist upon a woman's right to choose celibacy, to live communally, and to do meaningful work. They demanded and received great loyalty from their members and were in turn deeply supportive of each other. Despite defections, the orders maintained a very high standard of religious life, proving convincingly that women could lead women, live together, and work for the greater good of the church, the people, and God. The Evangelical organizations had a more limited impact upon Victorian women, but they too offered important training in leadership and opportunities to exercise responsibility. A religious community empowered women, validating women's work and values in a world that seemed materialistic, godless, and male. As a Methodist sister urged the readers of *Young Women:*

> We have a large unworked force, a great untried resource, in that half of humanity which is only just beginning to realise the extent and significance of its mission, and of its relation to the whole. . . . When I hear prophecies of the evil to come, I lift up my eyes to the heights of our mighty womanhood with the conviction that it is over there that to-morrow's sun is going to rise. If only the young women of to-day would awake to the great possibilities that lie before them, and to their own responsibility to respect them.[105]

The Victorian religious orders offered single women a great challenge: to make active, amid the alien poor, fallen, and sick, their religious ideals of self-sacrifice and service. These women believed that with prayer and hard work they would reach "the heights of our mighty womanhood." Although not every devout woman felt a formal community necessary for her work, the ideals lived out by the sisters and deaconesses gave evidence of woman's power in community. The other communities discussed here were never so complete, but each embodied some of the characteristics and ideals of the religious orders.

3

Reformed Hospital Nursing: Discipline and Cleanliness

The history of nursing naturally calls to mind Florence Nightingale and her leadership in revolutionizing hospital care. Although reform work had begun before Nightingale made her imprint, and though many others assisted her, she was the dominant ideological leader of reformed nursing. No other nineteenth-century occupation for women had a standard-bearer of her stature, fame, and importance. From her sickbed Nightingale attempted to supervise the modernization of nursing, along with advising high-ranking government officials on army reform, sanitation in India, and hospital architecture.[1] Nightingale and her protégés desired no less than a completely new career for educated women. Nursing was to be turned into a profession for single women of impeccable moral standards. Nurses who drank, accepted tips, catered to the whims of favorite patients, and lacked training were to be replaced by devoted and disciplined paragons of womanly service. A discrepancy between this high ideal and the realities of late nineteenth-century hospital care was inevitable, but in the course of time nursing did become a respectable occupation for educated single women.

At midcentury hospital care varied enormously, from the small, homelike privately run hospitals to the vast, prisonlike workhouse infirmaries. But in the forefront of medical care were the voluntary hospitals that served the poor and working class and had attached medical schools with teaching specialists. In spite of resistance from the old guard, scientific discoveries were welcomed by their most advanced doctors; change was in the air. Nightingale and her followers believed that if they concentrated their reforming efforts upon the most influential hospitals they would ultimately have a wider impact than if they started with the most retrograde or smallest. They could speak to the govern-

ing boards of the large voluntary hospitals on terms of relative social equality and therefore could assume a greater acceptance of
their new training programs and of upper-class trainees. The decision to focus on these hospitals meant that conditions in other
kinds of hospitals changed very slowly, that relatively few women
received a modern training, and that reforms proceeded from the
top down. I have concentrated on these new nurses' training
schools in the major voluntary hospitals because they opened the
profession to educated single women. Although largely untrained
working-class women in unreformed hospitals or in private nursing remained the norm throughout the nineteenth century, the
small numbers of upper-class women seized the leadership of reformed nursing and set the standards by which all nurses were
judged.

Reformers necessarily downgraded the skills of the old-style
nurses. Some, who had spent years in a single ward, possessed
considerable skill gained from watching the same cases time and
again. The work was considered suitable for untrained, older working women, whose only requirement was a willingness to do hard,
unpleasant tasks. The pay, in London about a shilling a day with
some food and beer, was good for unskilled women.[2] They had virtually no time off, though a special staff, even less trained, was
hired for night watching. No nurse could expect a room of her
own; she had a cot in some corner, in or near her ward or possibly
in an attic dormitory. Nurses were expected to purchase and prepare their own food in their wards, along with the special diets of
the patients. Bad as reformers claimed conditions to be, they were
no worse than those of a maid of all work, who toiled similarly
long hours and slept on a pallet in the kitchen. Nurses had the
advantage of friendly company in the patients and a work routine
that was long, but only intermittently arduous. After the floors
had been scrubbed, the coal fetched, and the patients seen to, periods of rest could be found. But conditions that might satisfy a
"skivvy" were hardly suitable for a middle-class spinster.

Educated women could win a place for themselves in the hospital world only by insisting upon their superior morality and skill.
From the beginning they had to win over the educated public to
the idea of their own daughters' engaging in nursing and to make a
space for themselves in the rapidly modernizing voluntary hospitals. Reformers argued for the moral influence of ladies in the cor-

rupt environment of the hospitals. As Anna Jameson told her readers,

> We may at least hope that a man who has been thus tended by gentle and superior beings of the other sex, will hardly be so ready as theretofore to make women the victims of his levity or brutality; what he did not spare for the sake of mother or sister, he may perhaps, in some hour of temptation and selfish impulse, spare for the sake of those who bent over him when "pain and anguish wrung the brow," and whispered low the solemn words of peace, of patience, of divine hope and comfort, while laying the pillow under a poor fellow's rough head, or holding the cup to his parched lips.[3]

A life of hard work under difficult conditions was transformed ideologically into fighting for spiritual regeneration among the poor patients and respect for educated working women among the doctors and general public. Power, self-fulfillment, and moral duty could all be satisfied by serving the sick.

Unlike the other occupations discussed here, nursing alone faced complex problems of gender, class, and status. Schools, colleges, and settlement houses were run by and largely financed by women, but voluntary hospitals were always run by men and financed by public donations garnered by men. The patients were generally content with nurses from their own class. The doctors, who were consolidating recent gains in status, did not welcome an invasion of self-important ladies from a higher social class. Parents were often horrified at the notion of their daughters' working in centers of sin and sickness. Women were dependent upon the reforming spirit that was sweeping medicine, but they had to establish their own separate sphere of influence. The complicated struggles with doctors and the traditional structure of nursing did not lead to the creation of real communities of women, as with the other occupations discussed here; rather, a strict hierarchy dominated by a single woman head prevailed. In spite of a rhetoric of power, nursing leaders controlled only their own corps of women.

The history of modern nursing can be divided into two general periods, the "pioneer age," dating from the late 1850s until the late 1880s, and the "mothering age," from then until the achievement of nurses' registration in 1919. The first generation had the enormous task of recruiting and training a different kind of woman, and then of cleansing the hospital wards of dirt, corruption, and old-style nurses. Not surprisingly, they saw themselves as soldiers—officers—in the fight against disease. They set the standards and the structure of reformed nursing. Nurses were to have a unique and vital place in the modern hospital. As William Farr argued,

> A devoted nurse, well taught in hygiene, and knowing practically the nature and accidents of various kinds of sickness, deserves, as Miss Nightingale has shown, a place next to the doctor; indeed medical treatment can only be effectively carried out through the agency of good nurses.[4]

Reformers, however, found that they could survive only by creating space for the new nurse under, not beside, the doctor. Even then it was always a difficult relationship, with doctors controlling the nurses' curriculum and working conditions and sometimes the matron herself. The second generation shifted the emphasis away from military metaphors to maternal ones while simultaneously strengthening the control of women over women; a narrower sphere of influence was accepted. By the late nineteenth century nursing had, if anything, an excess of recruits and goodwill and so could enforce the ideology of an earlier period much more thoroughly. Throughout both periods the class superiority of the largely upper-middle-class leaders of nursing gave them the confidence to push ahead with reforms, however unpopular. The changes they advocated coincided with larger social changes that favored their methods; progress during the last forty years of the century meant a strong work discipline, control of the disreputable poor, and the greater regimentation of life in general. The ideological success of the nursing leaders was due in large part to the combination of traditional female values with modern ideas about work.

Training Leaders for a New Profession

Reformed nursing had its roots in the high-church religious revival of the 1840s and 1850s. The new Anglican sisterhoods, as described in the previous chapter, saw nursing the sick poor as one of their prime objectives. Lydia Sellon's care of cholera victims in Devonport, as well as the nursing order of St. John's (founded in

1848) in London, had brought much favorable publicity to the High Anglicans. The ancient tradition of the religious vocation of nursing appeared to be revived in these selfless sisters. Similar reforms were being undertaken by Roman Catholic nuns in France and Lutheran deaconesses in Germany. Pastor Fliedner's deaconesses' training center at Kaiserswerth became something of a mecca for English reformers seeking a model for changes in England.[5] Although all these orders, in England and on the Continent, put little emphasis upon formal training, they set new standards of cleanliness and conscientiousness. When Nightingale went to the Crimea in 1853, twenty-four of her thirty-eight nurses were from Anglican and Roman Catholic religious orders (the Evangelicals refused to send anyone). The women's success in the Crimea brought fame and a renewed public interest in nursing as a vocation; both the medical reformers and the religious orders benefited from their achievement.

Nursing was so closely linked with religious commitment in the minds of the educated public because no one could believe that anyone but a sister would be willing to do the work. As a journalist in the *Pall Mall Gazette* cynically declared, "If the sight of the chasuble and the odours of incense are a delight and a support to a woman who is just going to pass her day at the bedside of cholera and fever patients, why should we complain?"[6] The sisterhoods, moreover, had the added advantage of doing the work "in a peculiarly admirable way" without pay, so that hard-pressed hospital funds could be used elsewhere.[7] Even if they were religiously suspect, they did not disturb middle-class prejudices about ladies' working for money. But Nightingale condemned the sisters as contentious among themselves and with the patients and doctors; she felt that too many preferred spiritual healing to relieving physical misery. Although Nightingale once said that the ideal situation would be a religious nursing order under lay control, upon her return from the Crimea she fought for an independent lay "order" of nurses trained in a lay hospital.[8] In this she was supported by most of the advocates of reformed nursing, who came from Evangelical or Nonconformist backgrounds and wished to wrest nursing leadership from the hands of the High Anglicans. They wanted commitment without incense, but they unanimously agreed that religious inspiration was essential if gentlewomen were to consent to a lifetime of unpleasant work.

Florence Nightingale herself drew a fine line between excessive religious zeal and a vocational commitment to nursing. When she wished to attract more upper-class women to nursing, she used as her model the intensely religious Agnes Jones, who had died of typhus contracted while nursing the sick in the Liverpool Workhouse Infirmary. In less than three years Jones and her twelve Nightingale nurses, according to Nightingale, had brought cleanliness and order to over a thousand sick paupers. With her death nursing had its martyr, and a new standard of woman's ability to bring about *"moral* sanitary reform."[9] As Nightingale eulogized:

> The founders and pioneers of almost everything that is best must be martyrs. But these are the last ever to think themselves so. And for all there must be constant self-sacrifice for the good of all. But the distinction is this—the life is not a sacrifice; it is the engaging in an occupation the happiest of any. But the strong, the healthy wills in any life must determine to pursue the common good at any personal cost—at daily sacrifice.[10]

Nursing was to be transformed from the most menial of women's work to the most exalted through the commitment of pure and selfless women. Jones herself lamented, "When one seeks training in other than a Christian home, there is in public institutions so much to keep back, and so little to foster spiritual growth."[11] She clearly would have preferred a religious nurses' training, had there been any alternative to the high-church hospitals; she longed for some kind of religious order for Evangelicals such as herself.

Agnes Jones, it was argued, had succeeded not only because of "daily sacrifice," but also because she had been thoroughly trained. Nightingale could give her no higher compliment than to say, "She went through all of the work of a soldier; she thereby fitted herself for being the best general we ever had."[12] If other middle- and upper-class women had similar aspirations, they had to expect the same kind of discipline. When Nightingale opened the Nightingale School of Nursing at St. Thomas' Hospital, London, in 1860, she modeled the training on that of the army. She had chosen St. Thomas' as the site for her new school because she trusted the matron. Appointed in 1854, Mrs. Wardroper had already begun reforming the nursing staff when Nightingale selected her as her "general." Together they set up a detailed agenda for each probationer, including not only a minute accounting of her time, but also a general monthly assessment of her progress and moral character. Minor infractions, such as "making eyes" or wearing untidy uniforms were severely punished.[13] Like an army recruit, the probationer was given new clothes and was virtually cut off from contact with outsiders; her time was filled with work, regulated exercise, and study. She was, in the words of Agnes Jones, "immured" for twelve months.[14] But the result was a soldier ready to do battle against dirt, disease, and sin.

Probationers were plunged into a grueling hospital day, even by the strict standards of an Anglican novitiate. An early "pro" at St. Thomas' described a fifteen-hour day with short breaks, seven days a week. She rose at 6:00 a.m., had breakfast, and from 7:00 to 8:00 made fourteen beds and washed each patient. At 8:00 the ward sister came on duty and read prayers. Until 9:30 the probationer washed all utensils, including the dressing bowls, spittoons, and bedpans. At 10:00 she helped give out lunch (a light snack), assisted with dressings, and generally helped until 12:45 and dinner. This was eaten as quickly as possible to make room for a little rest. In the meantime, the sister and ward nurse served dinner in the ward and took turns going for their dinners. At 1:30 the probationer returned to help prepare patients for the doctor's rounds with his students. The sister attended him with an inkpot, while a pro carried a basin of water so he could wash his hands after touching each patient. The more eager would listen carefully to what he said, hoping to learn a bit more about medicine. At 3:30 the probationers were given an hour and a half off and then had an hour for tea. At 6:00 they returned to the ward to wash the patients and prepare them for the night, including dressings, poultices, liniments, and so forth. Often a new patient was admitted at this time. At 8:30 the long day ended and supper was served. Prayers were at 9:00, after which a pro was free to snatch a few moments for relaxation, letter writing, or study. Lights were out at 10:30. Lectures were given in off hours, sometimes as late as 8:30, and studying had to be done in the scanty free time.[15] If the house sister caught a pro studying when she was supposed to be exercising outside, she would reprimand her. Probationers served for periods of three months in different wards, including a tour of night duty where they learned to serve breakfast, roll bandages, and complete any work left undone by the day nurses. A complicated schedule of times off gave the pro an occasional free afternoon at the discretion of the ward sister. The regimen was clearly intended to weed out all but the most determined.

Military training was necessary because of the extreme differences between the clean, pure new nurses and their environment.
The sources of contagion were poorly understood, but Nightingale had seen the death rate of injured soldiers plummet when she
had the hospitals at Scutari thoroughly cleansed. Illness was
closely connected with sin.[16] Like the sisters reforming prostitutes, nurses had to be prepared to fight more than simple fevers
and broken bones:

> Nursing is warfare, and the nurses are soldiers. . . . Sin and its
> consequences—disease, suffering, degeneration, degradation,
> death—seem to fill the foreground of the view, and we want a
> strong mind to face them bravely, and to look through and
> beyond.[17]

Cleanliness not only would help the sick body to repair itself,
but it would also inculcate new standards, moral and physical, in
the patient. The nurses too would benefit, like the sisters who
scrubbed floors, from the purifying influence of the hard work.
The strong activist strain of Victorian religion found its natural
outlet in images of lady nurses as Christian soldiers in the battle
against disease and degradation.

The emphasis upon cleanliness and discipline was part of a
larger struggle reformers faced in making space within the hospitals for the new nurses. By giving hygiene a vital role in the patient's return to health, Nightingale carved out an area of expertise for her new nurses. She argued that neither the doctor nor the
nurse cured a patient; only nature could do so.[18] The grave responsibility of creating the right conditions for nature rested upon the
nurse. At a time when trained nurses were often unwelcome, this
separation of care from cure gave them a distinct task. These arguments were undermined, however, by the fact that the doctors
first decided who was sick enough to be placed under their care.
Moreover, the defense of cleanliness and hygiene was largely based
on an obsolete scientific model, in which diseases were seen as an
outward sign of bodily imbalance rather than as the result of contagious germs.[19]

Nursing ideology originally empowered educated leaders—
ladies—to take on the reform of society as a whole through reformed nursing. Nurses actively fought not only filth and illness
in the hospital, but also the environment of illness—poverty,
drink, and sin. It was an exciting and attractive alternative to the

narrow medical model of the doctors, who increasingly limited themselves to the care of bodies. But within the confines of the modernizing hospitals, a specifically female vision of extended medical care could not survive the growing power of the scientific approach combined with the consolidation of the doctors' control over medicine. The early claim for the nurse's autonomy—her unique mission—was lost. As Gamarnikow has pointed out, nursing gradually became redefined as fulfilling the doctor's orders and performing housework in the wards.[20] Grand notions of hygiene "became limited to the sanitary aspects of patient care."[21] The failure of women to establish their own intellectual space within the medical world was concealed by their success in controlling the prevailing ideology of vocational nursing. But nursing leaders had only a limited voice in their probationers' curriculum, as well as their working conditions. They were forced to defend vigorously the one area doctors had left them—the discipline of the women under them.

In defending their own bailiwick, nursing leaders used military metaphors both to train their nurses and to establish the right of women to supervise women in a world controlled by men. They scrupulously defined themselves as a separate "corps," working alongside the doctors in the battle against disease; but they were determined to keep control over their own troops. A leading American nurse spoke at the Chicago World's Fair in 1893, warning that, although the medical doctors were "undoubtedly the superior officers," they should not rule the nurses' school:

> The private soldier in the ranks and the officer in command have the same profession. The officer is also a soldier and knows every detail of the common soldier's work and life. The nurse and physician have different professions. The doctor is not a nurse, and only now and then is one found who fairly comprehends the actual matter-of-fact realities of the training school. On this fundamental difference rests the claim of the school to be ruled, as an educative and disciplinary body, by those of its origin.[22]

To an outsider Lavinia Dock's reasoning appears disingenuous; surely both doctors and nurses have a similar duty, returning the sick to good health. Respect and power, however, could be gained only by exaggerating the differences between treatment (doctors) and care (nurses). In effect, nursing leaders argued for a distinct, separate, and unequal place for women in the modern hospital—subordinate to the medical profession but controlled by themselves.

American leaders were still defending their right to a separate domain as late as the 1890s; Nightingale had been arguing more or less successfully for the separate control of nursing in the major English hospitals from the beginning. As she said in 1867,

> It is quite, quite impossible (and it is not only my experience, but that of all Christendom) for the discipline, the internal management of Sisters and Nurses to be in any other hands but those of *one* female Head. No man can or ought to interfere with it. Nothing but indiscipline can ensue.
>
> The whole reform in Nursing both at home and abroad has consisted in this:—to take all power over the Nursing out of the hands of the men and put it into the hands of *one female trained* head, and make her responsible for everything regarding internal management and discipline being carried out.[23]

In time every English hospital with a training school confronted the issue of how much power should be invested in the hands of a single woman matron. Many, though never all, English hospitals came to follow the Nightingale model. These hospitals were ruled by a kind of triumvirate of the matron, the hospital treasurer, and the chairman of the hospital's governing board.[24] All decisions in regard to the female nurses were made by the matron, whose power had to be continually defended both within and outside the hospital world. As with mother superiors, the public distrusted women in authority, and any errors of judgment were magnified.

A religious sister who was elevated to the rank of mother superior generally had the full assent of her order and could count on its loyalty even in the face of public damnation. Such was not the case for the reforming matron, who had to fight an uphill battle within the hospital and also conquer misunderstandings among the general public. Although gentleness was extolled in a nurse, a matron was supposed to behave like a general, regardless of personal feelings. Mary Cadbury, a Nightingale nurse, found it difficult to ignore criticism and bitterly commented, *"Men* may be stupid, the students and Doctors, but women in a hospital never seem expected to be so."[25] In 1879 the governors of Guy's Hospital appointed as matron Miss Burt, who had reformed the Leicester Infirmary. She immediately announced a plan of shifting sisters (the heads of wards), nurses, and probationers around the wards so they could gain more varied experience. This was consonant with the hygiene model, which emphasized knowing all aspects of health and sickness, but was in direct opposition to the medical efficiency the doctors desired. Her decision led to open revolt by the staff doctors and a public squabble about interfering nurses. Burt herself was hardly a model of tact, claiming that the old nurses were untrained, took money from patients, did not keep patients clean, spent their time off in public houses and music halls—and wore jewelry.[26] The governors supported Burt, issuing a printed ultimatum on 7 October 1880:

> That the Medical Staff having persisted in ignoring the Matron appointed by the Court and confirmed in her appointment after patient investigation of all complaints against her, while she, on her part, is willing to submit herself obediently to the orders of the Physicians and Surgeons in all matters directly affecting the treatment of any patient, this Court finds that it is the attitude of the Medical Staff which impedes the harmonious working of the Hospital.[27]

The two doctors in opposition resigned, and victory was claimed for the matron. More important, however, were the elevation of Burt to equality in governance with the governing body and the medical staff, and the acknowledgment of her control in all matters regarding the nurses.

Social superiority and indomitable will characterized the lady probationers who rose to positions of authority at very young ages during these pioneering years. Ambition clearly played an important part in attracting these women to nursing; even though they spoke continually of self-sacrifice, they reveled in the responsibilities and challenges of hospital reform. Few other vocations, even that of headmistress or mother superior, offered such a grand opportunity for effecting visible change in a male-dominated world. The formidable Eva Lückes became matron of the London Hospital in 1880 at the age of twenty-six and remained for thirty-nine years. She became the leading opponent of state registration of nurses and an advocate of Nightingale's concept of nursing as a vocation. Her family's military experience served her well as she shaped not only the largest hospital in London, but also the course of nurses' training. Even her adulatory biographer admitted that, "Under an exterior of great feminine charm she had an iron will, which neither spared herself or other when this ideal was in danger."[28] Her chief rival was Ethel Gordon Manson, who became matron of the prestigious London hospital St. Bartholomew's in 1881 at the age of twenty-four. Manson was convinced that a voice had summoned her to the position in spite of her relative inexperience; she clearly offered the governing board social class, confidence, and administrative ability beyond her years.[29] Indeed, in six years she modernized the nurses' school and established the three-year training period for regular probationers. After her marriage to Dr. Bedford Fenwick she became the prime spokeswoman for state registration and uniform standards of training for all.[30] Strong-willed upper-middle-class women, a tiny but influential minority, set the tone and standards of the profession.

In spite of rapid promotion and the challenge of a cause, in the 1860s, 1870s, and 1880s nursing did not attract large numbers of recruits. The unsavory reputation of hospitals combined with the dubious status of even reformed nursing made it a questionable occupation for sheltered middle-class women. Nightingale chafed that so few were willing to follow Agnes Jones. She was utterly impatient with "the enormous Jaw, the infinite female ink which England pours forth on 'Woman's Work.'"[31] She knew she had founded a worthy occupation for unemployed ladies, if only they would discard false notions of propriety:

> It makes me mad to hear people talk about unemployed women. If they are unemployed it is because they won't work. The highest salaries given to women at all we can secure to women trained by us. But we can't find the women. They won't come.[32]

But even the domestic servants, in whom Nightingale put more faith, did not come forward. Until the late 1880s reformers struggled to meet the growing demand for trained nurses without changing their standards of social class, leadership abilities, or vocational commitment. Recruits to noninstitutional and specialized hospitals grew, but they did not have to undergo the grueling training demanded by reformers at the leading voluntary hospitals, nor could they expect to move into a nursing career that led to a matronship.[33] During the pioneer days nursing did draw a handful of well-to-do and confident young women who became leaders, such as Lückes and Manson. But the majority of recruits were neither from the solid middle class or upper classes, nor from the servant class. Most appear to have been drawn from the lower middle class, from families with enough money to educate their daughters but not enough to support them all their lives should they never marry. The result was a discrepancy between the dominant ideology of nursing—the self-sacrificing lady officer, extolled by reformers—and the realities of recruitment.[34] Regular probationers thought they were moving up in status by becoming nurses, while their leaders continually worried about the possibilities of a lady's moving down.

Class snobbery remained explicitly a part of recruitment, in spite of these realities. Although some of the new training schools, including St. Thomas', had begun with a single course for everybody, they all soon had a two-tier system similar to the sisterhoods. Lady probationers paid £1 per week for up to one year's training, while regular probationers were paid £12 to £20 per year during their three years' training. Although the regular probationers were always in the majority, the matrons of voluntary hospitals put much of their faith in women from their own class, whom they hoped would become leaders at other, as-yet-unreformed hospitals. As Nightingale pointed out, "Unquestionably the educated will be more likely to rise to the post of Superintendent, but *not* because they are ladies, but because they are *educated*."[35] This shrewd estimate was turned into a self-fulfilling prophecy by matrons who frankly preferred ladies of known social status, regardless of their nursing capabilities. Everything was done to encourage lady probationers to take the leadership role that their social class naturally assigned them. At many hospitals a lady pro, no matter how inexperienced, could temporarily take over a ward, over the heads of more experienced ward nurses. And, of course, she could expect to move rapidly into a matronship upon completion of her training, especially if she required no regular salary.

The ladies who did respond to the call, however, were not always suitable. Too many were religious zealots or unaccustomed to hard physical work. Many women lacked sufficient confidence to become leaders or were bigoted and self-important. Mary Cadbury, a teetotaler, never missed an occasion to inform the doctors who passed through her ward about the evils of drink. Since brandy and other stimulants were routinely prescribed, her advice was hardly welcome. Nightingale herself often imposed taxing responsibilities on a lady probationer as soon as she had completed her training. Maria Machin was one of those who proved unable

to bear the weight of these duties. In 1873, after her year's training, she went to the Montreal General Hospital to start a new
school and to supervise the nurses. Five years later she was asked
to leave, having been found extravagant and unable to control the
nurses. Nightingale then got her the position of matron at St. Bartholomew's. But she failed as miserably as before, and for the same
reasons; within two years she resigned and escaped into marriage.[36] Machin's failure is a good reminder of the discrepancy between the reformers' expectations and hospital realities.

The continual calls for military discipline and religious vocation indicate how precarious a hold the new matrons had over
their nurses. The open revolts Machin faced, it was thought, could
be controlled only by the ruthlessness of a Burt. Sometimes the
old nurses, and occasionally some of the new ones, were caught
taking a nip from the brandy prescribed for the patients.[37] Young
nurses, even from good families, were not always controllable.
Mary Cadbury dropped all her training in obedience and self-
discipline when she found a doctor uppish. As she wrote home
after one quarrel:

> Next morn I woke feeling as if I were bruised all over, it came
> to me very clearly to write Miss Hill [the matron] and say that
> I felt the doctor had so insulted me that unless he apologized I
> did not feel I could stay unless he would alter his conduct
> towards me altogether for I had borne a long time with it.[38]

When Miss Hill sided with the doctor, Cadbury told her, "I
didn't know what my father would say when he heard all," and she
tendered her resignation.[39] Eventually matters were smoothed
over, but Cadbury's keen sense of her social position was typical
of the first generation of lady nurses. Despite her eagerness to pioneer for other Quaker women, Cadbury had no compunction about
calling upon her father's position when questioning the authority of her matron and an uppity doctor. Margaret Lonsdale, the
daughter of a bishop, published a blistering attack on Guy's Hospital in the widely read Nineteenth Century in 1880, alleging that
the doctors opposed nursing reform because "[t]he presence of refined, intelligent women in the wards imposes a kind of moral restraint upon the words and ways of both doctors and students."[40]
In comparison with the other hospitals, Guy's seemed to her too
slow in accepting reforms emanating from ladies. Nightingale
was continually writing to her nurses, urging them to be more pa-

tient, lest they lose all possibility of improving the hospitals where they worked.[41]

Older women were preferred as recruits because they were less sexually attractive and therefore less likely to take their complaints to the doctors and be championed by them.[42] Any flirtation between a nurse or probationer and a doctor was supposed to lead to instant dismissal, but a matron (or her spies) could not be everywhere at once. Fortunately high-mindedness sometimes went with a sense of humor. One lady pro delightedly described her relations with the medical students to a friend,

> All the students that are put on as surgeon's dressers or as recorders of cases that I have seen yet are very nice fellows. We are not supposed to have anything to say to them except in connection with the work but when you are standing for half an hour at a time helping with their work it is not in human nature to be silent so if we are very anxious to learn anything about the case before us there is a good opportunity of plying them with questions. If they are young beginners and we know better than them how to do what they are sent to do, we cock-crow over them finely, you may be sure, which is rather unfair, but they are just as glad to learn from us.[43]

In spite of the rhetoric of moral superiority, many lady probationers were proving the far more valuable point that men and women could work together without the loss of respectability on one side or intellectual freedom on the other.

High expectations must often have met an impasse—patients did not want Bible readings or the continual cleaning around their beds; the old nurses ignored orders or practiced subterfuge; doctors were impatient or gave contradictory orders. Change was slow and erratic. The life of Mary Cadbury (1839–96) reflects these difficulties far more realistically than the ideological fanfare of the famous. Cadbury trained very successfully at St. Thomas', and in 1874 she agreed to help reform the workhouse infirmary at Highgate. But she took an immediate dislike to the Highgate matron and hated the male patients and lower-class nurses. Everything seemed a sharp contrast to the well ordered and obedient troops of nurses and patients at St. Thomas'. She wrote home disconsolate about the realities of reforming a hospital, "There is no one that I see to speak to, this is loneliness such as I have never had it before, and you know [as] I have a social disposition that it will be a fight before I get used to it. The more I know my patients the more I shall feel it."[44] Less than a year later she gratefully accepted the position of sister of Mary Ward back at St. Thomas'. But she repeatedly disputed with Mrs. Wardroper about proselytizing against drink among her probationers, and she favored the lady probationers over the regulars. After a favorite doctor died, Cadbury quarreled again with Mrs. Wardroper and left to try district nursing. Four years later, feeling that she had to better herself, she accepted the post of matron of the Liverpool Parish Infirmary. She arrived without administrative experience and found the work grueling and unrewarding. Within eighteen months she resigned, after having been away on her only extended vacation during this time. She went on to become matron of the West Street Hospital, Sheffield, and the Queen's Hospital, Birmingham, small hospitals without prestige.[45]

For all her cares and failures, Cadbury was conscientious, honest, and hard working—a model new sister, if an inadequate matron. She made a home in each ward she supervised, urging those under her to remember their religious duties. For her, drink was a social illness that she should work to cure, even as she helped to mend bodies. Her wider vision of the nurse's vocation often resulted in narrow hectoring rather than actual reform, but her intentions were at one with an ideology that empowered women to reform the world. Indeed, she may have chosen nursing as a career because it provided her with a substitute "pulpit" (however incongruous this might be for a Quaker), where she could preach and convert.[46] Certainly nursing gave her a satisfying position of superiority in relation to the wealthy Quaker women she saw at meetings:

> I felt so shabby at meeting this morning. Friends seemed to dress so, but it was a nice meeting till it came over me how wonderful and good it was that God should let me be in work which was so entirely to my taste and in which I am so happy. So many people have to do what they dislike and it seemed so much more interesting a life than that of these young and middle-aged ladies at meeting, not to have to dress, nor make calls, nor always be sociable with people, and then the feeling that some people didn't invite you when you thought they ought and so on.[47]

Cadbury found both religious justification and personal power in her work—an almost ideal combination for a Victorian single woman.

Yet by the late 1880s, all was not well with the original model of the reforming upper-class nurse. Respectability had been won, but women remained marginal to the powerful medical world. As arguments for the nurses' autonomy failed, nursing leaders tightened their hold upon those they trained; a woman's world ruled by a few at the top became the goal. In the process the larger vision of reform that included reforming the sources of disease was modified to encompass only areas that were more readily controlled. Progress came to be measured in such symbols as the large separate living quarters erected for nurses, rather than in the reform of specific hospital practices. Although women continued to be trained in military style, publicly the nurse's image shifted to that of a nurturing but distant mother figure. A section of the nursing leadership attempted to impose state registration, three years' training, and public examinations upon the profession. All of these changes met with opposition from within nursing, the medical profession, and the public, while criticism was mounting against the very gains made by the new nurse.

A Disciplined Mother

After they had won the support of their hospital governing boards, matrons such as Lückes, Manson, Burt, and Wardroper concentrated their efforts on improving the training, living conditions, and respectability of the nurse. Their writings were primarily directed toward nurses and women interested in becoming nurses, rather than the medical establishment. Scientific learning was downplayed not only to avoid competing with doctors, but also to keep nursing a womanly occupation. Medicine advanced rapidly during the closing years of the nineteenth century, especially in the areas of surgery and diagnosis, both of which would be closed to nurses. Higher status was gained by delegating some of the routine cleaning chores to ward maids and giving nurses greater responsibility in carrying out the doctor's orders. But as Gamarnikow has pointed out, this only emphasized the subordinate position of women in the medical hierarchy.[48] Such duties were rationalized by the increasing use of family metaphors, comparing the doctor to a father and the nurse to a mother. Since discipline could not be lessened among the ranks of nurses and probationers, the actual training in the voluntary hospitals continued to be along military lines, while life in the wards was to take on the aura of a family.

By the late 1880s the most famous nursing schools were turning away candidates and could pick the best from among hundreds of applicants. Nursing began to take on the classic contours of a woman's occupation: overcrowding, stagnating wages, uncontrolled entry, and widely varying standards of training. Paradoxically this change was accompanied by a steady increase in prestige. The relatively rapid shift from an unattractive to a popular occupation can be explained by many factors. The demand for trained nurses increased by leaps and bounds. Hospitals were modernizing and expanding; the best wanted a better class of assistants who could handle the greater responsibilities of modern medicine. The upper classes still avoided entering a hospital, but they too wanted better care; they came to expect a higher standard of private nursing. Actual contact with a trained nurse in one's own home often removed some of the stigma attached to the position. The steady increase of middle-class women in paid occupations of all sorts made it more acceptable to work for pay. Finally, the propaganda of the pioneers had effectively created the image of nursing as an exciting vocation for the idealistic woman. A little nursing became fashionable among the upper classes. By 1892, Nightingale was complaining, "Our trial is not crucifixion, but *fashion*. Nursing has become the fashion: and it brings in all sorts of amateur alloy and public life instead of inner life."[49]

Fashion brought in the lady probationer of the period 1885–1919, but necessity and idealism attracted the regular probationer. Nursing had increased by only 14.5 percent between 1861 and 1871, but it grew by 50.8 percent between 1881 and 1891 and from 24,821 in 1861 to 77,060 in 1911.[50] Although fewer in number than teachers, shop assistants, or clerks, nurses formed one of the largest occupational groups of women by the late nineteenth century. And as reformers loved to remind their audience, it was the one respectable job that did not compete with men.[51] In the 1860s and 1870s nurses' salaries were high in comparison with those paid for much other work available to women; the dearth of trained workers made advancement rapid. But by the 1890s salaries had shrunk in comparison with those in teaching or social work. Matrons earned from £100 to £300 per year with room, board, and laundry. Pay for sisters and nurses was much less. A sister's salary started at about £30 and rose to a maximum of £55, with uniforms, laundry, room, and board worth about another £20. A regular nurse could expect to earn no more than £20 to £25 per year, with the same additional perquisites.[52] As in school-teaching, promotion in a voluntary hospital came rapidly or not at all, making such alternatives as district, private, and school nursing popular for their greater freedom and shorter hours.

Virtually every form and length of training was available; with no state examination, minimum standards, or outside controls anyone could start a training school. Short day courses were particularly popular. If a woman later found that she had to work for pay, she could easily find work as a private nurse, whereas other professional occupations usually required more training. Once again it was argued that ladies did not need to train as long as other women because of their superior general education.[53] Throughout the 1880s *Work and Leisure* published advertisements for suitable part-time and day courses in nursing, as well as articles on the opportunities available for lady nurses. Not surprisingly, few other records survive of these small private nursing schools, convalescent homes, and doctors who performed an important educational task imperfectly by the standards of yesterday and today. Dilettantism among upper-class women was vigorously fought by Nightingale and other matrons, anxious to have professional women taken seriously. Any lady seriously interested in nursing knew that she had to undertake a residential training course at a reputable hospital, but many received their first initiation into the world of medicine from these shadowy institutions.

Entry into a voluntary hospital training school in the late nineteenth century was both very easy and very difficult, depending upon one's social class and determination. A short literacy test was usually required, along with a long application form. Matrons liked to emphasize their selectivity, and certainly filling out forms tended to discourage the less literate or confident. Every matron prided herself on her ability to assess character during the short personal interview, although most of the time was spent on pro forma matters. An applicant who appeared in too-fashionable clothes or without gloves might be refused admittance. There seems to have been no correlation between the matron's interview and the candidate's success, nor were matrons ever blamed for the high percentage of failures.[54] Recommendations from two or three ladies and a minister were also required. They were expected to comment on the candidate's maturity and moral character, narrowly defined as sexual purity and honesty. Nevertheless, respectability, which included such intangibles as accent and dress, could be a slippery matter for those in the lower reaches of the middle class; much depended upon the matron's prejudices and the hospital's needs when admitting a woman who lacked the clear credentials of a lady.

Maturity was defined as being over twenty-three, though in reality applicants appear to have frequently entered training at twenty-one in all but the most popular hospitals.[55] Many women interested in nursing spent a year or two in a fever hospital or children's hospital, where untrained women were welcome at nineteen. The simpler work (and lower pay) provided a good introduction to nursing. Since education commonly ended at fourteen or younger for working-class girls, the high age was a means of discouraging their entry and attracting better-educated girls from the middle class. But even the middle-class girl ceased her education at sixteen, or at most eighteen. Matrons preferred to think that the women they wanted did not have to work between the end of formal education and entry into nurses' training. They insisted that the time could not be better spent than at home, learning elementary cookery, housewifery, and care of the sick.[56]

Not every applicant for nursing school, however, was a model daughter. For many hospital work seemed more attractive than a sisterhood as an escape from a useless life or an unhappy home. Honnor Morten, in an autobiographical sketch of her nursing experiences, described her motivations as a seeking after "the real":

> Deliberately I offer up to the great God of Knowledge all that remains of my youth and innocence, asking in return only the right to face life as it is; only freedom to see and hear; only contrast to make clear the colours of the land I leave behind.[57]

Beneath her rhetoric lay a desire to see life that was ordinarily hidden from a middle-class girl. She found cases of venereal disease, delirium tremens, malnourished children, and tubercular mothers that more than met her expectations. Family opposition simply increased a woman's desire to become a nurse. Mary Cadbury laughingly wrote her supportive mother about meeting with relatives, "who were not a little afraid even to speak to me, 'cos especially for fear I might give . . . some infection. They evidently didn't approve of my being here and wanted to know how long I was going to stay, but such things don't discourage one, but rather the opposite."[58] Similar shocked responses from family members were recorded by devoted nurses well into the twentieth century.[59]

Despite the intense propaganda calling for self-sacrificing, religious women to become nurses, many women had a healthy sense of personal commitment that did not include either the romance of Honnor Morten or the martyrdom of Agnes Jones. The author of an account of nursing for a feminist journal in the 1880s begins with the hearty comment,

> My intention of devoting my life to nursing the sick had its origin neither in the abstract desire for self-sacrifice nor a more peculiar wish to contribute personal service to the alleviations of human sufferings. . . . I recognised from the first that I sought not another's but my own good.[60]

A strong sense of self-worth carries the narrator through the often onerous and petty tasks required of her during her training, and soon she becomes a happy sister. But *Work and Leisure* remained in a minority in its commonsense approach to hospital work. Far more attractive to the public was the romantic perspective that argued that no lady became a nurse until she had been jilted or lost all chance of marriage.

In painting its cheerful picture of the possibilities available for ladies in nursing, *Work and Leisure* stressed not only the career ladder open only to ladies, but also the strict divisions maintained during training between lady probationers and the regulars. Although all the probationers worked together in the wards, the ladies were often excused from the more unpleasant tasks, such as sweeping, cleaning spittoons, and night duty. In the larger nurses' homes, ladies were given private rooms. They sometimes had a separate sitting room and always ate at a different table. If they had to wear a uniform at all, it was more stylish and distinctive. At the Middlesex Hospital the lady probationers were required to wear a four-inch trail, so that when they knelt beside a bed the student doctors and male patients could not see their ankles. The unsanitary and annoying cloth was a nuisance the matron refused to alter.[61]

Once admitted to a reputable training school, a probationer of whatever class faced a year of hard work similar to that at St.

Thomas' in its early days. Although working days were gradually shortened until most probationers had a ten-hour day, excluding breaks, and nurses worked twelve to fourteen hours, the overall focus on practical experience and cleanliness did not change. Before 1910 only three hospitals offered a preliminary training school of six to eight weeks. Hospital administrators were reluctant to add any unnecessary expense, so that a probationer had to pay for her expenses during this time; if she failed, the hospital lost little. Any formal education continued to be squeezed into off-hours. In a sense, the failure to address the issue of proper training in anything like a thorough manner "solved" the problem of how much scientific training a nurse should have.[62] If the emphasis was upon her moral probity, domestic skills, and selflessness, then formal training could be minimized and the three long years of ward duty would be appropriate. At a time when scientific training was becoming more and more essential for understanding medicine, nurses were exhorted to remember that they practiced an art, doctors a science.[63] More practically, nursing schools had neither the funds nor the support of the medical staff to increase the formal education of their nurses.

Ethel Gordon Manson had first established a three-year training period at St. Bartholomew's in the 1880s because she wanted to raise the prestige of her training school. The extended period, which included only one year of course work, soon became a financial necessity for the expanding hospitals. One of the ironies of reformed nursing was how few fully trained nurses actually did bedside work in the best hospitals, not to mention the worst. Wards were generally staffed with one sister, one ward nurse, and three or four probationers for approximately thirty to forty beds (or as many as a hundred in workhouse infirmaries). The sister supervised the others, administered prescription medicine, and acted as an intermediary with the doctor. She, unlike the probationers, rarely changed wards. The ward nurse, with more than three years' experience behind her, supervised the cleaning maids and the night nurses, who were usually the second- and third-year pros. The probationers had little time to master more than the rudiments of their work in three months, before going on to another ward. Patients who had been recuperating for many months often knew the ward routine better than a new probationer.

For a gentlewoman, nursing meant a peculiar role reversal. Instead of being served by working people, she served them. As the matron of the Glasgow Royal Infirmary warned,

> Our poorer and less fortunately placed brethren with whom you will now come into contact have not had your advantages, and must be dealt with in a loving and helpful spirit. Any superciliousness on your part will be keenly felt by them and resented. Meet them as fellow-creatures, not as inferior beings, remembering that it is a mere accident of birth, and not personal merit of your own, which has placed you in different circumstances.[64]

Sick and helpless working people were not only less frightening, but also more manageable; stripped of their familiar surroundings, they were forced to follow a regimen alien to their habits. Yet even as she ordered her patients around, a nurse had to keep her distance. All patients were referred to by number, and nurses frequently changed from side to side in a ward, lest they get to know anyone too well. Probationers could be sent to the matron for spending too much time with a patient or granting special favors. This could be difficult in a children's ward, where a child might want to have its medicine given by a particular nurse.[65] Probationers were encouraged to see nursing as an extension of mothering yet were positively discouraged from making friends with the patients.

In spite of this contradiction, the ward, under the guidance of a wise sister, was defined as a home. Americans who visited English hospitals noted how sisters "often remain for a working lifetime at the head of their households as contentedly as a mother at the head of her family," creating a "home-like, serene and cheerful atmosphere."[66] In a sense, sisters had enormous power, just as a mother had. They could ignore an intractable patient, flatter a busy doctor, and control the information each received. The nurses were younger sisters, the patients their children, and the doctors the fathers. This comparison, as Gamarnikow has pointed out, was made quite frequently in contemporary nursing journals. In 1894, for example, *The Hospital* editorialized,

> In the bearing of a nurse toward her charge there must be something of the indulgence of a mother for her child; that is why women are better nurses than men. . . . It is astonishing

what can be done with gentleness, especially when dispensed by a woman, and as the medical man is there, I think it would be well if the so-called firmness, when needed, were left to him. She can always invoke the physician's orders for the refusal of any unreasonable request.[67]

A few years later readers were reminded, "The best nurse is that woman whose maternal instincts were well developed. . . . The connection between mothering and nursing is very close."[68] In a rival paper, The Nursing Record and Hospital World, exactly the same language was used. E. J. R. Landale wrote, "to the truly vocated Nurse her work is her life, her home is her ward, the sick are her children. She troubles herself very little about money, too little indeed for her future good."[69] Endless changes were rung on the metaphor of the nurturing, motherly nurse. Ironically, Nightingale herself by the 1890s had shifted from her earlier militarism to a gentler relationship with her nurses. She loved to address the probationers at the Nightingale School as her "dear children," signing her letters, "Mother Chief."[70]

Like any family, power was distributed unequally. Eva Lückes reminded nurses and probationers that "we cannot do better than to regard the set of wards as a united family of which Sister is the head. Her interest in all is assumed as a matter of course. No one would think of ignoring or defying her wishes, though they would gladly turn to her for help in difficulty."[71] But a thicket of unwritten rules came between the sister and those under her. A probationer never spoke to anyone until spoken to; she could not use certain staircases and had to appear before her superiors in a clean apron. She was expected to serve tea to everyone else first at mealtimes. In some hospitals it was bad manners to ask for seconds, so the probationers were often left hungry after gulping down their meals under the eyes of the waiting nurses who had been served first. Humiliation seemed to dog the inept. Bedpans still had hollow handles in the 1920s. Ida Holford had the misfortune to slip in front of her dragonlike ward sister while carrying an armload back to the sluices:

> With a short, mad peal of wedding bells for the damned, they hit the floor in front of me, and through their hollow handles the contents were freely sloshed over the shoes and stockings of the almighty one, while—as one woman—the ward craned forward in breathless and fascinated appreciation.[72]

But there were lighter moments. A St. Thomas' probationer had to help her kindhearted sister conceal a drunk patient, who had been permitted out to "buy some Christmas cards."[73] Nevertheless, the continual harping on the importance of a familylike atmosphere bespoke the opposite, a world of severe discipline and secret infractions, abuses and unhappiness.

A major problem was the education of the probationers, which was largely in the hands of the ward sister. Most sisters were so overworked that when a pro had a particular aptitude for a job she was not encouraged to try something else; the smooth running of the ward took precedence over teaching the inexperienced and awkward. Here again a rhetoric of moral duty concealed the realities of hard routine work. E. J. R. Landale described the great responsibility of being a nurse to the readers of *The Nursing Record and Hospital World*:

> The capacity for so training Probationers, and for wisely dealing with various characters, presupposes in the Sister a well trained and disciplined mind—and a controlled nature, yet one of deep sympathies. . . . Sisters [should] be chosen not only for their excellence in ward work, but for that higher moral force and excellence which will fit them to rule and influence their subordinates wisely, and for their highest good.[74]

Some sisters could live up to this ideal, but in an occupation chronically short of qualified workers, most fell short. Tired and overworked, they used discipline to cover mistakes and to enforce order. Moreover, even the most adroit might have had trouble juggling the dual role of army officer and sympathetic mother. If she took her duties seriously, a sister could not risk intimacy with those under her. The sister was, after all, controlled by her "general," the matron, and any confidences might find their way back to her. Mrs. Wardroper, the first matron of the Nightingale School, resorted to an unfortunate system of encouraging confidences and gossip. She may have felt more in control of the nurses, but the morale of those under her was poor.[75]

Descriptions of life in the nurses' home sound like a combination of boot camp and boarding school. Homesickness and shared miseries united probationers. Looking back, old nurses remembered midnight feasts of tinned sardines and cake from home, washed down with milk and tea stolen from the ward. A St.

Thomas' nurse remembered fifty years later her horror at meeting
the matron late one night when she was carrying a teapot of milk
back to her room.[76] Working and living together so intensively,
each class developed a temporary corporate loyalty, identifying
with each other and helping the weaker to succeed. Just as in
boarding schools and colleges, probationers were discouraged
from making friends outside their own entry group. As late as the
1930s C. M. Harker found at her training school that "batches of
students . . . were judged rather like wine: there were good vin-
tages and bad."[77] Each group soon learned to take pride in work
well done. Even the comic songs echoed duty and hard work:

> We do all the dirty work
> The Ward Maids will not do
> Clean lavatories, bathrooms
> And scrub the patients too
> We slave like heathen niggers
> But somehow get some fun
> One's life feels all the sweeter
> When one's duty has been done[78]

But the bonds formed during a year of labor were weak; nurses
were slow to form associations similar to the alumnae organizations of educational institutions. St. Bartholomew's was the first,
in 1899. A probationer was encouraged to develop loyalties first
to her profession, second to her school, and only third to her
classmates.

Perhaps the probationers found it so difficult to see the wards as
homes because they were there for only three months. But they
also may have recognized a truer family metaphor for describing
ward life: it most closely resembled an upper-class wife and her
domestic servants. Even the nurses' uniforms resembled those of
a servant. Although the maids did all the scrubbing and heavy
carrying, much hard physical work remained to be done by the
pros. In addition to daily bed making, they were expected to dust,
empty and clean bedpans, scrub down the lavatories, and bathe
patients. No one thought of laborsaving devices, so the heavy
screens placed around a patient for privacy did not have wheels
until the twentieth century. A particularly onerous domestic task
was the annual counting of supplies. All linen had to be marked
and counted, all cutlery and every supply of bandages, medication,
and soap accounted for; the turnout was reminiscent of spring

cleaning in a large country home. An elaborate system of borrowing and remarking kept the required number of items on hand for
the matron's inspection. Wards were generally in pairs, so that if
ward A's utensils were marked in red, the sister could negotiate
with ward B to change a few items temporarily from green to red.[79]

In an angry attack on Elizabeth Garrett Anderson, the first
woman doctor, for failing to see the difference between a domestic
servant and a nurse, Florence Nightingale wrote,

> The situation of a Head Nurse in a hospital is one quite pecu-
> liar, as far as I am aware, in the world. In a man's ward, she is
> the only woman in real practical charge of grown-up men.
> [Queens have been in official fictitious charge—but] the Head
> nurse of a man's ward in a civil hospital has the absolute
> charge of the actions of thirty or forty men at every moment
> of the day and night—besides those of three or four women
> nurses in a position peculiarly exposed to breaches of de-
> corum and discipline. The character that can really and effec-
> tually fulfill this charge is a rare one.[80]

Despite Nightingale's claims, Garrett Anderson was probably
right. The well-trained nurse no longer scrubbed floors, but a passion for cleanliness and discipline overrode other considerations.
A probationer sent to wash soiled bandages day after day might be
forgiven for feeling that her "training" served little purpose but to
humiliate her. Sisters who followed Nightingale's edicts invariably found cleaning—especially filthy utensils—to be good discipline. In a hospital "woman's work" was as rigidly defined as in
the wider society. What power a woman had was through an em-
bodiment of the womanly ideal of giving to others—of controlling
the men in her ward through benevolent despotism, as the motherly grande dame of Victorian fiction.

The result was not a family, such as could be found in the boarding schools or settlement houses, but rather a rigid ordering of
women that masqueraded as a family while mimicking the medical hierarchy under which the nurses labored. The constant rota-
tion of probationers from ward to ward, the class divisions in the
training home, and the exploitative work all acted to inhibit a
sense of community among women nurses. They associated their
life together with stringent and often unnecessary regulations enforced by ancient and unrelenting battle-axes. They stole pleasures in cold bedrooms rather than face the cheerless common

room shared by all. Meals were remembered as dreary and hasty affairs, without relaxation of discipline. The very high drop-out rate—seldom less than 30 percent from the very earliest days through World War I—seemed to cast a pall upon those who succeeded.[81] Although they might feel special because they had survived, many probationers upon completion of their training were angry at the waste of some of the keenest women.[82] The vocational argument, used so unrelentingly by the first generation, covered too many problems for the second generation to accept their lot uncomplainingly.

Saints with Clay Feet

The Victorian public adored womanly self-sacrifice. Nurses captured the public imagination; they were surrogates for those who could not or would not give up their own lives for others. In an age that was widely condemned for its materialistic and self-seeking character, women—and especially nurses—carried the burden of morality for others. Nurses were as close to saints as a Protestant country could have. In 1888 the *Westminster Review* warned that "a sentimental glamour has been thrown over the services rendered to the sick" and called for better working conditions, improved pay, and pension plans for all nurses. But the author could not resist striking a sentimental note in his conclusion, reflecting the symbolic role of nurses:

> These are the women who carry, wherever they go, an atmosphere of noble labour and unselfish enterprise which brings to this work-a-day world a gleam of the glory to come. . . . The influence exercised far and wide by a nurse is almost unbounded, and if she be actuated by the fervent love of humanity which urges many women to undertake this work, she can carry everywhere with her a glorious torch to light all upwards towards more sublime and unselfish aims.[83]

Carrying a torch lighting the path to heaven was an awkward position for even the most idealistic. But it was especially uncomfortable when criticisms of nurses poured in from both the public and the profession itself.

Amid the general admiration of the self-sacrificing nurse, criticism pinpointed the class conflicts inherent in the model of the reformed nurse. For the educated public, the very success of the

10. *"Sweet Girl Graduates at Home."*
The homelike atmosphere of Byng
Hall, University of London, is
emphasized to counteract popular
fears of "masculine" intellectual
women. (The Graphic, *1884.)*

*11. Constance Louisa Maynard
(seated, left) with fellow students from
her Girton Prayer Meeting, ca. 1873–
75. Courtesy of Westfield College,
University of London.*

*12. Royal Holloway College cocoa
party, ca. 1910. Courtesy of BBC
Hulton Picture Library.*

13. The cast of Mostofus, *the going-down play, Somerville, 1912. Courtesy of Somerville College, Oxford.*

14. *Schoolgirls walking in a crocodile,*
1903. (G. R. Sims, Living London,
1903.)

15. *Miss Beale and the College Staff,*
1878. Note the Gothic building in the
background. Courtesy of Cheltenham
Ladies' College.

*16. Cheltenham Ladies' College
archery team, ca. 1890. Courtesy of
Cheltenham Ladies' College.*

*17. "'Oh, I love you—I love you!' she cried." A schoolgirl declares her love to a favorite teacher. (L. T. Meade, *The Manor School*, 1903.) Courtesy of the Osborne Collection of Early Children's Books, Toronto Public Library.*

new nurses led to higher expectations. Many trained nurses upon completing their probationary training became private nurses, a position that placed them in unique proximity to upper-class family secrets. The manners of a lady, especially in regard to discretion, were expected, along with the selfless service of a family retainer. Some nurses clearly did not live up to such an ideal, and stories began to proliferate about those who took advantage of their patients, or were callous, or simply lacked good manners.[84] Although private nursing was better paid and less exhausting than hospital nursing, a nurse had to tread a fine line in a world that insisted upon a working-class workload and ladylike manners. A professional nurse was not a devoted spinster aunt or daughter, but neither was she a domestic servant. An older generation of nurses, ever ready to see a falling away from their standards, tended to side with upper-class critics. Their solution, like that of those who hired the nurses, was to call for a better class of nurses and to urge probationers to greater heights of self-sacrifice.

But criticism by outsiders was pale in comparison with the controversies that wracked reformed nursing around the turn of the twentieth century. For the first thirty-odd years of reform, attacks had been made against the old nurses and the general organization of hospitals. Improvement only led to further criticism—this time of the pioneers. So much had been promised that when nursing fell short it evoked angry accusations and counter accusations. At the root of the complaints was a sense that nursing had not yet achieved its appropriate professional status. A major public battle was waged for and against state registration and examination of nurses. But an equally important, though more disorganized, criticism was against the nature and conditions of reformed nursing itself. Isolated voices repeatedly complained about the poor pay, execrable living conditions, and long hours of nurses; those engaged in the battle over state registration often dismissed these commentators as lacking in commitment. Yet ultimately, theirs was the voice of the rank and file and therefore needs to be heard more clearly.

In their eagerness to turn nursing into a suitable profession for ladies, the matrons of the London voluntary hospitals bent all their efforts toward "raising standards." At its simplest this operated on the principle of "more is better": more years of training, more rigorous regulations, more discipline.[85] But underneath this was a commitment to nursing as an occupation exclusively for the single gentlewoman. Asserting that "a well-born woman will more easily enter into the feelings of her patients than a woman who belongs to the lower orders," Lucy M. Rae in 1902 called for the exclusion of all but those of the right social class:

> The matter could be easily accomplished if hospital officials would recognise the fact that the question of "class" is at the root of the evils in the nursing profession; there might then be some chance of a remedy.[86]

Such a "remedy" would have left the workhouse infirmaries and all but the elite hospitals empty. A position of snobbish social and moral superiority had been taken by the pioneers and was adhered to through generations of matrons at the voluntary hospitals. Even the respondents to Rae did not question her assumption that a lady was morally superior; they simply argued that some women were innately "lady-like."[87] In spite of the martyrdom of Agnes Jones or the allure of district nursing, the mighty training schools were designed to train ladies to go into private nursing or to head wards in equivalent institutions. Their only concern with other forms of nursing was how to bring them under their own control.

The intensely hierarchical medical world only encouraged this snobbery. Although historians have tended to portray the anti-registrationists as advocates of the common nurse, a closer look at the arguments on either side shows little to distinguish them. When Ethel Bedford Fenwick first proposed the state registration of nurses in 1887, she advocated a three-year nationally devised training program at accredited hospitals of no less than one hundred beds. These requirements, however unrealistic, would raise nursing to the status of a middle-class profession. During the ensuing forty years, after the formation of various rival organizations, a major government inquiry, several parliamentary bills, and a great deal of public back-stabbing, this demand remained unchanged. The antis, led by Eva Lückes and Sydney Holland of the London Hospital, with the powerful behind-the-scenes support of Florence Nightingale, were not in favor of a more democratic system; they simply wanted to retain control of their own training program and nurses. Many matrons from provincial hospitals favored registration because they thought it would make their nurses equal to those from the socially prestigious London schools. General practitioners opposed registration because they feared their clients would prefer the cheaper nurses to them. For the elite who led the battle on both sides, special standards—whether registration or a certificate of performance—would mark the superior nurse. Even after some of the antis formed an organization in favor of a diluted form of registration, agreement could not be reached; the government stepped in and prepared its own state registration bill. The product of compromise, it passed in 1919, satisfying no one. In the words of the nursing historian Monica Baly,

> By its own folly the profession had handed over the control of the standard of entry and the requirements for the basic training to the government, and of course to the ultimate control by people who had the responsibility for keeping the hospitals staffed as cheaply as possible. . . . the first hallmark of a profession—that it controls its own standard of entry and training, was lost.[88]

A major difficulty the proregistrationists never faced was the very large number of untrained or minimally trained nurses that would be thrown out of employment, decimating the ranks of the ordinary hospitals, should state registration be imposed according to their high standards. In 1901 some 63,500 women and 5,700 men (mostly in mental hospitals) were nurses. Of these about 25,000 had had some training, but only about 10,000 "would have satisfied Florence Nightingale." At most 5,000 were trained ladies. More than 42 percent of the 67,000 female nurses and midwives were over forty-five, with more than 6,000 over sixty-five.[89] Yet the leaders of state registration continued to advocate nursing as a vocation for single women between the ages of twenty-five and fifty. The antis, on the other hand, had little to offer because leaders such as Lückes assumed the superiority of training at elite hospitals like their own. Lückes offered no alternative solution either for training the thousands who could not afford to attend an equivalent institution or for preventing the flooding of the market, which would undermine the occupation as a whole. The class bias of reformers, whatever their position on state registration versus vocational commitment, hindered any realistic improvement of nursing, and thus women lost control of its course.

The drawn-out and acrimonious fight for registration concealed or deflected concern for the continuing difficulties of hospital nurses. Despite an obsession with cleanliness for the patients, the nurses' living quarters were often dirty and their food was often inadequate. Plain food went with plain living, but insufficient food appears to have been due to poor planning and inexperience. Like the early principals at the women's colleges, many matrons were chosen because they had the right social connections rather than for their experience in food management. The elaborate system of times off and on made it difficult to keep the dining room clean and the food fresh. Roasts, hot and cold, with potatoes and pudding, made up the bulk of every meal; little variety and much starch depressed everyone, but especially the lady probationers. Agnes Hunt found it difficult to eat breakfast with the stench of stale beer and cheese pervading the dining room.[90] Several Nightingale nurses remembered their dismay at discovering they would be served only one plate for all courses. Fortunately in 1900 a particularly obstreperous probationer declared the custom "disgusting" and proceeded to eat her pudding off the back of her plate. She was reprimanded, but the next week extra plates were provided.[91] An investigation into conditions in the London Hospital in 1890–92 revealed a pattern of overwork, poor food, and insufficient attention to the nurses' health. *The Nursing Record*, under the editorship of Bedford Fenwick, used the occasion to attack Lückes and the London Hospital's policies. A thinly disguised serial novel savagely maligned her for capriciousness, indifference to her nurses, and unsanitary living conditions.[92]

Poor living conditions could be improved only with additional resources to build better nursing homes. When Nightingale started her training school she assumed that all trained nurses would live in or near their wards; training homes were only for probationers and for dining. But many voluntary hospitals, which served a working-class population, were in poor neighborhoods; it would have been unthinkable for a respectable woman to find lodgings in such communities. Moreover, schoolteachers, college teachers, paid settlement workers, and religious sisters all expected to live in their workplaces. Respectable nurses clearly needed their own home, a part of, but apart from, the hospital. Eva Lückes's greatest triumph was to open a modern residence for her two hundred–odd nurses.[93] Unfortunately these homes were all too often run on the same strict disciplinary lines that were applied to probationers. Nurses were often forbidden to visit their rooms when off duty, except when going to bed; night passes were extremely restrictive, so women could rarely attend a concert or lecture. Mature women were increasingly restive under such a regime.

Ideally the nurses' homes were communities of warmth, encouragement, and relaxing recreation. Since nurses had so little free time, a few matrons made a point of bringing culture and recreation to them. During its pioneer days the Nightingale School held soirees and poetry readings. Wealthy donors to the hospital were asked to take nurses out for afternoon rides in their carriages. By the end of the century at Guy's the probationers were encouraged to join the swimming or tennis teams or to participate in the hospital choral society.[94] But as in so much else, recreational and cultural opportunities for nurses varied enormously. A nurse who trained at St. Thomas' reminisced about how frequently she took the bus to Baker Street, which cost twopence, round trip, and was just long enough for her to get plenty of fresh air and rest during her two-hour afternoon break.[95] Agnes Hunt in 1890 found that the West London Hospital, Hammersmith, gave nurses two hours off every other day, with no provisions whatever for the use of this paltry free time.[96] Middle-class women who were accustomed to the pleasures of church meetings, tea parties, and concerts found nursing antithetical to the development of any cultural life.

During the early years of the twentieth century, just as nurses' homes were gradually beginning to loosen their rules, modernists were questioning the very idea of living in. Lucy Ashby in 1908 suggested that living a few hundred yards away from the hospital would broaden the horizons of both probationers and nurses:

> In the first place, it would raise the nurse, in the matter of freedom, to the *status* of the typist and the clerk. And why not? It would fit her for work by giving her a little time for play. The nurse wants to feel that she can visit a theatre or attend a family party occasionally without being accused of frivolousness, and jeopardising her chance of promotion thereby. She wants a little time which she can call her own.[97]

But the demand for a life outside the hospital collided with the most deeply held beliefs of the reforming generation. One indignant reply to Ashby argued, "if a woman can't live 'in,' work 'in,' eat 'in,' and even think 'in,' she should choose different work with fewer demands."[98] The cornerstone of reformed nursing had been a total commitment to hospital work. Any falling-off from this ideal was seen as a traitorous capitulation to lower moral standards. In effect, women nurses had to be superior or they lost all credibility.

Unrealistic standards continued to plague nursing. A woman was not considered mature enough to enter training until twenty-three or twenty-five; she was then expected to immure herself in a hospital for twenty-odd years, only to retire prematurely at forty-five or fifty. As early as 1876 the *Victoria Magazine* had rhetorically asked, "Is it a career likely to tempt a woman of culture, to commence at 25 upon wages which an incompetent servant maid of eighteen will not take, and to end her working life—while still in her prime—upon less wages than a head-nurse or a 'plain cook' can demand and easily obtain?"[99] Many women who might have preferred hospital work for its greater variety were forced to choose private nursing because of the better pay and longer working life. Like teachers, nurses over fifty were supposed to be too physically debilitated and mentally rigid to continue working. Just as a doctor reached the apex of his career, a nurse was considered to be on the decline and incapable of new responsibilities.

Early retirement from hospital work raised the insistent question of how a woman was to live from fifty until her death. In 1887 Henry Burdett organized the Royal National Pension Fund for Nurses in response to the publicity surrounding the death of a nurse in a workhouse. The nurse had contracted typhoid in her ward; permanently disabled, she could no longer work and died penniless. The fund offered both health insurance and a pension scheme and was supported by rather high premiums for nurses and donations from sympathetic individuals. Membership in the fund was never widespread, and most hospitals offered no pension scheme whatever or insisted upon twenty years' service for eligibility.[100] Many hospital nurses, upon compulsory retirement, went into private nursing; that 6,000 women over sixty-five in 1901 were still actively engaged in nursing testifies to the longer work life of many nurses. A few women were able to open private convalescent homes or boardinghouses for private nurses who were between cases. But poor pay and the lack of pensions remained important grievances among nurses until well into the twentieth century.

Although demand was high, trained nurses had little control over entry, working conditions, and pay. Nursing leaders themselves exploited the Victorian belief in woman's self-sacrificing nature at the price of decent pay and working conditions. The poor food found in nurses' homes was consonant with an image of spirituality, the long hours with vocational commitment, the poor pay with religious motives. The reforming *Nursing Record*, for example, opposed recommendations to shorten a nurse's hours, arguing in an editorial, "I can imagine nothing more trying than an eight hours' shift. At the end of twelve hours, one hardly knows how to go and leave the worst cases, the interest and anxiety over them is so great." [101] Understaffing and poor pay were both justified by arguing that better conditions would attract the wrong kind of woman.

Class prejudice divided the ranks of nursing, but even if they had been united it is doubtful that women could have achieved the power base they sought in the early years of reformed nursing. All other women's occupations were based upon a "separate spheres" argument, in which middle-class women worked with women or children or the poor but never worked daily with their professional or social equals. Nursing alone grappled with creating a sphere for women amid a male world while seeking to eliminate working-class women who had no such pretensions. By the end of the century upper-class leaders had impressed their image of nursing upon the profession itself, tightly controlling those under them so as to create the false sense of a powerful all-female sphere within the medical world. Certainly hospital matrons had great power, but only over those directly under them; lower-class nurses whom they distrusted still dominated numerically.

The very high wastage rate among probationers, the frequent loss of nurses after completion of training, and the high turnover of lady probationers meant instability at the bottom of the hierarchy, in sharp contrast to the longevity at the top. Matrons and sisters rarely changed, and they spent their energies consolidating what power they had, controlling those who changed frequently or resigned. A classic situation of the fundamentally powerless developed. The little power of those at the top was strengthened until it became a virtual stranglehold upon those under them. Probationers assuaged their frustrations by gossiping about their leaders and collecting stories about their abuse of power. One pseudonymous account described "Saint E.," a sister who went to morning and evening church services but skimmed the cream from the patients' milk for her cat and forced the probationers to do all her work.[102] Doctors, who held the real power in the hospital, were idolized as distant patriarchs, while the women often despised each other. In a situation that should have encouraged close working relationships—ward care—nursing fostered dogged survival.[103] A. H. Stoney described her probationary years at the end of the nineteenth century as "life on a treadmill," with "cruelty and humanity hand in hand," overworking the nurses to serve the patients. But unlike many, she argued,

> Do not blame matrons and sisters, however, as so many nurses seem inclined to do. There may perhaps be individual instances of tyranny and petty, needless exactions; but on the whole they are fine, fair-minded women, who are compelled to get work done as best they can, the work required by the committees and visiting staff. It is not their fault if their workers are too few.[104]

Others were less charitable. The ridiculously high standards set for nurses, and especially sisters, meant that those who fell short were subject to continual criticism. The ultimate failure of the military metaphor was the inability of nurses to unite for a larger ideal.

Nursing more than any other occupation discussed here was dependent upon the male medical world for acceptance; from the beginning it had to carve out a special sphere of influence under exceptionally difficult conditions. But in focusing on the status of nursing for the few upper-class single women, the mass of hardworking nurses were left by the wayside. State registration and the control of entry into the profession obsessed leaders who should have been fighting for shorter hours, better pay, and adequate pensions. Since the arguments for hygiene as woman's special field were undermined by advances in medical science, the occupation itself never fully broke from its domestic-service origins. Nursing leaders failed to enlarge or consolidate their power. Instead they turned inward, fighting to retain their control over those in training while disparaging those who might settle for less discipline. Class prejudice and sexism collided to create a weak secondary occupation rather than the strongly united corps of women so celebrated in the pronouncements of nursing leaders. Nursing demonstrated the limitations of a separate female world that lacked an effective power base within its own domain.

CHAPTER

4

Women's Colleges: An Independent Intellectual Life

In 1935 the detective-story writer Dorothy L. Sayers published *Gaudy Night*, set in "Shrewsbury College," a nostalgic version of her own Somerville. She describes the women dons with great affection, half-envying, half-satirizing their high-mindedness, gentle naiveté, and intellectual honesty. The heroine is continually struck by the kindness of these single women, who watch after each faithful servant and poor student, carefully distributing limited funds:

> "Yes—[Agnes] was Head-Scout in your time; yes, she has left. She began to find the work too much for her and had to retire. I'm glad to say we were able to squeeze out a tiny pension for her—only a trifle, but as you know, our income has to be stretched very carefully to cover everything. And we arranged a little scheme by which she takes in odd jobs of mending and so on for the students and attends to the College linen. It all helps; and she's especially glad because that crippled sister of hers can do part of the work and contribute something to their small income. Agnes says the poor soul is so much happier now that she need not feel herself a burden."[1]

The "untiring conscientiousness" of the women leaders ensured that "nobody's interests [were] overlooked or forgotten, and an endless goodwill made up for a perennial scarcity of funds."[2] Sayers found that women's traditional role of caring for the needy was carried on with feminine delicacy and shrewdness, without loss of intellectual zeal and objectivity. But her dons are too unworldly to understand vengeance, passion, or married life. By the interwar years the women's colleges seemed to be genteel ivory towers untouched by the massive political and social changes around them. Yet during the nineteenth century, the admission of women to the universities was seen by such feminists as Alice Zimmern as "the keystone of the arch, without which the rest of the fabric could have neither stability nor permanence."[3] Without access to all levels of formal education, Victorian reformers believed, women could never enter the professions, train other women and girls, or prove their worthiness to vote. Education was their foundation for further change.

The movement for women's higher education was part of a much larger "revolution of the dons," in which both Oxford and Cambridge were transformed into modern teaching and research institutions. Just as the reform of women's legal status came about within the context of larger legal changes, so too did the women's colleges grow in an environment of curricular and organizational reform at the two major universities. Male reformers brought from the public schools a high ideal of personal service to their colleges, which included a commitment to teaching and close student relations. Coaching, which had long been in the hands of outsiders especially hired by the students, was gradually brought into the colleges.[4] Women, whose prior education had often been erratic, were early beneficiaries of this reform in teaching.[5] The ideological debate at the time was between the traditionalists who favored a liberal education that focused upon character development and the modernizers who wanted an education that would prepare the young for the professions, with an emphasis upon the pursuit of new knowledge—of research. Women were drawn to university training for both of these reasons, and as will be seen, the character of the first two women's colleges reflected these differing priorities.

The leaders in the movement for women's higher education were almost exclusively drawn from the professional middle class, in alliance with supporters from some of the leading northern commercial and industrial families.[6] Men who had risen in status and financial security through formal education recognized its value in preparing their own children. With little inherited wealth or social influence, the doctors, lawyers, and clergymen asserted the superiority of training and examinations over other criteria for judging public worth.[7] The founders of the women's colleges wanted educated daughters and wives; if their daughters did not marry, a college education would doubtless help them find better teaching positions. Higher education for women fit into the plans of feminist reformers eager to expand the educational and job opportunities of women, but it is best characterized as part of a wider movement of middle-class reform. The liberal intelligentsia during the second half of the nineteenth century transformed education and the professions in England; middle-class women were part of this larger movement.

Although the students came from every level of the middle class and included a few from the gentry, the women's colleges were solidly middle class in their ethos. Learning—for both men and women—was always seen as part of a larger purpose, for service to God or mankind. Clearly many women entered college in order to improve their job prospects, but many also sought time for uninterrupted study. In comparison with their brothers, women could add little prestige to their families by attending college, nor could they look forward to a leadership position in the civil service or a profession. College study meant a time of shared learning and living before returning home or going into teaching. Although some snobbery was unavoidable, life within the women's colleges was remarkably free of the class divisions that plagued both the sisterhoods and nursing.

Higher education for women began modestly. Queen's College was founded in 1848 by the Reverend F. D. Maurice and the Governesses' Benevolent Institution to provide training for governesses so that they could obtain better salaries. In the following year Bedford College was founded by Elizabeth Reid, a determined and unswerving feminist who insisted that women play a major role in its governance. Both colleges were almost wholly nonresidential and placed much emphasis upon making up deficiencies in their students' education. They paved the way for higher education at a degree level, but notions of providing a separate environment for women, in which full-time study and independence from family duties would be key elements, were rejected. This ideal, routinely considered the best possible education for young men, was achieved only in 1869 with the founding of Hitchin, later Girton, College. Residential colleges, in spite of their late start and small enrollments, were an important alternative to the traditional family for single women. I am specifically concerned here with the corporate life of the residential colleges at Cambridge and Oxford, Royal Holloway College and Westfield College. These institutions shared with the two pioneering colleges a history of slow gains, small numbers, setbacks offsetting victories, and most of all, severe financial constraints. They never had enough money, enough books, enough trained leadership, and in the early days, enough students; only at the end of the nineteenth century did competition for entry become fiercely competitive.[8]

But higher education for women is also a story of great personal advances. The colleges offered a unique opportunity for intellectual women to join others who shared their delight in study; they were expected to take responsibility for their own time and studies, unlike either churchwomen or nurses in training. Even though women were tightly circumscribed by regulations and chaperoned off grounds, within the precincts of the colleges they were freer and more independent than in any of the other institutions discussed here. Those who planned a career in teaching (and fully half did) were better prepared intellectually and emotionally for a life dedicated to teaching girls. They slipped naturally into the new high schools and boarding schools, providing leadership and role models for generations; the corporate values learned in college were taught to the young, emphasizing, as chapter 5 documents, a wider duty than the family. Women who attended college with no intention of working afterward found courage through intellectual discipline to work more effectively at home or to convince a reluctant father of the importance of work for women. For both kinds of women, college was a glorious interlude, a special women's space in which duty to self and community took precedence over all outside obligations. Residential colleges offered untold opportunities for friendship, contact with some of the best minds of the times, and intellectual freedom—privileges that were rare in even the most advanced professional families.

Small Beginnings, Great Responsibilities

The roots of the residential women's colleges at Oxford and Cambridge were similar in many ways to those of the two London precursors. Educational reform had begun in the late 1840s, gathering strength through the 1850s and 1860s. Each decade saw the opening of new secondary schools for girls, the launching of various lecture series for ladies, and the admittance of girls to nationwide examinations; and finally came the founding of the two women's colleges in London. These small beginnings laid the groundwork for major reforms in women's education during the years 1869–87.[9] The women's colleges were a natural, though by no means easy, step for middle-class liberal reformers.

Supporters of women's higher education thought largely in terms of giving women an opportunity to participate in university life, to hear lectures, and to pursue a regular course of study, without necessarily taking any examinations. Women without systematic education would clearly find it difficult to undertake the Oxford or Cambridge honors examinations, based as they were upon years of classical and mathematical training. If women failed these exams, they might confirm beliefs about women's intellectual inferiority. In 1866 the examining body of the University of London, which at the time had no faculty or formal courses, offered to give women a special examination. After some debate, this examination was then given for ten years, until 1878, when women were admitted to the same examinations as men. But Emily Davies (1830–1921) was afraid that accepting an inferior and separate examination would cut women off from the opportunities available to men.[10] She forged ahead with her plan to open a college where women would study for the Cambridge "Tripos" examinations. She optimistically hoped to raise £30,000 and to attract some twenty-five students. But her pamphlets, letters, and talks brought only a cautiously favorable response in middle-class circles; few were willing to commit themselves until they had seen the experiment in action. Davies finally opened her doors in 1869 with six students and £7,000 in pledges.[11]

In the meantime the reforming Cambridge professor Henry Sidgwick had approached Anne Jemima Clough, a leader of the North of England Council for Promoting the Higher Education of Women, about founding a residential hall for those interested in attending lectures connected with the Higher Local Examinations.[12] Clough agreed in 1871 to become the residential head of a house Sidgwick had rented. For Sidgwick women's higher education was part of his larger scheme to reform outdated requirements at Cambridge. He encouraged his students to bypass the stultifying examination requirements and to take the new courses emerging in science, philosophy, economics, and history. Davies, however, insisted that her students follow exactly the same course as the men, which meant taking the compulsory Greek examination and the Tripos examination within the stated limit of three years and one term. She also strongly encouraged her students to tackle mathematics and classics rather than the low-prestige newer subjects. Many angry letters were exchanged between Davies and Sidgwick. In the end her belief in standards identical with men's was fully accepted, but for years she fought an isolated battle, convinced that even her friends did not support her.[13]

When Davies opened her college she did not know whether or not women would be permitted to take the Cambridge examinations. Her students had to prepare for each exam with the hope that the examiners would agree to look over their papers. Fortunately permission was granted at every level, and in 1872 three women successfully passed the Tripos exams, each gaining unofficial honors in her subject. It was an enormous victory, for it proved that erratically trained women could fulfill exactly the same requirements as men and do creditably in their exams. In 1874 two students from Sidgwick's Newnham College passed their Tripos. These triumphs were somewhat marred by the continued animosity between Davies and Sidgwick. Davies remained an outsider both literally and metaphorically during her long years of association with Cambridge. This gave her the strength to see beyond petty, local quarrels, but it also excluded her from the insider's knowledge skillfully used by Sidgwick. In 1881 Sidgwick was able to maneuver through the university syndicate an official agreement to admit women to the examinations. They were still denied permission to attend university lectures and refused the degree, but they were at least ensured a permanent position on the fringes of the university.[14]

At first Cambridge had been more welcoming than Oxford toward women, but in the early 1870s the situation changed. In 1872, when Oxford fellows were permitted to marry, the town soon filled with intelligent, reform-minded couples, eager to extend the benefits of an Oxford education to women.[15] In 1873 a group of women, with the help of two popular dons, T. H. Green and Mark Pattison, formed a committee to organize lectures for women. By 1878 another committee was investigating the establishment of a residential hall to enable women outside Oxford to attend the Higher Local lectures. Religious differences had led to the formation of a separate committee, headed by the principal of the new Keble College, for the express purpose of founding a Church of England hall. In 1879 the Anglican Lady Margaret Hall and the nondenominational Somerville Hall opened. For many years they were only residential halls, while the Association for the Education of Women (AEW) made all the necessary arrangements for lectures and examinations. As with the Cambridge students, at first women were not permitted to attend the men's lectures; sympathetic dons had to give the same lecture twice. LMH students went to a small hall over a bakery, so that knowledge mingled with the smell of fresh bread. Early students took a Women's Examination, similar to the Cambridge Higher Local, but in 1884 permission was given to take some of the men's examinations, and by 1894 all exams except medicine were open to women.[16] The original two Oxford colleges had fewer problems than those at Cambridge, perhaps because they had learned from their predecessors, perhaps because they were given fewer choices in regard to examinations.

In the minds of most English people university education meant Oxford or Cambridge, not the examining body of the University of London. Nevertheless, Bedford College, upgraded to a college in 1878 when London opened degrees to women, grew steadily as a largely nonresidential institution. So too did Royal Holloway College (1887) and Westfield College (1882). Royal Holloway, founded by Thomas Holloway, who had made his fortune in patent medicine, was unique in having a very large and magnificent building and a substantial endowment. For many years it mainly attracted students reading for the Higher Local Examinations or simply studying for a few years with no intention of taking a degree. Westfield, founded on Evangelical Church of England principles, with required Bible classes, drew mainly future missionaries and teachers. Despite an overworked staff, poor libraries, and inadequate laboratories, these colleges offered many of the same freedoms and opportunities as the more prestigious and better-known Oxbridge colleges. By 1897 women were largely accepted as part of the world of higher education, albeit a peripheral and minor part. The Women's Institute proudly compiled a listing of the total number of women at each university in the United Kingdom in 1897, including the number who had taken the London B.A. examination. The following numbers were in attendance at the women's colleges:[17]

Girton (Cambridge)	109
Newnham (Cambridge)	166
Somerville (Oxford)	73
Lady Margaret Hall (Oxford)	48
St. Hugh's Hall (Oxford)	24
St. Hilda's Hall (Oxford)	17
Bedford College (London)	192
Westfield College (London)	44
Royal Holloway (London)	111

In the early days few parents were eager to send their daughters away to college. It was expensive and seemed superfluous except for those intending to teach. Even in this obvious occupation the number of jobs for the college-educated were limited in the 1870s. Only the more farsighted saw the steady growth of secondary education over the next fifty years. Although colleges aroused less hysteria than sisterhoods, they were opposed for much the same reasons. The chief difficulty was the widespread belief that young women should not leave their homes except under dire economic necessity. Many were certain that college would alienate well-to-do young women from their families and lead them to prefer the society of friends their own age. Indeed, Davies ruefully wrote one supporter,

> I will try to be respectful to parents, but how is it possible to describe College life without showing how infinitely pleasanter it will be than home: It is a weak point which I am utterly at a loss to defend. I do not believe that our utmost efforts to poison the students' lives at College will make them half so miserable as they are at home.[18]

Single women who became Anglican sisters established the priority of religion over family demands. Those who became nurses proved that women could work with men without loss of status. But those who sought residential higher education were most clearly serving their own needs, creating their own space. In a world that deified a woman's life of service, Davies's ambitions for Girton necessarily raised suspicion among those she approached for support. Nevertheless, the colleges benefited from feminist agitation for better education and more recognition of women. For some fathers sending a recalcitrant daughter to college seemed a simple and safe way to pacify her—far better than having her traipsing around the slums or wearing herself out in a hospital.

All of the early founders recognized the dangers of presenting too attractive an alternative to the family, but the other colleges took a different tack from Davies's. They minimized notions about college life as a separate world for personal growth and maximized its resemblance to the traditional family. The prospectuses of both the Oxford halls declared that they would share "a common life with the way and tone of a Christian family," with Somerville substituting the word "English" for "Christian."[19] Elizabeth Wordsworth, principal of Lady Margaret Hall for thirty years, ran the hall like a large upper-class family; she always referred to her students as ladies. While Emily Davies discouraged her Girton students from becoming involved in the social round of Cambridge, Wordsworth expected hers to help her at teas and to escort her to the many social events of her Oxford circle.[20] In order to save the cost of fires, LMH students sat together in a common room, generally chattering to each other as they worked; every Girton student was supplied with a scuttle of coal a day, ensuring the freedom to study in privacy or to entertain special friends. Newnham College retained a system of separate dining rooms for each of its halls so that the dinner hour more closely resembled a large family gathering. A. J. Clough, like an elderly aunt, fussed over her students' health and worried if they did not write home regularly.[21] Davies, on the other hand, started her college with a "high table," in imitation of the men's colleges; the first mistress and her assistant were to eat at a raised table, while the five students sat below in a row looking up at them.[22] In the long run neither the imitation of a men's college nor the family-style model proved suitable for the women's colleges, but many years were spent floundering, looking for the right style of corporate living.

Some of the differences in perspective were reflected in the architecture of the individual colleges. LMH with its comfortable, large red-brick building for many years resembled a pleasant country home; the long garden down to the Cherwell added to this sense of rural peace. Girton College, in contrast, was purpose-built in imposing deep-red brick Gothic, imitating the men's colleges, even though it took years before a quadrangle was completed. Newnham was, perhaps, the most fortunate in its choice of architect; Basil Champneys, a leading exponent of Queen Anne architecture, took a personal interest in the college's buildings.[23] He managed to combine a sense of collegiate life with a wholly feminine atmosphere; his white-trimmed brick buildings were pleasantly inviting. Internally the colleges were rather spartan, as befitted a generation determined to use its new opportunities to serve others. Donations of furniture and fittings from women supporters, however, gradually improved the appearance of the common rooms, so that parents were reassured by the homelike atmosphere of their daughters' residence. The surroundings, like those of the new boarding schools, bespoke permanence, seriousness of purpose, and the same solidity that marked the middle-class families from which the bulk of students came.

One of the effects of this emphasis upon family-style colleges in all but Girton was an almost excessive amateurism about finances and administration. Uncertain relations with the university combined with the small size of their institutions left women principals very much on their own to muddle through the management and organization of the institution and their students. Principals were chosen not for their skills as bursars, though they were often expected to fulfill such duties, but because of their social connections, ability to get along with contentious committee members, and general interest in young people. Bookkeeping could be quite haphazard; Henry Sidgwick's wife soon took over Newnham's books when she saw Clough's efforts. Charlotte Toynbee, one of Wordsworth's volunteer assistants at LMH, simply insisted that the students pay her again after she lost the box containing their fees for the term.[24] A scholarship student of 1884 who came from a large London high school was struck by the "extreme amateurishness" of Somerville, combined with an enormous amount of attention paid to each individual's academic work.[25] Since the colleges had so little money and were so small, it was impossible to invest money or engage in long-term planning that might yield larger funds. In such circumstances, finances remained painfully simple.

Few principals had had any experience in running a household, much less a growing college filled with obstreperous young women and servants. Elizabeth Wordsworth was assisted by a battery of loyal Oxford wives. Bertha Johnson, in charge of domestic details at LMH, firmly announced, "I *never* buy any lard, and never allow cooking butter; any butter that is wanted the cook has to contrive out of odds and ends."[26] Not surprisingly, many early students remembered studying amid the pervasive odor of burnt fat. Reminiscences from all of the colleges echo Virginia Woolf's comments about the appalling food at Newnham in the 1920s. The food was so bad at Newnham in the mid-nineties that eighteen students sent a formal complaint to the principal.[27] A little later a group formed a secret L.S.D. society, which stood for "Leaving Sunday Dinner," but also implied the pounds, shillings, and pence they were willing to pay for a good meal once a week.[28]

Food obviously held the same low priority for academic women as for nursing leaders. The first principal of St. Hugh's appears to have considered an interest in food to be bordering on the sinful. Joan Evans described C. A. E. Moberly as a person of "amazing insularity":

Like many women of her age and class, our Principal had no conception of either comfort or beauty . . . our rooms were deplorably furnished, and our food ordered without intelligence and cooked without care or supervision. . . . Never in my life have I eaten so much reasty ham and over-salt salt beef, more wooden carrots and more tasteless milk puddings, than under her regime; and there was a mysterious sweet that appeared on Sunday evenings, apparently made from the remains of other puddings stuck together with custard, that the whole College knew as the Ancient of Days.[29]

For a sophisticated and internationally famous historian, Moberly's indifference to food was symbolic of the cultural limitations of a woman's college. But for an earlier generation, poor food had been symbolic of intellectual freedom and an indifference to the economic necessities of a poorly endowed institution.

Victorian single women usually lived in institutions if they left their families, so they had few opportunities to select and prepare their own food. This freedom, so important in our own day, was seen as a laborious task for those unfortunate enough not to live in a boardinghouse, institution, or home. Who one ate with mattered far more than what one ate. Mealtimes, in spite of the poor quality of the food, were important public events in the colleges. Teatime and late-night cocoa parties were occasions for special friends, but dinner in particular was an occasion for formal attire and a sharing of community life. Social skills, particularly conversation, and not the actual content of the meal were emphasized. Thus, the shy or socially marginal were encouraged to learn from their more confident peers under the wing of kindly principals. Madeline Shaw Lefevre, first principal of Somerville, kept a close watch over her students, lest they miss the social benefits of Oxford. One scholarship student remembered:

When interesting visitors came to see the Hall she invariably brought them to my room and drew me into conversation with them. If we had a garden-party or other function I would be sent off to show round and entertain one of the most formidable guests; in fact I see that she tried deliberately to cure my shyness and to draw me out of myself.[30]

During her final term Shaw Lefevre insisted upon lending her suitable clothing and escorting her to the annual degree-giving ceremony so she would not miss this most magnificent of Oxford ceremonials. This student was grateful to learn the social manners of an upper-class Victorian lady. But these habits angered women such as Joan Evans and Virginia Woolf, who saw such behavior as a continuation of the secondary status of women. They noticed the wealth that made fine food possible at the men's colleges and the breadth of contacts that made for intellectual discussion at dinners, not simply good manners. They were angry at women who were content to watch rather than participate in the feast of Oxford and Cambridge.

The 1890s saw a shift away from graciousness and bad food toward professionalization and bad food. The colleges were beneficiaries of the improved teaching in high schools, which produced many more and better-trained students; greater general acceptance brought more donations from interested persons. Changes can also be seen in the hiring of a new type of principal. In 1889 Somerville hired Agnes Maitland. In the following fifteen years she doubled the enrollment, built a library and extensive housing, and hired a full staff; the latter action meant a decisive break with the AEW's inefficient methods of arranging lectures and tutors for all women students. Symbolic of her efforts was the decision in 1894 to change the hall's name to Somerville College, "implying the desire of the Governing Body to raise it above the level of a Hall of Residence."[31] Maitland's successor, Emily Penrose, proceeded to concentrate on raising Somerville's academic standards. A scholar herself, she saw the need to develop advanced studies and to prepare for the day when women would receive Oxford degrees. By 1914 Somerville was refusing students who would not take all of the degree requirements; in 1920 Somerville had by far the largest number of women ready to receive the B.A. degree without having to repeat any required work.[32]

Even before Penrose, however, Somerville and the other women's colleges recognized the need to establish studentships for postgraduate studies. As early as 1883 students at Girton were calling for resident graduates. In the early 1890s past students began a fund for an endowed studentship, but funds grew very slowly. In 1897 a nonresidential Pfeiffer Studentship of £40 was offered, but no progress had been made toward residential scholars. In 1901 Ethel Sargant sharply pointed out the lack of intellectual growth at Girton:

> The truth is we do not sufficiently realise that the experimental stage is past. . . . Now that college life has left its

stamp on a generation we may fairly seek to criticise the system in order to amend it. The great defect in it is that in the effort to satisfy University tests we have neglected the pursuit of learning for its own sake. Such an omission may be pardonable in the youth of a college, but if we continue to train successive generations to look on a good place in the class lists as the only end of University teaching, we shall justly be considered as money-changers in the Temple.[33]

An older notion of higher education as a time for reading, for the development of character, had first given way to the pursuit of certification for a profession; now Sargant was asking Girton to follow the men's colleges and see learning in the modern sense of a center for the pursuit of original knowledge. Sargant's plea was met by a donation of funds for a woman immediately to take up a studentship for three years and by further contributions to the slowly increasing fund for an endowed studentship.[34] Newnham from the 1880s had occasionally given a one-year postgraduate studentship, especially in the natural sciences; by 1900 funds had been established for two three-year research fellowships. The renowned classical scholar Jane Ellen Harrison was the first to hold one.[35] The first Mary Somerville Research Fellowship was awarded in 1903.[36] Each of these moves was made in part to answer those who accused women of being incapable of furthering human knowledge. By the early twentieth century the more forward-thinking colleges—whether for men or women—had clearly moved beyond the earlier models of a small family or boarding school and were professional, modern academic institutions.

These changes, however, were not always made as smoothly as outsiders might have hoped. For many principals the dual process of winning acceptance from the wider community while gaining on-the-job experience was often a difficult one. Like headmistresses, hospital matrons, and mother superiors, they did not always act with tact, decisiveness, or flexibility. Neither did male heads of colleges, but they were usually under less pressure to prove themselves and could rely on past models and traditions. Most principals accepted the separate-but-equal model, working within the constraints imposed upon them by a male university and female respectability. Although the women's colleges were remarkably successful in giving the necessary support to women seeking an independent intellectual life, they were often run by women of extremely conventional social attitudes. Girton had the most difficulty in finding a principal, and over the years the governing board consistently chose even more circumspect leaders than the less militant institutions. After several temporary mistresses (Girton's term for principal), including Davies herself, in 1874 A. F. Bernard was appointed; she held the post for nine years, until her marriage. An austere and well-mannered woman, she neither asked for more authority nor used it, and so was eminently satisfactory from Davies's perspective. But her distant manner and narrow interpretation of her position alienated many students, who wished either for a warmer, more motherly leader or for a more dynamic feminist. At her retirement two early students were finalists for the position. The committee chose the unimaginative Elizabeth Welsh over the charismatic Louisa Lumsden. The power at Girton remained in the hands of Davies and her committee for many years because she alone had the ambitious vision of Mother Emily Ayckbowm or Dorothea Beale and was willing to pursue it at whatever price.[37]

The cautiousness of the women principals may have been the natural outcome of the scholarly life, which studies history rather than makes it, but the timidity of so many brilliant women cannot be explained so simply. The most obvious explanation is the double bind faced by all pioneering women. Despite often erratic schooling, they had to be equal to if not better than men intellectually, while not losing one iota of their feminine respectability.[38] Conforming to both norms was an arduous and not always reconcilable task, made more difficult by the weight of medical opinion against women's education. Anxiety that too much learning would unsex a woman was widespread, fanned by Social Darwinists concerned about "the decline of the species" and by doctors convinced that time spent studying would drain maternal energy.[39] Their repeated allegations of possible infertility, brain damage, or mental breakdown from overwork put the reformers on the defensive.[40] The sense of being present on sufferance made everyone especially careful about social mores. Fear of opposition narrowed the causes on which educationalists would speak out. Emily Davies dropped her support of women's suffrage lest she jeopardize the future of Girton. Josephine Butler gave up her educational work after she began agitating for the repeal of the Contagious Diseases Acts. University women followed "the conventionalities of the age" even more firmly than other career women lest they attract further negative criticism; Constance Maynard, first mistress of Westfield College, justified such behavior as "the best possible shelter for the new aspirations."[41] But it locked women into a rigid mold of respectability when they might have gained more by daring more.

The obvious success of college students in later life was one of the best arguments against scientists, medical men, and Oxbridge misogynists. Many a pioneer found such a struggle exhilarating in the name of future opportunities for women. But after women had silenced the most vociferous opposition, they could not alter their marginal status at male universities. Even at the University of London, ostensibly open to both sexes equally, fellowships were often awarded to men over women. At University College the women students had an awkward and inferior common room for many years. The women lecturers could invite their male colleagues to lunch with them at their senior common room, but not vice-versa.[42] Important contacts and information were obviously missed by the women faculty. In all-female sisterhoods or girls' schools, it was easier and more acceptable to fight vigorously for one's community. These institutions had separate goals and did not generally imitate their male equivalents. The women's colleges, however, identified closely with their universities; their founders, with the possible exception of Davies, wanted a better education for middle-class women, not a revolution in social relations. Once a foothold had been established, little effort was made to expand into other areas; this task was left to the women students after they had completed their studies. Hedged in on all sides by social and economic constraints, they bought intellectual freedom at the price of political timidity, a frequent fear of change and a dislike of innovation. Ironically these were often characteristics they shared with their male opposition.

The Students

The women principals were on surer ground when they came to define what one of Girton's mistresses called an "abode of disciplined freedom."[43] Like all the leaders of other women's institutions, the leaders of higher education hoped to offer a new kind of community, an alternative to the family or spinsterish isolation. But their community was temporary—a brief interlude of growth and preparation before going out to serve others. Agnes Maitland, principal of Somerville, addressed the National Union of Women Workers in 1894, criticizing the family for the narrow, selfish view it encouraged in women. She argued before that large organization of middle-class philanthropists,

> I believe that the colleges and halls for women are training generation after generation of students in a truer, wider unselfishness than women have hitherto known.
>
> Their experiences in college teach them to understand what life in a corporate body must of necessity be, what are the responsibilities and duties of those who share its benefits; they learn what true union is, how absolutely we are members one of another, how certain it is that if one member suffers all the others suffer with it. . . . personal unselfishness, individual rather than communistic, is a plant that often flourishes exceedingly in college life. Gifts and graces are exercised towards each other that sometimes have been unhappily dwarfed or ignored at home. The often beautiful unselfishness of tutors and lecturers, not long since students themselves, strikes a high note.[44]

Maitland's message of social service and community was particularly attractive to middle-class women of the late nineteenth century. College life was, for a short period of time, an ideal combination of self-development and preparation for future service. As such, it met the needs of many young women eager to contribute their skills to a wider society. As a young Quaker studying for the Newnham entrance examination explained to a friend, "I think work like yours and mine just now gives one rather a feeling of selfishness—the aim is so very definite and so entirely for our own immediate advantage. But then how often a man's business must seem so—and our final aim is not selfish."[45] To do good for others increasingly meant formal preparation of oneself.

Women entered college for a variety of reasons. In the early days many were older women who had been teaching and wanted to improve their skills. Others came for more inchoate motives. Louisa Lumsden, in her late twenties, seized the opportunity to go to Hitchin, the forerunner to Girton, the very first year it opened; she was utterly bored with the social round of her aristocratic Scots family and longed for some purpose in her life.[46] Mary Paley was engaged to an officer who had been sent to India. In his absence she studied for the Cambridge Higher Local Examination. When he returned they found they had nothing in common, and the engagement was broken; she was then free to take up the scholarship she had been offered by the newly founded Newnham College.[47] A few years later Jane Ellen Harrison arrived from the distinguished Cheltenham Ladies' College, where she had received top marks in all her exams and classes. She disliked her step-mother, and her father, recognizing her unusual intelligence, found further education for Jane kept peace with both women.[48]

Constance Maynard had spent seven years filling her life with projects—painting, reading, teaching Sunday School, and learning Greek—after she came home from boarding school. She was ec-static when her father let her go to Hitchin in 1872 for a year, which was later extended to three. She fell in love with the college and all the women in it, waking each morning "with a sort of sting of delight," eagerly plunging into her work. She and the other students were happy "in the glorious conviction that at last, at last, we were afloat on a stream that had a real destination, even though we hardly knew what that destination was."[49] But she was also shocked to discover that not every student came with the same idealism as herself. One wealthy girl had been placed in the college to keep her out of the way until an eligible man could be found. Another was clearly unstable. In spite of their differ-ences, however, all of the early students were swept along by their sense of a shared adventure, demanding the very best of them.

A later generation still sought college entry as a means of gain-ing independence and sometimes faced indifference or animosity from parents. Lynda Grier (1880–1967) had no formal schooling until she became an external student at Newnham in 1904; a year later, to her astonishment, she was offered a scholarship. Her pe-tite and attractive mother never took her studies seriously and would not give her a room of her own. She insisted on sharing Grier's bedroom and study until her death, when Grier was forty and a highly respected acting professor of economics at Leeds. Throughout her youth the partially deaf and ungainly Grier felt unwanted by her mother and convinced of her own intellectual and social incapacity. She made few friends in Cambridge, but later, when principal of LMH, she turned her shyness into an as-set, drawing out shy and awkward students with her understand-ing and warmth.[50] Just before World War I Vera Brittain found her mother deeply pitied by her Buxton neighbors when informed that her daughter planned to go to Oxford. Her parents were chary of giving her any assistance while she prepared, but her brother's encouragement helped her to persist in studying Latin and mathematics in an unheated study.[51] What Brittain experienced in 1912–14 had been described fifty years earlier by Constance Maynard as her mother's "pat, pat, patting down of all ambition."[52] Although their opportunities were greater by Brittain's time, the intellectual life of women was still largely irrelevant to most middle-class families.

Both Maynard and Brittain overcame any lingering guilt about family duties during their college days, but the ill health that plagued some women was symptomatic of unresolved conflicts. At the end of the first year at Hitchin Davies wrote to one student encouragingly, "I should think you will find it a help in struggling with the mistaken tenderness of relations to have some set work to do [during the long vacation]. If you are beaten in the unequal fight, I hope that at any rate you will get a good rest."[53] Anna Lloyd neither studied nor rested, and she returned in broken health for only one more term before yielding to her older sisters' pleas that she take up the family duties of a maiden aunt. Some fifteen years later the asthmatic Winnie Seebohm entered Newnham full of high hopes. But her asthma continued to bother her, and her loving family insisted that she return home—where it promptly became worse. Her doctor ordered a rest cure with no reading, no work, and no activity. In agony she wrote a Newnham friend,

> I always want everything so *frantically*, and I'm always *just*
> the person that can't have them! And I see lots of other people
> who might have them easily and don't care to, won't even take
> the trouble to put out their hands to take them, while I am
> stretching out my arms lovingly and panting for them and
> they are always hung out of my reach! Is there some great
> lesson of life in all this, do you think?[54]

A month later she died from an asthma attack, hoping to the very end to return to Newnham. Her biographer speculates that she was killed by a combination of insecurity and overprotection that made it impossible for her to break away from her family. Many women who were eager to stretch themselves intellectually were reluctant or unable to pay the emotional price. Friendship and work in the college community could not compensate for possible estrangement from family and society.

Well-brought-up Victorian and Edwardian girls did not, theoretically, need to develop a strong self-image. They were intended to remain quietly at home until the right man should appear. Yet we know that this was not necessarily the reality of middle-class life. Struggling against or supported by their families, countless isolated women pursued a lonely path. In fighting the dominant ethos of the times, a woman had to have a sufficiently positive sense of herself and of her sex to let her believe in improvement and change. Women like Anna Lloyd and Winnie Seebohm staunchly advocated higher education for women, but they could not overcome their own personal conflicts and "the mistaken tenderness of relations." The leaders of women's higher education hoped that the colleges would provide a breathing space where women could test themselves and grow personally; they believed that the result would be a more mature and useful person. Agnes Maitland neatly balanced personal independence and home duties in her description of college as "a blossoming time for character," when later "the blossoms do and should bear after fruit for home life."[55] In the words of Constance Maynard, it would give women the opportunity for "the assertion of personality and the endurance of the consequences of action" in a relatively protected environment.[56] For most college was enormously liberating, but for some it was terrifying.

At times the discussion of the benefits and liabilities of a college education for middle-class women has the same air of unreality as the attacks on careers for single women. The economic necessity that might drive a young woman from a respectable family to seek further education was largely ignored. Nevertheless, many women went to college primarily because it meant greater job opportunities and better pay. Their initial investment was high. In 1899 fees varied from £35 per eight-week term at Girton for room, board, and tuition to £15 per eight-week term at St. Hugh's for room and board, with an additional charge of £4 to £5 for tuition.[57] Scholarships were few and rarely covered all expenses; moreover, three eight-week terms left one with a great deal of the year at home, to be fed and clothed by one's family. After paying approximately £100 per year for three years, a woman could expect to receive that same amount as a beginning teacher at a good high school or £60 to £70 with room and board at a boarding school.[58] Such remuneration after a very heavy investment made full-time higher education a difficult proposition and explains why so many early students had taught before entering college.

From the very beginning the women's colleges included a relatively wide range of young women from the lower middle to the upper levels of society. Students were highly conscious of who belonged to their set and who did not, who might safely be asked home and who not. The most obvious division seemed to be between those who came from wealthy families and attended for the love of learning and those who came in order to obtain a better teaching post. The latter group were generally poorer, more earnest, and less sophisticated. Frances Mary Buss of the North London Collegiate School encouraged her ablest students to go to Girton, lending them money and coaching them for the scholarship examination. When the first three of her students entered Girton in 1875 they were commonly known as "the Bus-ters" because of their schoolgirl manners and less cultured backgrounds.[59] Like the men's colleges, there were always "in" and "out" groups, determined by sports, intellect, money, or some current fashion. Patronizing condescension was so common as to be a part of the ordinary day of "An old Newnham Student" writing for a popular girls' magazine in 1903. Coming late to breakfast, she has the bad luck to sit with "Miss Brown, a North Country 'fresher.'":

> At first I am rather stiff and bored with her (Miss Brown is not quite, quite—you understand), and we converse very stupidly about the weather and the thickness of the bacon; but by-and-by, I let myself go, and become quite witty and brilliant on the subject of Miss Hill's new blouse. The next stage is that Miss Brown becomes confiding and asks me how it is some people get invitations to parties in the town. I say I presume that most of us have had a cousin or brother or friend at Cambridge, and through them we have one or two introductions to dons.
>
> Miss Brown says she supposed it was that way, but just wondered if it would be any good putting your name down anywhere!
>
> I shake my head emphatically at this.[60]

Fortunately the routine of work took precedence over class differences; hard work could be a wonderful anodyne for lonely North Country freshers. The daily work schedule at the residential colleges was established early in all of the colleges. Women who had been to boarding school were delighted to find that they no longer had to account for every hour of their time, while those who had studied at home were pleased to find themselves working to some purpose with like-minded individuals. The day began at 7:00 a.m. with a jug of hot water delivered to one's door; the hated cold-water baths of boarding-school days were now optional. Prayers were at 8:00, followed by an informal breakfast and the reading of mail and the morning papers in the common room until 9:00 or 9:30, when all the bedrooms would have been cleaned and the beds made into sofas. Some students had lectures in the mornings, some were free to study. Lunch was designed to fit the different schedules and was served from noon to 2:00 or 3:00; no matter how pressing one's work, it was necessary to sign in at each meal. Afternoons were spent on hockey, boating, and long walks, though the science students always had laboratory work. They formed a separate group, with their leisure time from 5:00 to 7:00, when everyone else was back studying after their tea-break at 4:00. Dinner was at 6:00 or 7:00, depending upon the college.[61] At Royal Holloway it was quite a formal occasion, with the principal leading a procession of staff and students through the long corridors; each person had earlier arranged for a dinner partner.[62] Afterward students had coffee with the staff in their rooms. The period immediately after dinner was for socializing and special-interest societies; these included such weekly highlights as dancing (among themselves only), debate, "sharp practice" (a kind of comic debate), and literary clubs. These activities were followed by another hour or two of intensive study; at 9:30 the round of formal cocoa parties began. At Girton a tray with milk, tea, and a bun was served to each student in her room. "Tray," as it became known, was slang for sharing one's tea and bun with friends in someone's room. Close friends met each evening to discuss the day's events, as well as every sort of intellectual and social question.[63] Bedtime was early, though a few continued to work late. One Newnhamite confessed that she usually completed her essays just in time for the 2:30 a.m. pickup at the college's post box.[64] At LMH, on the other hand, the gas (and later electricity) was turned off at 10:30; any student caught up or wandering the corridors after this time was reprimanded.

Despite a general lack of funds, the founders of all the colleges felt that each woman must have her own room. Davies, for example, refused to spend money on landscaping yet insisted upon a bedroom and sitting room for each woman when Girton's first building was built. Limited funds were then turned into an asset; the colleges supplied only the minimum of furniture and expected each student to do her own decorating. Several shops did a thriving business in secondhand furniture and ornaments, and each woman had the pleasure of displaying her own preferences for the first time. Many students testified to the education in taste they received from their fellow students. Most important was the psychological sense of independence this interior decorating gave each woman; she felt truly liberated from her boarding school and family, free to express herself and experiment. College provided women for the first and sometimes only time in their lives with a small space that they could completely control. Only the very wealthiest hospitals could offer their lady probationers a single room, and such rooms, unheated and undecorated, were used only for sleeping. A college student's room was her home, her private domain.

The privilege of a private room went hand in hand with a strong sense of corporate identity. College meant lifelong friendships and a community of united women. From the very beginning each college had a rich variety of songs, customs, and rituals, binding students to each other and the institution. The Girton pioneers made up songs about each other and their college that were sung at all special events. As late as the 1920s freshers were regularly taught the college songs once a week after dinner. Girtonians cheered the final-year students before their Tripos exams with charades, specially composed songs, poems, and other treats. The hearty send-off encouraged the women, who faced a long trip into Cambridge and then the wait for a runner to bring copies of the exams from the men's examination room.[65] Although some songs were meant to encourage rivalry in sports, most simply emphasized the pleasures of being at college. A thread of defiance and joyousness runs through the women's rituals, from the songs to the mock parliaments before women had the vote. Generations of Girtonians happily sang,

> "Girton my friend, you are young, are young,"
> Said Cambridge old and grey,
> "And it is not meet that a tree whose growth
> Is centuries old, should plight its troth
> To the mushroom birth of to-day, to-day,
> To the mushroom birth of to-day."
> But full and clear falls on the ear
> The answer of Girton for all to hear;—

"You may say us Yea, you may say us Nay,
But the tide has turned and we've left the bay,
We've crossed the bar and we've felt the spray
Where the winds and waves have their freest play,—
We like it, good Sir, and we'll have our way!"[66]

College women believed the future belonged to them—and
their songs, clubs, plays, and sports all proclaimed this.

Defiance toward outside criticism built confidence in and loyalty to the new institutions, but it was only one aspect of students' rituals. Equally important were those traditions that built a
shared history among them. These were of two types: one emphasized the ordinariness of the students, their traditional, feminine
domesticity, while the other focused upon what made them special, their lives together and their studying for a better future for
women. As early as 1886, only seven years after its founding, the
principal of Somerville praised a student's article about life there,
noting especially "your remark about the comradeship which exists between all—even those who are least intimate." But she was
also keenly aware of the fragility of their traditions and the need
for each generation of students to carry them on: "I trust that
your article will help present and future students to realize that
something has been built up for them and given in trust by their
predecessors—and they may add to or lessen the good tone which
they find there by words or acts."[67]

Rituals of domesticity were clearly intended to reassure parents
and the public (and the women themselves) that higher education
would not cut them off from their peers and families. A typical
example might be the annual Christmas parties or jammaking. In
1883 the *Girl's Own Paper* praised Westfield College for its homelike atmosphere:

At the college . . . there is bright companionship in the study,
together with the charm of English home life, and it would be
hard to find a happier group of girls than the fourteen students
now in residence. Affecting neither strange opinions nor
strange attire, they pass from the lecture-room to the tennis
court, or country ramble; from the social tea-party to the
quiet hour of reading, each in her own pretty study by her
own fire-side. . . . One afternoon all amused themselves making marmalade, and very good marmalade it was, as I can as-

sure those who doubt that domestic accomplishments
flourish on such soil.[68]

Three years later Maynard wrote a play similar to those she had
participated in as a Girton student, for private performance only,
to commemorate Westfield's first three B.A.s (London). Each of her
students dressed as a character known to Dr. Johnson and recited
for the three pioneers. Everyone was then cheered with songs,
cakes, and tea.[69] Cakes, tea, and homemade marmalade or jam remained favorites among students for many years of celebrations.

Somervillians, as Shaw Lefevre sensed, were especially keen on
building a tradition of comradeship. A particularly important college ritual was the Somerville annual going-down play, written
and produced by the third-year students during the two-week interval between finishing their exams and finding out the results.
The play always parodied favorite tutors, students, and Oxford
characters. In 1912, for example, the students put on *Mastofus*,
starring "Fritilla," a student who fritters away her time and also a
pun on the women's magazine *Fritillary*. She is plagued by Fine
Clothes, Gaudy, Good Intentions, and Little Results. Other students parodied included Stodger, accompanied by Memory, Notebooks, and Sleepless Nights and the athletic hearty Flannelette,
aided by Health and Jollity. After a series of comic examination
questions, poor hardworking Stodger receives a low pass and Flannelette an unexpected first.[70] Like the college songs, these plays
were filled with references to college life and the spirit of adventure it engendered. For many years Wordsworth wrote comic plays
for LMH students that were very similar to the Somerville student productions. The first, *The Apple of Discord*, wittily played
upon the idea of Paris's award of the golden apple, but with the
prize "The golden fruit of learning which till now / No woman's
hand has plucked from mystic bough."[71] Such rituals flourished
until after World War I, when virtually all university societies became coeducational.

The wider college community was vitally important to women
students, but individual friendships were the most treasured aspect of residential life. At last they could choose their own friends
rather than relying upon their families. The process of becoming
friends, however, was highly formal, with careful gradations between each of the three years. A series of written invitations to
cocoa or coffee from second and first years to freshers opened the

fall term. A fresher could not invite anyone above her to cocoa until her second and third term, when she busily repaid all the hospitality she had received. While cocoa in the evening was de rigueur for second years, third years were expected to serve coffee on Saturday afternoons. In the days before instant coffee, this could be quite an art—or a disaster, as one woman remembers, from watching her friend pour hot water into a cup with a spoonful of coffee grounds.[72] After a decent interval a friend might "prop," that is, propose to call you by your first name, if you would do the same to her. This was done only in the privacy of one's rooms and very rarely between first and third years. As ridiculous as these formalities seem, they gave each young student an enhanced sense of maturity. They also established a sharp line between school and college as well as being a relatively painless way of introducing women to corporate living. And the students themselves could laugh at the customs. In 1889 Girton freshmen were asked to write an "Examination in Things Not Generally Known," which included such questions as "Give an exhaustive opinion of the merits of the Second as compared with the Third year, using both personal observation and hearsay evidence to support your remarks," and "Classify the College, as far as you can, in respect of (a) Manners, (b) Appearance and *chic*, (c) Qualities as Hostess."[73]

Reminiscences of college life during the early days always compare the many regulations under which young Victorian women lived in comparison with the freedom of more modern times. Yet these restrictions were similar to those of a well-regulated middle-class household.[74] Daughters, however, were demanding unheard-of freedoms to think, travel, and move about alone. The first students were in the vanguard of making such demands, and they were often a trial to their guardians. As Henry Sidgwick recognized, the spirit of freedom grew as the intellect expanded. In December 1871 he wrote a friend:

> Peace reigns again I believe; the only point that has occurred of an inharmonious bearing is that Miss Kennedy yearns to attend Ward's Anglo-Catholic ritual by herself and we refuse— that is Miss Clough does, I being Jorricks. My own feeling is that we ought to run all risks that Liberty brings with it; but I keep silence, assuming no responsibility that is not thrust on me. Restraint of Liberty is our rock ahead, I foresee.[75]

Emily Davies, ever fearful lest her project flounder on the rocks of reputation, kept a tight rein on her students. She did not trust their judgment in matters relating to the governance of the college; she vetoed all student proposals during her many years as secretary of Girton's governing committee. Unlike the more confident Sidgwick, she complained bitterly about the independent spirit of the students, exclaiming to Barbara Bodichon, "Is it not vexing to see such a spirit shown? I am afraid we shall have no lasting peace while any of the pioneers remain."[76] Yet within the walls of the college, women were remarkably free; an American commentator described "the internal discipline" of Girton as being "as slight as possible."[77] And after all, regulations also controlled the public conduct of the male undergraduates, who were expected to be inside their colleges by 9:00 p.m.; a special police force roamed the streets looking for miscreants.

Freedom within a limited space, nevertheless, inevitably led to a questioning of its limits. Surely a respectable young woman could try an Anglo-Catholic church on her own, just as she might at home. But where was the line to be drawn? And how permanent was it? Some regulations fell quickly, while others lasted well beyond their time. Oxbridge dons soon tired of giving separate lectures to women, but into the twentieth century, a woman could not attend a mixed event unchaperoned. For many years chaperoning provided a small income for retired ladies. Visiting the men's colleges was made as difficult as possible, while visits from brothers and other close relatives to the colleges were equally hedged in. Students were constantly reminded that "the brother of one is not the brother of all."[78] No friends were permitted to share tea with one's brother. Equally difficult was proper attire; women could not be seen practicing sports outdoors, so their fields had to be well protected. Girton was not landscaped for several years, so all passersby could see everything going on. During the winter students were limited to the gymnasium and to running in the long corridors. Violent pillow fights and chases up and down the stairs were popular ways to work off energy after a long day's studying.[79] LMH was fortunate in having property that swept down to the Cherwell, giving them ample private space for sports as well as access to the river for boating.

The women's colleges suffered from no unwanted publicity or scandal in their early days; students were too careful themselves to jeopardize their pioneering institutions. But general assent to Victorian rules of conduct was strained by the early twentieth century. The excessive concern for the proprieties of genteel life seemed childish to some. One Newnhamite of 1901 was furious when her brother could not watch her hockey match; she promptly labeled the principal as having a "horrid mind." Only after she left college did she feel a part of the adult world.[80] Regulations could also sometimes be bent, as one young lecturer discovered at the very pious Westfield:

> Probably around 1911 or 12 one of the general students, older and much more sophisticated than most of us, wanted to be away for the night (or possibly two) in the term. She was known to be well connected, and could hardly be refused, but Miss Richardson [the vice-principal] was worried and said as much to me, in a sort of questioning way (for I had been on friendly terms with the lady). For the moment I was puzzled, but glancing at her troubled face, I suddenly understood, and said, "You don't mean—surely not," and she said, "Yes"—after a short silence we spoke of other matters. I had a feeling that not much escaped her; also that she could learn much from even brief encounters.[81]

By this time women were overtly and covertly breaking the college's rules; yet they were not substantially changed until after World War I. One Newnhamite of 1918 bragged of breaking all the rules "except for getting in over the railings at night, and that was not out of respect for the rules, but for my clothes."[82]

By the early years of the twentieth century, as chapter 7 demonstrates in regard to suffrage, women were in open revolt against their society and often felt little gratitude toward the pioneering women of higher education. Irritation with outdated regulations rose to the breaking point. The high-minded thinking and dowdy dressing of the lecturers was frankly unappealing and was representative—like the bad food—of limitations, not freedom. The role model so painstakingly constructed by Victorian feminists to give meaning to spinsterhood did not attract this generation. At the end of the war, the Newnham Debating Society cheerfully voted in favor of the motion "That Woman's sphere is in the home" in order to shock their elders.[83] By this time, moreover, many of the most thoughtful students were becoming pacifists, while the staff was ardently patriotic. For some students nothing seemed more out-of-date than their unmarried lecturers. How had this happened in less than fifty years?

Intellectual Leaders of Women: College Staff

Even at the height of disagreements between students and staff
after World War I, students repeatedly attested to their respect and
admiration for individual lecturers, no matter how much they
might disagree with them en masse. The reputation of the woman
lecturer was high throughout the period 1870–1920, but she was
a more attractive role model at some times than at others. The lecturers at the women's colleges faced the same problems as all
single women of this period. The sense of being discounted in the
larger society had inspired the first generation of pioneering
women, but later generations, inheriting a secure if minor position in the world of higher education, were reluctant to agitate for
further changes. The women Dorothy Sayers portrayed in 1935
were long-standing stereotypes. Lecturers fell into three familiar
categories: the traditional schoolteacher, the emotional and motherly, or the intellectual and asexual; and for a very few, a unique
and even revolutionary style combined feminine and masculine
traits. The majority appear to have been comfortable in combining a strong independence of style and thought with an equally
strong sense of social proprieties. All three types shared a common disregard for politics and feminist issues, and it is this perhaps more than anything else that irritated so many early-
twentieth-century students. They asked how women who had
benefited so much themselves from the gains of the women's
movement could be so indifferent to the struggles students faced.

From the beginning women lecturers had an anomalous position in relation to both their students and the university; their
status was largely derived from traditional deference rather than
any ascribed professional position. They received no recognition
from Oxford or Cambridge and very little from London; for many
years lecturers suffered the indignity of being denied equal access
to university laboratory space, library privileges, and participation
in university governance. They also had no voice in the syllabus
or examinations for which they prepared their students. Intellectual contacts with lecturers outside the colleges were minimal for
many years. A woman in science, for example, could participate
only with great difficulty in the major scientific debates of the
times; she had to depend upon her social contacts rather than her
scientific achievements. At her college, a tutor's time was taken
up with many tasks better suited for a boarding-school teacher.

Tutors were expected to act as chaperones and to socialize with students at all meals. The financial constraints of the women's colleges left all of them with very heavy teaching loads and little time for research. Yet the life was still enormously attractive for intellectual women, who devoted their entire lives to a single college, willingly forgoing the privileges and salaries of headmistresses.

For the fortunate few—never more than a dozen at each institution—college life was an unparalleled combination of private space, public amenities, and shared interests. The college, moreover, gave the advantages of a small flat, maid service, meals, and a garden, without the commensurate responsibilities. Most of the lecturers had had some experience with the difficulties of studying alone at home or trying to pursue a course of research without support from an institution; academic life simplified all the trials of the lonely pursuit of knowledge. The very great advantages women derived from living together have been well described by the classicist Jane Ellen Harrison, who lived for twenty years at Newnham:

> I have a natural gift for community life. It seems to me sane and civilised and economically right. I like to live spaciously, but rather plainly, in large halls with great spaces and quiet libraries. I like to wake in the morning with the sense of a great, silent garden round me. These things are, or should be, and soon will be, forbidden to the private family; they are right and good for the community. If I had been rich, I should have founded a learned community for women, with vows of consecration and a beautiful rule and habit; as it is, I am content to have lived many years of my life in a college.[84]

Like so many of her contemporaries, the agnostic Harrison thought in terms of a consecrated order of women as an appropriate metaphor for the beauty, independence, and community college life bestowed upon women. It was a passionately positive idea of celibacy and intellectual dedication.

Descriptions of college life turned naturally to the dominant metaphors of religion and the family. For someone like Harrison, the image of a religious order conveyed a sense of austerity, independence, and objectivity that accorded well with her sense of the intellectual priorities of a college. For other teachers, however, it seemed most natural—most feminine—to think of the college as a home where one was fortunate enough to work and live in the same place. Elizabeth Wordsworth never saw LMH as anything but a home for young ladies, arguing as late as 1893, "My own ideal is a college consisting of moderately-sized groups of students, each of them small enough to have a somewhat homelike character."[85] Although she accepted the expansion of LMH beyond her preferred size of forty students, she always regretted her consequent inability to know each thoroughly.

The students who looked to their lecturers for leadership alternated between seeking an independent model and the more familiar family model. Emily Davies never fully understood her students' need for leadership and community; she expected Girtonians to spend all their time studying. When Louisa Lumsden, the first resident tutor, sided with the students against her and the governing board, Davies was shocked and dismissed their complaints as irrelevant. Lumsden, who felt that she gave essential care and leadership to many floundering students, left in a huff in 1875.[86] Sara Burstall, a student only a few years later, remembered it as a time of great loneliness:

> The lack of personal guidance or stimulus, intellectual and moral, from older and wiser women was a serious weakness then in the College: it arose not only from the inevitable paucity of staff, but from what seems to have been a definite aim to leave the students free to develop in their own way. Sentimentality was a deadly thing, influence belonged to schooldays, and personal relations at college might lead to these. The value of the tutor in the men's system . . . was ignored. I knew what such influence could be from my own experience . . . lofty, intellectual, absolutely free from sentimentality, full of power "to warn, to comfort and command." There was in Girton of 1880 no such friend to whom one could go for counsel and consolation.[87]

Gradually a counseling system was built up, so that new students did not flounder but were directed in their studies and daily lives. Even so, many students remembered prewar Girton days as a time of too much independence but too little guidance, too much chaperonage but too little tutoring.

The earnest and well-meaning tutors who followed the fiery and erratic Lumsden were forerunners of what became the dominant stereotype of academic women—dowdy, ineffectual in daily life, but brilliant scholars. Anecdotes about such women abound, offering a slightly more attractive alternative to that other popular stereotype of the successful single woman, the dominating head-mistress. Alice Gardner, Newnham's first history lecturer, was notorious for her dull teaching of a subject just coming into its own at Cambridge. She padded around the corridors in felt slippers and a disheveled dress, rather shocking some of the students by her private appearance in public places.[88] But in sharp contrast to her was Mary Paley Marshall, who briefly lectured at Newnham. She had done exceptionally well in the Moral Science Tripos as Newnham's first honors student, and she then went on to marry her teacher, the famous economist Alfred Marshall. She was an outstanding role model for students still uncertain about whether one could combine intellectual work and marriage. Winnie Seebohm wrote home after her first lecture, ecstatically describing her,

> She *is* a Princess Ida. She wears a flowing dark green cloth robe with dark brown fur round the bottom (not on the very edge)—she has dark brown hair which goes back in a great wave and is very loosely pinned up behind—very deep-set large eyes, a straight nose—a face that one likes to watch. Then she is enthusiastic and simple. She speaks fluently and earnestly with her head thrown back a little and her hands generally clasped or resting on the desk. She looks oftenest at the ceiling but every now and then straight at you. She looks at Political Economy from a philanthropic woman's point of view, and talks to each separately about the books we might read and the other subjects we are working at.[89]

Tutors who came straight from Gilbert and Sullivan were rare, but the best made a point of presenting their subject from a womanly perspective. Serious-minded students, including Seebohm, felt this to be far more important than one's physical appearance, however bemused they might have been by the "not elegant" Gardner.

Living under the constant scrutiny of dozens of critical young eyes must have been somewhat daunting for even the most self-possessed. The lecturers were judged by the impossibly high standards we always reserve for those we admire; students wanted them to be intellectually superior but personally accessible, bringing together better than any ordinary woman the emotional and the intellectual. A good many young tutors found it difficult to combine their personal lives with their teaching careers. A young woman at Newnham complained about the exhausting effort of making conversation at dinner after an afternoon of tutorials.[90] A teacher at Royal Holloway, anxious to prepare for classes, had to throw out two students at 10:00 p.m., after two hours of coffee and chitchat. The next day the second year came around and apologized, explaining that she couldn't leave before the shy third year, as it wasn't done.[91] Such social rigidities were self-enforcing; each side held up its rituals, keeping distance and privacy within a very limited circle. The resident tutor represented the triumph of intellect over female emotions, for she had less room for the legitimate expression of emotion in her work than a schoolteacher or settlement-house worker. As a result, most were devoted to their families and a few select friends. They held tightly to the ideals and life-styles they had learned as students and were oblivious to fashion and change. For a woman tutor, her greatest struggle and greatest triumph was combining in a positive way the traditional definitions of the feminine and the masculine. Beneath the adherence to social proprieties and rigid intellectuality lay the potential for balancing the emotions and the mind.

The woman who best represents this struggle for balance, and whose teaching and publications most triumphantly vindicate it, was Jane Ellen Harrison (1850–1928). Harrison had been a brilliant early student at Newnham, but her revolutionary spirit had frightened the authorities, who appointed her best friend classics tutor. She spent fifteen years in London lecturing and studying classical archaeology, anthropology, and languages (by the end of her life she knew some eleven living and five dead languages, believing strongly that one could understand a people only through its language). In 1898 she was invited back to Newnham; the next fifteen years were to be her most intellectually fruitful. Along with men much younger than herself, she revolutionized classical studies, that high-status male preserve of Oxbridge.[92]

Harrison turned classical studies upside down by insisting that the rational religion of the gods was rooted in primitive chthonic cults. She argued that ritual practice precedes myth, that actions are rationalized only after they have long fulfilled human emotional needs. Her brilliant insight was based upon a wide knowledge of contemporary anthropology, folklore, and comparative religion, but it was rooted in her feminine sensibility. Harrison built upon the Victorian belief that woman's nature was fundamentally different from man's. She felt that women were more "resonant" to social and racial needs because they were more in touch with their emotions. Men were more "insulated," and therefore more capable of pure thought, but less able to understand the essential nature of people and things.[93] Her research, in effect, confirmed her temperamental bias toward the primitive and emotional as more authentic and vital than the rational and reasoned.[94] Her highest praise was reserved for those "able to know without ceasing to feel," and she constantly reminded her friends and students that "to feel keenly is often an amazing intellectual revelation."[95] Unlike other scholars, both male and female, she refused to cut herself off from her richest source of ideas, her feelings. But she also passionately supported the necessity of combining male "insulation" with female "resonance." As she explained in a paper given with her closest collaborator, Gilbert Murray:

> I never looked to man to supply me with ideas. He might accidentally, or as often happened, we might flash them out together. Thoughts are self-begotten by some process of parthenogenesis, but there comes a moment when alone I cannot bring them to birth. If companionship is denied, they die unborn. The moment, as far as I can formulate the need, is when you want to disentangle them from yourself and your emotions . . . then, you want the mind of a man with its greater power of insulation. . . . To talk over a thing with a competent man friend is like coming out of a seething cauldron into a well-ordered room.[96]

Harrison's personal life also expressed what she saw as the female principle, not only in her friendships, but also in her lifestyle. Once someone was a friend, he or she was promptly given a pet name, sometimes from her current favorite language, more often that of a figure drawn from pre-Socratic Greece. Gilbert Murray was Cheiron, the wise, kindly centaur, or Thêr, meaning sage or wise. She signed her letters to him as Ker, an underworld sprite. She kept a bear with glasses and an umbrella on her mantel, symbolic of her theriomorph. The bear had a double meaning for her, representative of both old-fashioned learning (his name was Herr Professor) and of ancient, primitive ritual.[97] To call someone "bearish" was the highest compliment, for the animal represented fidelity, strength, and imagination. Harrison's male friends indulged her love of whimsy and archness; they appear to have found it a relief from the scholarly and repressed behavior expected of them. She took advantage of being a woman and of being permitted to express a wider range of feelings publicly. She happily admitted to the Murrays, "I am by nature rotten with superstition and mysticism," but she also added that she could not do "good things . . . because for me that way madness lies."[98] Half-joking, half-serious, Harrison refused to follow the conventional path of goodness, lest she become bogged down in the stereotype of what a woman should be. She knew the roots of her own genius rested in the irrational—not surprisingly, she was one of the first in England to recognize Freud's importance. At her best she used her intuitive imagination harnessed to her immense learning.

Harrison's balance was sustained by passionate friendships with men and the security of living in a female community. She admitted to falling in love all her life; she always had a male scholar with whom she could consult and share her work. She could be a very stormy friend, given to extreme demands and emotional crises, even as she gave so generously of herself and her learning. It was difficult for her when her younger collaborators married, leaving her feeling isolated personally and intellectually. In 1908, after nearly a decade of close work together, Francis Cornford announced his engagement. Harrison was devastated and sought refuge at a small seaside resort in East Anglia. From there she was able to write a painful letter of reconciliation to his fiancée:

> About work. Yes the world *is* a ruthless place & sex the most ruthless thing in it. Thank you for seeing that. I am just now faced by the blank unalterable fact that for more than 6 months Francis has not cared & could not care at all for the work that has been for years our joint life and friendship—but I have faith to believe it may not always be so. While it *is* so it is better that he & I should *not* be together. I also absolutely believe that you reverence work—tho' you could not as yet understand nor can he how—late in life—work & friendship come to be the whole of life. I trust you always.[99]

The last years of Harrison's life were spent with a student, Hope Mirrlees, who shared her enthusiasm for Russian (she had dropped her Greek studies during World War I) and language play. In this final relationship the roles were reversed, with Mirrlees playing the stormy, needy novice and Harrison the wise bear. But friends felt Mirrlees was controlling Harrison, insisting upon her vision of the world without Harrison's largeness of purpose and intellectual brilliance.[100]

Harrison was too controversial a figure to fit comfortably into a conservative academic field, but at Newnham she was overwhelmingly admired. There she received the confirmation of her intelligence and attractiveness that was sometimes difficult to find in the male world of the classics. Her teaching and lecturing were legendary, commanding wide audiences. She always wanted her students to feel the impact of a religious ritual or artifact; in addition to lantern slides and reproductions, she sometimes called on someone to provide sound effects. She could scare an audience quite effectively with unexpected roars of ritual bulls.[101] She frankly preferred young and overconfident students to crabbed academics her own age, and she encouraged them in the same audacious theorizing she did herself.[102] Her pronounced originality came from a sensibility that was ever fresh to experience and thought; she never hesitated in pronouncing new theories. She expected her students to think as boldly as she did but gave them the space to go in whatever direction they wanted. One student remembered her gratefully in a letter on her retirement:

> You flashed into my life like some new planet. You stood for all true magic and mystery of the unknown. You lured us on to the quest, tho' you gave us no clue to it—you were disturbing, but that was what we wanted—you never posed as an *authority*—as omniscient like most teachers do. You taught us the thrill and passion of intellectual things—the thrill that could be even stronger and more constraining than being in love! You *did* pull down our idols—you often made me afraid. I did not know *where* you were leading me! But, oh how I blessed you. What sparks you struck out of our dull clay.[103]

Harrison loved to create sparks in her students—and in academic circles. After one particularly sharp exchange, an angry male classicist wrote to a friend, "Never was such an audacious, shameless avowal of charlatanism, debauching young minds wholesale, and that too in a generation whose loose thinking has been doing immense harm to national life and international politics."[104] Harrison would have enjoyed knowing that so much importance was attached to a woman who taught classics. If he could have seen her cheerfully mixing soup, stewed prunes, and meat at high table, his prejudices would have been confirmed—but for her, it was all part of making unexpected and original connections.[105]

Harrison could not have survived so well without the support of Newnham; indeed, she speaks with revealing briefness about her lonely fifteen years in London.[106] She had found at Cambridge a satisfactory resolution of contrary elements, which resonated brilliantly in her work. But even during her most productive period, Harrison felt the limitations and pain of being ancillary—a maiden aunt, a spinster friend. Behind her jubilant wordplay and childlike enthusiasms lay an insecurity only partially resolved by friendship and intellectual success. In the same poignant letter of reconciliation written to Cornford's fiancée, Harrison revealed her sense of special names, and most especially, the implications of "aunt":

> About names—how strange & wonderful they are. I think one will always—in the New Jerusalem—have official names for public use & one's secret names for those who are near to one, known only to a very few. . . .—a secret name should mean only just one's personal relation that no one else could have and the public name is just a label. . . .
>
> Jane is a dignified label for me—but I want you to drop 'Aunt.' Aunt & Uncle have to me always a touch of comedy & even farce about them—perhaps you won't agree. You know not what being a real Aunt is. I don't think it is much of a relationship anyhow, I mean, I find that with my real nieces, I have to make separate friends with them individually or not if I am to have any real relation. Anyhow I am not yr *real* Aunt—& you are not my real niece—you are first & foremost the child of my friend whom I chose for myself & who is gone & *that* is more than any *un*chosen relationship and you are my friend for yr own sake—so let our label be Jane. One cannot always find a *real* name—it either comes or doesn't come & it is useless to hunt. . . . the real names are flashes of sudden intimacy & contact, caught in a moment & then kept for always.[107]

Harrison sought to avoid the pigeonholing of unmarried women into the role of aunt; by insisting upon only personal relationships she tried to turn necessities into choices. Her "public name" was that of a distinguished classical scholar, but her "real name" was known only to close friends, admitted into her life with all its confusions, hesitations, and brilliancy.

Harrison was exceptional in her revolutionary style and intelligence, but her struggle to combine the intellect and the emotional, a career and a personal life, was faced by all academic women. The very security of the college community could envelop the less adventurous, cushioning them from struggle and change; sometimes it must have seemed that the timid survived best. Each hard-won triumph could easily become obsolete. Harrison did not resolve her life until she was in her fifties. Louisa Lumsden was never able to hold a position of authority without provoking controversy, yet in her old age she became a popular and doughty fighter for suffrage. By then she was old enough to be deferred to by the younger generation but still angry enough to rally women to the cause.[108]

Constance Maynard (1849–1935) is an excellent example of a woman who successfully combined a rich emotional life with public achievement. After an unusually narrow religious upbringing, Maynard found the intellectual freedom of Girton in the 1870s exhilarating. Her enormous happiness, however, was jarred by the strong currents of agnosticism and modern biblical criticism she found there. She became determined during her student years to found a college that would offer women the same freedom to learn as Girton did, but without the religious struggle she had undergone.[109] Financial support from two wealthy religious women gave Maynard the means to open Westfield College in 1882. At first she had to fight to justify its existence, while also trying to find students interested in pursuing learning in a Christian atmosphere. Her Evangelical supporters would have preferred a high school or a mission school like the Pennefathers' Mildmay Institute, and educationalists were dubious about Westfield's intellectual standards. Many of the early students, like those at Royal Holloway, did not stay for a degree course, but Westfield gave them essential encouragement in their careers. Mary Alice Douglas, the reforming headmistress of the Godolphin School, remembered "with undying gratitude" the year she spent at Westfield as a scholarship student. She had met Maynard at a garden party given by Bishop Walsham How, and after hearing about the new college, she thought, "I wish I could beg, borrow, or steal, and go to that college."[110] Conscious of the difficulties of those who hoped to be "Christian witnesses" at home and abroad, Maynard initiated an elaborate chain-letter system to keep in touch with students after they had left Westfield. The community of friends first developed at the college was kept through a lifetime by means of her efforts.[111]

Maynard, first as a teacher in a boarding school and then as the head of her own college, found satisfaction in a series of passionate friendships both with students and with fellow teachers. For her, as for many single women, friendship was seen as completing a life's work, as validating the decision not to marry, to have a career, to help a wider sphere than one's immediate family. As such, a special relationship was the single most important emotional tie to an institution or organization; virtually every community discussed here nourished and was nourished by the homoerotic friendships of women. We cannot now fully answer the question of precisely how sexually aware the participants were, but surely some were while some were not. Although a religious or spiritual vocabulary frequently masked personal desires, women consistently spoke of their love in terms that replicated heterosexual love. Quite unselfconsciously women referred to their relationships as marriages, complete with the exchange of rings and promises of lifelong fidelity. Such relationships were tied by a love that implied, and sometimes openly avowed, feelings that went beyond simple attraction. Indeed, the frequent emphasis upon the power of the emotions suggests an understanding of what we now label as sexual desire; commentators would probably not have argued so forcefully for the control of the emotions if they had not recognized their sexual source.[112] Sexual passion, if not physical sexuality, characterized a special friendship.

The responsibilities of leadership weighed heavily upon Maynard, and within a year of founding Westfield she had persuaded a young Quaker student from Newnham to transfer. Anne Richardson entered in 1883 and brought with her a close friend, Frances Ralph Gray, who was hired to teach classics. Soon Ralph, as she was called, Anne, and Constance were locked in an emotional triangle. Their love for each other united them against the barrage of criticism the college initially faced, but it also divided them when feelings flared and love was not returned. Constance expected Anne and Ralph alternately to behave like dutiful daughters under her leadership and to be her equals who would support her in troubled times. Anne and Ralph themselves veered between demanding a more professional relationship and wanting close friendship. Sometimes they were flattered to be called upon for so much advice, but at other times they behaved like angry daughters. Trivial slights were blown out of proportion and hurt feelings exaggerated. On one occasion Ralph violently accused Constance of failing to respect her; correcting elementary Latin had eroded her sense of personal worth. She later apologized with equal vehemence, telling Constance, "Mistress, you are wonderful! Your *perfect* magnanimity after I spoke like that,—oh, it is lovely, it is *most* Christian. I love you truly. Yes, I *do!*[113] Beneath Ralph's childish outburst was a desire to be treated as a professional, but Constance interpreted her unhappiness in personal terms and sought in it some cause for the failure of their friendship.

Ralph and Anne often felt at odds with Constance's leadership. They both found that they had to give her advice, while she took the credit—or neglected important administrative duties in favor of religious talks with the students. Ralph's unexpected attack pointed to a problem that Constance never overcame: a reluctance to admit and use her authority openly. When she turned to Anne or Ralph for support, she denied the difference in status between them, yet she was their superior and determined their working conditions. They continually felt frustrated by her unwillingness to give orders and direct answers. Constance could not be unkind to people, and so she ended up being untruthful. Her behavior was no different from that of many a Victorian lady, and in circumstances calling for her sympathies with those younger or less educated than herself, she was enormously effective. But she could not adapt herself to the more modern, impersonal, professional methods of relating to teachers and students.

When Constance fell in love with Ralph, she clearly wanted the same kind of total love she had earlier experienced with Louisa Lumsden, but within a religious setting.[114] During Ralph's early days at Westfield, Constance poured all her pent-up affection upon her. At first flattered, Ralph supported her through two years of close confidences, then abruptly withdrew. The reason for this is unclear because Constance's diaries for 1887–1900 have been destroyed, but presumably it was a question of Constance's excessive emotional demands. The sexual implications of these demands were never fully articulated, nor was Ralph's sense of denied autonomy. In 1886 Ralph moved out of Westfield to an apartment, and then in 1888 she went on holiday with Anne; each move took her further away from Constance's embrace. Yet in 1891 she returned to Westfield and seems to have hoped for a renewal of their relationship. Constance painfully recorded in her diary her overtures:

[Ralph] was not well, and I went up to see that she was rightly attended to. As I left she said with gentle hesitation, "You never bite my fingers now, as you used to do." "Oh no, never," I replied lightly. "And you never snarl and growl like a jaguar when you can't express yourself. I never heard anyone growl as well as you." "No," I said, "it's useless. I've been cured of that." The sweet low voice went on, "And you never rock me in your arms and call me your baby." "No," I said in the same even tone, "I've been cured of that too." "Oh!" she said, with quite a new meaning, "oh, I see." Here was a spot too painful to be touched, and I said, "Goodbye, dear," and left the room. I will not go into the desolation I felt when alone again. I was like a pot-bound root all curled in upon itself, like an iron-bound bud that has lost the spring, and now no rain and no sunshine can open it.[115]

Ralph's questions reveal the degree of physical intimacy between adult women who lived and worked closely together. No matter how much women, and especially religious women, might call their friendship "spiritual," they were keenly alive to its earthly component. Unlike the school raves discussed in the next chapter, women of the same age could not so easily conceal from themselves their erotic attraction—their uncontrollable and pleasurable feelings—for a favorite. An intimate friendship permitted a range of feelings that enhanced the partners' sense of love and radiated out to the other women with whom they worked, and ultimately to God. The loss of sexual play with Ralph meant the loss of these vital connections for Constance.

All the rest of her life Constance mulled over why she had failed with Ralph. In spite of the strong sexual undercurrent of their relationship, she divided love and sex along strict gender lines, assuming that sexual feeling could only be heterosexual.[116] Constance was forced to fall back on analogies with the family, recognizing in part that at Westfield she was the husband in the public sphere but preferred to be the wife in the private sphere. Ralph, in contrast, appears to have sensed the sexual connections that Constance ignored; at the very least she disliked her extreme emotional demands. As she explained to the heartbroken Constance,

it was a long time before she really loved me, and could tell
Nannie [Anne Richardson, the vice-principal] and me so, but
that she did at last, deeply, very deeply. Yet she saw there were
two sides to me—one independent, practical, hard-working,
wholly devoted to the College, and this she loved, the other
"something wrong." Yet *this* was the side I seemed doomed
nearly always to be in contact with.[117]

Anne told Constance that Ralph had come to the conclusion
"that in personal absorption there is a danger and a wrong that she
can scarcely express."[118] Ralph could be teasingly close first to
Constance and then to Anne, but she gradually pulled away from
her friends, favoring the pursuit of her own career. We cannot
know what Ralph Gray lost by narrowing her personal life in order to bring it in line with a presumed religious duty or her public
responsibilities, but her solution became the admired pattern for
teachers in the early twentieth century. Professionalization for
women often meant the imitation of male values, including the
suppression of feeling.

Even when they were most flourishing, women's homoerotic
friendships were not easy or simple. Although free of the "deviancy" label, they had other difficulties, reflecting the problematic
relationship of the professional single woman with the wider
world, her friends, and herself. Modeling themselves upon heterosexual marriage, women could not easily escape its stereotypes of
behavior and expectations. Immersed in old ideologies and patterns, women replicated relationships that had been born out of
powerlessness. Even as she sought public recognition for Westfield
and its students, Maynard tried to domesticate her friendships,
students, and the internal organization of the college. Ralph gave
up the domestic for the public, refusing a personal life at Westfield
for a highly successful career as a headmistress. The continuing
struggle to build a new family, to develop a new kind of homoerotic friendship that met the different needs of a public life, often
left the first generation of college-educated women brittle, cold,
or overemotional.

Maynard's intense involvement with her friends was curiously
like Harrison's, despite the very different personalities of the two.
The price both paid for their independence was often extreme
emotional dependence, leading them to demand too much from
others. Both women found happiness in old age through an emotional involvement with a student. Although Harrison had avoided

having a conventional home all of her life, she spoke of Hope Mirrlees as her "ghostly daughter," evoking an intimate family relationship she had never had as a child.[119] The student Maynard loved at fifty was her "white bud" whom she was privileged to open into "passion pure in snowy bloom."[120] Harrison had entered adulthood seeking the freedom to know far more than the freedom to act; as Harry C. Payne has pointed out, her scholarship was a successful synthesis of sex in intellect.[121] Maynard's lifelong goal was the teaching of religion in intellect; her college offered devout young women the freedom to know. However uneasy their blend of emotion and intellect, Harrison and Maynard never lost sight of the importance of combining their intellectual work with their emotional needs. They refused to deny both parts of themselves, and throughout their lives they recognized the necessity of friendship and work.

Both Harrison and Maynard were highly successful women by any standard, leaving permanent memorials in research and higher education. Their success was due in part to their unwillingness to compromise, to fit into any ordinary stereotype of the single woman. Their failures arose out of their strength; because they had worked so hard to break a new path for themselves and other women, they were not always flexible or confident. They are unique in their accomplishments but representative of the first generation of Victorian women who benefited from higher education. They had the training and the courage to forge ahead—but more important, they also had a supportive women's community behind them. However disappointing individuals within that community might be, they never lost their faith in its importance to them and to all women. Harrison admitted, "It is absurd, but when a girl isn't happy at college I feel it somehow as a sort of personal insult."[122]

College was a golden time when a woman could expand, be herself, try new friends, new ideas, new personae. But beyond that, it opened opportunities for the future, seized by so many women, following the example of Harrison and Maynard. In the words of a distinguished Girtonian, higher education "meant the right of a large class of women to an honourable independence; it opened out another possibility of a respected and self-respecting life."[123] "An honourable independence" for women is both a modest and a revolutionary achievement; its realization was made possible by a small band of determined women.

5

The Reformed Boarding Schools: Personal Life and Public Duty

If only every girl would go to school and stay there long enough to learn the corporate virtues, in two or three generations we should realise Utopia.[1]

Teaching was the most important occupation for single women throughout the nineteenth and early twentieth centuries. Elementary education, especially after the Education Act of 1870, grew by leaps and bounds, but even the much slower growth of secondary education provided new job opportunities. For women who were able to go to college, secondary-school teaching was a natural and respected career. If they were fortunate enough to obtain a position at one of the new reformed boarding schools that started in the last third of the nineteenth century, they could recreate the ideal combination of work and community that had characterized their years at a residential college. Teaching in a boarding school was a special challenge because women were expected to inculcate through their teaching and through their daily lives the new, more public values espoused by pioneering educationists. Older, domestic ideals continued, but the new woman—teacher and student—was expected to take a broader view of her responsibilities and to combine school loyalty, public service, and a reasonable interest in academics.

The boys' public schools of the nineteenth century were clearly in opposition to the Victorian family.[2] However much the elite praised the family as a bulwark against the pressures and deceits of the public realm, they sent their children, especially their boys, away from this nurturing environment into the harsh world of the public school. The sons of gentlemen had to be toughened if they were going to become leaders of the empire, business, and politics. Matters were less simple for girls. On the one hand, reformers of girls' education were concerned to establish the importance of corporate values; their special emphasis upon public duty was modeled upon the leadership training boys received. But on the other hand, they recognized that the majority of their girls would become wives of the bourgeoisie, and so family values could not be wholly neglected. The result was a curious amalgam that bore slight resemblance to either the boys' school or the Victorian family, in spite of the ideological borrowings from both. Repeatedly we find that girls' boarding schools claimed to encourage both family ties and familylike behavior, and yet they were in actuality encouraging codes and behavior antithetical to the traditional family.

In every complex society the socializing of children and adolescents contains contradictory ideologies and behavior. Many of the contradictions of the new girls' schools were never resolved but were held in a fruitful, or disorienting, tension by individuals. For most women the combination of public service and private life under the same roof was immensely satisfying. The chance for prestige and effective reform among those of one's own social class changed teaching from a last resort to a natural choice. Indeed, the opportunity to combine the intellectual and the personal and be paid for it seemed almost "magical"; as one leading educationist said, "Economic independence is, after all, one of the requisites of a full and happy life . . . [but] I should have been glad to do the work for nothing."[3] Working with close friends among the young could be immensely satisfying, especially when one felt the school to be in the vanguard of important changes for women. The new boarding school became one of the most supportive of communities for a single woman.

Nevertheless, tensions were inevitable in the enclosed world of a boarding school where work and community were so closely linked. These tensions were aggravated by the tendency to think of one's school as a family, even though its actual organization was very different from any nuclear family. It was sometimes difficult to draw a clear line between appropriate work behavior and personal needs. Both teachers and students were left without an adequate language to build a new community. Moreover, educated women themselves often felt conflicted about their own ambitions and personal needs. The lack of role models for both headmistresses and teachers also aggravated problems of authority. The pressures to "realize Utopia" led headmistresses to establish careful distinctions between themselves and the staff, the staff and the students. All normal power relationships found in a family were intensified in subtly different ways in the hierarchically ordered single-sex boarding school.

For students, the busy life of a boarding school seemed to offer few relaxations from duty and communal loyalties. During term time a boarding school, moreover, was among the most enclosed of institutions, isolating the residents from both their families and the larger public world for which they were presumably preparing. The new education cultivated a modern individuality; a girl was encouraged to take responsibility for her actions, to recognize their consequences for others. She was to become a self-controlled autonomous being within the larger public world of the school, in preparation for the atomized world of capitalism. At the same time, a girl was encouraged to find personal intimacy through intense friendships. Private needs and public duties became enmeshed in the web of school discipline.

Boarding-school life was built upon a series of paradoxes: distance and intimacy, self-development and repression, discipline and freedom all combined to encourage a self-sufficient, intensely emotional and achievement-oriented world. I am specifically concerned here with the nature and impact of such schools as important all-female communities that were controlled by independent women, who socialized girls into community life and corporate values. The lives of the teachers, who spent a lifetime devoted to a single institution, shaping its character and that of their protégées under the firm hand of an admired headmistress, are examined in detail. The changing subculture of the girls, their friendships with each other and the teachers, and the rituals of their daily routine are considered in terms of the delicate balance between authority and friendship, distance and intimacy. The importance of friendships for both girls and teachers is analyzed, showing their special nature within the confines of the boarding school while recognizing their importance for other women's communities such as colleges and settlement houses.

New Standards, New Teachers

Old-fashioned girls' boarding schools, which had flourished since the early eighteenth century, continued to serve the wealthier classes as finishing schools until the end of the nineteenth century. Run by poor widows or spinsters from the genteel classes, they had few academic pretensions and many social ones. All

were run on the model of an enlarged family; the numbers admitted rarely exceeded fifteen or twenty. No effort was made to separate girls according to age or level of knowledge. Most of the girls
spent only two or three years at such a school, sometime around
the age of fourteen. The cost varied enormously, but a very high
ratio of students to teachers made any extras—normally music
and languages—costly. Although often expensive and academi-
cally weak, these small schools offered many advantages to students and teachers, for they gave single women financial independence and girls a chance to live away from home among their
peers.[4] But however genteel and supportive these "ladies' seminaries" might be, they did not meet the needs of a rapidly indus-
trializing society.

Both boys and girls of the nineteenth century faced an acceler-
ating process whereby childhood and education were prolonged in
preparation for greater autonomy and individualism in adulthood.
The reformed schools, with graded work, sports, and public duties
for both sexes, were better prepared to train children for a new future. The traditional schools had left boys to fend for themselves
among a horde of other boys, while girls were left wholly dependent upon adult guidance. In the 1870s, 1880s and 1890s many
new secondary schools were founded, all committed to higher, or
at least more regularized, academic standards, classes streamed
according to age, examinations, a flat, limited fee, and trained
teachers. Reformers at first had to fight an uphill battle to convince parents to invest in their daughters' education. Many could
not afford even low fees (all secondary education was fee paying)
after they had paid for their sons; others feared that the new-style
schools would make their daughters discontented or argued that
they needed their help at home. The elite boys' schools always
had far larger enrollments and endowments.[5] Nevertheless, by the
end of the century, more girls than boys over twelve attended secondary schools. In 1898 approximately eighty thousand girls over
twelve were in secondary schools of varying quality, but only sixteen thousand remained beyond sixteen, with as few as two thousand remaining until eighteen.[6] The schools flourished and overcame opposition simply because they met a perceived need among
the middle and upper classes, provided an excellent outlet for
restless daughters, and offered a better and cheaper education than
many of the old seminaries.

The bulk of these new schools were private. In 1898 some 70
percent of the girls at the secondary level were in private schools,

and about one-seventh of these were in private boarding schools, the elite institutions of secondary education socially and culturally.[7] Education for the middle and upper classes of Victorian England was closely linked to issues of status; those who were new and insecure about their class status found in the education of their children the safest and most effective means of establishing their right to a place among ladies and gentlemen. Since the upper classes had traditionally sent their children away to be educated, boarding schools carried clear social cachet. Numbers of rather dubious schools were opened for both boys and girls during the late nineteenth century to meet the need for cheaper boarding schools that might still inculcate a façade of the gentility associated with the ancient public schools.[8] The girls' schools could not, of course, compete in regard to longevity, much less in prestige or traditions, with schools like Eton and Harrow, but they made up for these deficiencies by other means. Dorothea Beale, for example, would not accept girls whose parents were in trade at the Cheltenham Ladies' College. Hannah Pipe, a Methodist schoolmistress, found that her particular vocation "was to get hold of these girls with money and without refinement from their earlier years, and to open their eyes to all that is best in this life and in that which is to come."[9] By placing such a strong emphasis upon moral training at a time when high morality was equated with social superiority, the more expensive girls' schools quickly established their social importance. Smaller, less prestigious schools generally succeeded by imitating the more famous and larger schools. Thus we find that the new boarding schools of the last thirty years of the nineteenth century became important both as a means of establishing one's family credentials and as a socializing force that transmitted traditional class values. Middle-class families who could afford to do so sent their girls away to school, however briefly. Within specific schools we find girls coming from a relatively homogeneous social background, but different schools were available for every level of the middle and upper classes.

The reformed boarding schools became popular, however, for an additional reason, only indirectly connected with status. By the late nineteenth century public service had become fashionable, so that the ideals promulgated by the reformers coincided with the desires of parents. As Winifred Peck has said in regard to the popularity of such reformed schools as St. Leonards and Wycombe Abbey,

It was an age of philanthropy, of social work, of church work, of the stirring of the suffrage movement. The more serious society ladies were amongst the leaders. . . . They began to feel that their daughters well disposed of at boarding schools would leave them even freer for their activities, and that girls in a school like Wycombe would learn to carry on the torch and devote their lives to public service even more whole-heartedly than their elders.[10]

Boarding schools that encouraged public service not only were convenient for parents; they were equally important for teachers. Even those who had no taste for philanthropy, a woman's traditional public occupation, could find respect and usefulness serving the daughters of the upper classes. A classroom, or a house of boarders, could mean independence and personal fulfillment that had not been so readily possible for earlier generations of governesses and teachers. Boarding-school teachers were more likely to see their work as a lifetime career and home than day-school teachers. For those devoted to teaching, it represented the best combination of public service and motherhood. At the height of the suffrage movement, Winifred Mercier, a leading educationist, wrote a friend about her belief "that the most womanly women I know—womanly in the best sense of the word, and more motherly than many mothers—are also those who have done the most public work, have had the least sheltered lives, have devoted themselves to their careers most."[11]

However much they might have agreed on the importance of girls' learning new public duties, reformers were less clear about the content of the new education. Debate focused on what should be taught (not only academic subjects, but also moral and social values), how it should be taught (large or small schools, day schools, resident mistresses, nonresident masters, etc.), and by whom (men or women, and at what level of formal training). Intellectual standards, however, could be raised only so long as traditional social standards were maintained; respectability was once more the essential cloak for change. Feminists, led by Emily Davies and Frances Mary Buss (the founder of the eminent day school the North London Collegiate), called for training as similar as possible to that of boys; they feared that any other kind might be considered inferior and devalued. But parents objected to a curriculum too narrowly based upon the classics and mathematics, and it was difficult to find trained teachers for these subjects. The majority of educational reformers did not wish to see girls compete with boys but preferred an education that gave women "more power to make the home what it should be."[12] Social graces and husband-hunting were to be replaced with noblesse oblige and godliness.

Ideologically the new schools were all committed to the moral, intellectual, and physical training of girls, although individual schools differed on priorities. Those with any academic pretensions grew to at least one hundred, and more usually two hundred, students, with some growing as large as nine hundred. During the early days of reform, roughly 1860 to 1890, greater emphasis was placed upon moral-intellectual reform, under the leadership of Dorothea Beale, headmistress of the Cheltenham Ladies' College from 1858 until 1904, and a leading spokeswoman for academic standards combined with religion and gentility. She opposed external examinations and prizes, arguing that "a spirit of rivalry" and "the desire for distinction" would run counter to the moral training of education, which should lead to "the true woman's ornament of a meek and quiet spirit."[13] But when the benefits of an outside check on academic standards became obvious, Beale quickly capitulated to both exams and prizes. Within the precincts of the school serious work habits were encouraged; the teachers kept their distance and did not invite students to approach them on other than academic problems. On the other hand, the independently run boardinghouses surrounding the College were much more intimate in their organization, with their heads fostering mother-daughter relationships with their favorites. Thus, professionalism and domesticity were kept sharply divided, yet both were a part of each girl's day.

Other schools, such as Roedean, founded by the Lawrence sisters in 1885, or St. Leonards, founded in 1877, placed greater emphasis upon honor and duty in lieu of godliness and gentility. Louisa Lumsden and Jane Frances Dove, the first and second headmistresses of St. Leonards, opposed the emotionalism that they felt characterized ladies' seminaries, and so they used sports and other team activities to encourage school loyalties. Physical fitness and public duties rather than gentility and academic work were emphasized. In these schools students built emotional ties with a favorite older student, a prefect or sports leader, rather than with their housemothers. In spite of these differences in comparison with the more religiously inclined headmistresses, all of the girls' boarding schools followed a similar pattern of daily work. The actual character of an institution, however, tended to become a reflection of the preferences of the head and her teachers.

The new values of these reformed schools were embodied in the buildings themselves. Although virtually all of the schools began either in a townhouse or in a country house, as soon as funds were available, new buildings went up and old ones were thoroughly remodeled. A drafty country home might serve, but its rooms were altered to become dormitories, classrooms, a dining room and, most important of all, a great hall so the whole school could meet together for worship, announcements, and important events. Each room had its special purpose. A modern school looked like a school, not like an enlarged family home. Tastes differed, of course. Dorothea Beale preferred the Gothic, so successive additions to Cheltenham brought more turrets, pointed arches, and stained glass. Long corridors (never to be run down), cold rooms, and plain food seem to have characterized all of the schools. These physical surroundings were echoed in the rise of uniforms at the end of the century, as well as in school colors, hymns, and customs. Physical surroundings, personal apparel, and school rituals, and perhaps inevitably teachers, all came to bear the recognizable stamp of a particular institution.

The first reformed boarding schools were led by pioneers equal to any of the hospital matrons or mother superiors. These women had not had the educational opportunities that they made available to a new generation, but they possessed enormous organizational skill and a keen sense of what parents wanted and students needed. Remote and dedicated figures whose notions of appropriate leadership for adolescents are antipathetic to the present, they are now unfortunately stereotyped as formidable women of overweening ambition.[14] Formidable and ambitious they might have been, but they also never lost sight of a greater end: the permanent foundation of their school as a community for training girls. Like the handpicked hospital matrons, they were the visionaries who translated a new kind of formal education and community into reality, working day by day with recalcitrant students, untrained teachers, and suspicious parents. In the early days they could not be sure that their methods would actually produce a better, more sensible body of women. The leading headmistresses did everything they could to gain favorable public opinion and to ensure success within their schools. A religious sense of vocation, and of adventure, sustained them. Several wrote pamphlets and articles demonstrating the physical health and religious piety of their students. They lectured teachers, students, and parents regularly on the necessities of high personal and academic standards, self-discipline, and physical health. While headmistresses insisted upon the importance of esprit de corps for their students and teachers, they could never become part of the corps, but remained ever the leaders. Little evidence survives of the internal struggles the leading first-generation headmistresses underwent, but surely their intensity, high seriousness, and total commitment speak of both gains and losses personally.[15]

The rewards of autocratic leadership were obvious. Most headmistresses, unlike hospital matrons, had minimal difficulty in gaining the respect of governors and parents. Each generation of parents appears to have become progressively more submissive to school regulations. In 1864 Dorothea Beale had spoken in favor of day schools, lest girls lose the essential moral training only a mother could provide. By 1879 she had taken moral leadership and was reprimanding the parents of day children for their permissiveness in regard to study habits and bedtimes; they were instructed to follow the school's regulations in such matters.[16] Lucy Soulsby, a follower of Beale, repeatedly reminded her girls that their first duty was to their parents, but when a parent overruled her on a frivolous matter she was outraged:

"You were not at School in the morning yet you were at a party in the afternoon? I suppose your Mother suggested it? You had no business to *allow* your Mother to do such a thing!!"[17]

By the 1890s new regulations began to appear, informing parents that they could not visit their children during term time, or could visit only once a term if permission was granted in advance. When the mayor of a town asked that his daughter return to St. Leonards a day late so she could attend an official ceremony, the headmistress wired back, "Now or never."[18] A generation earlier no head of a ladies' seminary would have dared to do such a thing—or faced "never" with equanimity. The new headmistresses wanted respect and deference based upon their expertise, not their inherent gentility (though they laid claim to possessing that too).[19]

In spite of inevitable criticism, the managing of parents, governors, and students was often relatively easy in comparison with building a corps of trained and committed teachers. Proper learning could not go forward without well-educated and respected teachers. Headmistresses were looking for women who would devote themselves entirely to building the new institution, who were thoroughly educated in their particular subjects yet were still ladies. In return they promised self-respect and approbation within the walls of the school, the excitement of training a new generation without the rigidities of an established system, and a community of committed teachers and eager (more or less) students. By the late 1870s, Dorothea Beale had started one of the first teachers' colleges, enabling older students to stay on for systematic training and to prepare for the University of London (external) B.A. examinations. She provided her teachers with opportunities for study and travel, congenial housing and the leisure to prepare lessons thoroughly. Such privileges were unheard of in the old days, but so too was the degree of commitment demanded. Beale called Cheltenham her husband and was shocked when any teacher wanted to live out of sight of the college.[20]

Teachers were recruited largely through personal contacts and from the pool of the brightest and neediest students at the school itself. This was not considered inbreeding, but rather was seen as an opportunity to further the specific goals and ethos of the school. Most girls began as pupil-teachers in the lower grades at the school they had attended. Then they applied for a scholarship to one of the Oxbridge colleges or else attended either an independent teacher-training college or one attached to the school itself, such as at Cheltenham. For poorer students the opportunity to go on in their studies and to receive formal training under an admired head was more than welcome; it seemed to open out worlds of opportunity. Beginning as a pupil-teacher, an ambitious girl could study for an external degree from the University of London and rise to a respected position in the small world of her school.[21] In effect, she was assured a steady income and secure niche without the sacrifices her teachers had made. Many women spent a lifetime in devoted service under a headmistress they had first known as young girls.

Self-development, a relatively novel idea for dutiful daughters, collided with deeply ingrained beliefs about family obligations. In spite of their ostensible support of the family, headmistresses were part of the modern "male" world in their concern to develop individual opportunities over traditional family demands. The emotional closeness of an adolescent girl with her mother had been naturally loosened by years at school, but this did not alter fundamental loyalties. A girl who lacked family support of some kind, with even the most powerful headmistress on her side, could rarely pursue further study and work. Although training would ultimately lead to a better job and therefore a means of helping the family, young women were sometimes more anxious to alleviate their mothers' immediate burdens. Grace Hadow in 1893 was offered a two-year pupil-training scholarship by her beloved headmistress, Clare Arnold. In a long letter to her older sister she debated between her desire to stay and her fear of making her mother unhappy:

> Speaking purely selfishly I should be *miserable* if I thought of Mother working so hard, and longing for me, and I able to come and not coming. Miss Arnold spoke of my being more use to her bye and bye if I stayed, but I don't think so. I know it was frightfully selfish of me to let Miss Arnold write [Mother], I am very sorry now. It ought not to be so hard to give up anything for Mother. It is not, but God knows it felt *so* hard to decide which was most useful. . . . Impress upon Mother that I am *glad* to come home at Christmas. I have thought and prayed and wrestled over it and I think it must be best. It is no real sacrifice, it could not be to do anything for her. I should never forgive myself if I neglected any chance of making her life easier. I must leave. I *want* it.[22]

"Selfishness" was the culprit here. Hadow felt selfish about letting her mother know indirectly how very much she wanted to stay, and yet equally selfish that she did not have the right feelings about rejoining her mother. Since both school and home taught the importance of self-sacrifice made in the right spirit (though often for different ends), Hadow felt obliged to want what she clearly did not want. Fortunately, after six months at home Hadow's older brother persuaded her mother to let her return. From these modest beginnings she went on to a distinguished career as a college teacher and administrator, although always with breaks to help her family at home. She resolved her fears about her possible selfishness by dividing her time between two incompatible duties, teaching and home.

Grace Hadow's twisting and turning in an effort to feel as she ought could be resolved only by outside intervention. When she returned to Truro High School, she did so under the strong conviction that she was following her religious duty. For both the pioneers and Hadow's generation, religious dedication inspired self-discipline and gave teaching a higher ideal. In the early days it had been widely assumed that no lady chose to become a governess or teacher, so the first generation of reformers repeatedly spoke of teaching as a special vocation. This concept persisted well beyond its origins under the leadership of such women as Beale and Soulsby. Beale welcomed each new teacher with a private interview, prayer together, and a solemn adjuration to "look Higher."[23] Soulsby, as headmistress of Oxford High and Manor House School, continually urged her teachers to see their work as important as that of a minister, for they too were dealing with souls.[24]

The ideals the headmistresses wished to inculcate in their teachers and students often took the form of symbolic representations, religious or otherwise. Beale constantly reminded those under her of past female role models, such as saints, queens, and various allegorical figures. A favorite of hers was the gentle warrior Britomart from Spenser's *Faerie Queene*. In the late 1880s she had stained glass windows installed, including Britomart and other allegorical favorites. She recommended to the Cheltenham Old Girls' Guild that they choose the daisy as their flower, because it was "one of God's hieroglyphics, telling us of the inward light that lighteth every man coming into the world, bidding us to look up to Him, assuring us of His presence in our hearts."[25] Most heads, however, preferred more contemporary heroines as exemplars. The Mary Datchlor School installed stained glass windows in the 1890s that included only leaders in women's education, reminding one and all of their recently won opportunities.[26] Other schools filled their walls with illustrations of such contemporary heroines as Grace Darling, Florence Nightingale, Agnes Jones, and Agnes Weston. All were deeply religious women who led public lives of self-sacrifice.

Such different personalities as the devout Lucy Soulsby and the agnostic Jane Ellen Harrison felt the need for a community of teachers, dedicated to learning and teaching. In 1872 a group of high-church teachers formed the Society of the Holy Name in order to help like-minded teachers and to propagate the vocational view of teaching. Hopes that the Society might become a formal order were never realized, but the organization attracted a dedicated minority that met regularly for retreats.[27] Beale held retreats called "Quiet Days" for her teachers and had hopes of founding an

order of teachers. That she did not must be one of her few failures.[28] Religious belief was often the underpinning of a single
woman's work outside the home in the nineteenth and early twentieth centuries, so it was natural to seek out others who wished to
consecrate the mundane routine of the classroom. As Winifred
Mercier wrote in 1908,

> Education is a religious act, for it should increase the element
> of fellowship in the world, and not only because it is the
> quickening in the individual considered alone, of the higher
> nature over the lower. If education is not a religious thing,—a
> spiritual thing—it should be cast out upon the dung-hill, for
> it will corrupt the world, the salt has lost its savour.[29]

Differences clearly existed between the teachers who saw their
work as a vocation and those who saw it as a respectable profession for single women. Yet each group was united in a sense of the
importance of teaching. Those wishing to professionalize teaching were equally eager to make inflated calls to duty, only with an
emphasis upon the woman teacher as an important representative
of a new profession. By the end of the century Sara Burstall, the
headmistress of the Manchester High School for Girls, could confidently assert, "Parents have to realise that the teacher is an expert professional and is entitled therefore to the deference shown
to the skilled professional opinion of the doctor, lawyer, or architect."[30] Claims such as these necessarily led to a shift in the self-
identity of teachers. Individual women, if they followed Burstall,
were encouraged to see themselves as modern, autonomous leaders in an important field but to subordinate their personal conflicts and needs. While religiously inclined leaders had attempted
to resolve possible conflicts between the private and the public,
the professionals increasingly assumed a division between the
two. "Duty" became more narrowly defined as the conscientious
performance of work; one's personal life, as long as it was respectable, was left to oneself. The teaching profession has historically
moved in this direction, gradually dropping most requirements in
regard to an individual's private life. But in the process, as with
nursing, teaching for women became defined in modern, male
terms as an occupation, rather than a vocation that was part of a
larger move to purify and uplift the young, the poor, and the sick.
    Decent pay and working conditions might have helped to sus-
tain the ideals of the pioneering generation longer. But unfortu-

nately for women, neither one matched that of their male colleagues. A sense of vocation, whether religiously or politically inspired, had to be a substitute. Although life at the prestige boarding schools, discussed most fully here, was usually quite good, the minor schools could be appalling. In the early twentieth century Amy Barlow taught for eight years at a school where she never had more than a third of a bedroom, ate stodgy food, and was given endless additional duties. Her pay was so small that most of it went for clothes and train fare home during vacations. Her only real holidays were invitations from students.[31] Barlow's waking hours were consumed by simple drudgery that should have been done by servants, such as checking the girls' laundry or supervising the dining room. With virtually no time off, she had to find her relaxation in participating in the girls' athletic competitions. In 1917 she left to replace a male teacher at a boys' preparatory school. There she found "so much more air to breathe, more time for everything and much more freedom. It took me a long time to realise that every 'feverish minute' had not to be used to the uttermost."[32]

As with nursing, during the pioneering days trained women willing to devote themselves to a new institution were few. Promotion was therefore rapid, with many young teachers going to head new schools. Those with university training could command rather high salaries, starting at about £120 and rising to £220. Headmistresses usually started at £200, plus a capitation fee of £1 per pupil.[33] But the growth of new schools slowed down and few teachers left, so that by the 1890s openings became fewer and fewer. The normal situation for female employment asserted itself again; an excessive number of candidates applied for every job, giving schools the opportunity of picking the most qualified and of lowering salaries to meet costs elsewhere. An ambitious woman could no longer count on a headmistresship, since so many young heads had been appointed only twenty or thirty years before. In spite of repeated pleas to set minimum salaries of £100 and up, according to training, few schools offered this much. Starting salaries were more usually £70 to £80 nonresidential or £40 to £60 residential for a college-trained teacher.[34] Frances Dove was offered £130 per annum by Cheltenham in 1875 when she completed the Natural Science Tripos at Girton. At Wycombe Abbey, which she founded in 1896, the highest salary she paid any teacher was £120.[35] Yet it cost about £100 to attend one of the Oxbridge colleges for three eight-week terms. To add insult to the low pay, a

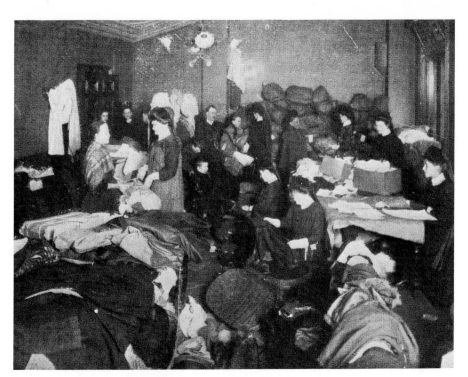

18. "Preparing Gifts of Clothing for Poor Families in Bad Times," ca. 1900. (Samuel Chadwick, The Church in the City, *1910.) Courtesy of the City of Manchester Public Libraries.*

19. "Browning Hall, Entertaining the
Cripples," 1903. (G. R. Sims, Living
London, 1903.)

20. "In the St. Mary's Working Girls'
Club, Stepney," 1903. (G. R. Sims,
Living London, 1903.)

*21. Helen Gladstone (seated, center)
with her staff, Women's University
Settlement, ca. 1901–6. Courtesy of
Blackfriars Settlement.*

22. *Suffrage militants disrupt
Parliament from behind the grille of
the ladies' gallery, 1906. Note
Christabel Pankhurst* (seated, center).
(Graphic, *1906.*)

23. *Woman chalking "Votes for
Women" on pavement, 1908.*
(Graphic, *1908.*)

*24. Removing a Women's Freedom
League member chained to the grille
of the ladies' gallery in Parliament,
1908. (*Illustrated London News,
1913.)

25. *Emily Davison's funeral, June
1913, the last time the suffragettes
took over the streets of London.*
(Illustrated London News, *1913.*)

26. *A debate at the Pioneer Club,
1903. (G. R. Sims,* Living London,
1903.)

27. *A dance at the Honor Club,
Fitzroy Square, 1903. (G. R. Sims,*
Living London, *1903.)*

teacher could be dismissed at virtually every school without any reasons being given, and often without notice. No pension schemes were included, so money had to be saved out of a small salary.[36]

Without university training or with only a teaching certificate, a woman could make little progress in secondary education. Yet until 1925 the board of education did not pay for training. The refusal to provide assistance came partly from traditional government parsimony toward education, but it also had class and economic roots. If middle-class women were willing to pay for their own higher education in order to edge out their less fortunate sisters in an already overcrowded field, subsidies appeared unnecessary. And, indeed, many women like Grace Hadow began as pupil-teachers and later found a way to go on to university. Moreover, the cost of professional training acted as an effective barrier to those who might not qualify as "ladies" and would therefore be suspect as teachers of bourgeois children. However difficult it was for women such as Amy Barlow to find a good job, college-educated women sought out secondary-school teaching as the most attractive option available from a very short list. In spite of the efforts of Nightingale and other reformers, nursing remained somewhat suspect as a career; social work rarely paid; and religious work was often too confining. The reformed girls' schools were growing in size and status, and teaching was still seen as a natural extension of woman's traditional role. But hand in hand with the new opportunities secondary-school teaching offered went the melancholy fact that educated women had virtually no other option. From 1871 to 1893 Girton, Newnham, Somerville, Royal Holloway, and Alexandra College (Dublin) had matriculated a total of 1,486 students; 680 became teachers, 208 married, and 11 entered medicine.[37] Over half the students at Newnham had become teachers, but the college also had the highest percentage who had married. Education was not an opening up of wider opportunities as it so often seemed to the pioneers or to the young, but a narrow staircase leading to more education as an ill-paid—but respected—teacher.

Discipline and Community: Boarding School Life

Discipline was the cornerstone of all the new communities for women. We have already seen the powerful discipline under which religious sisters worked and the minute regulations governing the lives of probationers and nurses in the large voluntary hospitals. The relative freedom of college students came only within the walls of their own institution; outside it they were guarded by a plethora of conventions and rules. A similarly pervasive discipline permeated the daily life of the new schools, affecting everyone. The emphasis upon discipline seems almost extraordinary, given how eager many women were to take up the new professions and how willingly they submitted to regulations that would enhance their respectability and status. The distrust with which headmistresses viewed their own teachers was often a matter of dealing with an unknown and untrained quantity. But this is not a sufficient explanation for the conformity expected by leaders of marked originality and independence. The nineteenth century can be seen as a time in which regulations increasingly permeated all aspects of life; but, as I indicated in the chapter on nursing, educated women in particular benefited in many cases from this process, for they not only were subject to discipline, but also were empowered to discipline others. In the reformed boarding schools we find discipline over self and students to be particularly important, but also full of paradoxes and contradictions that do not yield to simple explanations.

Discipline carried important symbolic overtones, signifying the educated woman's ability to behave in a rational, professional manner both personally and publicly. The control of one's personal feelings meant self-respect and power for Victorian women, who had so long been considered incapable of reason. Self-discipline meant maturity, autonomy, and privilege. Greater self-development depended upon greater self-control, greater distance from others. This new distance shifted sexual and emotional satisfaction away from familial models and toward individual discipline. The self-disciplined woman could enter public space as a recognized expert; she could face an uncomprehending public or angry parents or a reluctant school board. In effect, she created her own space, controlling others through her own visible self-confidence. She was privileged to enter specifically male worlds on behalf of women, becoming a spokesperson for the silenced. Thus, strong bodily self-control, strong personal self-discipline, meant freedom for the independent single woman.

The discipline of others gave privacy and autonomy to teachers while also enhancing their prestige. Schools maintained this discipline through the enforcement of a clear hierarchy of authority. At college a relatively homogeneous group of women were united by the common bonds of the scholarly life. In the settlements, a similar group of women worked together as virtual equals while maintaining class distinctions in regard to the poor whom they served. Secure within the confines of either a college or a settlement house, women of roughly the same social background and age could live together as equals, with minimal distinctions. But when actually working and living with unequals—children or the sick—teachers and nurses naturally used discipline as a means of establishing and enforcing distance. Discipline over others, rightly administered, proved that women could exact obedience from other women and girls and create a harmonious community.

Schoolteachers obviously had many good reasons to accept the discipline imposed upon them. Obedience brought success at work, and in difficult times it indicated a sensibility that could rise above petty regulations or even the abuse of power. Headmistresses had a distinct notion of proper behavior and little compunction about invading a teacher's classroom or private life. Caroline Rigg, the first head of the Mary Datchelor School, crisply informed her governing board, "I am sorry for Miss—, she is the one weak member of a strong Staff, and I should be glad to have the weakness removed."[38] On another occasion she reported that a teacher "has responded most heartily to my remonstrations and that all her work this term shows a great improvement, while her temper and spirit have left nothing to be desired."[39] Alice Ottley, the well-known head of the Worcester High School, after her weekly staff meeting read an elevating book to her staff while they sewed for a charity.[40] This was a universal evening ritual in boarding schools, but the staff may have resented being treated like children. Indeed, some teachers did wilt under the regimen. A generation of ladies who had worked at their own pace, choosing what to teach and what to skip, could not be expected to take kindly to the new ways. Others found the work itself too confining. Louisa Lumsden, one of the first three women to take the Cambridge honors examinations, lasted only eighteen months at Cheltenham. She found the endless correcting of elementary Latin lessons too tedious and left to found St. Leonards.[41] Many women, of course, had no choice but to soldier on.

Soldiering on was exactly what teachers were expected to do. Teachers faced a large group of girls who were keenly aware of their foibles and weaknesses. Lucy Soulsby admitted that much of teaching involved a deadly routine combined with the delicate balancing of discipline and encouragement. She urged teachers to take heart in remembering their duty, described in military and religious metaphors,

> If we believe that each lesson as we give it is the Master's marching orders for us at that moment, it does not matter that we feel our delivery dull, our discipline weak, our information very limited. . . . when you are face to face with the enemy and the trumpets sound for an attack, you must use what weapons you have, and leave it to your Captain, who ordered you to fight at that particular moment, whether you stand or fall. Half the nervousness which spoils many a lesson would vanish, if the teacher felt more strongly that the battle was not hers but God's.[42]

Soulsby's exaggerated language is reminiscent of the exhortations leveled at nurses. But fighting disease as a trained soldier somehow seems more appropriate. To compare a classroom to a battlefield only turns the children into the enemy—hardly the effect Soulsby had in mind, as a keen advocate of esprit de corps. Alternatively, dull or unprepared students could be seen as sinful, and the teacher as the voice of conscience. An adversarial relationship is implied, rather than the old, familiar family model of the past. Unconsciously Soulsby undermined the authority of the family and replaced it with the powerful teacher, commanding her pupils to do her bidding in God's name.

A teacher, female or male, had a double task of teaching lessons and building character. At the best and largest schools teaching involved only one's speciality, though teachers were always expected to help wherever they were needed. The core curriculum usually consisted of Scripture (almost invariably taken by the headmistress), mathematics (one of the major innovations of the reformed schools), French, English literature, history, some geography, and a second language. Following Dorothea Beale's lead, most schools had a four-hour morning, with a short break in the middle; classes were one hour apiece. Afternoons were spent on "extras," including dance, music, drawing, or returned lessons (i.e., redoing assignments that did not reach a minimum standard). Calisthenics were included several times a week in the mornings; only at the end of the century did organized team sports become common afternoon activities. Science was also late in being adopted; women teachers of science were rare and laboratories expensive. Changes in curriculum remained minor until after World War I, except for adding more science and Latin, and housewifery in lieu of embroidery.[43]

Classroom work itself could be intimidating. Many first-generation teachers had been trained almost wholly at home and had had little school experience or knew only their own school's routine. Even for a later generation, surrounded by a web of regulations, holding the attention and interest of a group of adolescent girls was not easy. Since women could not use the corporal punishment of the boys' schools and were often uncertain about their own authority, an exaggerated trust was placed in rules and busy-work. Students were on their honor in many schools to write down their misdeeds in a large book that was examined weekly by the headmistress. A common method of control in schools run by Anglican sisters was weekly confession. The more conscientious students carried notebooks in which to mark down their various "sins." At Margaret Nevinson's convent school, "Very often the silence of our dormitory (for no word was allowed to be spoken after Compline) would be broken by the preface: 'This is strictly necessary, has any one seen my sin paper?'"[44] Although the new schools prided themselves on having gotten rid of the petty and stifling rules of the old-style schools, in reality they often had far more.

A teacher had three methods of disciplining students without direct recourse to the rule book: pleas based upon personal affection, the authority of the head, or school loyalty. The first method had been universally used in the unreformed schools and was generally in disrepute as breeding favoritism. But it had by no means died out in the new schools. Constance Maynard was a great believer in personal talks with stubborn girls, but her success with larger groups was distinctly below standard:

> there was a grand sparring-match between two of our hot-headed girls at one of my Drawing-lessons; so I took them [on] a walk, one on each side of me & talked a bit, & was delighted with the generosity of their response, & it was all made up. But on the other hand it was complained that at my Physical Geography lessons the children made a great noise, & sometimes too I let the fires down & the rooms got cold, & then a disapproving word or look from Miss Lumsden [the headmistress] made life a burden. I felt myself unfit for the life

demanded of me, & yet, hard as it was, I found I was making it selfishly easy, leaving Frances Dove all the strictness and correction, & myself reaping affection & pleasure. This was no conscious arrangement, but so it turned out, & it made me feel annoyed with my position.[45]

Teachers were expected to remind students of their higher moral duty or of the school's honor, but concrete emotional appeals were often easier and more effective than abstract principles.

Reporting a girl to the headmistress was usually a tacit admission of personal failure, resorted to only in dire straits. Maynard was heartily rebuffed when she took her problems to Lumsden. M. V. Hughes found that her first head was a martinet who frightened staff and students but that her second was far worse, for she left the staff to bear the entire burden of discipline.[46] Lumsden, although she disliked mediating between the students and her teachers, also had problems with discipline. She found it difficult to find the happy medium between ignoring minor infractions and overreacting, so that some of the older girls openly flouted her rule. The humorless calls to duty issued by so many headmistresses betray a certain lack of confidence, as if only by continual exhortation could teachers and students be expected to achieve the necessary self-discipline.

A later generation of headmistresses disciplined by means of an honor code and prefects, but even they did not trust the innate sense of honor of girls as much as boys were trusted at their schools. Winifred Peck felt that the prefects had too much responsibility without the power to hand out penalties at Wycombe Abbey. The conscientious worried excessively about minor infractions, while the successful gained an inflated sense of themselves.[47] Indeed, some heads thought more of their prefects than their staffs and commonly told them about policy changes before the staff heard.[48] One retired teacher, after a lifetime in boarding schools, concluded that schools were run either for the teacher or the pupil. When they were run for the pupil, the teachers were overworked, underpaid, and without adequate authority.[49] From the perspective of the teachers, the prefects could undermine their authority—and with it the delicately balanced school hierarchy—or they could be a necessary implement to it. Giving prefects power, however limited, had the effect of distributing discipline throughout the community. For teachers, anxious to preserve their autonomy amid the crowded, busy life of school, pre-

fects helped to keep an important distance between the younger
students and themselves. They could then act more effectively as
remote adjudicators of justice, performing admirable intellectual
tasks and leading lives to be emulated by the bookish.

By the end of the nineteenth century the most important single
method for binding girls into a band of loyal students was sports.
They were a perfect answer to critics who felt that girls were too
physically weak to study as boys did. They also channeled the
emotionalism and "herd instinct" of girls into a "healthier" esprit
de corps. Frances Dove believed that girls had relatively few opportunities to practice "the principles of corporate life" aside from
the playing field and should therefore be encouraged in every way
to participate in team sports. For her, games were

> a splendid field for the development of powers of organisation,
> of good temper under trying circumstances, courage and deter-
> mination to play up and do your best even in a losing game,
> rapidity of thought and action, judgement and self-reliance,
> and above all things, unselfishness, and a knowledge of corpo-
> rate action, learning to sink individual preferences in the
> effort of loyally working with others for the common good.[50]

Team sports were representative of the new freedoms available
for girls and women at the end of the nineteenth century. At their
most obvious they meant a continuation of the childish privilege
of running about in a short skirt along with the more adult pleasure of group activity. Running up and down a hockey field in a
gym tunic was exhilarating after the restraints of walking two by
two in a crocodile (respectable exercise for schoolgirls at ladies'
seminaries). Girls' clothing, as reformers knew, was symbolic of
their position in life; the more stultifying their lives, the more
complicated their clothing. The simplification of apparel and the
downgrading of concern for clothes in girls' schools before World
War I had a liberating effect for most girls, freeing them at least
slightly from social constraints. Yet this freedom was clearly limited, just as it was at the schools. Although it was universally admitted that girls were easier to teach and to discipline than boys,
they had far stricter regulations. The constraints were obviously
training for the future—for when they would be in the real world,
which consistently limited women's roles as firmly as their clothing did. The freedom of the gym tunic was as temporary as schooldays were.

Discipline for both students and teachers operated in two distinct but complementary spheres—school hours and house hours. During the day while at school, teachers and students were part of a modern, professional world, learning skills and relating to each other as trainer and trainee preparing for the public world. After "work," students were part of a house in which they lived for their entire stay, among some twenty-five girls, under a house head. Like the college halls, this world also inculcated the new values of personal autonomy and corporate action. Girls and teachers were bound to the new order by means of respect and affection; the overt discipline of the classroom subtly blended with a more effective means of control. In the early twentieth century the house system was enthusiastically endorsed by the head of St. Leonards in a manner reminiscent of Frances Dove's definition of team sports:

> At first the house seems to [the newcomer] a refuge from the larger world of school; it soon becomes an opportunity. It is exhilarating to be one of a company. All sorts of things become possible in co-operation which have not been worth while alone. The experience is like that of a mediocre solo player who suddenly finds she can share in a symphony: it becomes worthwhile to practise—and to play in tune.[51]

Girls learned to work with others, to subordinate their private selves to public demands, while at the same time they strengthened their own specific talents.

At Cheltenham the houses were run by poor ladies for a profit; fees varied from fifty guineas a year to over ninety, so class distinctions were still quite obvious to those who cared about such matters. While at school the girls worked under a discipline of silence and order (no talking was allowed except in classes) among hundreds of students. But once away, they were back in a familiar world of the cosy boardinghouse. The two systems led to problems. Some housemothers tried to compete with Beale for time and loyalties. A few were utterly incompetent; Beale had a better eye for social class than for character, and on one occasion she fought a lawsuit with an irate housemother who had come to her with high military connections.[52] By the 1880s Beale began to take greater control of her houses, working closely with trusted housemistresses; by 1896 the school owned—and controlled—all thirteen houses. School discipline and house discipline were finally at one. Other schools learned from Beale's mistakes and kept their houses firmly under the headmistress's control. At St. Leonards the most effective teachers were given houses, which became their lifelong homes, where many a woman "found a satisfaction that made her definitely content to accept this work with its human appeal in place of some more distinguished administrative post."[53] Margaret Haig Mackworth (Viscountess Rhondda) flourished at St. Leonards under the aegis of her attractive and sophisticated housemistress. For her Julia Sandys set a standard of manners, good taste, and ethics that she tried her whole life to emulate.[54]

The St. Leonards house system was modeled more closely after the boys' public school system than the houses at Cheltenham. By the 1890s any school wealthy enough and large enough to afford separate houses followed the lead of St. Leonards. Here we can see most clearly the ways the family model, adapted by all the reforming communities of single women, was transformed. At St. Leonards the housemistress took on the double role of father and mother; she was to provide the leadership for the girls under her both at home and in the school. They were bound to her as her children and so were called by her surname, like a wife or daughter, in the public arena of the school.[55] The housemistress embodied leadership qualities formally belonging to men, for she played an active public role as a professional in the school, a microcosm of society; but in her house she was the nurturing, wise mother. The division between the public and private, male and female was kept, yet altered. The houses themselves were both private homes and public domain. Thus, students were encouraged to see their house as their home and yet to behave in a public manner while at home. This particular combination is perhaps best seen in an anecdote: After an especially riotous occasion in her house, Julia Sandys reminded her girls that they did not live in a public house, but that they "must always remember that this was a public house."[56] Public behavior in private places was especially good training for girls who would later combine marriage and public service or become wives of England's leaders.

The whole ethos of the houses was intended to be "healthy minded." This covered a variety of evils, best described as a refusal to indulge in slang, secrets, and silliness. Housemothers kept a sharp eye out for these schoolgirl sins. At Cheltenham, when a housemother caught a student using "slang and unladylike expressions" she was reported to Beale and had to write a letter of apology to her mother. The first version was not sufficiently contrite, but several scenes and many tears later, a revised version was dispatched to her astonished mother.[57] After the expulsion of two girls for cheating,

> The night they went Miss Caines spoke to us all after prayers, and said what a grief all this had been to her & Miss Beale, & how they hoped it would be a lesson to us, that we would try more in future to choose what was right & resist what was wrong. She said a good deal more which I cannot remember, & cried dreadfully, seeming thoroughly overcome. I think we most of us resolved to do better & be more earnest in future.[58]

Caines obviously felt that only by emotional appeals could she make her girls realize the magnitude of their sins, yet the grief seems wholly one-sided. The sinners only half understood what the fuss was about, while the disciplinarians publicly mourned their ineffectiveness.

Silliness was presumably eradicated by hard work and team sports, but secrets proved more difficult to root out, symbolizing as they did irreverence and uncontrollable desires. At midcentury the most feared secret was masturbation. The forthright—and unreformed—Elizabeth Sewell sternly told her readers that it was "not the *learning* together that makes girls school-girlish; it is the *living* together; the being herded like animals in one fold;—the sense of sham and pretense, the fact that the decencies of life are disregarded in the bedroom."[59] Girls in early adolescence, if put together, were bound to follow their curiosity into evil areas; only through careful management could they be kept innocent and pure.[60] Indeed, Sewell felt that women's education had to be carefully supervised from the cradle upward. When a girl reached her teens she would then be more ready to accept family priorities and would not be enticed away by friendships or impure conversation. She would have been shocked, but hardly surprised, to learn from a former student at Cheltenham that "The conversation of certain pupils was like any barrack-room, and they naturally tried to get hold of new girls as recruits."[61] Sewell only hinted at what could be said openly about orphan girls. The Sisters of the Church were forced to expel a group of older girls "who had been found guilty of immoral habits which they spread among the younger ones."[62] The pervasive hysteria about masturbation that appears to have swept periodically through boys' boarding schools touched the girls' schools more lightly. Nevertheless, reading between the lines, one senses the same fear of bodily knowledge. Girls were encouraged, rather, in priggish obedience to dormitory rules, while sexual matters—secrets—were deflected into spiritualized, but highly public, crushes.

The very discipline that seemed to despise feeling and behaving in an overtly emotional way actually encouraged a kind of sexual expression that was double-edged. If one's daily life demanded a public mask, a carefully cultivated sense of duty to the group, then one found refuge—an assertion of selfhood—through homo-erotic friendships. Far more effective than Sewell's perpetual vigilance was an internalized system that exalted self-control and obedience to a distant loved one. Sexuality found expression not through masturbation or dirty stories, but through a disciplined love.

Distance and Desire: Schoolgirl Friendships

A more pervasively disciplined life meant simultaneously a breaking down of the division between public and private and the encouragement of an emotional life dependent upon distance and discipline. Girls who attended boarding school were surrounded by rules, within which they were given a good deal of freedom and autonomy. For those who fit, such as the blissfully happy Winifred Peck at Wycombe Abbey, life could not have been better; she loftily informed her doubting brothers that she "belong[ed] to the most wonderful school in England" and was allowed to talk with friends and play games to her heart's content.[63] But underneath this new freedom was a swift-moving corporate life that encouraged subsuming of the individual's personality and the admiration of a few select leaders. Similar divisions were faced by teachers. Work in a boarding school meant the assertion of self, a pulling away from traditional family responsibilities and the creation of new ones. Personal self-development meant greater loneliness and yet a greater chance to form close friendships. The admiration of a young girl or teacher for an older prefect or teacher in authority was a crucial element in school life that often continued into other all-female institutions. Such relations could be disruptive of school routine—an assertion of individuality that broke the corporate ethos—or a necessary part of it—a means of ensuring group loyalty. In either case, they were an exploration of self that encouraged self-knowledge and individuality—in other words, a separate identity, apart from the group.

Greater self-development depended upon greater self-control, greater distance from others. This new distance shifted sexual and emotional satisfaction away from familial models and toward individual discipline. Bodily self-control became a means of expressing self, or the fulfillment of desire. Love itself was not displaced but focused upon a distant object, while nonfulfillment—sacrifice—became the source of personal satisfaction.[64] The emotions were focused upon a distant, inaccessible but admired student or teacher, or even the headmistress; differences in age and authority created a distance that intensified desire. The loved one became the object of desire that found its expression through symbolic acts rather than actual physical closeness or even friendship in an ordinary sense of daily contact and conversation. Distance was a means of deepening a pleasure that preferred nonsexual fulfillment. Indeed, full sexual fulfillment would have meant a failure of self-discipline and therefore of self-identity. The strong self reveled in its own control.

An intense friendship was an important step in growing up; it was also a valuable alternative to flirtations with the opposite sex. As one writer explained, "perhaps not even her acceptance of a lover is a more important era in the life of a young girl than her first serious choice of a friend."[65] Such friendships taught girls intimacy and socialized them into the world of women. Indeed, Victorians found them an important means of reinforcing a girl's identity with her mother at a time when she would ordinarily be breaking away from her.[66] Late marriage reinforced the need for such an identification. Adolescent rebellion was to be circumvented by keeping a "good" friendship within the family circle, ideally leading without conflict to a happy marriage.

Yet this was rarely the reality, or we would not have so many contemporary warnings against close friendships that disrupted families. Lucy Soulsby urged her students, "Remember to feel for your Mother; see how natural and loving her jealousy is, and spare it by constant tact—instead of being a martyr, feel that it is *she*, and not *you*, who is ill-used."[67] Desire was to be transformed into "discipline and self-denial, so as to develop all the possibilities of nobleness."[68] Nonfulfillment was the key to improving one's passionate attachment, for as Soulsby cautioned, "outside self-chosen affections burn all the stronger for repression and self-restraint; while home ones burn stronger for each act of attention to them and expression of them."[69] Opposites—family duties and personal pleasures—could be brought together through iron self-discipline, which would yield a double reward. One did not give up love, but used it to further self-knowledge and self-control. The proper use of friendship could actually enhance the development of personal autonomy without loss of family ties.

The control of passionate friendships for familial and social ends was promulgated by virtually every reforming headmistress. Friendships were not labeled deviant until the early years of the twentieth century. Rather, only their excess, the uncontrolled, was labeled as wrong. Any public display of affection or excessive demands upon either oneself or one's beloved was condemned. But heads confidently assumed that they could channel passions into school loyalty or youthful idealism. As Sara Burstall explained in a textbook on English high schools for girls, romantic friendship

should be recognised, allowed for, regulated, controlled, and made a help and not a hindrance in moral development. . . . A woman's life is, moreover, largely concerned with emotion; to suppress this will be injurious, to allow it to develop slowly and harmlessly, in respect or even reverence for someone who is older and presumably wiser than the girl herself, is not injurious and may be helpful.[70]

Burstall defined homoerotic friendships in terms of woman's traditional sphere, as an encouragement to marriage. "Raves," as they were called, or "gonages" (for gone on) could be encouraged as long as they did not risk the balance between authority and self-control that characterized girls' schools. Thus, homoerotic friendships were an important means to maturity.

The emotional triangle of the mother-daughter-friend was broken, or at least loosened, when a girl went away to boarding school in early adolescence. Freed from the immediate jealousy (or demands) of her mother, a young girl often found a surrogate mother in an admired older student or teacher. Rather than loving a student her own age, she sought a representative of the new disciplined life of the school. Sometimes this was someone who had been assigned to mother her, to teach her the norms of the school.

A woman who attended the Godolphin School in the 1870s remembered, "The older girls had to 'mother' a small one. I think I must have 'mothered' the lot, for my nickname was 'Grannie.'"[71]

Raves thrived on two apparently contradictory elements—public affirmation and secrecy. Public affirmation came through the continual discussion in school of favorite students and teachers. But secrecy helped to confirm and heighten private pleasure and the creation of an internal world of nonfulfillment. Fantasies of self-service and self-sacrifice were fostered by the very distance between the lover and the loved one. For most young girls emotions focused on the head girl or games prefect or a favored young teacher—all remote, yet familiar and publicly admired figures. These individuals could be seen daily, yet rarely in private and even more rarely in any kind of intimacy. Such situations encouraged a life lived largely through symbolic acts and symbolic conversations. The very distance created by the school's hierarchy assisted in the growth and sustenance of raves.

The thrills of being gone on someone could be discussed endlessly among peers, adding delicious excitement to the routine of school. A series of raves appears to have gone through most boarding schools at regular intervals. Boarding schools encouraged a kind of public voyeurism, with admiring girls dissecting the clothes, conversation, and appearances of a favorite. Theodora Benson remembered, "What endless discussions of tactics and strategy we used to hold after supper!" Unaffected herself, she enjoyed passing out advice to her "afflicted friends," even though they rarely took it.[72] Girls made public their most private desires not only because of group encouragement, but also because through talking they could make impossible fantasies more real. Moreover, even the most trivial act of service—helping the loved one put on her coat or cleaning the blackboard—could gain significance through later conversations. Self-fulfillment came from the endless articulation of each newly aroused feeling, each action, each hope, before an admiring audience.

But secrecy was far more important, for it reinforced self-control. Every girl had her special, secret acts of homage, special ways of betraying her own desires to herself and the loved one. Within the limited and confined world of the boarding school, certain acts took on important symbolic significance. The most common form of devotion was to make the beloved's bed or to buy her flowers or candy.[73] Every act became freighted with a sense of service and self-abnegation. At Cheltenham a ravee indignantly claimed that she could fill her rave's hot-water bottle better than her rival could.[74] These acts of service never involved physical contact, but they were a means of penetrating the private space of the loved one, of entering her room and secretly making it more attractive. One's presence was then felt by one's absence. Every ravee, indeed, hoped that her good offices would be noticed even as she did her work in secret.

An essential pleasure for those who loved a remote figure was the very distance itself, which gave room for an enriched self-consciousness. Without gratification, countless fantasies could be constructed, a seemingly continuous web of self-examination, self-inspection, self-fulfillment. In her autobiographical tale *Olivia*, Dorothy Strachey Bussy contrasted her agnostic family and the dreary Methodist school she had attended with the overwhelming pleasure of her French school. Sent there at sixteen, she soon fell under the spell of her French teacher, Mlle Julie. In the voice of Olivia, Bussy described "a curious repugnance, a terror of getting *too* near" her, lest mundane facts interrupt the rich emotional life she enjoyed within herself. She especially savored the moment before she entered Mlle Julie's room:

> It seemed an almost superhuman effort to open it. It wasn't exactly fear that stopped me. No, but a kind of religious awe. The next step was too grave, too portentous to be taken without preparation—the step which was to abolish absence. All one's fortitude, all one's powers, must be summoned and concentrated to enable one to endure that overwhelming change. She is behind that door. The door will open and I shall be in her presence.[75]

A love such as Olivia's was passionately self-involved, for it opened a wide range of emotions to be experienced in solitude, especially nights when she listened to Mlle Julie's footsteps in the corridor, hoping she would stop and give her a good-night kiss.

Every ravee hoped to receive some sign that she had been picked out from among the many admirers for special attention. Having won the "competition" and found that her love was reciprocated, a rave's emotions took yet another turn. Greater intimacy was sought, though not necessarily in private, for secrecy was created in the public domain. The two lovers found means of speaking silently to each other, of sharing words and thoughts that could not be, and would not be, talked about in the general strategy sessions among peers. The secret sharing of a private world in a public place became a major source of pleasure, for it affirmed the love while never removing it from the realm of self-discipline. Indeed, self-control itself was heightened and embraced as a pleasure by the very creation of private understandings. Olivia felt certain of Mlle Julie's love after hearing her read a poem to the class:

> It was to me she was reading. I knew it. Yes, I understood, but no one else did. Once more the sense of profound intimacy, that communion beyond the power of words and caresses to bestow, gathered me to her heart. I was with her, beside her, for ever close to her, in that infinitely lovely, infinitely distant star, which shed its mingled rays of sorrow, affection and renouncement on the dark world below.[76]

The distance between the lover and the loved one is bridged not through consummation, but rather through a unity of sorrow and self-sacrifice.

The rave flourished on a paradox of fulfillment through unrequited love. Had Olivia and Mlle Julie come too close, they might have found the tensions of love unsupportable. So much of the emotional life of a ravee centered on a world of fantasy, out of time and place, on some "infinitely lovely, infinitely distant star." Only there could the love remain safe and unchanged. And yet the very act of falling in love precipitated a crisis of identity in which the ravee moved inexorably toward an increased self-awareness. This new stage, however, involved a kind of reentry into the temporal world, where love had to face the buffetings of daily life. Olivia's sorrow came from a sense of the impossibility of sustaining her love anywhere but in her imagination.

However much each ravee might sustain her love on slight indications of favor and her own imagination, she still hoped that her homage might be repaid by another symbolic act, a vital reward that temporarily bridged the distance between the girl and her beloved. An admired teacher or prefect was ordinarily given social permission to kiss all younger students. Every night Penelope Lawrence, head of Roedean, kissed each girl in her house good-night; Saturdays she kissed the whole school. She possibly used this moment to check each child, but the hurried, physically active days of the students hardly suggests such sensitivity on the part of school administrators. More probably she was simply incorporating an aspect of family life into the residential homes in order to encourage, however vaguely, a family atmosphere.[77] Olive Willis, when she started Downe House in the early twentieth century, shed the innumerable regulations she had hated as a student at Roedean, but she kept the symbolic good-night kiss.[78] Such a gesture was so drained of its meaning that it became a means of distancing intimacy, of reminding the girls how far they were from home. Yet for the couple involved, on special occasions the kiss was reinvested with meaning, carrying overtones of transitory fulfillment. A virtually meaningless social gesture regained its original meaning and became a private, yet public, expression of love. The mother-daughter moment became a special act of kindness by the loved one, promising untold, unrealizable, future happiness.

The school authorities could not always control the raves that seemed to sweep through many schools, and indeed, they often did not wish to do so. When they did try to intervene, their efforts were usually clumsy and ineffective. Lilian Faithfull, headmistress of Cheltenham during the early years of the twentieth century, felt that the best cure for raves was to share one's friend with everyone. Girls were advised that if their emotional attachment did not improve their work, play, and "general power of helping others," it should be "root[ed] out with unhesitating courage and unwavering will."[79] She encouraged a public airing of opinions on raves, believing that rational discussion was the best preventive. Her advice was an updated version of the Victorian precept of sacrificing self for the good of others. Yet for most girls a rave offered a unique opportunity to practice a self-sacrifice that was far more rewarding than the "general power of helping others." The subversive elements of a rave could not be so easily controlled as Faithfull hoped, for it was a more satisfying expression of the same emotions school authorities attempted to channel into corporate loyalties. Possibly public ridicule was more effective. Olive Willis, headmistress of Downe House, had a teacher write a satirical play about raves when she found them too popular for her taste. She played the part of a student admirer in such a comic way that her students were shamed into recognizing what she considered to be their immaturity.[80]

Neither comedy nor "unhesitating courage" by the authorities or the students was likely to stamp out raves. At Roedean during Rachel Davis's time, school raves so dominated that the head,

Penelope Lawrence, decided to have the games captain speak before the entire school on the subject. Her short lecture condemning such "sickening *nonsense*" left the students temporarily chastened, but her admirers loved her even more for her courage. Davis shrewdly diagnosed why raves dominated Roedean:

> it can hardly be called a disease unless it reaches a feverish and inflamed condition. Unfortunately this is nearly always brought about by the clumsy fingers of the unloving, which, in school, as well as outside, must always interfere with what they do not understand. In truth the world has always been afraid of love, and until it can be made to realise that here is the one thing that is right and beautiful in all its shapes persecution followed by distortion is bound to carry on its work.[81]

On the fateful night after the games prefect spoke, Davis's passion for an older girl was held up to ridicule by a particularly nasty housemate, who sought attention by puncturing the idealism of others. If attention could not be gained by having a rave, it could be won by mocking those who did. Yet the very vulnerability implicit in being gone on someone increased the deliciousness of the feelings. To suffer both inwardly and publicly gave both oneself and one's love greater importance—and fulfillment.

The recipients of so much emotion reacted in a variety of ways, sometimes using it to further their own self-image, or simply ignoring it, or channeling it into school loyalty. But quite often the feelings expressed by a younger student or teacher for an older woman were reciprocated. The rave became an opportunity for mutual spiritual growth, under the leadership of the older woman. In the 1870s and 1880s this often meant an Evangelical awakening to God's love through a shared earthly love. For a later generation of teachers a specific religious commitment had gradually become a generalized sense of duty, public and vaguely Christian. Sexual attraction was transformed into a special spiritual duty, intensifying both the love and the responsibility for the younger teacher or student.[82]

Many teachers felt an awe-inspiring love for their protégées, caring for them more intently than many mothers. In the late 1870s while teaching at St. Leonards School, Constance Maynard fell in love with a series of admiring students. Concerned about balancing the public, academic standards of the new school with her own sense of Christian behavior, she sought a resolution by concentrating on the moral welfare of her favorites. She wrote in her diary, "Looking at Katherine, all the mother in me wakes & I think how tender I would be of letting any evil in on a mind such as that, so quick of apprehension yet at present so lovely so sensitive so pure."[83] Maynard's concerns focus not upon any possible evil actions or temptations that might harm her favorite, but rather on evil thoughts. She was as caught up in a moment of adolescent innocence as any admiring Victorian male, cherishing the girl's beauty while only barely recognizing that such a moment must pass. The potential for disappointment and failure was intrinsic in such a perspective, regardless of the student.

Self-fulfillment for Maynard and other teachers like her came through a spiritual leadership that met the younger girl on the same plane of idealization, without making overt the differential in power that underlay their mutual attraction. Reading aloud, exchanges of letters, and private talks took on the same symbolic importance for them that bed making and flower giving had for the ravees. Some of Mlle Julie's happiest moments were reading French classics with her favorite students. Private talks, of course, offered intimacy without loss of distance, for the teacher or older student retained her privileged position of moral instructor. Minor sins, school infractions, and spiritual struggles could be discussed at great length, encouraging a self-examination that became grounds for further intimacies, confessions, and avowals to do better. Passion was transferred to a spiritual realm, which then made it more accessible, more manageable, and yet also more satisfying.

Letters were an especially important means of communication between teachers and their admiring students, bridging the distance between the rave and the ravee. Shy students who feared speaking directly with someone they loved could pour out their affection in letters. In turn, teachers who were anxious about their public, professional role could break their silence through letters of advice, consolation, and love. Letter writing, however, also reveals the ways love functioned to disrupt and accentuate the distance between the family and the school. Many girls begged their raves to write to them during the holidays, to give them advice while they were away from school and in the midst of numerous worldly temptations. Maynard became deeply involved in the spiritual life of a favorite student, Mary Tait. The adolescent

Mary found her life at home to be "distasteful or a bore," and she hated her family obligations. Maynard wrote exhorting her to greater self-discipline and self-sacrifice. The correspondence gave both a sense of moving out of the mundane and into the rarefied atmosphere of spiritual strivings. Just before the end of the Christmas holidays, Mary wrote, "'You can't think how delicious it is to know you are pleased. It is awfully severe sometimes to do what is right, but I always think of you & it becomes quite easy to do it.'"[84] Maynard, in turn, prayed for Mary, carrying her letters with her "as a secret, unaccountable source of gladness of heart."[85]

Mary, however, began to wilt under the pressures exerted by her teacher. After Constance reprimanded her for a poor effort on her drawing class exam, Mary wrote back, "I was not aware that Drawing was a subject of such extreme importance. . . . I *am* indifferent to everything except that you should not take everything I do so much to heart."[86] Constance was heartbroken, interpreting her rejection not as stemming from the fickleness of an admittedly spoiled girl, but instead as involving the loss of a soul. She wrote in her diary, "Oh, Mary, Mary, I loved you, *loved*—do you know what that means? . . . Oh, my child my child, are you lost to me indeed? and I was the link through which you were dimly feeling after a higher life—are you lost to that too?"[87] Mary had sought to overturn the discipline of her family life; she was naturally reluctant to embrace the discipline Constance's love offered her. She escaped into her circle of adolescent friends, leaving Constance as forlorn as any rejected mother—or lover. Idealized self-control and spiritual seeking did not satisfy Mary, but Constance based much of her emotional life on this combination.

Constance's misery and confusion over Mary's rejection raises the issue of the power differential in school friendships. Although the older woman had the greater power over the younger, she also had the most to lose in admitting her love. She gained most by keeping the relationship distant, by fostering self-control within herself and the ravee. When she bridged the inequality between them, she risked not only rejection, but also a loss of spiritual leadership. Many teachers found themselves, like Constance Maynard, swayed by their love of a younger student.[88] Indeed, the emotional center of the relationship almost inevitably shifted to the ravee as soon as the attraction between the two had been acknowledged, because so much emphasis was placed upon her spiritual growth. The older woman was then in a position of self-sacrifice, giving moral guidance and personal love. But an under-current of sexuality could undermine her distant authority, leading to a closeness that revealed the girl's power over her. The implications were frightening because they brought to the surface conflicting needs of power, autonomy, sexual desire, and spirituality.

Constance Maynard learned from her experience with Mary Tait, and several years later, when she fell in love with another student, she cautioned her new love,

> I told her how the capacity for loving always meant the capacity for suffering, & how I should expect the utmost self-control from her; I should expect it continuously, I said, & never say Thank you, for I belonged to the cause, the object, not to the individual, & all Students must be alike to me. And then, coming closer yet, I told her that self-control was not needed for the sake of appearances only, but for our own two selves, for real love, "the best thing in the world" could be a terribly weakening power . . . we both agreed that a denial such as this enforced upon one part of our nature, was a sort of genuine satisfaction to another part, to the love of order, of justice, of doing something great & public.[89]

Maynard's advice catches exactly the combination of loving through self-discipline, of satisfaction through the suppression of desire, that characterized the late nineteenth and early twentieth century rave. When not carried to "excess," a friendship such as she described coincided happily with the desire of headmistresses, teachers, and parents that a rave be a spiritually uplifting experience.

Constance's expressed desire for self-imposed control was not always reciprocated. A ravee might prefer to retreat back into her own untouched fantasies, or she might use the love she had aroused for further emotional power and sexual exploration. The rave could not always be contained on the spiritual level; indeed, its very expression was rooted in earthly acts of love, however mediated by a spiritual vocabulary. In the midst of counseling self-control to a student she loved, Constance did not notice the jealousy she aroused in other students. The very next term she was confronted by a hysterical student who could no longer hold back "the hopeless, perfectly self-controlled love which had evidently brought her into this state." On the doctor's advice, Maynard coaxed the deranged student into her room and away from the other students. She then had to lie down with her on her bed, which gave the girl the opportunity to grasp her tightly and to declare that they were now married. In "solemn tones" she insisted, "We are two no longer. I am part of you & you are part of me. I know all your thoughts by instinct. We can never be separated. Two souls for one forever."[90] The next day the girl was quickly taken away and returned to her family for care, and Maynard lost sight of her. Freed from parental restraints, the girl appears to have become unbalanced, although her expressions of passionate love never went beyond a parody of lovemaking. However much a rave depended upon the imagination, virtually every girl wished for some sign that she had been singled out for special attention. As Maynard's preference for another student became obvious, the girl may have lost hope. Hysteria became a way of breaking through to her beloved teacher; when mad she could relinquish self-control and permit herself to act out the full expression of her love. Maynard, on the other hand, never felt that her declarations of love were anything more than the product of insanity, bearing no relation to the "sweet converse" she enjoyed with her favorite.

To judge from one fictionalized account, students were not always alone in their inability or unwillingness to place limits on their homoerotic love. In *Olivia* Mlle Julie's "marriage" to Mlle Cara could not tolerate the strains of adolescent adoration, and so the school was broken up. In the midst of this messy "divorce," Mlle Cara died by what appeared to be suicide. Olivia's deeply idealistic love for Mlle Julie provided meager comfort in the days that followed. Mlle Julie's farewell to her beloved Olivia, just before going into exile, both warned of and praised lesbian love:

> "It has been a struggle all my life—but I have always been
> victorious—I was proud of my victory." And then her voice
> changed, broke, deepened, softened, became a murmur: "I
> wonder now whether defeat wouldn't have been better for us
> all—as well as sweeter." Another long pause. She turned now
> and looked at me, and smiled. "You, Olivia, will never be vic-
> torious, but if you are defeated—" how she looked at me!
> "when you are defeated—" she looked at me in a way that
> made my heart stand still and the blood rush to my face, to
> my forehead, till I seemed wrapped in flame.[91]

Mlle Julie, Olivia, and the others involved in the tragedy of "Les Avons" school recognized and gloried in the sexual roots of their spiritual love, but they also insisted upon containing it through self-control.

But *Olivia* is fictionalized autobiography. Writing fifty years after the events, in the mid-1930s, Bussy portrayed her love for the real-life Mlle Julie, Mlle Souvestre, as wholly spiritual, and assumed her teacher's greater self-awareness. What Bussy remembered, and what she knew or felt at the time, must remain two different things. Moreover, she appears to have added the tragic finale, for no published evidence exists that Marie Souvestre's lover committed suicide; Mlle Souvestre did not close her school, but transferred it to Allenswood, near London, and hired Bussy to teach Shakespeare. Perhaps Bussy revenged herself upon the past by such a reordering of events; she never labeled her love as deviant, but she interpreted victory as suppression, not expression.[92] Yet her book—dedicated to the memory of Virginia Woolf—is a poignant homage to an enduring love that was never replicated with the same strength, power, or beauty.

Sexuality, Spirituality, and Power: Friendships among Teachers

Few homoerotic friendships between students and teachers could have had as disruptive an effect as Olivia's for Mlle Julie. The very transitory nature of so many student-teacher raves points to one of the chief difficulties of such first loves. They were considered, by definition, to be preliminary to marriage and therefore to be encouraged as a preamble to "the real thing." While heterosexual interests, much less concerns, were continually minimized within the school precincts, in time girls left school, came out, and generally married. An earlier love was left behind. Yet many teachers continued to love those of their own sex, finding in it, as discussed in chapter 1, a solution to the dangers, perceived and actual, in heterosexual love. For these women, a career and friendship went hand in hand. In spite of their sexual roots, friendships between teachers were, like raves, described in spiritual terms. They were also sometimes based upon the same unequal power relationship, but with the same reworking of the family metaphor found in college friendships. Whatever the language of love, many young professional women formed lifelong friendships in college or in their first teaching job.

Schools were obviously among the most supportive environments for the friendships of independent women because an emotional relation between a student and teacher was frequently the impetus for a career of dedicated service, rather than a preamble to marriage. No one thought it odd that a young woman might want to continue to live and work with an admired teacher; frequently this unequal relationship matured into one of great mutual support and admiration. For example, Grace Hadow's brother encouraged their mother to permit her to become a student-pupil under Clare Arnold, headmistress of Truro High School, because "Her hero-worship for Miss Arnold is another point in favour of acceptance."[93] Arnold some fifteen years previously had exchanged letters of religious belief and love with Constance Maynard; her own headmistress, Dorothea Beale, had advised her during a time of difficult religious questioning. She could now guide the youthful Hadow, teaching her "we are looking to eternity for the judgement of our work."[94] The conjunction of religion and idealized love gave meaning to the discipline of teaching. Hadow and other young teachers found it natural and right to submit to those they loved.

The friendships of Constance Maynard are in many ways typical of first-generation college-educated teachers. Not only was she deeply involved with Mary Tait, but she also was herself in a similar unequal, adoring relationship with her headmistress Louisa Lumsden. Although the new institutions, such as boarding schools, gave single women far more scope for personal friendships, they were still immersed in the old ideologies and patterns. Indeed, the effort to model the new boarding schools on the traditional bourgeois family, however distant the reality was, demonstrates the dependence of pioneering women upon known female models.[95] Since they worked in what they saw as a family—their school—they naturally turned to the most forceful women leaders as "husbands," the most nurturing as "wives," and the students as "children." Lumsden had intervened on Maynard's behalf and forced the wayward "daughter" Mary Tait to apologize; the incident strengthened her love for her vulnerable "wife." Yet, the schools were not families and, indeed, unconsciously subverted the family. Thus many women who thought they wanted "marriage" with a dear friend were caught in conflicting and changing languages, values, and modes of behavior.

On the surface it may seem that adult women's homoerotic friendships were, as they have been labeled by psychoanalysts, immature. Rather, they should be seen as an effort to balance three problematic areas: sexuality, spirituality, and power. All three existed in highly mediated forms for a Victorian single woman. She was expected to express her sexuality only after marriage, to follow a clergyman's lead in religious matters, and to have no desire for direct power outside the family sphere. Such limitations, already discussed in chapter 1, are a crucial backdrop for understanding women's friendships. Not surprisingly, the closed world of the boarding school made the expression of and tension among these three areas more intense. Greater opportunities meant greater conflicts.

A close look at the relationship of Louisa Lumsden and Constance Maynard will show the ways sexuality, spirituality, and power underlay their unequal "marriage." Relations between Louisa and Constance were particularly strained because of their deep love, going back to their days at Girton together. But Constance, a devout Evangelical, could see her relationship with the agnostic Louisa only in narrowly religious terms. In the early stages Constance kept hoping that she could gently lead Louisa back to belief; she repeated to herself in her diary Paul's injunction, "The unbelieving husband is sanctified by the wife" (1 Cor. 7 : 14). But every time she mentioned religion, Louisa burst into a tirade about God's permitting the suffering of innocent children and animals. Night after night Constance lay in Louisa's arms praying for her, but she could not bear to feel Louisa's distance and would always beg her for forgiveness:

> The coolness was so unendurable that in the evening I asked her forgiveness, though I hardly knew what for, & at once she became so sweet, so gracious, that I seemed almost drowned in the sense of the overpowering beauty of living day & night for one heart alone. Work, friends, pleasure, everything shared, & then the long, long clasp of living love that needs no explanation. . . . If this noble heart submitted to Christ, I think I should never wander more.[96]

Constance's plight was emblematic of the structural problem of the new "families" of professional women. Too much was expected of a single relationship—"Work, friends, pleasure, everything shared" gave no room for disagreement. The very privacy and freedom women such as Louisa and Constance had could become entombing, suffocating, rather than liberating. When distance was lost but inequality remained, the relationship had to be continually renegotiated, reworking the family analogy over and over. Constance deflected the difficulties of living in an unequal, adoring relationship to problems of belief. Louisa wanted perfect sympathy and understanding for her strivings to understand the world, while Constance tried to keep her within the confines of Evangelical Christianity. Uncertain of their public roles and often afraid of public criticism, each woman demanded certainty from her love.

Louisa had longed to be a man and was convinced that she was not made for happiness—a conviction that she turned into a self-fulfilling prophecy by her uncertain temper. But with Constance she felt happy and effective; as she explained one evening to her, "I have been thinking over everything, & I am only *too* happy; my work, my home, my wife, all are good & I am satisfied. I *think* I have never been so happy in my life before."[97] Constance was thrilled with the attention she received from the "noble, leonine" Louisa, but she often felt consumed by her love and pitied others who had fallen under her sway. Constance's brief stay at St. Leonards was marked by a sense of shared wretchedness, experienced by all the teachers who loved Louisa but feared her temper. Jane Frances Dove, the shy and awkward daughter of a village clergyman, adored the aristocratic Louisa and had secretly tended her fire, made her bed, left flowers, and performed other services for her at Girton. Louisa, however, disliked her self-abnegation, which reminded her of an adolescent rave. But she had no qualms about accepting Dove's services as her second-in-command and left many onerous tasks to her. Maynard, Dove, and several other teachers were attracted to Louisa's very irrationality amid building a new female code of rationality and order. Although she gave charismatic leadership for the new values, she bound others to her by her expression of powerful, unreliable emotions.

Publicly Louisa and Constance were typical upper-class ladies of severe manners and distant demeanor. But privately their society permitted, and they experienced, a wide range of emotional behavor with intimate friends. The very distance and self-control demanded of them in public rebounded to make moments of intimacy more precious; friendships bore the entire weight of the emotions. Pent-up anger, frustrated ambitions, and constrained sexuality all had to find their outlet through a single friendship. Flowers, billets-doux, pillow fights, and games, along with countless kisses and tears, marked the courtship and "marriage" of Louisa and Constance. Life with Louisa brought Constance the heights and depths of love. While at St. Leonards she easily turned down an offer of marriage. Despite her grief, Louisa was shocked and kept urging her to reconsider. Constance was deeply moved by her reaction:

> "You have helped to raise one profession that needed it, go now & do the same for another!" & ever between [sobs] she strained me to her heart as if nothing could ever separate us, saying, "But what *shall* I do without you? It is not what you teach, though I don't want to undervalue that, it is what you *are*, both in the School & to me personally. This I can never replace. . . . I am the worst person in the world for you to talk to, for I believe married life to be really the happiest, & I long for it for you, though the loss to me is beyond words." She has been called "hard & intellectual"—but to me it is at times as if she was made of nothing but the deepest love. . . . I knew she loved me, but not with such a force that was almost terrible. It was as if I had waked a sleeping lion.[98]

In her autobiography Constance recalled those days vividly, remembering, "As I put on my cloak and went off to School I used to hug myself & think, 'Now I know what love is!' & anything Dr. Robertson offered seemed timid & colourless in comparison."[99] For a brief period Constance's desire for emotional reassurance— for intimacy and fulfillment within the public realm of the school—was met by Louisa's passionate love. But their religious differences were irreconcilable, and Constance left to found West-field College.

The passionate intensity of Louisa's and Constance's love for each other can be fully recorded because we have Constance's diaries. Other relationships between lifelong friends are less easily examined, but they were clearly crucial to the growth and sustenance of many school communities. The three older Lawrence sisters who founded Roedean were so close that they became known jointly as "the Firm." Another five sisters studied under their older sisters and then taught at Roedean themselves for varying lengths of time; only one married. Several sisters also had lifelong friends with whom they retired after working together for decades.[100] A more unusual case is the friendship of Olive Willis, headmistress of Downe House, with Maria Nickel, an eccentric, multitalented Polish refugee. Engaged in 1910 to teach chemistry and geography, Nickel refused to correct any papers, but instead poured her energy into the many odd tasks of the new school. She ended up as the school's architect, chauffeur, and handyman. To save valuable space, she refused a room of her own and slept on Willis's bathroom floor. Even when she poisoned a new teacher's dog in a jealous fit, she was kept on, bullying, protecting, and assisting her beloved head.[101] Willis seems to have had Lumsden's charisma in attracting talented women who would work under her for very little pay. Her biographer speaks with admiration of Lilian Heather, who acted as vice-principal for many years, handling all the school's finances: "Her affection was not without possessiveness, and clashed sometimes with the claims on Olive of other friends, but her whole-hearted devotion of her brilliant talents to the service of the school, and her willing acceptance of boring tasks, were remarkable."[102] Downe House prided itself on encouraging eccentricities and discouraging schoolgirlishness, but it may not have been entirely successful in either.[103]

Most friendships were less colorful, but few were without their complications. Friendships between equals—two or three teachers—were certainly as important, and as common, as the more unequal "marriages" described here. But they also had fewer emotional complications, unless careers took radically different forms or beliefs changed. These less tortured friendships provided private space and support within the confining world of the boarding school. Young women teachers, knowing that marriage was unlikely or unattractive, developed a large network of independent women friends. Society permitted very limited relations with men for proper young schoolteachers, while similar responsibilities, enthusiasms, and goals united them with their colleagues.[104] Women lived and worked together during term time and then vacationed together, enjoying freedom of movement and emotional satisfactions that would never have been possible within a family. Indeed, they were often more loving and stable relationships than a family. Winifred Mercier, at her first teaching post in Edinburgh in 1902, became lifelong friends with two women teachers, J. K. Borland and K. Scott Moncrieff. She and Borland, in the Highlands, wrote for their friend to join them. When she could not,

> We went up a high hill yesterday covered in places with great patches of snow on which in a fit of vandalism we wrote our names and picked out the largest and smoothest patch to write K. S. M. on, which somewhat soothed our feelings. . . .

If you cannot leave home, could I, should I, might I be of
any use in your stead, so that we could change places for the
last week[?] [105]

Vacations together provided a joyous break into freedom, away
from the confines of respectability and adulthood. "Donald," as
Borland was known to her friends, provided Winifred with her
first real home. Lewis Mercier had never been able to earn a living
for his family, and they had been forced to live with various relatives all her life. Later, when Winifred was earning enough money
as a Girton College don, she rented a home for her father and
mother and supported them until their deaths. But her real home
remained with Donald. Similar long-term friendships can easily
be documented; all were accepted without the questionable overtones they later acquired. [106]

Winifred and Donald shared more than a passionate liking for
each other; they also found in each other a sympathetic ear on
every possible concern. Women teachers did not have many opportunities to discuss frankly and freely their special concerns, ambitions, and confusions. Families, like Winnie Seebohm's overpro-
tective family, too often suggested quitting or returning home
rather than struggling and confronting a problem. Alternatively,
like Mercier's, they insisted upon extra attention, nursing, and
other services, to the detriment of a daughter's career. Headmistresses were sometimes themselves the source of a difficulty
or lacked sympathy with issues that did not directly concern the
school itself. Winifred and Donald made a habit of drawing brief
sketches for each other of the day's absurdities in teaching;
grading papers was interrupted by wrestling matches and jokes.
Through letters and conversations they tested ideas and actions
that might be tried out at a future date and for the present provided relief from the constraints they felt in their work and home
lives. One August, in the midst of studying for the external London degree and caring for her perpetually ill mother, Winifred passionately wrote,

Donald, wouldn't you like to go to America, Canada, or the
great wide west? where perhaps there might be more chance
of finding out what manner of being you were?—where there
is more room, more freedom, and one is not so hide-bound by
conventions—where you could get nearer the soil, and as I

said before, not be stifled by artificialities and habits and conventions, your own and other peoples'. Oh wouldn't you like
it, wouldn't you? wouldn't you? [107]

Later, when Mercier became a leader in the reform of teacher
training colleges, she retained her enthusiastic exploration of
ideas and alternatives; rather like Jane Ellen Harrison, she used
her fame to give her the freedoms she had not had as a young
teacher. She felt free to express her likes and dislikes, and, in the
words of her biographer,

> Now and again her affectionate demonstrativeness would em-
> barrass her more conventional friends, and she would use it as
> a weapon against them. When two of them teased her about
> some trifle in a London restaurant, she quelled them by say-
> ing, "If you say that again, I'll kiss you both, at once." They
> knew she would be as good as her word. [108]

Mercier was able to "find out what manner of being" she was
through the combination of an active career in teaching and
college administration and a satisfying private life with Donald,
her support in difficult times, tester of ideas, and enthusiastic
vacationer.

The Public Criticism of Friendships

By the early twentieth century female sexuality came increasingly under examination, and traditional notions about the asexuality of single women were discarded. It was no longer so readily
assumed that women had little or no sexual feeling, and their
deeply emotional lives were seen to have sexual roots. One of the
natural results of the new educators' emphasis upon careers for
women, public responsibilities, and professional behavior was a
blurring of the clear distinctions between the female, domestic
world and the male, public world. As women gained a voice in the
public sphere, their single-sex institutions came under attack.
Opposition was especially voiced in regard to teachers, who had
power over the next generation. At the height of the militant suffrage campaign, Ethel Colquhoun "regretted that the influence of
mothers has been so largely superseded nowadays by that of the
female celibate pedagogue." She described the teacher as someone
whose

life is full of minor irritations to all but the born teacher, restricted within narrow limits and often monotonous, with very few plums and a scale of remuneration leaving little margin for the pleasures of life. . . . Unhappily it is to this class, on whom changing social conditions have laid such a heavy burden, that the young girls of to-day look for guidance and for their philosophy of life.[109]

Hostility toward women focused upon student-teacher relations, which were interpreted as the distorted use of sexual power. Friendship between teachers was stigmatized as abnormal, and raves were attacked as permanently distorting. The preferred form of friendship was less exclusive, less extreme. Warnings were regularly published about the phase all schoolgirls went through of fastening their emotions upon an admired teacher; students were encouraged to channel their energy toward serving the school, and teachers were advised to discourage any intimacies.

Schoolgirl raves were the first of women's friendships to be questioned. The best-known treatment of a lesbian teacher-student relationship of this period now is D. H. Lawrence's description of Ursula's infatuation with her teacher in *The Rainbow* (1915), in a chapter titled "Shame." But the most famous contemporary attack was Clemence Dane's *Regiment of Women* (1917), a vicious and effective portrayal of a power-hungry lesbian. The brilliant but psychopathic thirty-five-year-old Clare Hartill preys upon the generous and warmhearted nineteen-year-old teacher Alwynne. Hartill encourages her students to idolize her, pushing their intellectual and emotional interests into areas that amuse her. When she becomes bored, each in turn is discarded and another protégée taken up. A brilliant girl of twelve becomes overstrained when she is cast aside and commits suicide. Alwynne blames herself for the girl's death until her handsome cousin Roger reassures her and teaches her the nature of true love. Roger, meeting the passionate and distorted Clare, thinks:

She did not understand Louise, whom she had killed, nor this loyal and affectionate child [Alwynne], whom she was driving into melancholia, nor anyone it appeared, nor anything, but the needs of her own barrenly emotional nature. . . . He was horrified at the idea of such a woman, such a type of woman, in undisputed authority, moulding the mothers of the next generation. . . . He had never considered the matter seriously, but he supposed she was but one of many. . . . There must be something poisonous in a system that could render possible the placing of such women in such positions.[110]

Several stormy scenes later, Roger marries Alwynne, and Clare is left to brood alone about her "unnatural" nature. The book, possibly written out of personal experience, became widely known as an important exposé of single-sex education. Unlike boys' schools, girls' schools were never wracked with revelations of homosexuality, but their teachers could suffer the same growing suspicion about too affectionate or conscientious a friendship between teacher and taught.

The schoolgirl-teacher friendship fell under attack for numerous reasons. It was, as Colquhoun and Dane understood, deeply threatening to the nuclear family, for it fostered a very different kind of relationship from the traditional one a girl had with her mother or a wife with her husband. The schools had failed to replicate the family atmosphere they praised because the self-control they advocated was not equivalent to the suppresion of self recommended by mothers. The latter was an unconscious sacrificing of personal wishes and desires to the ambitions and goals of husbands and families. But self-control implies a conscious control of impulses that have reached awareness through an atmosphere conducive to self-examination. The result of this process was self-knowledge and self-development. Put simply, single-sex homo-erotic friendships undercut the family. The heightened self-knowledge implied by such a relationship pointed in the direction of personal autonomy and independence, an independence that few heterosexual relationships, including Roger's traditional marriage with the "affectionate child" Alwynne, could sustain.

Only a man can break the power of "heart-ill" Clare in *Regiment of Women*, but single women teachers were under attack not only from outsiders like Dane and Colquhoun, but also from within their own ranks. The social Darwinists, along with conservative social commentators, worried about the falling birthrate among the upper classes; some headmistresses responded by recommending compulsory domestic science courses for girls in lieu of pure science. At the same time social scientists were enshrining contemporary attitudes as scientific truth in pioneering studies of adolescence. Girls were considered to be weakened by puberty and therefore to be discouraged from hard intellectual work. The argument was increasingly put forward that since marriage and children would be the careers of most girls, all should be trained for these tasks. Converts were made even among those who had benefited from reformed schools. Both Lilian Faithfull and Sara Burstall, leading headmistresses, spoke out in favor of domestic science for girls in secondary schools.[111] Burstall in particular encouraged girls to think of marriage as their future rather than the path she had taken to Girton, teaching, and an active public career as headmistress of Manchester High School for Girls. In 1907, a year before girls were imitating their brothers as "Girl Scouts," she wrote in opposition to camps, arguing that girls were needed by their mothers at home and had no use for such experiences as they would be at home, not in the wider community (or part of a single-sex community) during their adult lives.[112] The Board of Education's 1923 Report on Secondary Schools succinctly defined the change in attitudes, suggesting that in the recent past "old and delicate graces had been lost, and the individuality of womanhood had been sacrificed upon the austere altar of sex equality."[113]

Teachers were placed in a particularly difficult situation during these years. Just as marriage was once again being exalted as woman's best and happiest haven, local education authorities were routinely imposing bars on married women's teaching. Girls were being taught in the most obvious way that they could not have both a career and marriage. For two generations women had successfully fought to establish teaching as an honorable choice, not a place of last resort; in the 1920s, when large numbers of women could not marry because so many men of their generation had been lost in World War I, teaching was redefined as a dumping ground for old maids. The virtues of duty and self-sacrifice, of self-control as a source of freedom, echoed hollowly after the travesties of the war. The final blow against single women was the demise of a large feminist movement that had given many a support group and had validated their lives. An unmarried schoolteacher could not easily stand up against the combined attack on female friendships, women's careers, and the loss of the organized women's movement.

The fragility of the pioneers was exposed in a most damning fashion—their calls to sacrifice, duty, and honor, to teaching for the love of children and the respect of society—could not be sustained in the new "open" society of the 1920s. The respect women's teaching had briefly commanded was never completely lost, but teaching was certainly never again so happy a resolution of a single woman's desire for a satisfying public and personal life. Boarding schools in their prime were probably the most successful of all women's total communities; they were widely used by the well-to-do, admired by thousands of readers of girls' stories, eagerly attended by the luckier, and affectionately remembered by old girls. But when major changes struck the upper classes, girls' boarding schools were not sufficiently flexible, in spite of a few nonacademic subjects, a few male teachers, and very gradually more contacts with the outside world.[114] Frozen in time, girls' schools became subject to satire and amusement—and worst of all—irrelevance. When other options became more readily available for both girls and women, schooldays were remembered differently, accentuating changed standards of individual autonomy and behavior. What had been liberating for one generation— Winifred Peck adored rushing about on the hockey field—became stultifying for the next. By the 1950s, as Judith Okely has so poignantly documented, girls' boarding schools were so narrow and out of date as to destroy all that had once been intellectually exciting and socially freeing; school, and especially hockey, forcibly reminded the students that they were inferior to men and always would be.[115] Such a fate may have been avoided by some of the better schools, but the importance of boarding schools as a socializing force for girls and women decidedly declined after World War I. The snob appeal remained, but not the public voice.

6

Settlement Houses: A Community Ideal for the Poor

[S]mall bands of the votaries of culture and decency, planted and rooted in the soil of London, wherever vice and horror grew thickest, would by their very presence purge the air and destroy evil elements, as the stronger microbes devour the weaker in the bodily frame.[1]

During the middle years of the nineteenth century outstanding individual women such as Mary Carpenter, Louisa Twining, and Octavia Hill had pioneered new approaches to philanthropy in child welfare, workhouse living conditions, and model housing. Women had always been active in charity, willingly giving of their time and money, but the increasing wealth and leisure of middle-class Victorians freed even larger numbers of women to take up the cause of the poor.[2] In a society severely divided by class, men had fewer and fewer contacts with people outside their own class other than at work, while women increasingly crossed class lines through their philanthropic activities. Charitable organizations united middle- and upper-class women and gave them greater access to poor women and children; since women were less identified with economic exploitation and political power, they were more readily accepted into the homes of the working class and the poor. During the second half of the nineteenth century philanthropy grew by leaps and bounds in response to the growing recognition of widespread poverty, inadequate housing, and social dislocation brought about by industrialization and urbanization. Although rooted in woman's traditional role of succoring the poor, philanthropy was closely tied to the increasing bureaucratization of the social services. As charity organizations and government institutions came to provide more and more services, skilled professionals were necessary to guide and train the veritable army of volunteers. In 1893 it was estimated that some twenty thousand women were "maintaining themselves as paid officials in works of philanthropic usefulness in England, while at least twenty times that number, or about half a million, [were] occupied more or less continuously and semi-professionally in similar works."[3] Women entered philanthropy in such large numbers to fulfill one of their most important duties to themselves and other women: "As civilisation advances, as the social interests and occupations become more and more complicated, the family duties and influences diverge from the central home,—in a manner, radiate from it . . . the woman becomes, on a larger scale, mother and sister, nurse and help."[4]

Unlike traditional charity, which assumed that the rich were busy and the poor could wait upon them, nineteenth-century charity assumed that the poor were busy and the rich should go to them.[5] This meant long hours trudging through back alleys and lanes or waiting in dreary workhouses and hospitals to seek out the needy individual. Such work was very labor-intensive, and any success meant an ever-increasing need for volunteers. But women believed passionately in the importance of personal friendships and would not willingly adopt the more impersonal methods of the larger charities and the government. Indeed, many of their strongest battles were fought against such organizations because they built institutions so large that the individual child or aged person received no individual love or attention. Women worked to foster more personal help through such organizations as Louisa Twining's Workhouse Visiting Society, Mrs. Nassau Senior's Metropolitan Association for Befriending Young Servants, and Maude Stanley's Girls' Club Union.[6] No matter how professionalized women's philanthropic organizations became—and most of them began to hire a small number of full-time workers very early— women were determined to keep philanthropy personal and individual. Gifts and money necessarily played some part in all charity, but the primary goal for most women was the reestablishment of a network of friendships across class lines, between women of shared interests and concerns. The bitter isolation of institutional life or of a large city or a strange job was to be overcome through personal contact between rich and poor.

Visiting the poor obviously gave the well-to-do a purpose in life; certainly it was very popular. By the end of the century an upper-class woman who did not do some kind of volunteer work would have been an anomaly among her friends. And for single women, such work had become a respectable alternative to idleness. But boredom alone cannot explain why so many women willingly visited the slums, week after week. In a society that emphasized service to a higher good—one's country or religion—it was immensely satisfying to feel an active part of the charity movement. While one's brother drilled with his cadet corps in the name of the empire, visiting the poor could seem equally important, if not quite so glamorous, when done in the name of God and country.[7] Slum life attracted overprotected women who had wanted adventure and excitement away from their dull respectable homes. The experience women gained in hospitals, workhouses, and settlements prepared them to play a role in public affairs in a way that no school or college could. All the most active women charity workers served as poor law guardians and on school boards, as well as in lesser government offices. They saw themselves as representing the interests of poor women and children with no voice or vote. When agitation for women's suffrage was revived during the early years of the twentieth century, women could point to their effective leadership at the local level as well as their widespread experience working with women and children of different classes. Such public service proved women worthy of the vote.[8]

The large number of charitable organizations run by women laid the groundwork for the settlement houses discussed in this chapter. We have already seen in chapter 2 the importance of working with the poor for Anglican sisters and Evangelical deaconesses. By the 1880s, when settlements were first founded, educated single women were eager to be a part of a movement based upon personal friendships, which had always been a cornerstone of women's charitable work. The idea of a residential home amid the people one worked with especially appealed to those who had gone to boarding school or college. They had benefited so much from the experience of corporate living that a settlement seemed the perfect means of carrying this ideal into a wider world. A settlement implied the improvement of the people not by missionary work, but rather by personal example. As the heroine of a Newnham College novel explained,

the world still awaited regeneration which one of their colleagues at Girton (they would at least give the credit of the remark to Girton) had prophesied would come from "three consecutive generations of single women." If by that the Girtonian meant that the world needed unattached women—women without family ties—prepared to work wholeheartedly in the service of their fellow-creatures on boards of guardians, on school-boards, on parish councils, their Girton friend was right. And nowhere, perhaps, was women's work more urgently needed than in the social settlements of great cities. . . . What was wanted, she thought, to help to set the world right, was a greater sympathy between those for whom the world was all golden gates of glorious opportunity, and those for whom it was but a gray prison wall.[9]

The roots of the settlements for women were both revolutionary and evolutionary, domestic and public. During the years from the late nineteenth century until after World War I, the work of middle-class women settlers—helping poor women and girls—changed from social outreach to social welfare. But women always remained ideologically and practically distinct from their male counterparts, bringing to the slums both different services and different goals.

Disciplined Philanthropy

The settlement movement began when Canon Samuel Barnett and his wife founded Toynbee Hall in Whitechapel, London, in 1884. Built in memory of Arnold Toynbee, who had pioneered living among the poor in the East End, the settlement's chief aim was to foster friendship between the working class and the best of Oxford and Cambridge students. Barnett saw the working class as a dull, undifferentiated mass, devoid of culture; he hoped to bring the young students—the finest of contemporary culture—into contact with workers to enrich their lives. Art, music, and education were of primary importance at Toynbee Hall; friendship, not charity, was the watchword.[10] Barnett insisted upon the primacy of culture over religion and thereby broke with the many religious missions in the East End. A mission was intended to bring people closer to God, but a settlement brought them closer to each other.[11] At a time of great and fearful social divisions, personal friendship would be more effective with the working class than preaching Christianity from a distance. Ideally, a settlement was nonsectarian and encouraged religion by example. Barnett's experiment quickly attracted some of the most idealistic students at Oxford and Cambridge, and soon women were planning their own settlements.

Barnett and the many young men who stayed briefly at Toynbee

Hall were the ideological leaders of the English settlement-house movement. They publicized the staggering amount of poverty in the East End of London, the need for better cooperation with the poor, and the importance of political reform. For men a brief sojourn in a settlement was an excellent opportunity to gain more experience of life before going on to a career in law, religion, or public service. So many of the architects of the welfare state and early Labour party spent time at Toynbee Hall that George Lansbury sardonically commented, "men who went in training under the Barnetts . . . could always be sure of government and municipal appointments. . . . [They] discovered the advancement of their own interests and the interests of the poor were best served by leaving East London to stew in its own juice while they became members of parliament, cabinet ministers, civil servants."[12] Young Oxbridge graduates who stayed at Toynbee Hall or one of the other men's settlements taught classes in the arts and other impractical subjects, or offered free legal advice, or learned local politics by serving on the poor law board. In effect, men gave the expertise they had gained through the privileges of class— knowledge of the classics, legal training, or political confidence. In return, they laid the foundations for a career that often touched only peripherally upon social service.

Such options were not open to women. Women, too, brought their social skills to bear upon their slum work, but rather than using their education (many of the early volunteers had been to Oxford or Cambridge), they emphasized a nonprofessional shared women's world. Their child centers, prenatal care, and girls' clubs assumed that women could always reach across class barriers to help each other. Although the women's settlements, like the men's, were plagued with short-term residents and a lack of continuity, their volunteers used their experience as an initiation into social work, not as a stepping-stone to another career. The men accused the women's settlements of resembling training colleges rather than true settlements. While women wanted experience in specific jobs—care of the handicapped, casework, or club organization—men emphasized "undifferentiated helpfulness."[13] Women social workers carved out an area of service for themselves that was explicitly antitheoretical and proinstinctual; in doing so, they continued notions about women's special domestic sphere. Unlike Jane Addams and her American cohorts, they had little other choice, since men had already preempted the intellectual and ideological work of the settlements. The women settlers did gradually come to see themselves as professionals with a distinct identity, but this early disjunction between men's work and women's work meant that their expertise was limited to "women's issues."

The men's and women's settlements differed not only ideologically, but also in the physical appearance of both the settlement itself and the members. Emily K. Abel has pointed out that Barnett's ideal settler possessed the same qualities as the ideal Victorian lady.[14] The working class was to be influenced by the Toynbee Hall resident's presence, rather than his actions; he would create an atmosphere of loving patience and kindness, so that the feckless and undisciplined of the neighborhood would come to see the virtues of better behavior. Their reward would be genteel evenings of tea with cultured conversation. Beatrice Webb noticed that Canon Barnett was "like a strong woman," while his wife was "the more masculine of the two."[15] The women settlers did, indeed, develop a more forthright style, for they had to take initiative, to organize and lead the many different clubs they started, whether for mothers, children, or adolescent girls. Obviously a lady's class background had given her some experience in organizing the lives of servants, but in a slum, a lady became tougher, more capable—and more public. Toynbee Hall was designed to look like an Oxbridge college, complete with a quiet, green quadrangle. Other less famous (and wealthy) men's settlements were more modest but still aspired to this physical layout. Not surprisingly, the women's settlements looked like an urban home. Usually starting with the rental of one building, expansion simply became a matter of knocking connecting passageways into the building next door or renting an empty building down the street. Money was spent to further the social services, not for the buildings.

The ideological roots of the women's movement were not with Canon Barnett and Christian Socialism, but with the practical work of Octavia Hill and the Charity Organisation Society. Hill (1838–1912) was one of the most respected reformers of the previous generation. Beginning in 1865 with a block of houses purchased with funds from John Ruskin, she had built up a small empire of model tenancies. Hill took the property and tenants she received and slowly remodeled both, working under the principle of regular personal contact between the rent collector and the tenant. Tenants who did not pay their rent promptly were dismissed, but those who stayed were supported in a variety of ways. Work was found for the unemployed, apprenticeships were sought for children, and instruction was given in housewifery and home decorating. Over the years Hill had trained a large number of lady volunteers to oversee the properties, each week collecting the rent and using the occasion to assist—or interfere—in the affairs of the tenants.[16] Her greatest pride was her guarantee of 5 percent return on investment in model housing; this was about half what most slum landlords made and so was scarcely an inducement for any widespread acceptance of her methods. She was more influential, rather, as a spokesperson for effective improvement among the poor without charity.[17]

Octavia Hill was a founder and firm supporter of the Charity Organisation Society, that key organization in Victorian philanthropy. Founded in the late 1860s as an umbrella organization for overlapping charities in London, the COS quickly developed an effective style of charity in tune with the dominant ideology of self-help. Both Hill and the COS opposed "indiscriminate charity" as undermining the self-respect of the poor and encouraging them to seek hand-outs rather than work. COS assistance was never given without prior investigation; volunteers were sent out with a questionnaire to each family, and a case report was written. A committee then decided who was deserving of aid and who was not. Any evidence that family members could help each other or that anyone drank meant automatic denial. The respectable few who were helped were given thorough and careful assistance with follow-up investigations and reports.[18] The poor loathed the attitude of superiority permeating the COS and applied for aid only when driven to it. In turn, the COS hated and campaigned against all organizations that simply gave money away to the poor. This usually meant the Salvation Army and the Sisters of the Church; in the eyes of the COS they concealed the true nature of poverty and diverted funds from those too proud to beg.

When Octavia Hill was first approached about helping to found a women's settlement, she was rather lukewarm. She feared that a residential house for single women would take them away from their families and lead them to prefer work among the poor to their primary duties.[19] Moreover, she believed that the gently born needed the rest and recuperation available at home, well away from the sights and sounds of the slums. Canon Barnett also opposed women's starting settlements. He was afraid that women would take over the movement and drive out the best men, just as they did whenever they entered any field in large numbers.[20] His fears turned out to be only partially correct; by 1914 women outnumbered men by 246 to 189.[21] More women than men were free to work full time and eager to take up the work. They simply could not be stopped. The strain of commuting to the East End or across the Thames and returning late at night, in addition to the frustrations of part-time work, brought volunteers into the women's settlements. Moreover, the COS and other charitable organizations were calling for more volunteers on the spot. Hill bowed to the inevitable and throughout her remaining life worked closely with the Women's University Settlement, founded in 1887 in Southwark, near some of her largest blocks of housing. Barnett, on the other hand, remained a distant publicist, more concerned with ideology than with the day-to-day work of women's settlements.[22]

Not all the women's settlements were tied as closely to the principles of the COS and Hill's rent collectors as the Women's University Settlement, though virtually all of them drew their ideological strength from this wing of the social-reform movement. Less easily categorized were women settlers drawn to the slums out of socialist or pacifist convictions. Visionaries such as Eleanor Rathbone, the McMillan sisters, and the Lester sisters often worked alone or with only a few close friends, pioneering a single reform. Open-air schools for the physically weak, school health inspections, kindergartens, and pre- and postnatal baby care all owe their origins to farsighted women who fought against contemporary attitudes (and parsimony) in regard to health care, child development, and education.[23] Although they were deeply influenced by the newer ideologies of socialism and Tolstoyism, these women also drew strength from a kind of Christian millennialism that emphasized working for a radically different and better future. Writing after her sister's premature death in 1917, Margaret McMillan summed up her life,

> Looking below the surface of my sister's life and labours, I feel that one impulse—the desire to prepare and make ready—obscurely impelled her always. . . . She strove even throughout the storm and stress of her last years to make ready a new environment for the children of to-morrow, to open up new

centres for students of varied orders, to cut and clear some bit of the road that leads to world-harmony.[24]

In spite of suffering under misunderstandings and attacks locally and nationally, the McMillan sisters never doubted that they had to push forward in changing not only preschool care, but also the state's responsibility to its new generation.

Distinctions between the workaday social workers and the visionaries are in some senses artificial. The settlements attracted idealists, willing to sacrifice their security and ease for work among the poor, to be neighbors to the needy. The military metaphors, so readily adopted by reformers in nursing and teaching, were replaced by metaphors of disease and of empire. The cultured middle-class volunteers would purify the stained slums of England by their very presence. Neighborliness would "purge the air and destroy evil elements." Cleanliness, both real and metaphorical, became a crucial symbol. Middle-class standards of cleanliness were rigorously enforced in all of the experimental nursery schools and kindergartens, and some club leaders refused admittance to girls who had not washed before coming.

Colonialism was an even more pervasive metaphor. The settlers in the slums would colonize the "natives," teaching them not only cleanliness, but also new standards of speech, deportment, and manners. An admired warden was described as the perfect leader of a settlement:

> If some one were wanted to take entire charge of a newly conquered territory, how well she would fill the post! She could teach the natives all things necessary for their moral and physical well-being: design their houses, lay out their gardens, and teach them how to sew and to cook. She would use the resources of the land for their general edification, and without any commotion or disturbance would soon make the place into a self-respecting well-doing colony.[25]

Settlers confidently assumed that they would be welcome wherever they went and therefore unlike men could "conquer" "without any commotion or disturbance." Many slum dwellers knew perfectly well that their living conditions were dreadful and welcomed the help provided by the settlements; but the assumption that filth meant cultural and moral depravity was often galling. Even the visionaries shared the colonial perspective, though they had less faith in individual action and more in state legislation. The McMillans ran their nursery from 8 : 00 a.m. to 6 : 00 p.m. and preferred to keep their children overnight when space permitted; they did not trust sending delicate children back into their homes, however much they may have missed their families. Nor did they trust mothers, who had to be taught principles of cleanliness, nutrition, and health.[26]

The colonial metaphor had powerful reverberations for middle-class women. Emigration to Canada or Australia meant adventure, freedom, and space for their brothers. Tied more closely to their families, women could find freedom by "emigrating" to the East End. As Octavia Hill pointed out in 1889,

> [T]here are comparatively few parents who do not recognize for their daughters the duty of sympathy and of rendering such service as other claims permit. With [this] different ideal of life, customs have altered in a marked manner; it used to be difficult for a girl to walk alone, and it was considered almost impossible for her to travel in omnibuses or third-class trains. The changes in custom with regard to such matters have opened out fresh possibilities of work.[27]

Charitable work gave women freedom to walk and move in areas that were previously forbidden. Neither teaching, nor nursing, nor even mission work permitted women so much spatial freedom. The streets of the slums, away from upper-class men's eyes, were theirs; no matter how much they might be teased by little boys or abused by drunks, they carried a kind of immunity along the streets of the drab slums they sought to uplift. Settlements, like the colleges, discouraged fashionable dress and pretentious manners; the artificialities of society could be dispensed with in order to reach out to the more "natural" poor.

At the same time, however, settlers worked to limit the freedom of the "natives," or to remove them from their environment. Clubs and other organizations were started to get children and adolescents off the streets and into a more salubrious atmosphere. All reformers were strong advocates of removing weak and disabled children entirely from their homes, lest they be destroyed by disease—and moral infection. Flora Lucy Freeman wrote a number of tales of "girl life," all portraying the many pitfalls a poor girl was likely to fall into if she did not secure a safe position as a domestic servant in the country.[28] The very environment that freed middle-

class women was considered too dangerous for children and liable
to poison adolescents that were not brought into the settlement's
clubs. Children were sent away to the country in the summer, orphans to training centers, and girls into domestic service, all to
get them at least temporarily out of the slums. Yet sooner or later
all had to return to their own homes and make their way among
members of their own social class. Reform of the slums meant
spatial freedom for the settlers, spatial confinement for the natives.

Middle-class women could safely colonize the slums because
they brought with them the structures and beliefs of their own
class, the educated upper-middle class. Neither the idealism nor
the self-confidence of a new generation of educated women could
be satisfied by the amateur philanthropy of their mothers. Settlements were a particularly appealing solution in both America and
England, for they promised public leadership and professional yet
womanly work. The loyalties of college women to their college
and friends were strengthened by a sense of being different from
their peers, of being better prepared to take up public responsibilities. The fellowship of college life could be broadened to reach out
to the poor, as Ethel Hurlbatt, principal of Bedford College, London, explained:

> To women the enjoyment of University life brought home a
> knowledge of the infinite power and force that lie in the idea
> of association . . . [of] fellowship with those associated with
> us in study, but differing from us in experience, in the object
> of their work, and in the destinies that await them. . . . If this
> fellowship were of value in a life of study, would it not be of
> infinite service in social work, in the efforts directed towards
> making society a better society, and especially in that particu-
> lar effort of Settlement work—to raise the standards of social
> work among the poor.[29]

College women brought to the settlements their traditions of
community life and professionalism. The settlements appealed
most to those colleges and schools that emphasized the womanly
virtues of public life. Of the four Oxbridge colleges, Newnham and
Lady Margaret Hall were the most active. Anne Jemima Clough
invited Mrs. Barnett to Newnham in 1886; her speech and the enthusiasm of two Newnhamites already working in the slums
launched the fund drive for starting the Women's University Settlement. Lady Margaret Hall contributed to both the WUS and its

own settlement in Lambeth, founded in 1897. The more overtly feminist and intellectual Girton and Somerville sent volunteers and made donations, but their involvement remained more perfunctory.[30] The leaders of Newnham and LMH hoped that their students would be educated to be better wives, mothers, and Christian women; Emily Davies, on the other hand, urged direct competition with men in all areas of education and training. Settlement houses attracted women who wished to help other women to fulfill themselves as women without competing directly with men.

For some twenty-five years settlements were seen as an exciting and worthwhile adventure, attracting some of the very best young people. In an autobiographical novel published in 1901, all of the most thoughtful Newnham students consider joining a favorite old girl who has started a small settlement in a London slum. Her vivacity and eager commitment to a life of action inspire each student to dream of following her path:

> The lovely animated face, with the big gray eyes, the laughing mouth, and the glorious crown of curly red-brown hair, had taken the quiet little student's beauty-loving heart by storm. Vi's talk too—what a new world it had led them into, away from their narrow, sheltered world of books and tennis, academic successes, and college gaities, to the bigger, wider world of men and women outside, with its grander outlook, its greater issues![31]

Vi's best friend, an heiress, finds peace and fulfillment in spartan living and patient work with children at the settlement, while another friend finds that contact with "the feeble and downtrodden" gives her the patience to continue living at home, helping her aging father. Elizabeth Wilson Grierson's *What the Other Children Do* (1912) sends two well-to-do girls to live with their Aunt Marion at a settlement for six weeks. The sisters are chastened by the poverty of children their own age, but inspired by their unmarried aunt's rich and meaningful work. Fiction obliquely revealed what many sensed, namely that the settlements were more effective in meeting the needs of educated single women than those of the slum dwellers.

The romanticism of fiction was not entirely untrue. Honnor Morten, after her nurse's training, opened a settlement in Hoxton with two friends from Bedford College. They reported living in a three-room flat in "a rather gloomy block of artizans' dwellings," where they offered general help to their neighbors. In order to minimize class distinctions they did all their own housework. When they received invitations to Christmas parties in the neighboring tenements, Morten could say, "We feel now we really do stand on the footing of friends and neighbours."[32] In an autobiographical study, she described the pleasure of being "[r]ight in the centre of life [where] I sit in my little room and wait. Walk up, Romance, walk up!" She had the satisfaction of finding that she was working at odds with the local church:

> Romance walked up first in the shape of the curate; I
> curtseyed to him and dusted a chair for him with my apron.
> But he looked suspiciously at the Botticelli and returned the
> soup-ticket to his waistcoat pocket. I told him I didn't go to
> church, and then somehow, I don't quite know how, I found
> myself explaining to him that God wasn't a man, but a Spirit,
> and ought to be spoken of as "it."[33]

Some time later they invited the curate to supper, but he was shocked to be offered Chianti and cigarettes. Morten, following the path of other settlers, was elected to the London School Board; she successfully brought school nurses to the poorer elementary schools and had baths installed in the schools for the retarded. But eager to push her belief in egalitarian Christianity further than was possible in any urban institution, Morten left Hoxton for Sussex, where she started the Tolstoi Settlement for physically handicapped London children.[34]

Many settlements began under the enthusiasm of an individual such as Honnor Morten, who actually lived alone for a year in Hoxton before convincing her Bedford College friends to join her. The Women's University Settlement was launched as a joint-colleges venture, but its first warden, Alice Grüner, had already been living in a London slum with a friend for several months. So few women had had any such experience that they were looked upon as important leaders. But this did not mean that the corporate ideal of school or college was lost; indeed, all of the settlements made a point of linking with an institution, such as a church or a school. Students or parishioners could volunteer to work in "their" settlement, as well as raise money for it. One of the most active groups was the Cheltenham Ladies' Guild of former students. When the Guild began in 1884 it was formed not only to keep old friends in touch with each other and the school, but also "for the sake of widening our sympathies, and strengthening our hands for work outside this circle [of old pupils]."[35] Four years later members voted unanimously to "undertake some work" in the Guild's "corporate capacity." They overwhelmingly agreed, against the wishes of Dorothea Beale, to start a settlement. An East End parish "of the better sort" was decided upon, and a nurse volunteered to head the settlement, working at her own expense.[36] The settlement opened in 1889, but its early years were exceptionally difficult. The first warden died in 1893 from diphtheria caused by faulty drains, and donations from Guild members were inadequate to meet the costs of new drains and the rent. Fortunately the Guild rose to the occasion. In time a new home was found and named "St. Hilda's East." In late 1899 an experienced resident of the settlement and active COS worker, Marion Bruce, became warden. She remained head of Cheltenham's settlement for thirty-two years, providing the necessary continuity and experience for its success.[37]

St. Hilda's East was fortunate in its longtime warden. Other settlements faced repeated difficulties between volunteers and the warden, or the warden and the settlement's executive committee. A little over a year after the WUS had begun, a group of committee members wrote Alice Grüner about "a widespread feeling amongst members of the Association that life at the Settlement is made so unnecessarily depressing and unhappy that they will not work there themselves nor ask their friends to do so. Some even, it is to be feared, prevent others from helping." They went on to accuse her of "neglecting ordinary conventional politeness," losing her temper, imputing wrong motives, and "insisting on compliance with your directions in unimportant details." Grüner replied in a long and bitter letter, arguing that "work among the more degraded poor is necessarily depressing to a beginner," that she had been forced to take up work that short-term volunteers had left undone lest the settlement lose all credibility, and that she denied all other allegations. She then handed in her resignation, which, after further skirmishes, was accepted.[38] Grüner herself was obviously very difficult to work with, asserting her superior knowledge on all occasions. But she was at least partially correct in her anger. In fourteen months the settlement had started sixteen different projects, undertaken by seventeen workers, of whom only two were in residence for the whole year (Grüner and her original

friend) and only two others for over three months. Most volunteers came for only three or four weeks.[39]

The WUS floundered through a series of interim wardens, then
settled upon M. A. Sewell, an active COS advocate and experienced member of the executive committee. She served for nearly
ten years, and in 1901 Helen Gladstone, the daughter of William
Gladstone, was asked to become head. Helen Gladstone had served
Newnham College as a vice-principal for over a decade when she
left in 1896 to take care of her father. She was doubtless brought
to the settlement by those who remembered her devoted work for
Newnham. She came with a famous family name but had had no
experience working with the poor or with volunteers. The settlement's weekly "at homes" flourished under her graceful aegis;
many in the neighborhood wished to meet the Grand Old Man's
daughter. But even the appointment of a vice-warden to do all the
administrative work did not stop a steady decline in morale and
the quality of work done by the regulars. A subcommittee held
special hearings to answer objections of both volunteer and paid
workers. The charges were twofold: "that the present warden re-
gards and treats poor people from a different point of view from
what we are accustomed to," and that "if the workers are not to
look to the head for help why work in a settlement at all?"[40]
Helen Gladstone had the misfortune of heading the most profes-
sionally oriented of all the settlements, with many experienced
workers deeply committed to casework studies. Her old-fashioned
manners and noblesse oblige were admired, but extremely difficult to work under. Courtesy and fame were not sufficient in the
professionalizing world of twentieth-century social work.

Difficult or inadequate leadership paled in comparison with the
problem of finding reliable volunteers. Year after year the annual
reports of the settlements call for more volunteers and more donations. Students were encouraged to get to know their settlement
by means of summer outings or vacation visits; if they knew specific individuals they would contribute more regularly. Schools all
tried to inculcate an interest in the poor by annual picnics or visits. At Wycombe Abbey girls were encouraged to exchange letters
with their newfound friends. Winifred Peck noticed that their
"less fortunate sisters" managed to have several birthdays in the
year, "a signal for the conscientious to send off sweets and rib-
bons."[41] Picnics appear to have been rather more trying for college
students, if one Westfield College student is correct:

On Whit Monday we always entertained a large party of factory girls. They were as much a mystery to us as we to them,
one asking me where the gentlemen were that we waited on.
We explained that there were none, but we were here to be
taught. "Who pays you?" "We pay to be taught to work!!!!"
"Where's your bloke, Miss?" "I haven't got a bloke." "Well! I'd
thought you'd had a bloke Miss—."[42]

Large parties organized at the settlement itself were less awkward
occasions; the visitors helped to serve tea and buns, while the
members could easily entertain themselves. After an initial flurry
of interest, few students or old girls did more than donate a small
sum annually. But zealous settlement workers still hoped for
closer links between their old school and the settlement and continually encouraged donors to visit and, if at all possible, stay for a
short time. Dame Colet House, run by the St. Paul's School Union
for Social Work, had a reduced residence fee for Paulinas.[43] After
World War I the Women's University Settlement and Talbot House
invited Girton and Newnham students to spend a week during
their Christmas vacation in South London to see a selection of
settlement activities.[44] Such plans helped to build stronger links
with donors, but even so the settlements depended most upon
their residents and a core of regular volunteers.

Volunteers came to the settlements for many of the same reasons as the paid workers—curiosity, religious commitment, idealism, boredom, desire for adventure, or self-education. Many had
become interested in the settlement through hearing about the
work from enthusiastic residents. Others volunteered because
they wanted to be involved in important work and to remain in
touch with their school or college friendship network. A young
volunteer was trained on the job; her first work was usually investigating families for the COS or befriending a young servant girl or
helping with the girls' club. If she survived these responsibilities, she was encouraged to make a greater commitment, either
through temporary residence or by running a club or class on her
own. Relatively few volunteers could live for long in a settlement,
but virtually all did try to spend some time in residence. This
worked well when a volunteer's stay coincided with a permanent
resident's vacation, but all too often the warden was left with either too full or too empty a house. Work was started by residents
staying only two or three months, and when they left no one
could replace them. A few, unaccustomed to regular working

hours, were more bother than they were worth. Alice Lucy Hodson mentions residents who did not get up in the morning if they had worked a long evening the night before; her head would serve them breakfast in bed to shame them into more professional behavior.[45]

The leaders of the women's settlements were determined to turn philanthropy into a paid profession.[46] Within a short time of their founding, the Women's University Settlement and the Lady Margaret Hall Settlement both offered one-year training courses, linked to the COS's School of Sociology. Although part-time volunteers remained essential (in most settlements they outnumbered residents two or three to one), the focus was upon professional training in social work. Women often appear to have chosen a specific settlement because of its course or its specialty (the handicapped, children, medical care, etc.) rather than its links with a particular college or school. For example, the WUS in 1901 had eighteen noncollege and seven college residents (three from Newnham, two from Lady Margaret Hall, and one each from Somerville and Girton). The cost of residence, board, and training was £60 per year, a sum out of reach for all but the upper levels of the middle class, though one Pfeiffer Fellowship was offered. But since a college education was not a prerequisite, £60 may have seemed cheap in comparison with training for high-school teaching. Presumably women without money for formal training sought informal training through the various church missions. Even after training, a resident paid £30 to £35 a year for room and board, or a guinea a week for less than a month.[47] The warden received a salary of about £50 per year, and department heads were sometimes paid a small stipend. Only after World War I and the takeover of many social services by the government were social workers regularly paid.

Nevertheless, fulltime settlers, paid or unpaid, saw themselves as experts on poverty and welfare. They became invested in particular methods of work and sometimes lost sight of the "neighborliness" that was supposed to be the hallmark of a settlement. The class condescension that had characterized nineteenth-century philanthropy was being replaced by an equally invidious distinction, professional expertise. Moreover, paid workers felt superior to and apart from the erratic volunteers and donors. Settlements that had begun as a model of community living gradually became divided into the committed and the uncommitted, both struggling against the sea of poverty.

Descriptions of the women who worked in the settlements veer between the idealizations in fiction and a defensively comic insistence that women with a cause are normal. Alice Lucy Hodson sketches a number of familiar characters, including the busybody, the mournful depressive, the nervous enthusiast, the comfortable humorist, and the long-suffering martyr who finishes everyone else's tasks. They all seem excessively devoted and amateurish; the enthusiast was always going off to Italy to recuperate and leaving her work for the martyr. But the settlements also attracted very talented women who were fine administrators and organizers. Hodson wrote a reverential description of her warden, in contrast to the comic treatment of her peers:

> To describe the Head of the Settlement would be quite impossible, for she has so many sides that no one person can really know her. Were it necessary, she could, I fancy, do all the work herself, for from trimming hats to attending to small plumbing jobs, nothing comes amiss to her. She does all the housekeeping, and writes many letters; she seems to be on most of the committees in the neighborhood, and yet she has time to make covers for the chairs and weed the garden; she is studious, too, and fond of research work. Above all, she is a saint—but that is a secret.[48]

The power of the head derived from her domestic virtues brought into wider service; these, in turn, made her an effective colonist.

Social workers, however, became known as devoted and high-minded women who were rather unattractive to the ordinary educated classes. Reginald Kennedy-Cox described his first encounter with a woman worker in a tone of amused condescension:

> She was dressed in a greasy tweed cycling costume, and was nursing a poor sick, very sick, mongrel pup. She was really indescribably grubby, but her merry intelligent eyes flashed up at intervals behind thick steel-rimmed spectacles. The poor pup was too sick for her to move, but she nodded to a broken chair, and told me to draw close up to the fire, and we talked. She really was a wonderful woman, and I felt an awful snob that I should be repelled by the grime of her person and surroundings.[49]

Kennedy-Cox, in spite of his initial impression, was that rare individual, a committed male volunteer willing to lead the boy's club ("work . . . which was quite unsuited to a woman"); in time he became warden of the London Dockland Settlement and a well-known expert on slum youth.

Life at the settlements followed a routine that was familiar to all residents of boarding schools and colleges. Brief morning prayers preceded breakfast and the assignment of duties. Residents were given a fair amount of freedom to find their own work, especially after their initial training; the work was much more flexible than teaching or secretarial work. Mornings were usually spent in district visiting for the local parish church or on COS casework. The midday meal was not normally a group meal, permitting workers to attend both morning and noontime meetings. Afternoons were spent in study, classes, and preparation. At about 4:00 a whole series of activities began for schoolchildren and part-timers from the surrounding factories. Dinner was at 6:00 or 7:00; most residents hoped to get in a hot bath and change of clothes beforehand, especially if they had been out visiting and had had to tramp around wet and dirty alleys in long skirts. One of the sure ways of distinguishing a regular worker from a casual volunteer was by her clothes; the volunteer always came down to the East End dressed in feathers, trailing gowns, and other finery. Such clothing pleased the factory girls but was impossible to keep clean and inhibited one's freedom in walking through the neighborhood. The evening was always the busiest time of the day; a vast array of clubs, societies, and classes was offered. Most residents helped with at least one girls' club as well as teaching classes in sewing or accounting or some other less practical subject. At 10:00 everything was locked up, and the residents returned home for a well-earned cup of cocoa. As Hodson explained, "Yes, the work is hard, and it has an uncomfortable and yet satisfactory way of increasing."[50] Most settlements insisted that each resident take a whole day's rest away from the house once a week, but overwork plagued the conscientious.

Settlement house work combined familiar structures from college with new public freedoms. On the one hand, traditional middle-class formalities were retained, such as dressing for dinner, attending the theater, and generally enjoying cultural privileges. Aside from Honnor Morten's Hoxton Settlement and one or two others, women still kept servants and many of the comforts of home. One woman who had been a servant for the WUS before World War I remembered her days were marked by "Twelve grates before breakfast."[51] Imitating college life, each woman had her own room, with a fire. Indeed, Hilda Cashmore, founder and first warden of the Bristol settlement, based the daily life of the residents upon her experience at Somerville. She insisted that "a certain degree of formality . . . secured individual freedom and provided cover, a protection at need, from intrusion."[52] Privacy, the hard-won privilege of single women, was firmly kept as a necessity. Familiar structures and ways of behaving within the home helped to offset the strain of working with the poor day after day.

On the other hand, at work and on the streets women found that they could imitate their neighbors with relative ease. Simplicity of dress, food, and manners, followed by virtually every serious resident, did not undermine the basic assumptions of professional single women. Dedicated to service, they held the showiness of their less high-minded contemporaries in contempt.[53] Even certain rules of gentility could be abandoned by the more daring, although disapproval was shown toward those who "went native." None of the poor wore a hat and gloves in the summer, and a few settlers gave them up gleefully. Mary Simmons of the Bermondsey Settlement described her pleasure in living in a former public house. She and the other residents

> revel[ed] in a picturesque lack of respectability, and a freedom in being out of doors without having dressed for the part which is to me so congenial that the other day, when Mrs. Lidgett [wife of the minister] looked at me in doubtful surprise as I came wandering round to the Settlement with neither hat nor gloves, nor so much as even the hallmark of a sunshade, I couldn't think what she was going to scold me for now.[54]

Twenty years later, between the wars, Muriel Lester—after weeks of worry—worked up enough courage to go down Regent Street in the West End without gloves. To her relief no one seemed to notice.[55] Only in the East End could settlers discard the unnecessary without loss of respectability. They were free to go about the streets less fully clad because everyone knew they were ladies; no matter what they did, their accent, posture, and behavior all marked them out as settlers.

Working as a settler was often a stepping-stone to local politics and indirect access to the shaping of laws in regard to women and children. Large numbers of settlers serving on local governing boards, as well as a multitude of charitable organizations, gained more direct power than was possible in the female spheres of education and nursing or sisterhoods. Within the settlements women kept their all-female base, but outside they entered the many expanding areas of government services, charitable work, and various pressure groups. While women may not have achieved as illustrious careers as their male counterparts (or American women), they successfully carved out an area of expertise that gained them respect and a voice in social legislation. Whatever might be the gains for the poor—the focus of the next section—single women involved in settlement work found scope for their talents, satisfaction for their ambitions, friendship among equals, and a cause greater than themselves.

Measuring Success

How successful were the settlements among the poor? It is almost impossible to give a realistic assessment. The annual reports of each settlement up to World War I speak of increasing numbers attending various clubs, classes, and societies; the work seemed to expand, forever lagging behind the needs of the community. This is hardly surprising, given the small number of workers and the large populations they were trying to reach. The Robert Browning Settlement in Walworth served a population of 121,939 in 1896, crowded into one square mile; at that time they had four full-time workers and about a dozen volunteers.[56] We have little evidence of who attended settlement-house events, but certainly the educational side was most popular with elementary school teachers and clerks rather than workingmen. In 1905 Toynbee Hall reported that of the 644 members of its various clubs, only 25, or 4 percent, lived in Whitechapel.[57] The Women's University Settlement had approximately 100 volunteers and 25 residents in 1901 for twelve committees; but most of its work was service for other organizations, such as Octavia Hill's rent collecting, the COS, district visiting for the church, savings collection, and school management.[58] Like the twentieth-century scouting movement, settlements attracted a small core of faithful members and a much larger population that floated in and out of its various clubs and activities. The majority of the neighborhood was unaffected or barely noticed the settlers. But for the few who did join a club or class, the experience could be very positive.[59] The poor of the cities had interests as varied as their so-called betters, and for a minority the settlements offered previously unavailable opportunities.

One of the most popular projects for a women's settlement was a club for working girls. Most girls had little incentive to take courses because further training would not lead to a better job, and responsibilities at home made it impossible to study. A club, however, could be appealing to a "better set," eager to meet their friends and have a good time without getting into trouble with their parents. Most clubs were connected with the Federation of Working Girls' Clubs or the London Girls' Club Union, and organizers received practical advice and assistance through their publications and experienced volunteers. Clubs were aimed at thirteen- to eighteen-year-olds, though the larger ones sometimes included a separate group for unmarried women between eighteen and twenty-five. The clubs, held either at the settlement or at a local school, were open four or five evenings a week from 8 : 00 to 10 : 00; they offered sewing, millinary, singing, musical drill, gymnastics, dancing, and occasionally lectures. Admission was a penny a week, with buns and cocoa a halfpenny apiece. Teenage girls who had worked all day in a factory were usually eager for exercise and excitement, so no club succeeded that did not include dancing. Early reports from most clubs apologize for the lack of direct religious instruction or for the emphasis upon pleasure, but experience soon showed how desperately girls needed some escape from their factory and home responsibilities.

Experienced club leaders always cautioned firm rules and a modicum of self-rule by the older girls. The right balance between firmness and friendliness was often hard for middle-class volunteers to achieve. A report from Nottingham tells of a desperate evening in which two girls quarreled over the use of a thimble and ended up fighting, while their friends called out the windows for the local boys to come in. A few boys entered through the basement windows and had to be threatened with arrest before they would leave and the girls would calm down.[60] On the other hand, many ladies expected a wholly alien standard of behavior from their protégées. The *Girls' Club Journal* repeatedly advised volunteers against patronizing the girls, warning that "Some of the Club worker's difficulties she makes for herself, by her want of judgement, her lack of tact."[61] Given the wide discrepancy between the needs of the girls as perceived by the organizers and as perceived by the girls, it is no wonder that the most successful clubs tended to be led by a charismatic and devoted leader or else conducted through a process of self-selection that eliminated all but the quietest and most submissive members.

In the early 1890s Emmeline Pethick and Mary Neal broke away from the West London Mission and formed a small settlement of their own; most of their time was spent with a girls' club they named the "Espérance Club." At first they offered all of the usual club activities, hoping to give the hard-worked girls as much happiness as possible during their two hours at the club. But they soon found that they "could not close the doors on the world outside."

> The conditions, not only of the home, but of the factory or workshop had to be taken into account. It became our business to study the industrial question as it affected the girls' employments, the hours, the wages, and the conditions. And we had also to give them a conscious part to take in the battle that is being fought for the workers, and will not be won until it is loyally fought by the workers as well.[62]

Neal and Pethick encouraged their club members to report legitimate grievances to the proper authorities, and they gave regular lectures on basic economics and industrial conditions. They also had occasional debates with a boys' club, enabling the girls to discuss trade-union issues with the more experienced boys. Many of the girls who worked in the West End dress trade suffered from periods of overemployment and underemployment. In 1897 the club decided to open a model workroom, hiring girls forty-five hours a week at a minimum wage of fifteen shillings. Starting with five girls, they employed twenty by the end of the first year.[63] While Pethick looked after the economic and industrial education of the club members, Neal taught them English folk songs and dances.[64] The long-term success of the Espérance Club was due in large measure to the hard work and foresight of its two founders, who were unusually sensitive to the varied needs of the members. Both women worked within the context of the girls' club movement—they felt that the club should provide a home atmosphere for girls from overcrowded slums and should guide them in "the realisation of their womanhood."[65] But they were also sensitive to the wider issues of the times, and unlike many leaders, recognized the importance of training girls in "the social organisation of women," including trade unionism, the cooperative movement, and club life itself.

The problem of providing both instruction and relaxation was a difficult one not only at the clubs, but also at the mothers' meetings. The latter were popular because they gave overworked women one of their few opportunities to get out of the house. The most zealous settlement workers offered classes in baby care, nutrition, housewifery, and other skills they thought the neighborhood mothers needed. Some of these classes were frankly an effort to raise the standards of the race at a time when many members of the ruling class feared the decline of the English through poor mothering.[66] But more successful among the women themselves were the less ambitious affairs, usually including a short, cheery talk, the singing of hymns, and tea. The Robert Browning Settlement in Southwark had "Pleasant Tuesday Afternoons" for years following this formula. The PTAs, as they were known, became so popular that membership had to be limited to one thousand; average attendance was six hundred. Although both politics and religion were downplayed, in times of stress important issues were raised and acted upon. During the depression of 1902–4 the head of the Women's Section of the settlement suggested to the PTA women that they join with the women of Poplar and send a deputation to the queen, requesting work for their unemployed husbands. The London Trades Council and the Poplar Trades' and Labour Representation Committee organized the march of over three thousand women on 6 November 1902, carrying banners reading "Bread for Our Children" and "Work for Our Men." Browning Hall was in charge of the Southwark contingent, and most of its marchers were PTA members.[67] Less colorful, but no less important, were the small chapters of the Women's Co-operative Guild organized by different settlements. The Guild's emphasis upon self-education and self-government gave members their first opportunity to learn and practice the politics of their trade-union husbands.[68]

The settlements were most effective when they provided services the state could not supply; indeed, they paved the way for a state system of social services both in the training of social workers and in special services for the handicapped and for children. The Passmore Edwards Settlement, under the leadership of Mrs. Humphry Ward, set up a model school for the physically handicapped, including meals, physical therapy, and regular course work. The excellent results of the school were used to pressure the London County Council to establish similar schools rather than lumping the physically handicapped with the mentally handicapped and retarded.[69] Margaret McMillan's outdoor kindergarten and summer camp pioneered the health care of young children; her ideas on open schools for children under seven are now widely accepted.[70] Settlement workers, like an earlier generation of workhouse visitors, attempted to soften the harshness of the board schools. The severe discipline necessary to maintain order in classes of seventy children left little room for the imagination, much less for free play. The establishment of afternoon play groups at the settlements coincided with the efforts of the English Folk Dance and Song Society to introduce traditional English songs and dances into the schools. The society made ready converts among settlement women anxious to find an attractive alternative to the street games and bullying of slum children. "Sister Grace" Kimmins at the Bermondsey Settlement founded the Guild of Play to teach children under ten folk dances, songs, and medieval plays. The very oddity of the Guild's customs attracted children, who happily dressed up in quaint caps and aprons, danced around a Maypole, and crowned a May queen each year. Kimmins's insistence upon the importance of developing the imagination of each child was in direct opposition to the grim board schools in which the children spent their days.[71]

Grace Kimmins, however, was not content to provide only one alternative to the monotony of slum life. Only an unusual or very determined leader could gather together a group of disabled children and adults for weekly meetings under the title "Guild of the Brave Poor Things," with the motto "Happy in My Lot."[72] Kimmins started with weekly meetings but worked tirelessly to raise money to build an entirely new environment for crippled children. She opened the Heritage Craft Schools and Hospitals for Cripples at Chailey in Sussex in 1903.[73] Just as the McMillan sisters felt that the ordinary school hours were not long enough, Kimmins believed that her children could never be trained to their full capacity if they were not given a separate school. Ironically the upperclass public school was adopted by middle-class women as a solution to the evils of the slum. Just as young boys were sent away to boarding school, so too did reformers believe in sending young cripples away before they had been contaminated by their environment.

Obviously only the most disabled could be sent away permanently. But one of the most popular projects of the settlements
was the Children's Country Holiday Fund.[74] Middle- and upper-
class volunteers used their contacts in the country to find families who would take slum children for two weeks in the summer.
Slum families were encouraged to save during the year to help pay
for sending their neediest child on a holiday. The fund was always
inundated with more requests than could possibly be met. An experienced volunteer was put in charge of vetting the applications.
She soon learned to exclude bed wetters and those with severe
adenoidal problems, lice, or fleas; indeed, a fairly rigorous standard of cleanliness was insisted upon.[75] Settlers felt that such requirements encouraged better personal habits among families, but
some children must have been bitterly disappointed year after year.

Camps were an increasingly important part of settlement life,
teaching adolescents the benefits of corporate life as well as removing them to a more "natural" environment; like so many turn
of the century reformers, the settlers were firmly convinced of the
value of country life over the city. Even as freedom within the city
was being curbed, free access to the country was encouraged. Some
children were terrified by silence or by their first experience seeing birds, cows, and other animals out of cages. Lylie Valentine remembered all her life a week's camping trip at Mill Hill School
right after World War I:

> We went out to parties and for lovely country walks. Mill Hill
> boys were famous for cricket, so a match was arranged be-
> tween some Mill Hill boys and the Cockney Kids, including
> Doris and helpers. We won, and were so proud! It took me
> years to realise that they had let us win. Oh, that was a lovely
> holiday. We still talk about it and get a thrill.[76]

But holidays were brief, and the children had to return to crowded
homes and inadequate food. Indeed, nothing underscored the
enormous gap between the settlers and the slum dwellers more
than these brief interludes in the country. The women workers,
whenever they felt exhausted by slum life, could take a short
holiday in the country. But families had to save all year to raise
enough money for a week or two for their children; mothers were
lucky if they got a day at the seaside through the settlement. For
the more farsighted, conditions had to be changed at their root.

The search for more effective methods of combating poverty led the settlements to try contradictory solutions. In 1902 the WUS firmly informed its donors to stop donating old clothes because "It has not much faith in that form of charity which consists in giving away clothes, any more than it advocates giving away meals, and the result of this uncompromising attitude is an accumulating store of unwanted garments, and the temptation to inexperienced workers—and even to experienced ones—to give away what is in hand if only for the sake of making room for new arrivals."[77] At the same time Clara Grant, headmistress of a board school, started an "Old Clo' and Work Fund," requesting her friends to send her all the old clothes they could. The Fern Street School Settlement began in her small flat soon after she had decided to move into the neighborhood of her school in order to know the parents of her pupils better. Her unassuming settlement concentrated on meeting the immediate needs of the community; she served children's breakfasts, a friend ran a clinic, and a small food cooperative was started, in addition to the jumble sales. Everything was made use of, down to bundles of rubbish collected for kindling. In addition to such varied practical assistance, Grant started distributing "farthing bundles" on Saturday mornings to children below a certain height. Each child passed under an arch inscribed "Enter now, ye children small, / None can come who are too tall."[78] She or he paid a farthing for a bundle of miscellaneous goods that could not be sold separately, usually containing some kind of toy, cheap candy, yarn, bits of cloth, and other oddments. Grant's particular success was to offer a more modern version of charity with no attempt at reform or religion. She herself as a young schoolteacher had found "wonderous inspiration" at Toynbee Hall, where "Teachers, clerks, artisans, craving for themselves and (with the best of them) for their fellows, something nobler than the elementary school had given them, all met in simple, natural friendliness those who had enjoyed what we had missed."[79] Yet Grant did not attempt to provide similar opportunities for her neighbors, but rather met their more pressing daily needs. In this sense she ran not a true settlement house, but rather a cross between a mission and a relief center.

Although the women's settlements concentrated on providing goods and services that the state neglected, many workers also pressured the government to take over and regulate their work. After 1894, when the financial qualifications were removed, educated women and working-class men began to run more fre-

quently for the board of guardians. In 1885 there had been only
fifty women guardians; in 1895 there were eight hundred; and in
1905, twelve hundred.[80] Women also ran for school boards in increasing numbers, and in 1907, when they gained the right to
stand for local councils, many ran. The thankless task of attending endless meetings, preparing reports, and struggling for funds
fell upon many of the leaders of the settlement movement. Men
from both the left and the right tended to ignore women's issues or
to assume they would solve themselves as soon as family men
were taken care of; but when experienced women settlers spoke
out, men were forced to recognize the importance of meeting the
separate needs of women and children.

Settlement workers always emphasized their victories. But a
note of depression does creep in at times. In a report to Newnham
in 1899 two residents of the WUS admitted, "It is only by not letting our thoughts dwell on the absence of any immediate result of
work that we can go on visiting, week after week, the same home,
always finding it in the same condition of dirt and neglect and
wretchedness."[81] Constance Maynard gave up Bible reading to a
group of factory girls after only a few visits. On one occasion a girl
"called out loudly 'Cock a doodle doo!' & the whole long room
went off into shrieks of laughter." Maynard could find no way to
stop them, and so she quit. She was shocked by their rudeness and
thereafter confined her slum visiting to an occasional chat with
an elderly bona fide Christian.[82] Similar failures by settlement
workers were glossed over, so that reports only occasionally reveal
that a class enrolled too few or that a club faltered because of patronizing leadership. But the frequency with which club leaders
warned against condescension and rudeness and the strident tone
of many annual reports indicate strains beneath the optimistic
busyness of so many outings, clubs, and societies.

The more thoughtful slum workers were much less confident
about their ability to improve the lives of those around them or,
more important, to influence the local government to change its
punitive policies in regard to children or women. Some opposition
from male-dominated institutions, such as the poor law board or
parish clergy, could be exhilarating, reinforcing the settlers' belief
that they were pioneering more humane treatment of the poor.
But self-doubt, combined with opposition from those one was trying to help, could be devastating. Margaret McMillan wrote poignantly of the despair that threatened to overwhelm her sister

when no one seemed to want to prevent unnecessary illness in children:

> This is the place of the deep ford. Very deep and steep it is, the soft black yielding mass under the black waters of Poverty. At every step one goes down and down. At first it looked as if service would be joy. But it was not so. Real service is, in the beginning, and to the end, courage in going *down* and not turning back. . . . First in darkness and poverty and pain—yes, even in disgrace, for the pioneer cannot always equip himself well. He may have to bear reproach—just reproach—to despise the shame. The ford has *not* a good bottom—it has no bottom at all—the waters rise and rise.[83]

In the slums, McMillan implied, even the most confident and far-sighted lost their way, feeling that they and their project had no future. Muriel Lester found that she wept with fear the night Kingsley Hall opened in 1915; as a pacifist she knew she could expect little from her neighbors.[84] The sheer immensity of the work to be done, the indifference of public officials, and the animosity of local residents could make the life of a settler seem like an endless struggle. Even the most confident could not be sure that her vision was true, that progress could be made, and "that things get done somehow without trouble or suffering."[85]

Settlements by their very nature included a number of irreconcilable dilemmas. A major paradox was unmarried middle-class women advising working-class and poor wives and mothers how best to run their homes. Settlement workers were enthusiastic upholders of the home and its virtues and always worked to strengthen family ties. Yet they were walking evidence of the opposite; as independent, educated women they lived apart from their families and did not have immediate family cares. They—not mothers—advised on baby care, infant feeding, and the intricacies of raising children, though they had never had children of their own or brought them up on a limited and perhaps irregular income. Even as they advocated the strengthening of the family, they were fleeing their own. Some of the more realistic workers, such as Emmeline Pethick, simply admitted that the settlement or club provided an alternative to the overcrowded home and streets. Others insisted that their club work encouraged girls in home skills and discouraged them from breaking their family ties. In all cases middle-class values and definitions were enforced.

Male leaders, unhappy at the youthful, celibate image of the settlement worker, called for married couples from the educated classes to come and live in the slums.[86] Few, however, were willing to risk bringing up children there, where they might catch infectious diseases and a Cockney accent. As long as settlements brought enthusiastic young idealists into the slums they could not help but be artificial encampments, temporarily attracting by their very strangeness.

The age and unmarried state of most settlement workers could be an advantage in some situations, such as club work. Based upon their own school experience, women were convinced of the moral and social importance of developing a sense of communal obligation—of esprit de corps—among girls of all classes. Indirectly this would prepare them for suffrage and lead them to take a greater interest in political and economic affairs. It was universally agreed that the same things that made it difficult to develop a sense of wider obligations among middle-class girls held true for working-class girls. Family responsibilities, low self-image, and a general downgrading of women's loyalties conspired to make girls and women less interested in supporting each other and their community.[87] But working girls already often had a strong code of group loyalty that clashed with the definition of club leaders. Emmeline Pethick admitted,

> It is a distressing fact that a girl will sometimes deliberately throw herself away, and tread in the hard way of the transgressors, because her friend has chosen to walk in that path. If she sticks to her she may save her, if she forsakes her she is sure her friend will go altogether to the bad. The argument that she may lose her own soul in a bootless attempt has no weight with her. . . . The working girl has not yet realized the supreme importance of getting her own soul saved![88]

A worker at a religious settlement reminded her readers that the roughest girls were often the most "wonderfully true to their girl friends. . . . They will hold together, and defend one another to the last gasp, unlike the generality of women-kind, who are not famed for being true to each other."[89] Yet even when recognizing this loyalty, many club leaders wished to supplant it with virtues more in line with their own middle-class values. They found it difficult to build upon the working girls' group identity and to strengthen it because by and large they wanted to foster an identity with the girls' upper-class "betters." Valiant efforts were therefore made to wean girls away from "bad company" and to separate the well-behaved club girls from the rough outsiders. In the words of Maude Stanley, a leader in the girls' club movement, "We have not wished to take girls out of their class, but we have wished to see them ennoble the class to which they belong."[90]

It was all too easy to glorify one's uphill battle in civilizing the poor. Despite the repeated exhortations of Canon Barnett, Hill, and others, the poor seemed like an alien race, and not "just like you and me." Alice Lucy Hodson's description of her settlement house head as capable of civilizing a colony is typical of settlers who saw themselves as outposts or colonists amid a sea of raw natives. As late as 1915 a leading settlement worker could describe the movement as having a "peculiar influence" upon the neighborhood,

> Its workers are not uniformed; they go about as ordinary human beings, but the neighbourhood is quick to recognise the mysterious power given by educational and inheritance of education, and to do it homage. It means a great deal when our women call us 'ladies,' and in that word they express their sense of this power given to us by our happier growth. Because of this power they turn to us with a touching faith that we shall never be mean, or ungenerous or fail in knowledge or explanation. Because we live among them they regard us as of special treasure to be guarded and made much of. . . . Of course all this deference is hard to bear until one realises that it is just one form of the respect of the young to the old, of the pupil to the teacher. We are practically, older souls and therefore people turn to us with confidence and trust, and believe that we will understand their troubles.[91]

It is hard to imagine the cloistered products of Newnham and Lady Margaret Hall as "older souls" amid the grim realities of a London slum. Such romanticizing only underscores the enormous gap between the settlement and its neighborhood. The temptation to do good *for* others in one's own way and then to regret the lack of response was inevitable.

A more concrete difficulty that many older settlement workers were unwilling to face was the limitations of volunteerism. Very few middle-class women were able or willing to devote a lifetime to full-time settlement work without pay. Yet since so many accepted part-time voluntary work, social work remained underpaid and undeveloped as a profession. In 1896 the *Englishwomen's Yearbook* advised,

The woman who has means and leisure, even if she has but a competency of 80*l.* to 100*l.* a year, can choose her work. The Settlements, varying in character, offer perhaps the most attractive prospect for the majority. Congenial occupation, congenial companionship, reasonable comfort may be secured by the payment of 1*l.* weekly.[92]

A woman with an independent income of £80 to £100 was, indeed, free to choose her life-style, and congenial though the settlements might be, few lived there long except the paid staff. Sometimes a retired teacher or widow with a small pension could be a welcome addition to a youthful settlement, but each woman had to pay her way.[93] The WUS in 1912 launched an appeal through *The Times* for donations for "the continued payment of moderate salaries to certain heads of departments . . . to maintain a high standard of work and to train and use effectively the considerable amount of voluntary help which is forthcoming."[94] The salaries were indeed moderate, but so too were the numbers of professionals. Each year the WUS graduated some ten or twelve students from its School of Sociology into a world that offered few paid jobs. Like teaching and secretarial work, social work was overcrowded, with volunteers competing directly with professionals. Even though all serious social workers recognized the need for trained and paid professionals, the money was not forthcoming from donors, and the government had not yet taken up the work done by voluntary agencies. Before the state took over, settlers, as well as countless other "professional volunteers" served an important role in slum communities, providing services that were no longer done by traditional female networks. This intermediary stage concealed the true costs of social welfare, so that after reform legislation was passed, both local councils and the central government were shocked to find how expensive, and how widely used, their services were.

Sooner or later most thoughtful settlement workers were brought face to face with the incongruity of teaching folk dancing and Shakespeare to underemployed and hungry Londoners. Personal friendship was obviously an inadequate, or incomplete, solution to social inequities of such far-reaching scope as Charles

Booth's study of London revealed. If one-third of the population of the world's richest city lived at or below the poverty line, no individual organization could possibly cope with the situation.[95] Settlement houses, like the COS, had an investment in their own methods of approaching the poor; major government changes might make them obsolete. By 1906, when the Liberal government passed a series of bills extending the government's responsibilities for education, old-age pensions, and social services, the COS and several settlements opposed the measures vigorously, while some settlements and leading charitable organizations campaigned for such changes.[96] By 1910 the more political women settlers were turning to suffrage, arguing that they could not go on with their social work until they had a voice in Parliament. As an active suffragist and head of the Birmingham Women's Settlement, Cecile Matheson argued, "As a class social workers probably feel their un-enfranchised position more keenly than any body of women, for social workers have all the instincts of reformers, and to such political helplessness must ever be galling."[97] A new generation of workers could not easily choose between Clara Grant's simple charity and Octavia Hill's COS methods as solutions for the widespread hunger and ill health that they saw among the women and children of their neighborhoods. A political solution came to seem essential.

During the years before World War I numerous organizations studied the working and living conditions of London's working-class women. The Fabian Women's Group, founded in 1908, systematically investigated how wives and mothers spent the limited income they received from their husbands; the results, published in *Round about a Pound a Week*, conclusively proved that mothers could not feed, clothe, and house their families adequately on so small an income.[98] Studies by the Fabian Women's Group, the Women's Industrial Council, and the Women's Labour League, among many others, published detailed statistical reports of the pay, hours of work, and working conditions of factory girls, domestic servants, and shop clerks. By World War I the socialist argument for a wholesale change in the tax structure and in government services was widely known among the educated classes. These organizations, with their roots in the growing Labour party, had a profound impact upon legislative social reform. But they were theorists, not institution builders. None of their investigators lived or worked in the slums for any length of time, nor did they have much contact with the settlements, unless individual settlers were themselves socialists or Labour party members. Cooperation between settlements and political groups remained informal.[99] When a woman settler was a member of the local school board or poor law board, she brought her particular political beliefs to bear on such issues as school meals or outdoor relief; sometimes she agreed with the socialists, and sometimes with the COS.

The settlers were virtually all single women who were only peripherally active in sexually mixed political and social organizations. They had entered social work to help women and children and in many cases had pioneered child welfare, schools for the handicapped, and services for mothers. Their political activities were directly related to specific, local needs. The expansion of government services, which many considered necessary, left settlers in a difficult position, for they were becoming volunteers working for the state and its agencies. This had advantages if the council was cooperative and progressive, as Margaret McMillan found when she began her open-air nursery in Deptford.[100] In such cases, reforms could be institutionalized and live beyond a single reformer or experiment. But working hand in hand with a government agency could also mean more bureaucratic work and less personal contact with the poor. When the ideas of women settlers were accepted by the state, moreover, the women were given subordinate positions.[101] They were left to prepare the casework, run the centers, staff the offices, and do all the mundane tasks they had always taken on—but policy matters were largely controlled by men. Their failure to cement connections with the more politically oriented women's groups, and the failure of these groups to exploit the direct experience of the settlers, forced the settlement houses into the very position they had despised, as representatives of the state. The connections middle-class settlement workers had made with working-class girls and mothers shifted gradually from Victorian condescension to bureaucratic impersonality.

Settlement work was largely a thankless round of guilds, clubs, classes, and meetings. Yet it was also the testing ground for a new women's profession, giving many idealistic middle-class women new freedom and new opportunities. Werner Picht, in his thorough analysis of English settlements, declared that ordinary, decent women and men were being asked to take up work more suited to Franciscans.[102] But the settlements did attract a few saints, utterly self-forgetting rather than self-sacrificing. These rare and remarkable individuals had a more attractive vision of a better society than any hearty "pleasant afternoons" or charitable work. The atypical could be the most effective reformers, winning over both the poor and the powerful, as did the McMillans and Eleanor Rathbone.[103] The pacifists Muriel and Doris Lester are now virtually forgotten, but during the interwar years they revitalized the settlement movement in Bow. After ten years of voluntary work in the East End, in 1915 they started Kingsley Hall.[104] Doris pioneered kindergartens and outdoor schools for sickly children as well as organizing play groups, baby clinics, and other services for children. Her sister was the ideological leader of Kingsley Hall. As a member of the Poplar Council, she supported George Lansbury's struggle against increasing borough rates and cutting the school milk allowance. In 1928 she joined the "Brethren of the Common Table," in which she pledged to give back to the people all she had after meeting her necessities.[105] During all of these years she worked for the pacifist Fellowship of Reconciliation, hoping to avert another world war. Every resident at Kingsley House (it was sexually mixed—another innovation) during the interwar years agreed to the communal sharing of all income, housework, and responsibilities. Such idealism was rewarded by placing the seven or eight residents on call twenty-four hours of the day, with virtually no quiet or privacy outside their small chapel.[106] When Gandhi visited London in 1931, he insisted upon staying at Kingsley Hall rather than in a hotel. Muriel's Christian communism attracted many who could not necessarily live up to her ideals but who recognized her vision as one that illuminated their lives.[107]

The retirement and death of the Lester sisters left Kingsley Hall adrift, and like many earlier settlements, it has closed. But the settlement vision has not been entirely lost as social work has become a paid professional job. Personal knowledge of the community, its culture, and its leaders is considered essential for effective community work. Islington, for example, has moved its social workers out of the large office block of the council and into small rented houses dotted across the borough. Every social worker can walk around her or his neighborhood, staying in direct touch with those to be helped. The personal, individual contact is emphasized, even though the social workers return to their own homes after work. Nor has the role of middle-class women in social work

changed significantly since idealistic college students first discussed joining their brothers in the East End. The profession is
still underpaid and of low status, attracting mainly women of religious or humanitarian beliefs. Although the English women's
settlements never made the same impact upon society as their
American counterparts, they did open another vocation for educated women. They also demonstrated in countless practical ways
the viability of social reform. The better care of the mentally and
physically handicapped, the creation of summer camps and open-
air schools, neighborhood health clinics, job registries, and teenage clubs all owe their initiation to women working in and beside
the settlements. Whatever may have been the class limitations of
this generation of women, working during the years 1880–1920,
they were extraordinarily successful in laying the foundations for
effective social welfare. While the men theorized, the women
proved it could work.

7

Male Space and Women's Bodies: The Suffragette Movement

By the early years of the twentieth century middle-class single women could look back upon nearly half a century of agitation for better jobs, higher pay, and greater personal freedom. They had achieved much—the women's colleges were thriving, new high schools and boarding schools were opening, the contribution of women to public health and welfare was widely recognized as essential. But the press continued to mock the women's movement, diminishing it—as in more recent accusations of bra burning—to a demand among fast young ladies for a latchkey, that symbol of independence automatically given to their brothers. The family still weighed heavily upon single women, impressing individuals with the priority of family needs over personal development. The numbers of women who had gained independence and an adequate income were small.[1] Women had made little progress against political and economic inequalities. They were consistently paid one-third to two-thirds less than men for equivalent work, were often barred from employment if they married, and were generally discouraged from pursuing any career into the upper levels of management. Indeed, they had no voice whatever in such male preserves as the law, banking, commerce, and industry, even though they were often directly affected by the policies emanating from such powerful institutions. An increasingly complex industrial society needed the work of trained women but had successfully kept them from the centers of power.

The lack of the vote symbolized women's secondary status. The years immediately preceding World War I became the focus of the most passionate and concerted feminist attack upon male privilege; women created and sustained their first and most militant mass movement. The campaign for suffrage was almost as old as the women's movement; by the early years of the twentieth century women could vote in the municipal elections and hold elected seats on school boards and poor law boards. But these privileges only emphasized their unequal status. If women could so effectively hold positions of authority over children and the poor, then surely they could be responsible voters, to be granted suffrage on the same terms as men. The vote would bring women to the center of power and place them in a position to change the legal disabilities under which they suffered.

Middle-class leaders of the suffrage campaign during the nineteenth century had pursued a policy of regularly presenting private members' bills to the House of Commons from 1866, when John Stuart Mill had made the first presentation. But such methods had met with massive defeat in 1884, and for some twenty years afterward suffrage efforts were concentrated on low-key educational work among educated women, with an occasional attempt at breaching Parliament.[2] Suffrage was certainly alive and well among the more advanced women's circles, but all too few women seemed to recognize its importance.[3] These groups of women, however, were organizationally well prepared for the suffrage struggle when it began to mushroom; the long years of parliamentary maneuvering, party politics, and educational work laid invaluable groundwork. Despite almost universal hostility from the press, between 1906 and 1914 thousands of women converted to suffrage and pledged their time, money, and energy to its enactment.

Suffrage became the foremost women's issue, attracting countless new converts among apolitical women as well as focusing the work of many who had been active in a variety of other causes. The studies of poverty by socialist feminists were easily integrated into the demand for suffrage, as were the concerns of settlement workers. Charlotte Despard, for example, had been active as a settler, a member of the Lambeth poor law board, and a manager of two elementary schools in Wandsworth. She turned naturally first to the Independent Labour party and then to the Women's Social and Political Union as political organizations.[4] She had worked her way leftward through personal experience combined with a relentless hatred of injustice. Other women activists came from radical families that had long been associated with reforms, sometimes going back to the campaign against the Contagious Diseases Acts.[5] Millicent Fawcett, the leader of the nonmilitant suffragists, had for decades been fighting for suffrage as well as for educational and legal reforms; the umbrella organization she led, the National Union of Women's Suffrage Societies, welcomed both the experienced and the inexperienced. A woman could work locally or nationally, in a broad-based or a single-issue organization, as a full-time activist or as a silent partner.

Suffrage touched a responsive chord in so many middle-class women because they had been stirred by accounts of the sufferings of poor working women, the unequal legal position of wives and mothers, and the horrors of prostitution.[6] For each woman who had been able to work in a settlement house, there were hundreds who had been constrained from playing an active role in reform. Now they were given a concrete task—helping win the vote—that would lead to more far-reaching improvements. As Emmeline Pethick-Lawrence reminded her audiences, they were fighting for "Not the Vote only, but what the Vote means—the moral, the mental, economic, the spiritual enfranchisement of Womanhood; the release of women, the repairing, the rebuilding of that great temple of womanhood, which has been so ruined and defaced."[7] Victorian women had long claimed spiritual leadership—now they were insisting upon the centrality of this leadership, linked to legal, economic, and educational demands.

The sheer variety and scope of women's organizations devoted to suffrage, and ultimately larger social reforms, during the years preceding the war made it possible for an educated woman, married or unmarried, to find a group that met her needs. For example, the Actresses' Franchise League taught elocution to fledgling local leaders and put on plays and readings at suffrage meetings.[8] During the summers of 1908 and 1909 the Women's Freedom League sent a caravan of women through small towns, spreading the suffrage gospel.[9] The National Union of Women's Suffrage Societies (NUWSS) not only continued its policies of pressuring Parliament and its Liberal party friends, but it also staged marches, fund-raising bazaars, membership drives, and countless educational meetings. The most militant organization from the beginning was the Women's Social and Political Union (WSPU), which caught the imagination of a new generation of idealistic and impatient women. Its engagement in illegal and semilegal actions helped to publicize suffrage and contributed to the growth of the many different suffrage organizations. The reformist suffragists and the militant suffragettes both helped and hindered each other. Militancy politicized thousands of women, setting a new standard of moral and political commitment; but at the same time, it closed off the flexibility that was so necessary for parliamentary negotiations. Always a minority—few of the women discussed in the previous chapters became militants, though most supported suffrage—the WSPU is a study in extremes, in direct contrast to the moderation of the previous half-century.

The first public act of the WSPU set a pattern followed thereafter with increasing militancy. On 13 October 1905 Christabel Pankhurst and Annie Kenney attended a Liberal rally at the Free Trade Hall, Manchester, to ask Sir Edward Grey if the Liberal party would support a bill enfranchising women. He refused to answer their question, and they refused to leave until he did so. They were arrested and briefly imprisoned. The ensuing publicity, largely unfavorable, brought new recruits and an enthusiasm for women's suffrage that had never been seen before. Militancy was born. Christabel's policy was twofold: she repudiated the traditional method of introducing private members' bills and insisted upon attacking the government directly, demanding the acceptance of suffrage as party policy. Second, she exploited the free publicity created by committing acts that would lead to imprisonment and temporary martyrdom. As Andrew Rosen has said, the pattern was never varied until the outbreak of World War I: women openly courted arrest by committing acts of increasing violence against property, were jailed, and through passive resistance— hunger striking and forcible feeding—were made martyrs to the cause of "Votes for Women."[10] Their martyrdom brought more recruits, publicity, and funding. The Pankhursts' Women's Social and Political Union grew rapidly; the time had clearly come to present the women's political cause before the public with methods that had never previously been exploited by women.[11]

The militant suffrage campaign was a radical break with the Victorian women's movement, yet it was also its culmination. Victorian women had been trained for a life of serving others, of sacrificing self. The first generation of independent women had emphasized the importance of taking woman's spirituality into the public sphere. Religion had often provided the rationale for many of the causes discussed in the previous chapters. The military model, so readily called upon by leaders in nursing and schools, gave an internal discipline and sanction for difficult decisions. Those who had pursued careers as teachers or nurses or social workers had often found their reward in the pleasure of working with trusted friends; the pioneers had built new institutions that sent out generation after generation of trained women to take

their places in the ranks of working women. By the Edwardian period educated women were well accustomed to working together
and were ready for the greater commitment of a campaign. The
WSPU built upon this foundation of religious belief, military discipline, and the work community, but it tapped something deeper
—an extraordinary idealism that found its fullest expression in
the utter sacrifice of self for the cause. The fierce loyalty and
strength of the movement sprang from a spiritual self-confidence
that unleashed enormous energies not only for the vote, but also
for a total reconsideration of the role of women in society. Dr.
Mary Gordon, writing of Lady Constance Lytton's sacrifice to the
cause, argued,

> We do not know how it sprang into life; no one explanation
> is entirely satisfactory, certainly not the theory that it was the
> work of 'leaders.' It began all over the country, even in silent
> lonely places. It was a spiritual movement and had fire—not
> form. The Women's Social and Political Union leapt into being
> like a flame. It released vast stores of unconscious energy, just
> as the war did. It cohered fiercely, ignoring thinking, feeling
> and good order. It was not premeditated nor controllable—*it
> happened* at the bidding of the unconscious. It swept where it
> listed, and when its work was done it died down and out. . . .
> It always left behind a rebirth and a new situation. Such spiri-
> tual upheavals are always irrational, and irrational human
> types are swept into them as high priests. Con was seized and
> used. She was both flame and burnt offering.[12]

The fire of social change scorched, even consumed many, but no
independent woman was left untouched.

Underlying the suffrage campaign was an insistence upon radically changing the spiritual relationship both between women and
men and between women and society. The WSPU has been called
conservative because its leaders did not directly attack the class
and economic structure of society, and they presented what was
seen as an essentially Victorian sexual ideology. At a time when
class and sex were both being subverted, the WSPU's indifference
seems to place it in a nineteenth-century backwater, leaving its
incredible growth and militancy to such explanations as yellow-
press publicity or millenarianism or Dr. Mary Gordon's unconscious female psyche.[13] A closer consideration of its activities and
ideological statements reveals a conscious effort on the part of the

WSPU and many of the other suffrage organizations to forge a new spirituality, based upon women's traditional idealism and self-sacrifice but intended to reach out and transform not only the position of women in society, but that very society itself. Women were to become a force in the public sphere, to take over and control the public arena by the strength of their superior morality. This naturally meant a rigorous purity in regard to sexual matters, combined with a strong sense of bodily control; the integrity of the human body—degraded by forced feeding in prison—in turn symbolized the inherent spiritual force of each woman. In effect, the WSPU woman was willing to sacrifice her body through numerous and varied militant actions in order that her spirit might triumph. Her moral force (seen by some as moral violence) would bring justice to women and thereby give women space in the political arena, where they rightfully belonged. Not surprisingly, the WSPU spoke often of personal freedom, spiritual regeneration, and moral right triumphing over physical force. If we make the necessary mental leap into a world based upon noneconomic spiritual arguments, then the revolutionary ideology of the suffragettes becomes clear, along with their adherence to sexual purity. In this chapter, I shall therefore focus upon the metaphors of space and the body—the private and the public, the female body and the body politic—through which the spiritual sisterhood of the militants found expression. Each action of the militant campaign was symbolic of the state of women—and a move to alter that state radically.

The Call for a New Freedom

In early 1906 the Pankhursts decided to move their Women's Social and Political Union to London in order to be closer to Parliament and the centers of political power. They were soon joined by Emmeline and Frederick Pethick-Lawrence, a well-to-do couple long associated with social reform. The WSPU was ruled autocratically by Christabel, her mother Emmeline, and the Pethick-Lawrences; the leaders feared that their rapidly growing organization would lose its momentum if they became embroiled in the slow process of democratic decision making. Christabel justified her methods by comparing the WSPU to an orchestra, where each individual player was still heard, but subordinated her will to that of the conductor.[14] The four leaders controlled all major policy decisions, while permitting widely different levels of commitment from local chapters and individual members. At first they faced considerable opposition from within their ranks, and the non-militant suffragists boasted publicly of their democratic procedures, pointing out that they were preparing women for the vote by the form of their organization.[15] The WSPU's lack of democracy, however, had little effect on women who were eager for action. For the sheltered and wealthy Margaret Haig Mackworth, militancy had let "a draught of fresh air into our padded, stifled lives," bringing "adventure and excitement."[16] In spite of her later disappointment, the working-class socialist Hannah Mitchell could look back on her years as an activist and say, "all my previous life had been a preparation for this great experience."[17]

The WSPU organized thousands of meetings, soapbox rallies, street-corner sales of *Votes for Women,* and colorful marches throughout England. Until mid-1909 militancy was restricted to heckling Liberal party speakers at by-elections and demanding party support for a woman's suffrage bill. In less than three years the WSPU jumped from one organizer to seventy-five, with an income of £18,000 from subscriptions alone.[18] Then in June 1909, after Mrs. Pankhurst and eight well-known women were turned away from Parliament, government office windows were broken and 108 women were arrested. Most were later released, but one woman began the first hunger strike, protesting the continued refusal of the Home Office to grant women political-prisoner status. She was soon released, but at another prison women were forcibly fed. In July 1910 the so-called Conciliation Bill, supporting modified women's suffrage, passed by 139 votes in the House of Commons, but differences between the Lords and Commons led to the dissolving of Parliament. Rank-and-file WSPU members were growing impatient; the brutal breaking up of a suffragette rally on 18 November 1910, "Black Friday," further exacerbated a growing disillusionment with Parliament, compromise, and men.

A campaign of systematic window smashing began in late 1911. Following a second attack on exclusive West End shops, the police raided the WSPU headquarters on 5 March 1912. Christabel fled to Paris, where she single-handedly led the WSPU after breaking her close alliance with the Pethick-Lawrences. Henceforward the WSPU was a semilegal organization with a perpetually changing headquarters and deputy leadership. For two years a policy of arson and window smashing was pursued in the face of increasingly hostile publicity. In April 1913 the home secretary pushed through Parliament a bill giving the government power to release any hunger striker until she had recovered her health sufficiently to be rearrested. The "Cat and Mouse Act," as it was called, fed into the WSPU's insatiable need for publicity, as the "mice" proved to be remarkably successful in eluding rearrest and making dramatic appearances at meetings.[19] The WSPU's small band of militants was caught in a spiraling pattern of arson, arrest, hunger strikes, release, and rearrest. Operating as a guerrilla army, it had become increasingly out of touch not only with the nonmilitant suffragists, but also with public opinion, government policies, and the course of wider events. Then in August 1914 war was declared, and the Pankhursts abruptly called off their campaign.

By August 1914 the core of the WSPU was exhausted from hunger striking and the strain of an underground life. But their arson campaign had continued to grow for nearly two years; it is impossible to say how long they would have gone on without damaging either animals or people, yet escalating the level of destruction. Undoubtedly the last years of the WSPU's militancy had alienated more people that it had converted; but for those who had participated, life had never seemed more meaningful. For eight years—a long time by political standards—women had been at the center of public life. Early twentieth century England was a time of political upheaval. Labor unrest, the Irish question, and the suffrage campaign all assaulted the House of Commons, calling for incisive action and farsighted policies. Prime Minister Asquith and the Liberal party had responded with a combination of minor concessions, vacillation, and intransigence. All were guaranteed to infuriate those seeking redress. For middle-class and upper-class Englishmen it seemed as if the world they had known was under siege, imperiled as it had never been before. They reacted with fear and occasional violence against workingmen, the Irish, and especially the suffragettes. In sharp contrast, even at the end of the WSPU's militancy, the period for women was one of exultation, excitement, and the conviction of growing power and self-respect.

The repeated linking of spirituality with militant action by WSPU members came from the long tradition of women's and men's claiming moral leadership for women. Early twentieth century journalism frequently debated the materialism and lack of idealism of the times; concern was especially voiced about the corruption of public and private morals, with the decline of Victorian sexual mores and religious belief. The WSPU took this essentially conservative anxiety and heightened the division between its idealists and the publicly defined materialism of the age. Elaine Kidd could flatly state,

> Preachers are never tired of telling us that this is a materialistic age; but why do so few of them show any gratitude to those women who are, at this moment, engaged in a life and death struggle against the forces of materialism? I refer to the Militant Suffragettes, whose passionate idealism and daring imagination are in striking contrast to the sluggish respectability of the "plain man" who insists upon regarding them as criminals and lunatics.[20]

Despite claims to the contrary, the WSPU always saw women as superior to men. They were the carriers of civilization, both literally and metaphorically. As mothers, women had the high responsibility of training the future generation, a task that had never been fully recognized by men, as countless speeches on the connection between infant mortality, overworked mothers, and voteless women reminded the public. Now the militant's "passionate idealism and daring imagination" was a guide to civilization, bearing witness to a cause greater than self.

The WSPU combined the Victorian traditions of womanly self-sacrifice and moral leadership with the call to immediate action, demanding a very un-Victorian haste. For generations women had been taught to wait until the right moment for all kinds of reforms, ranging from suffrage to personal career choices. Florence Nightingale was in her early thirties before she broke away from her family, even though she first felt her call from God at seventeen. Both Elizabeth Wordsworth and Constance Maynard had had to wait many years before they found their niches in higher education; each Sunday they repeated their counsel of patience to an increasingly impatient audience of students. Now in the early years of the twentieth century, the WSPU told women that they had waited long enough. In this they were at one with the other suffrage organizations. When Mrs. Cobden-Sanderson, a longtime fighter in the nonmilitant wing, went to jail, she "turned to her comrades and said almost with a sigh of relief, 'We have talked so much for the Cause, now let us suffer for it.'"[21] Everywhere women shared this feeling—the time had come at last, and they need wait no more.

Although the militant suffrage movement emphasized the wider opportunities to do good that the vote would provide, it also spoke strongly about the vote as a source of woman's freedom. Women who had long "protested in their soul against the limitations which narrow a woman's life, and deny her opportunities of expressing herself in deed and action; against the limitations that restrict her energies and outlook," were reassured by Emmeline Pethick-Lawrence,

> A new word has gone forth. To the hearts of women all the world over a word has been whispered—the awakening word, Freedom. It is the word of the angel of destiny. . . . and his clear, high call will be heard by one woman after another, and she will rise up and follow the call, no matter how rough and unbeaten the track and how difficult the way—no matter to what class or community or nationality or creed she may belong. And the fellowship of women who have heard and have risen will grow more and more until it becomes conscious, and the joy of unity becomes a great strength.[22]

No one represented this spirit of freedom better than Christabel Pankhurst, who seemed inspired by "a deep, secret shame—shame that any woman should tamely accept the position accorded to her as something less than an adult human being—a position halfway between the child and the citizen. . . . Militancy to her meant the putting off of the slave *spirit*."[23] Christabel's speeches were filled with exhortations to independence, freedom, and action; she never spoke of woman's woes and helplessness, but talked of her equality and power.

Freedom was personal and psychological, reinforcing a sense of woman's spiritual leadership. The very vagueness of the word meant that it could be evoked repeatedly by leaders of every stripe. For some women it meant simply the vote, but for most it meant casting off the old ways and entering public space without fear. Since so many middle- and upper-class women had never participated in public political activities, simple actions such as chalking the pavements to announce a meeting or selling *Votes for Women* felt liberating. Indeed, freedom of movement came to symbolize the wider freedoms that women were seeking through the vote. The refusal of this freedom by the government, or by crowds of men at rallies, or by the doctors who forcibly fed the prisoners reinforced the belief that only spiritual superiority would conquer. The militants turned this superiority into a shield, protecting them as they entered public space, and into a weapon, altering public opinion as they asserted their rightful freedom. Freed from self-doubt and traditional inhibitions, the militants felt an inner freedom that sustained them like an "angel of destiny."

The urgency of the call "Rise up Women!" made the WSPU especially attractive to the young. Although some married women who had few family responsibilities were quite active in the organization, those who could commit the most time and energy were the unmarried young. Women who had no training for a job, or had dead-end jobs, or were waiting until they were old enough to begin a job were especially welcome. Virtually all of the full-time organizers were single women, and donations to the WSPU shifted from 45 percent unmarried subscribers in the fiscal year 1906–7 to 63 percent in the year 1913–14.[24] The WSPU broke with previous generations of feminists, emphasizing not experience or social connections, but rather youth and loyalty. Although the bulk of its membership was from the educated classes (working-class girls and women could ill afford the time and money, much less the risks involved in going to jail, and so remained a minority), class origins mattered less than a willingness to work, to commit oneself wholeheartedly. For those from families who opposed their activism, the decision to continue as an activist meant a painful break or countless battles at home. S. I. Stevenson, who hated her job and was estranged from her parents, found refuge in the WSPU headquarters, where "the sea of life was calm and truth shone unhindered."[25] The shy and self-educated Aeta Lamb, whose feminism "burnt within her with an ever-consuming flame," found happiness in working and speaking for the WSPU until her health broke from the strain of arrest and prison.[26] Charlotte Marsh halted a promising career as one of the first women sanitary inspectors; she went on to become one of the most sought-after militants, committing acts of enormous bravery and daring.[27]

The WSPU demanded a very high level of commitment from its cadre, yet it also rewarded them with a powerfully supportive community. Close friendships were formed under the pressures of political work. Emmeline Pethick-Lawrence found that traditional upper-class English reserve was thrown off under stress, and friendships that often lasted a lifetime might be formed overnight in a police station or prison. Mary Nesbitt, coming out of jail in May 1912, wrote a friend, "I was deeply impressed by the *wonderful* spirit of loyalty and love for the cause and for our leaders—all, irrespective of class creed or age, were unwavering, and I consider it the greatest and crowning honour of my life to have had two months, or nearly that, of daily and inspiring companionship with these noble women."[28] The greatest gift the WSPU offered its activists was self-discovery through shared danger, sacrifice, and friendship. Pethick-Lawrence reminisced in her autobiography, defining this special combination as the liberation of women of her generation:

> It meant to women the discovery of their own identity, that source within of purpose power and will, the *real* person that often remains throughout a life-time hidden under the mask of appearances. It meant also to women the discovery of the wealth of spiritual sympathy, loyalty and affection that could be formed in intercourse friendship and companionship with one another.[29]

The charisma of Mrs. Pankhurst, Christabel, and Emmeline Pethick-Lawrence drew forth the flame of total commitment from countless women.[30] It also frightened many more, who loathed their capricious, attention-getting tactics and resolute refusal to consider democratic procedures in policymaking. Teresa Billington-Greig, a founder of the WSPU, broke with the Pankhursts in 1907; she considered them to be utterly unreliable, "yielding to sudden tempests, they believe what they want and reject what they do not want to believe."[31] For women who were concerned to build a firm foundation for radical social change, the leaders of the WSPU were maddening in their utter reliance upon personal appeal, demagoguery, and drama.[32] But the rank and file of the WSPU were interested not so much in the wider economic and political issues as in the fiery commitment demanded of them. Years of unthinking loyalty culminated for Mary Richardson in the slashing of the "Rokeby Venus" at the National Gallery, in retaliation for the government's treatment of her adored Mrs. Pankhurst.[33] Other organizations and leaders were as committed to suffrage, but they lacked the Pankhurst flame that consumed the WPSU and made it shine so much more brightly.

Lady Constance Lytton described the impact of the WSPU leaders upon her in terms that were echoed by others:

> they represented something more than themselves, a force greater than their own seemed behind them. Their remarkable individual powers seemed illumined and enhanced by a light that was apart from them as are the colours and patterns of a stained-glass window by the sun shining through it. I had never before come across this kind of spirituality. I have since found it a characteristic of all the leaders in the militant section of the woman's movement, and of many of the rank and file.[34]

When Annie Kenney, a Lancashire mill girl, first met Christabel Pankhurst, she felt that Christabel had "lit the fire which consumed the past." She became her most devoted follower, describing herself as Christabel's "first-born Militant and mascot," while others dubbed her "Christabel's blotting paper."[35] She appears to have carried out all of Christabel's decisions, obeying her unquestioningly. Pethick-Lawrence found that Kenney's "complete surrender" to Christabel gave her incalculable power because she "was lit up with a spiritual flame."[36] In turn, Kenney's power and self-confidence attracted many middle-class women who were less confident than she. While Kenney was an organizer in the West of England, Mary Blathwayt, a colonel's daughter, eagerly served as her secretary, go-between, and domestic servant.[37] The years of militancy were some of the happiest for Kenney, Blathwayt, and others because they had found the perfect combination of absolute service and personal power.

Militancy meant a complete life change, as Annie Kenney intuitively sensed when she first met Christabel. It could free a woman to adopt a new religion and different dietary and living habits. Indeed, Elizabeth Robins, the famous actress and novelist, claimed that the cause itself was a religion:

> the woman suffrage movement has tapped those deep reservoirs of spiritual devotion and consecrated selflessness from which the world has, from the beginning, drawn its moral and religious strength[.]
>
> The truth is that the ideal for which woman suffrage stands has come, through suffering, to be a religion. No other faith

held in the civilised world to-day counts so many adherants ready to suffer so much for their faith's sake. Why not try to realise what this means?[38]

The thought that militancy, whatever its spiritual pretensions, could become an alternative religion must have frightened the enemies of the women's movement. Many women, however, found time to explore unorthodox beliefs. Theosophy, practiced by the leader of the Woman's Freedom League, Charlotte Despard, was very popular, because it appeared to offer an alternative to so much Victorian materialist thinking, was dominated by women, and emphasized spirituality as a force for social change.[39] Rachel Peace, in a series of prison notes written on lavatory paper to the music hall performer Kitty Marion, confessed to a kind of pantheism-cum-astrology. Though they had never met, she explained that her affinity for Marion was "in the stars":

> I wonder do you believe in the influence of the stars! I am frightfully keen about astrology and I think you and I must be under the Laws of the Universe and Life. . . . There are beautiful helpful spots constantly with us, guiding us, cheering us, helping us always when we try to live up to the very influence of similar stars, and that would account for a mutual understanding and common sympathy.[40]

Encouraged by Marion, she admitted that she was a "heathen" who prayed to Venus, who "gives us love. To us is given the power to give [to] each to gain love. Haven't you found it so in your life?"[41] This same sense of spiritual affinity with nature led many suffragettes to become vegetarians and to take up homeopathy. Underlying their search for a different set of beliefs and behavior was a desire for an alternative to a life designed and led by men. Just as a previous generation had sought to define communities of single women as "families," the militants sought to express their spirituality through a closer union with nature and with religions that gave room for the expression of what they saw as peculiarly feminine characteristics.

Joining the WSPU meant joining a spiritual army. The military metaphors, invoked so frequently in nursing and schooling, took on a different tone. By casting the struggle for the vote in terms of a battle, the leadership of the WSPU tapped into the rhetoric and idealism of the military. Moreover, many middle-class women had watched their brothers go off and fight for the empire in South Africa and India. Fighting for a higher cause—with the weapons of moral superiority—seemed a natural way to describe the struggle for the vote. The language, iconography, and ultimately the behavior of the WSPU portrayed an army at war with society. Christabel Pankhurst repeatedly spoke of battles, a war with the Liberal party, and army discipline. Both the militants and the nonmilitants were fond of portraying idealized Woman, dressed as a knight or goddess, leading civilization into a better future.[42] The National Union of Women's Suffrage Societies' weekly paper, *Common Cause*, pictured a woman in armor on its front page for over two years (1912–14); the allegorical figure carried a staff of "Wisdom" and wore "a sword of the spirit" as she blew her trumpet, calling other women to follow her lead. "The sword of the spirit" perfectly represents the symbolic war all suffrage women felt they were fighting, using the only weapons women had.

The leaders of the WSPU astutely tapped into the youthful desire for greater physical freedom and encouraged the exhilaration of battle among those who suffered from taunts, missiles, and unpleasant attacks wherever they attempted to speak in public. A "hardened suffragette" knew, unlike many women, that she could "take care of herself," while the inexperienced learned to overcome traditional womanly inhibitions and fears.[43] But as militancy increased, the metaphor of military action became a reality. Mrs. Pankhurst in particular was caught up in the danger and drama of the battlefield, often saying that she wanted to be tried for sedition; she was fully convinced that she and her daughter had brought the government to a standstill and that revolution was around the corner.[44] In such circumstances, they felt justified in demanding more and more from their advance corps. Increasingly in this guerrilla army, the ends justified the means. Helen Craggs, one of the first women arrested for arson, argued in court:

> I hold that militant Suffragettes stand in an analogous position to soldiers. You do not regard the latter as murderers because they fight in a good cause and neither am I as a militant Suffragist a criminal. Because I fight in a cause as good as any for which men have fought, I say, my lord, that I am morally guiltless.[45]

The militants became even more committed as their numbers decreased and their actions became more dangerous. Like guerrillas, they were ever ready to follow orders from their leaders, but equally likely to move in advance of them. Both hunger striking and stone throwing were undertaken without advice from WSPU headquarters. The autocracy of the WSPU contained a paradox: any woman who accepted militancy to the full followed the poli-cies of her leaders, but at the same time, she continually had to consider her position and use her independent judgment in decid-ing which actions to participate in and how.[46] She thus "took a forward step in self-emancipation which Christabel had always insisted was one of the main purposes of the movement."[47] Heroic action for the cause liberated the most devoted members of the "army."

Assaulting Public Space

When the militants behaved in radically new ways, they laid bare prejudices in both sexes, exacerbating the sexual division upon which Edwardian society was based. Although some writers did stress how attractive the new independent woman was, far more common were tales of young suffragettes' being led back to their natural course by love for a right-thinking man.[48] More se-rious was the undercurrent of innuendo that plagued the suffrage movement. Some came from the antisuffrage movement, ranging from male jokes to outright assertions of female monthly in-sanity.[49] Mrs. Fawcett, leader of the nonmilitants, spoke of a cam-paign "to whisper scandals against Suffragists in back drawing-rooms in Kensington to timid maiden ladies, who were told that the villainies perpetrated by the Suffragists were of so black a dye that details could not possibly be disclosed except to married women."[50] When she confronted the originators, they responded by blaming the WSPU. Such allegations only drew women closer to each other, but this in turn produced another set of attacks, against "an unsatisfied class of women," spinsters. Walter Heape in his book *Sex Antagonism* (1913) attacked this "Female army," claiming that if women were given the vote, "the authority and power hitherto held by the mothers of the nation would be largely usurped by spinsters and such a drastic change would be of vital importance to the race." He was convinced that these "waste products of our Female population" were subject to pathological derangement because "their generative system" degenerated through lack of use. Dredging up all the old arguments used against permitting women to pursue higher education, Heape heightened the very sex antagonism his book was meant to explain.[51]

The militants and men spoke different sexual languages. No man could believe claims of superior spirituality when he repeatedly saw women breaking the traditional boundaries dividing the sexes. Matters were complicated by the fact that the suffragettes dressed in a very feminine manner while forcing themselves into male space. When they sold Votes for Women on street corners or chalked pavements, women were horrified at men's reaction to their activities. Mary Richardson found that men came up to her ostensibly to buy a paper, but actually to whisper filthy language in her ear; although she retaliated by chasing them down the street, she ended many days feeling depressed.[52] Women felt that they had to make a sacrifice of their bodies for the cause through the public activities of attending Parliament, going on delegations, speaking on soapboxes, and selling literature; ultimately they might be asked to make the bodily sacrifice of prison and hunger striking. Such activities were all spiritualized by the suffragettes, but they breached the social distance between men and women and therefore left women vulnerable to sexual attack. From the male perspective, on the other hand, women appeared to be forcing themselves bodily upon male space and male consciousness—even into male arms, as crowds jostled and embraced in the many scenes before the House of Commons.

Suffragettes attempted to keep the privileges of social distance by retaining women's traditional clothing. The large-brimmed hats requiring numerous hatpins to stay in place, the upswept hairstyle that became disheveled at every public event, and the long, fitted dresses with lace and trimmings left the militants singularly unprepared for the scuffles that almost automatically occurred wherever they gathered. Obviously this fussiness about dress was a reaction against the stereotype of the dowdy and masculine "strong-minded" woman, which in the past might have put off possible converts. But Cicely Hamilton has argued that there also "may have been some connection between this 'dressiness' and the combative impulse, since soldiers, all the world over, are inclined to be fussy about their personal appearance."[53] Although Mrs. Pankhurst was eager to avoid shocking male prejudice, the impractical clothes had a more important symbolic value. She refused to concede that women had to become like men to be worthy of the vote; stylish dressing accentuated differences. The ethereal sexuality suffragettes projected emphasized the importance of femininity and feminine values even as women were performing unfeminine acts. The exaggerated stylishness was symbolic of women's bodily control, the very quality they thought men lacked. Men were to be taught women's claims by recognizing this controlled sexuality, swathed in layers of material. But because the militants encroached upon male space, they could not effectively prescribe the desired response to their femininity.

The most revolutionary aspect of the suffragette movement was precisely its insistence upon a female presence—even leadership —in male arenas. Earlier feminists had largely confined themselves to carving out a separate sphere for women or to pressuring for the reform of laws that specifically affected women and children. Now the WSPU was insisting upon the prerogative of women to enter the public, male world and to participate as equal citizens. On the one hand, this took the form of demanding the vote on the same terms as men. On the other, it meant political access to the streets, pavements, and hustings, but most of all the House of Commons. The numerous "rushes" on Parliament, carrying petitions to present to the prime minister, were clearly symbolic acts, intended to attract attention to forbidden public places. So too, the decision to sell *Votes for Women* on street corners and to set up soapbox meetings where women spoke to passing crowds were actions only socialist women had undertaken before. Now respectable middle- and upper-class women were refusing to remain at home behind closed doors and were claiming male space for women's purposes. They often met with fierce resistance, far worse than dirty words whispered in a saleswoman's ear. They could be repeatedly pinched, punched in the breasts, fondled under their skirts, and spit at in the face, have their hats pulled off, have rotten fruit thrown at them, and suffer other indignities.[54] The gentle and shy Mary Blathwayt found the courage to follow Annie Kenney into the public sphere; by 1909 she could record laconically in her diary,

> 8 June. Bristol. We were on a lorry and a large crowd of children were waiting for us when we arrived. Things were thrown at us all the time; but when we drove away at the end we were hit a great many times. Elsie Howey had her lip hit and it bled. I was hit by potatoes, stones, turf and dust. Something hit me very hard on my right ear as I was getting into our

tram. Someone threw a big stone as big as a baby's head; it fell onto the lorry.[55]

When middle-class women did not do as they were supposed to, or stay where they were supposed to be, the public assumed that they were fair game. Maud Kate Smith remembered the "fine yellow powder" that fell on the floor when House of Commons demonstrators returned from their expedition and took off their protective cardboard bodices.[56] Similar incidents of violence and its aftermath were recorded by virtually every activist.

This clash over public space is nowhere better illustrated than on "Black Friday," an event that shocked the largely middle- and upper-class constituency of the militant movement. On 18 November 1910 a large delegation of suffragettes met violence and brutality from policemen and the general public when they attempted to reach the House of Commons. For over six hours the police, bystanders, and suffragettes fought; in the end 115 women and 4 men were arrested. The newly appointed home secretary, Winston Churchill, was incorrectly blamed for an administrative decision by the police to use men from the East End rather than the more usual "A" Division men, who were familiar with and largely friendly to the suffragette delegations. The East End police were accustomed to dealing with the poor and had no compunction about treating the suffragettes with brutality and sexual aggression. But women, who were often the friends and relatives of M.P.s (the men the police were protecting), found such behavior shocking.[57] Black Friday brought into the open the sexual consequences of women's attempting to enter a male domain. In order to protect their public space, men were willing to permit, even encourage, the violation of woman's most intimate space—her body.

Women clearly could not compete physically with men, and indeed, they never wished to do so; the repeated public maulings served to confirm not their weakness, but the brutality of men. The natural corollary was the need for women in Parliament in order to improve the morality of men. Nevertheless, when the militants turned to window smashing, many women were relieved; they could break a single window and be immediately arrested, avoiding possible fights with the crowd.[58] Breaking windows also served the important purpose of demonstrating the weakness of established institutions. At first only government buildings were attacked, but in an effort to influence the insurance companies and major department stores, the militants went into the West End. In all cases windows broke quite easily and with a satisfying noise, reminding one and all of the fragility of male institutions. Moreover, the barrier between the inside (the government offices) and the outside (the women refused entry) was metaphorically destroyed, leaving a gaping hole (or boarded window) to remind others of women's position.

Pro-suffrage women were not always caught in a large crowd or left isolated to face a hostile audience around a soapbox or arrested for breaking windows. Both the militant and the non-militant wings took to the streets in unprecedented numbers, staging enormously successful marches, rallies, and parades. Mrs. Fawcett's National Union of Women's Suffrage Societies organized two large marches in the summers of 1910 and 1911, with women dressed in the clothing of their professions and carrying banners indicating their occupations or organizations. Some eight hundred women with degrees wore their academic robes—a fitting reminder, they felt, of women's gains over the past fifty years and of their right to vote as responsible citizens. In the 1911 march all the suffrage societies united to include the presentation of women's present-day achievements and their past accomplishments. Historical and empire pageants were included, with women dressed as such popular heroines as Queen Elizabeth, Godiva, Britomart, and Joan of Arc. This last was a favorite figure, seen as a model in her sacrifices for freedom; indeed, she was so popular that there appears to have been some quarreling about who would be Joan at various local pageants.[59] The WSPU trained a uniformed drum and fife band that led the small local marches as well as the more famous summer demonstrations through the streets of London. Starting in 1908 large rallies were held in Hyde Park each summer. The first great demonstration in June 1908 called upon women to wear the newly proclaimed WSPU colors, purple (dignity and loyalty), green (hope), and white (purity). Twenty platforms were set up, with famous suffragette speakers at each; seven separate processions marched into Hyde Park with forty bands. Thirty special trains brought people from seventy cities. Estimates of the size of the crowd ran as high as 500,000.[60] Such huge public events as these demonstrations, together with the thousands of large and small processions through the streets of London and many other cities, asserted the power of women to use public space for political purposes. Organized marches of uniformed or partially uniformed women were a show of strength as well as a means of developing self-respect and pride in women's history and culture. Moreover, they were a relatively safe way to keep the issue of suffrage before the public, underscoring the more colorful and dangerous demonstrations before the House of Commons.

The militants, however, were never content with simply asserting their large numbers and organizational skills. Their various illegal and semilegal actions were a means of crossing the invisible barrier keeping them from male political space. In October 1908 two members of the militant Women's Freedom League (WFL) chained themselves to the grille separating the Ladies' Gallery from the Commons; they then attempted to address the men below. Unable to detach the women, workers had to remove the grille, and the House was temporarily closed to visitors. The event was the culmination of a four months' vigil at the door of the House during all the hours the Commons sat, a mute but constant reminder of the WFL's request to meet with the prime minister.[61] The WSPU proved extraordinarily ingenious in getting into meetings forbidden to women (as a protection against interruption). In Bristol on one occasion two suffragettes hid themselves all night in the hall's organ loft in order to be ready to shout "Votes for women!" when the Liberal minister spoke.[62] Charlotte Marsh and Mary Leigh took axes, chopped the slates from the roof of Bingley Hall, Birmingham, and hurled them at the police and at Prime Minister Asquith's car.[63] In all of these cases the militants were physically apart, shouting down to a largely, even completely, male audience and demanding justice. Their exclusion from the political process was, in a sense, exaggerated by their position—they refused to participate in meetings until they could have their full rights in Parliament. If they were powerless, they did not wish to have a token show of influence, which their quiescent attendance at a meeting or a sitting of Parliament implied. Thus the symbolic acts of disrupting meetings by calling out "Votes for women!" came to hold a greater meaning for both the participants and the watchers.

Such actions also reinforced the militants' sense of being a guerrilla army of dedicated fighters. The purple, green, and white uniforms for special occasions set them apart from ordinary women, just as their illegal acts did. Militant women felt they were willing to take on tasks that others could not or would not do, in order to gain a female foothold in male territory. They believed that they had to be willing, like soldiers, to sacrifice them-selves even unto death. Here again the emphasis upon spirituality provided both a rationale and a means. If men confused the spiri-tual beauty of women with their physical bodies, women tended to the opposite extreme, confusing bodily sacrifice with spiritual ascension. The suffragettes believed that only by giving their bodies—the physical self—to the cause would they win the nec-essary spiritual victory that would enable them to enter the male political world.

Bodily Sacrifice

Between 1906 and 1914 over one thousand women went to prison for suffrage; thousands more were arrested.[64] Prison was the final goal of the suffragettes, symbolizing their search for justice and the injustice they met at every turn. Yet it was also their commu-nity, created through the fiery spirit that bound them together, de-spite fear, physical weakness, and long days spent in isolation. Going to prison was the self-transforming act that would alter not only the actor (the prisoner) but also the public. Isolated, yet united with fellow prisoners, the lonely martyr became, in the words of Mary Gordon, both the flame and the burnt offering, the self-fulfilled and the self-sacrificed.[65] A shared sense of awe and inspiration among both those who had been to prison and those who supported them gave all WSPU members a feeling of par-ticipating in history—in events that raised them above the ordi-nary and made them capable of unusual feats of courage and self-lessness. As one woman explained,

> "That is the greatest victory that we have won in this cam-paign, the conquest over all fear. I used to feel after the hunger strike and the forcible feeding, that at last I had succeeded in absolutely overcoming self. It gives one such a wonderful feel-ing of strength, that, combined with the knowledge that Truth and Justice are on our side, and must ultimately prevail."[66]

During the early days most women were imprisoned either for interrupting a political meeting or as part of a delegation to Parlia-ment. Procedures were soon developed to facilitate handling the increasingly large numbers arrested. The women were ordinarily released until a pro forma trial and then were given the heaviest possible sentence (WSPU propaganda always compared these sentences with the very light ones given men for sexual offenses, wife battering, and similar crimes). During the early days, women were required to wear prison uniforms, kept in separate cells, and refused all consideration as political prisoners. One of the most onerous aspects of wearing prison garb was the assignment of used clothing. Each week two identical dusters were handed out, one to be used as a handkerchief and the other as a neckerchief. Since their washing was inadequate, the more squeamish found this custom unsanitary and distasteful.[67] In July of 1909 Marion Wallace Dunlop voluntarily began hunger striking in protest against the failure of the government to grant suffrage prisoners political status. By September forcible feeding was used against hunger strikers, despite widespread public protest. In response, Winston Churchill formulated rule 243a, granting special privileges to prisoners of good character but without admitting the political nature of the women's protest. His temporary concessions lasted for a little over a year, when a recurrence of hunger strikes led to the renewal of forcible feeding, accompanied by more public protests. Then the passage of the "Cat and Mouse" Act in April 1913 brought food-and-water hunger strikes, forcible feeding, and another round of publicity and protest.

For the women who entered prison, the experience affected them deeply both personally and politically. The hardships acted to uplift most, though some found the isolation without privacy trying (wardresses could look through a peephole and could enter the cells at will), and the sense of powerlessness could be overwhelming for these middle-class women. The more cheerful found amusement in learning to scrub floors, circumventing regulations against speaking with each other or sending notes, and making up games. Some managed to write comic letters to the home secretary. Marion Wallace-Dunlop, for example, wrote asking for the use of pens: "Are you who are in authority at the Home Office unaware that the modern woman writes as well as sews? Perhaps you may be anxious to press upon us some permanent prejudice of your own in the form of the needle rather than the pen as a suitable implement for women. If this be so may I beg you to choose some other time and place for exalting the needle at the expense of the pen?"[68] But even in the best of times, under 243a, prison meant long hours alone, sustained only by the evening's dim echo of the WSPU band outside the gates and the daily group exercise period.

Yet hunger striking—an entirely voluntary act—was a far greater test of the spirit. S. I. Stevenson, who struck her first time in jail, recalled the experience vividly:

> I blushed with shame that the cup of tea should have such power over me. I kept going to it and looking at it—the steam fascinated me—(there wasn't *much* in the steam line). 'I'm not going to have any,' I kept telling myself. 'I'm only looking at it.' . . . My mouth was so parched it stung me. Now I have to record a sad, sad lapse. Without hardly knowing it I suddenly found myself again sitting over the tea. Would one little sip matter. Quite possibly no one was hunger striking. I stretched my tongue and curling it let it touch the level of the tea, in some sort as a cat lappeth, and drew it in. It was moist and eased my roof a little; I did not swallow at all. The wonderful relief it was to me—just that moisture on my tongue. Then I remembered. I covered up the teacup and buried my face in my hands. St. Augustine, all ye tempted ones, and Judas! I had fallen. A sip was as good as a swallow. In that dismal cell on that dismal November night a tragedy had happened. I had proved that I was not the stuff heroes are made of. . . . About ten minutes later the door swung open. My head was still buried in my hands in abject shame. A wardress tore off the coverings and handed the untasted (?) refreshment to a wardress outside. 'That's the seventeenth that hasn't touched anything,' I heard her say in gruesome tones to the other.[69]

Stevenson's apostasy was only momentary, but like all the others hunger striking, she found the mental torture almost unbearable. The physical pain was little after the first few days, but the mental strain wore many out. The slightest message from outside took on inordinate importance, as women lay alone thinking of Joan of Arc and Emmeline Pankhurst in order to keep up their courage.

As every prisoner knew, hunger striking was only the first step in their bodily sacrifice. They had to face forcible feeding two or three times a day. A doctor would arrive with a long rubber tube and three or four wardresses. They would hold down and gag the protesting prisoner, while he inserted the tube (often used again and again without cleansing) down either a nostril or if possible the mouth, and then would pour in a mixture of milk, bread, and brandy, sometimes including an antivomiting agent. Hunger strikers found the procedure utterly demoralizing, leaving them feeling nauseous, with cramps, headaches, and painful sores within their mouths, nasal passages, and even stomach. Most suffered severely from indigestion and constipation. But perhaps the worst was anticipating the arrival of the doctor. The agony of hearing one's comrades screaming in pain while waiting could be unbearable, and some women did crack under the strain. One prisoner described the whole ritual of offering food before the beginning of artificial feeding as an ironic reversal of Eve tempting Adam:

> the food, so delicious, so tempting, is offered by man to the woman, representative of her sex, and for the sake of her sex, she must refuse even to taste it. So the woman triumphs over the man. The offering is the lesser sin, but the acceptance is the greater, in this revolution of womanhood each woman strives to remove the old stigma of the story of Adam and Eve. She refuses to accept the position of subjection so disastrous to the race, both morally and physically, so great a barrier to progress and evolution.[70]

But as she reminded those who thought they might break the suffragette's spirit, "The stronger the temptation, the more uplifting is the feeling of victory."[71] Some women, such as Kitty Marion, found the whole experience too suggestive of forcible rape and struggled against being fed as long as their strength lasted. Others, such as Lady Constance Lytton, could hold nothing down and were left more dead than alive after each attempt. But like the male denial of public space for political actions, the physical assault upon the prisoner's body only strengthened the resolve of the sufferer. The men might insist upon keeping their control over women's bodies as well as the body politic, yet women turned these actions into symbolic victories. Although she might suffer the destruction of her body, each hunger striker knew that her spirit soared over the male political world and that moral force would triumph over physical force.

This spiritual victory, however, was purchased at great personal cost. Evelyn Sharp believed that the utter desolation she felt while striking "came from some indefinable revolt of the spirit against the violation of Nature implied in the voluntary starvation of Nature's great gift, the body."[72] For her, even as the spirit commanded the body to sacrifice itself for the cause, it revolted against her. Others were able to make a greater division between body and soul and to exalt their suffering in religious terms. Lady Constance Lytton felt "the rhythm of the world's soul calling us women to uncramp our powers from the thraldom of long disuse," and rejoiced at the opportunity prison gave her to join other women in self-sacrifice.[73] But the combination of enormous physical strain and family opposition broke the spirit of many hunger strikers. Even the steady support of Mrs. Pankhurst did not prevent S. I. Stevenson from succumbing to a nervous breakdown after her parents disowned her.[74] Lilian Lenton suffered double pneumonia and pluerisy after a feeding tube was accidentally inserted into her trachea; over fifty years later she still could not speak of the experience.[75] During the final phase of militancy Mary Richardson found the loneliness of underground life almost unbearable; weakened from chronic appendicitis and continual hunger striking, she became prey to extreme depression. The warmth and cheer of the suffragette nursing home was almost too much to bear after weeks of isolation in prison.[76] Rachel Peace wrote while in prison, during a prolonged hunger strike and forcible feeding three times a day:

> I am afraid I shall be affected mentally. I feel as if I should go mad. I have had nervous breakdowns before and now feel sensations of an impending crisis. Old distressing symptoms have re-appeared. I have frightful dreams and am struggling with mad people half the night.[77]

Fortunately she was soon released, but both Richardson and Peace shared a fear of madness, intensified by the government's efforts to commit the most frequent lawbreakers to criminal lunatic asylums.[78] The rhetoric of bodily sacrifice became a grim and frightening reality for women such as Peace and Richardson, yet they continued to seek martyrdom.

In spite of depression and breakdowns, the suffragette prisoners remained united and even created their own space and atmosphere of support. Time and again a suffering hunger striker was given a word or two of comfort secretly by a wardress, distressed by the brutality of forcible feeding. Regular prisoners told the suffragettes how prison conditions had improved once they started coming in regularly; moreover, they gave an air of hope to the place. As heartening as these incidents were, the suffragettes cherished most their successful efforts at keeping in touch with each other. Notes were passed by trading hymnals during morning chapel and, by the more skillful, during exercise time. Those in hospital could sometimes extract special privileges to talk or assist each other. During her first imprisonment in February 1909, Lady Constance participated in a hospital "jollification" for the departing Women's Freedom League prisoners. The nine sick prisoners and the wardress each contributed a recitation, culminating in Mrs. Pethick-Lawrence's recital of Olive Schreiner's "Three Dreams in a Desert," an allegory that seemed to them "a bare literal description of the pilgrimage of women. It fell on our ears more like an A B C railway guide to our journey than a figurative parable."[79]

After the relaxation of regulations brought about by Churchill, prisoners had more opportunities to spend time together, with shared work, exercise, and the freedom to have books and writing materials. At Aylesbury in 1912 Charlotte Marsh organized a sports day, complete with a potato race and a "concert" on combs and paper. Exhilarated by their freedom to talk together, the suffragettes renamed the prison "Simple Life Summer School," because so many favored a return to the land, physical culture, vegetarianism, theosophy, and, of course, social reform.[80] During a similar period at Winson Green Prison, Birmingham, the prisoners put out a comic magazine, dubbed the "Hammerers' Magazine." They included an advice column about how to deal with the Antis, how to collect a crowd when speaking outdoors (steal a baby from a pram or get a boy to drop pennies), how to lose weight (go to jail), and so forth. One woman, writing the "Health Notes in Hospital," bragged about training the doctor to understand "we are captives, not prisoners." But more important was the change to the large airy hospital room, poignantly symbolic of the change she and her fellow suffragettes were fighting for,

In a cell you have as companions to your pain and foes to your health, loneliness, oppression, secret fear—the silence which at home in illness is so grateful, is there full of suspicion. I remember even the rising sun thro' the small window teased me and I planned how I would keep it out—in here I chose a bed facing the dawn and many a morning I have lain and watched the golden light creep up my bed till I was bathed in it and I wondered at the difference of thought on the same subject. It has seemed to me like the dawning light of freedom in so many of us women's lives. We loved the light but in cramped surroundings or alien circumstances the light often proved a torment and a suffering. In the larger world of freedom—such as we twenty-five women make here the light grows and changes, and for my part I shall always remember these weeks as some of the happiest in a perfectly happy life.[81]

In prison each woman made "a larger world of freedom" for herself and other women—even as the public space of the male world was denied them, women found inspiration in creating freedom and space within the prison. Ironically, women had always fashioned a sphere of freedom for themselves under imprisoning conditions, whether within their own homes or someone else's or in a hated job. Now they could look to a real prison as liberating, opening up a new world of freedom.

No one symbolized this transformation from imprisonment in society to freedom in jail better than Lady Constance Lytton. Until her late thirties Lady Constance had led a sheltered life, caring for her mother and answering the demands placed upon a single woman from the aristocracy. Sylvia Pankhurst found that her prolonged dependency had made her almost childishly anxious about hurting others or putting herself forward.[82] Certainly to many she seemed like the finest, and last, flower of Victorian maidenhood. Her decision to participate in the militant movement pained her family and friends deeply; yet she found the strength to go forward into the most demanding roles. Like the pioneering Victorians before her, she had devoted long years to "spending herself in love's highest expression—which is Service," knowing "I do what is wanted of me now and in my home, but if ever the call comes, I shall never hesitate to follow it."[83] When the call came, she was ready for actions that would have daunted a far more liberated woman. Despite her poor health, in 1908 she led a delegation to the House of Commons and in 1909 threw a stone at Lloyd George's car in Newcastle, going to jail on both occasions. When she found that she received preferential treatment, in January 1910 she disguised herself as a working woman and was jailed in Walton Prison, Liverpool; despite a weak heart, she was forcibly fed eight times. She was released as soon as the authorities found out who she was, but not before irreparable damage had been done. She was imprisoned once again, briefly, but suffered throughout 1910 and 1911 with minor heart seizures, culminating in a stroke in early 1912. Although she lived until 1923, she could no longer participate actively in her beloved cause.[84]

During her brief career, Lady Constance became one of the most respected and loved of the suffragette leaders. Her utter selflessness, indeed, depreciation of her talents, combined with a loathing of snobbery and privilege, made her far more accessible than the powerful policymakers. She humanized the sacrifices made by the rank and file, giving them courage to carry on, and heartening others to emulate her. At her death a fellow suffragette wrote,

> Few things affected my whole vision of life more than [her] example. It made one ashamed of half-hearted faith, and of one's cowardice. It set a standard by which women felt they must measure themselves, and finding themselves wanting, felt that they must live more finely. That is what heroes and saints do for us, they lift up our standards of faith and achievement. I never saw her, except once in her beautiful youth, but, like many others, I feel to-day the same deep impulse of gratitude and love that we felt in the dark days when she lay in prison for us.[85]

Prison gave every woman, whether she went there herself or not, an opportunity to "live more finely," to recognize that women could undertake feats of courage and endurance equal to that of any man, and yet could say that they had hurt no one—man, woman, or animal—but themselves. The idealism of the WSPU found its highest expression in Lady Constance, whose pilgrimage lighted the path for countless others, yet was also representative of "the spiritual history of unnumbered women of our own [middle] class, which led to the breaking of shackles."[86]

While in prison Lady Constance found to her horror that she hated the doctors and wardresses that tortured her; to lessen this "moral poisoning" she tried closing her eyes when they entered her cell to feed her, so that she could not remember what they looked like.[87] Eventually she was able to overcome her hatred, but others were less able. A grim fanaticism overtook those who continued to hurl themselves against an obtuse government and increasingly hostile general public.[88] The militants resorted to one of two extremes: total bodily sacrifice through death or total bodily purity through female separatism. Lady Constance's hatred of the prison doctors evoked long-standing feminist fears of the medical profession; the passionate anger expressed against men during these years focused most often upon doctors.[89] Such well-known and loved feminists as Josephine Butler, the leader of the agitation against the Contagious Diseases Acts in the 1870s and 1880s, had identified immorality and the invasion of privacy with doctors.[90] A new generation of medical men were leaders in the antisuffrage movement as well as organized supporters of "rape" by means of forcible feeding. Animosity toward men was widely felt and expressed, but the greatest hatred was reserved for doctors.

The desire for complete bodily control contained within it a paradoxical admission of the very image women had been anxious to destroy, namely, the woman as victim. Although the suffragettes had insisted upon overthrowing the shackles of the past, they now embraced their victimization, attempting to turn it into a new, yet familiar, martyrdom. Bodily purity came to mean rejecting men and embracing death for the sake of the vote. Christabel Pankhurst's series of articles in 1913 in *The Suffragette* on "the great scourge," claimed that between 80 percent and 90 percent of all men suffered from venereal disease and warned women to preserve their bodily purity. Women were urged never again to sacrifice their bodies to polluted men, but rather to give them up freely to the cause in order "to possess their own souls."[91] For those most driven by the injustices women suffered during these traumatic years, this could only mean death. Many expected to die when they were hunger striking, but martrydom actually came through another dramatically public action. Emily Wilding Davison hurled herself in front of the king's horse at the 1913 Derby, calling out "Votes for women!"

Emily Wilding Davison's desire for the "consummate sacrifice" was part of the increasingly radical division between the WSPU members' spiritual ideal of a purified woman-led society and the male-controlled universe around them. All the regular hunger strikers, often on the edge of death, believed a sacrifice of their bodies would radically alter the balance of power between voteless women and the male government. Since they thought continually in terms of moral battles and spiritual transformations, they exaggerated the power of the symbolic act.[92] Davison, as a part of this cadre, was convinced that her death would demonstrate to the world the utmost that women would give and would thereby lead to the conversion of men to women's suffrage. The victimization of women, so vividly and successfully evoked during the Contagious Diseases campaign, was again brought to the fore.

But even more important was the act for women themselves. Some time before her death Davison wrote that the true militant would willingly sacrifice friendship, good report, love, and even life itself "to win the Pearl of Freedom for her sex." In highly charged language, reminiscent of Christabel's "Great Scourge" series, Davison embraced her lover, Death:

> "Cannot this cup of anguish be spared me," cries the militant aloud in agony, yet immediately, as if in repentance for having so nearly lost the Priceless Pearl, in the words of all strivers after progress, she ejaculates: "Nevertheless, I will pay, even unto this price," and in her writhing asks what further demand can be extracted from her.
>
> The glorious and inscrutable Spirit of Liberty has but one further penalty within its power, the surrender of Life itself. It is the supreme consummation of sacrifice, than which none can be higher or greater.
>
> To lay down life for friends, that is glorious, selfless, inspiring! But to re-enact the tragedy of Calvary for generations yet unborn, that is the last consummate sacrifice of the Militant!
> "Nor will she shrink from this Nirvana
> She will be faithful 'unto this last.'"[93]

Davison believed that men had "beautified and decorated the shrine, but they [had] kept it empty of the divinity which gave a significance to the paraphernalia of the shrine."[94] Men had forgotten the "mighty spirit," here identified as woman in possession of full freedom, as Christ on the cross. Davison's identification with Christ and his sacrifice was the most extreme statement of the WSPU's spiritual message. Nevertheless, she was not alone in seeing her actions as a religiously inspired sacrifice. Emmeline Pethick-Lawrence repeatedly spoke of the "saints" who had been forcibly fed, praising their "sublime" actions.[95] Lady Constance was sure that God was giving every hunger striker strength to face forcible feeding.[96] The language of the spirit came naturally to those who gave up their bodies to a moral cause.

The sacrificial acts of Davison and the hunger strikers reasserted the importance of ritual, prayer, and public praise to exorcise the demons of fear and defeat, as well as to lead women forth to the "Priceless Pearl," freedom. Davison's funeral on 14 June 1913 was the last large demonstration organized by the WSPU. At the time its leaders were either in jail or being hunted down, and its headquarters had to be moved continually to avoid raids.[97] Nevertheless, the WSPU was able to mount an impressive cortege through the streets of London to Euston Station, then her body was followed up to Northumberland for burial. Dressed in pure white, with the tall, blond Charlotte Marsh carrying a cross at the head of the procession, WSPU members walked silently through the lined streets of London, reminding all of their superior purity, faith, and loyalty. Maud Arncliffe-Sennett, who attended the funeral and followed the body north, was shocked at the irreverence of the general public, who kept calling out "The King's 'orse," seemingly more interested in the state of the horse than the dead woman. Her fears were confirmed when a man pretended to help her through the crowd, using the opportunity to take hold of her "in such an offensive and obscene manner that I literally shrieked out: 'Oh, Christ, to think you died for such as these!'"[98] When women met mockery, obscenity, and denial from men at every turning, they looked to Christabel's "great scourge" as an explanation for male behavior and their own desire for bodily purity.

The pawing and pushing by men whenever the suffragettes entered any public space frightened and angered women, leaving them eager for Christabel's message, "Votes for Women and Chastity for Men." For the militants men seemed to control the streets, the courts, and the prisons; they readily linked sexual impurity to the enforcement of woman's economic, political, and marital enslavement. Christabel, safe in Paris, could warn her *Suffragette* readers about the "infected soul" of Englishmen and the permanent loss of women's health from marriage with a polluter. In response to the few who argued that woman's chastity was the product of her past subjugation, she replied that mastery over self and sex were women's gains that would not be given up when their victory was theirs:

> Warned by the evils which the tyranny of sex has produced where men are concerned, women have no intention of letting matter triumph over mind, and the body triumph over the spirit, in their case.[99]

We cannot know how seriously her exaggerated statistics and health warnings were taken, but her insistence upon the modern woman's spiritual emancipation as a means to political emancipation must have struck a responsive chord.

In the heady days of the arson campaign Christabel's advice seemed appropriate to participants of an increasingly desperate struggle. Bodily preservation accompanied bodily destruction. Even as the hunger strikers sought death in prison, they were under special protection when free. Both the WSPU and Sylvia Pankhurst's breakaway East London Federation formed bodyguards to protect their leaders. On one occasion Mrs. Pankhurst successfully spoke from the balcony of a guarded house and then escaped between lines of the "Bodyguard" rhythmically swinging their Indian clubs.[100] Farce and tragedy seemed closely aligned as the government chased after recuperating suffragettes, who faced forcible feeding should they return to prison. The sexual connotations of the feeding heightened the women's sense of bodily integrity, while fighting against preying men ready to pounce upon them.

When war broke out on 4 August 1914 Christabel wrote in *The Suffragette* that the war was "God's vengeance upon the people who held women in subjection," and she called upon WSPU members to stand fast for the cause and womankind. Then abruptly on 15 August Mrs. Pankhurst sent around a memo exhorting WSPU members to place their energies at the service of their country.[101] *The Suffragette* reappeared, editorializing vigorously against the Germans and for Englishmen, their venereal state seemingly forgotten. The WSPU guerrilla army, toughened from years of discipline and sacrifice, transformed itself with remarkable ease into a fighting force for England. One of the most active arsonists, Charlotte Marsh, became Lloyd George's chauffeur; similar transformations occurred among other militants. Sylvia Pankhurst, however, continued to fight for the rights of East End women, and Emmeline Pethick-Lawrence became active in Jane Addams's international peace movement.[102] Divisions that had underlain the single-issue cause surfaced, and the women's movement entered a new phase.

Militancy had not gained the vote or its long-range goal of a spiritually regenerated society. Yet it did not fail its participants. They had successfully brought before the eyes of the general public a new vision of what society could be—and of how woman could behave. Women had sacrificed themselves in order to gain access to new spaces, public and spiritual, within themselves and the wider world. After the war, as the militants began to enter the widening sphere of public responsibilities, they kept alive their old vision through the Suffragette Fellowship. In the mid-thirties, under the leadership of Elsa Gye, the Fellowship sought to raise money for an Emily Wilding Davison memorial; her final sacrifice for the spiritual well-being of women seemed a central symbol to the remaining suffragettes.[103] Emmeline Pethick-Lawrence responded with passionate affection for a time when women had been willing to dare all for their vision of a better world:

> The inspiration of that movement enabled us to put into practice in our daily life some of the highest ideas expressed in philosophies and religions. It made the merging of self into the not-self easy and natural, instead of almost impossible. Sacrifices were made in the spirit of joy; deeds were done which could not have been contemplated had we not been lifted above the personal self. The remembrance of many deeds of courage and complete self-forgetfulness are revived as I write. I think . . . finally [of] the culminating act of self-immolation when Emily Davison threw herself in the way of the King's racing horse and cried for the last time, for justice for all women. . . . From that day onward the bounds of women's freedom have been extended ever more widely.[104]

Pethick-Lawrence's optimism seems misplaced some fifty years later, when so many ties still bind women far more subtly than the lack of suffrage. Nevertheless, the vision of the suffragettes casts its light along the path of our own generation's movement, inspiring many with the realization of what women will do in the name of freedom.

Conclusion

The political violence and moral claims of the suffragettes turned readily into patriotism, dissipating their vision of a society reformed by women. Militancy had united a community of committed women but had cut off other alternatives, other forms that might have lasted beyond World War I.[1] Yet all women's communities declined amid the national upheaval of the war and the depression following it. Emmeline Pethick-Lawrence's comments had a hollow ring in the middle of the depression, when few kept the suffrage spirit alive. Her emphasis upon the spiritually rejuvenating power of feminism was dated at a time when economic issues seemed to override all other political considerations. The breakup of the mass women's movement, and the consequent loss of center stage in the public's eye, had its roots in major historical, psychological, and ideological changes. The massive postwar backlash against any gains women had achieved both before and during the war, and the economic depression, forced women on the defensive. The assumption that women were morally superior, and the concomitant importance of sexual purity, came under assault, undermining one of the most cherished sources of the single woman's public power. Women's communities were attacked as emotionally and intellectually restrictive; their elaborate system of support and friendship was mocked as old-fashioned and possibly psychologically dangerous. Ideologically the political women's movement split between those seeking legal equality and those interested in protective legislation for women and assistance for mothers. These changes left women peculiarly vulnerable to the reassertion of traditional male-dominated political and economic structures.

The suffrage movement had brought women into public visibility in a new and unique way. But perhaps even more revolutionary was the entry of women into men's jobs during the four years of the Great War. Women worked as skilled engineers, munitions workers, agricultural workers, and chauffeurs and performed countless other tasks that would release another man for the front. Educated women were given leadership positions in the civil service, adminstering many of the new wartime bureaucracies. Women of every class proved that they could do a man's job; as one woman triumphantly wrote, "Girls are doing things / They've never done before . . . All the world is topsy-turvy / Since the War began." This takeover of male work left the men at the front feeling alienated and subtly emasculated.[2] When they returned home, the women were forced out of their jobs; yet during the postwar economic dislocation many men could not find jobs, nor could they regain their former ascendancy over women. To many social commentators and writers, women seemed to have done all too well without men.

In 1918 women over thirty were given the vote, largely for their war work. During the ensuing decade the nonmilitant women's suffrage organizations poured their energies into getting women candidates elected to Parliament and lobbying Parliament for the passage of bills seen as specifically women's issues.[3] The National Union of Women's Suffrage Societies changed its name to the National Union of Societies for Equal Citizenship (NUSEC), becoming in the process a key pressure group. Composed mainly of the middle-class leadership of the old NUWSS, the new organization sought social change through legislation. A number of immediate successes helped to sustain enthusiasm; moreover, feminists were united in the fight to remove the age bar on women's suffrage. Among the major victories of the 1920s that the feminists claimed were raising the age of consent for indecent assault from thirteen to sixteen, increasing the minimum amount payable by a husband or father in cases of separation or bastardy, raising the age to eighteen for the sale of intoxicating beverages, and starting a pension scheme for widows with dependent children. Although the handful of women M.P.s did not vote as a block, they did support this legislation and, indeed, in several cases had initiated it.

But the legislative reforms of the 1920s were deceptive. They were bought at the price of concentrating all energies on Parliament and electoral politics, to the neglect of building a larger constituency. The more open-ended models of political activity that complemented the many women's communities, begun during the Edwardian period, were neglected; women seemed to return to the Victorian notion that women should act politically primarily as a pressure group. Moreover, NUSEC—and the larger women's movement—struggled with serious disagreements about a future women's political program. A strong minority sought to focus NUSEC's efforts on removing the remaining legal disabilities women faced. Several other organizations were founded for the same purpose, including the Six Point Group, started by Lady Rhondda, a former suffragette, the Open Door Council, and the Equal Rights Council. The most active voices in all of these organizations were middle-class women, many of whom had been politically active before the war and had gained administrative experience during the war. They represented the traditional strength of the women's movement.

The leading opposition to the egalitarians were those under the leadership of Eleanor Rathbone, who fought for protective legislation and the payment of family allowances directly to mothers. Rathbone, as president of NUSEC from 1919 to 1928, attempted to pull the organization away from its liberal roots toward a newer, more modern notion of fighting to meet women's immediate needs—maternity benefits, child protection, and protection at work. In 1925 at the annual council meeting of NUSEC, she argued,

"Now the legal barriers are down, there is still some debris left which we must clear away. But we need not give ourselves up entirely to that, for women are virtually free. At last we have done with the boring business of measuring everything that women want, or that is offered them by men's standards, to see if it is exactly up to sample. At last we can stop looking at all our problems through men's eyes and discussing them in men's phraseology. We can demand what we want for women, not because it is what men have got but because it is what women need to fulfil the potentialities of their own natures and to adjust themselves to the circumstances of their own lives."[4]

Rathbone's chief opponent was Dame Millicent Fawcett, who fought family allowance schemes because she felt that they undermined parents' responsibility to their children.[5] But behind this opposition was concern that in minimizing the "debris" that still existed in terms of the legal disabilities of women, progress toward equality would not be made. Rathbone's efforts highlight the classic dilemma of feminism: how to unite the need for equality of opportunity and equality before the law with the demand for legislation to overcome the socially determined inequalities of women.[6] If women are the bearers of children and chiefly responsible for bringing them up, then—argued Rathbone to NUSEC—feminists must struggle to help change the laws to meet women's specific needs. For the egalitarians, this change seemed to imply the legal enshrinement of women in the home rather than doing everything to help them choose whether to stay there or to leave. But special legislation, or a subsidy for mothers, could be seen as a means of providing married women with economic independence.

As the movement for family endowment grew, it gradually lost its feminist roots.[7] Indeed, Rathbone herself was willing to compromise her feminism in order to get legislation passed that she felt was essential for children. Her work for the protection of women won adherents among the left, anxious to see women withdraw from the overcrowded labor market and concerned about the health of young factory women. The right, fearful of the nation's physical health in comparison with that of Germany, found the care and protection of children and mothers to be a good form of social insurance. Enormous and vital gains were made during the interwar years in establishing a welfare system that guarded the health of mothers and children. These gains, now under assault, should not be minimized, nor should the key role women played in the passage of this legislation. But these socialist and humanitarian feminists were absorbed into the larger political issues of the times and lost their specifically feminist perspective. The equal rights feminists, on the other hand, were gradually isolated and labeled bourgeois feminists, without relevance to society's immediate needs.

The differences that divided women during these years point to the difficulties of balancing two conflicting and contradictory ideologies during a time of declining power in the public realm. Women's unique understanding of social issues had always been one of the major arguments for giving them the vote, yet when these very issues became important, women were largely pushed to the background. Those women, such as Rathbone, who continued to be public figures, became isolated individuals rather than representatives of a women's organization. It is easy to blame the past and to argue that both issues—the extension of legal rights and the founding of maternity and child benefits—were important for women, and indispensable for future gains. Looking back, we can see that both groups, moreover, suffered from a further liability. Both had focused upon legislative reform and had hoped to assimilate into the male political world; they had therefore cut themselves off from a larger support network of women. Feminists found themselves especially vulnerable to defeat in the political arena and were soon seen by the political parties as electoral liabilities. Women themselves, in turn, did not vote as a block and seldom united on issues of shared concern; class, not gender, dominated voting patterns.

But even before the war, women's public and political presence was undermined in a variety of ways difficult to fight. Imperialism, while extolling the self-sacrificing single man who gave his life to tame some remote part of the empire, called for women to return to their traditional roles in the home. The eugenics movement attempted to reform working-class mothers and to pressure upper-class women to marry, lest the race lose its best stock. Just as women became most effective in the public sphere, medical and scientific opinion was undertaking its massive reevaluation of sexual mores.[8] The very success of single women in public life threatened the status quo; independent women were accused of sex hatred and pilloried for preferring their own sex to men. Amid a wholesale effort to revive marriage and delicate womanhood, single women and their communities were covertly and overtly attacked.

The power of single women had been strongest where it was most directly concerned with mitigating the impact of male-dominated industrial society upon the weak and friendless, or where it met an immediate need of middle-class women themselves. The social legislation of the interwar period was the culmination of many years of women's work at the local level, fighting for medical examinations for schoolchildren, school meals, the humane treatment of the elderly in the workhouses, and the extension of outdoor relief.[9] Women, however, had been least effective in their efforts to influence either directly or indirectly the organization of industry, the church, the military, or the government, apart from so-called women's issues. Without a separate economic base, women could not meet men as equals in the marketplace. Working-class women were employed in the lowest-paid, least skilled, and most unattractive jobs, where they could be easily dismissed or replaced. Middle-class women who had led the peace movement during the war discovered that they had no impact whatever upon the course of World War I. A major unsuccessful struggle within the Church of England during the interwar years was the proposal to ordain women. The efforts of women to gain a foothold in male centers of power were everywhere met with defeat or very partial victory.

Although women's communities had successfully met the personal and professional needs of many middle-class single women, they never overcame the general public's sense of their being a second choice, of being temporary until the right man came along. By their very nature, many women's communities were short term, such as boarding schools or college or nurses' training homes. For most women their days in such places were a pleasant interlude to be remembered with affection or humor. In contrast, men's communities, from the House of Commons to the meanest pub, were more permanent; social mores encouraged men to bond with each other. Women's communities were always smaller and poorer than the equivalent men's institutions. The largest of the women's residential colleges never grew beyond some two hundred students and a dozen tutors; the settlement houses rarely had more than ten or fifteen residents; and even the larger boarding schools had only forty to fifty permanent teachers. Women were slow to form "old girl" organizations and usually devoted time to them only when their own daughters attended their old school. Although married women continued to have strong commitments to their colleges or favorite charities, their contributions were necessarily more limited than those of their husbands to their schools.

This underlying instability was accentuated by the depression; the underfunded women's communities were especially hard hit. Donations fell off both because of the slump and because so many other issues seemed more important. Middle-class families were reluctant or unable to send their daughters to boarding school and college; jobs were few after an expensive education, and marriage remained the more attractive option. The settlement houses and religious missions had depended heavily upon volunteers, who could no longer afford to pay their own way or lacked the time to be regular workers. When the innumerable services performed by women in sisterhoods, settlement houses, schools, and hospitals came to be an important part of the welfare state, women came to identify with their profession rather than their specific community, further weakening institutional loyalties.

Poor pay and poor morale plagued women's communities during the interwar years. No longer at the forefront of social reform, they could only claim to be performing important services for little pay and less recognition. A major shortage of nurses led to an inquiry into how conditions could be improved; much of the blame was placed on the shoulders of the hospital matrons, for creating an unpleasant atmosphere in the nurses' homes and for insisting upon excessively rigid discipline. These criticisms, of course, had been made many times before. However true they might have been, the facts that nurses' training was woefully inadequate, that hours of work were still excessive, and that the pay was atrocious may have had an even greater effect on recruitment and retention.[10] Vera Brittain described "the educational veil" teachers were forced to take, criticizing school authorities and headmistresses for their demeaning regulations,

> At present the poor quarters and miserable rules which restrict assistant mistresses in England give little opportunity for that hospitality upon which outside contacts frequently depend. Until the conditions under which they live are remedied from within, it is the duty of every community to see that a more agreeable, more colourful and less solitary life is led by those all-important women who are so largely responsible for the ideas and ideals of the new generation.[11]

Ironically, community here has reverted to its more common usage, referring to the larger community—the town—in which the teacher worked. Brittain's "community" was no longer the school itself as a sustaining center for the personal and intellectual life of the teacher. The ideals of such pioneering headmistresses as Dorothea Beale and Lucy Soulsby were forgotten or obsolete by the 1920s. The unmarried teacher was seen as isolated from the wider social and cultural community and unable to escape because of her limited income. The teacher's position, for Brittain, was without freedom or friendship.

The frequent complaints voiced during the interwar years about outdated regulations and excessive discipline within women's working communities point to a weakness intrinsic in the original formulation of these institutions. Women's institutions had first been modeled upon the bourgeois family; when they evolved into something very different, women leaders had no alternative language or analysis of their worlds. Communities remained organizationally conservative, usually with a single powerful leader, a well-defined internal hierarchy, and considerable social distance between the women workers and those they served. The wide-ranging structual experimentation that has marked women's communities of our time had no attractions for nineteenth-century English women. Such experiments would have been impossible for respectable women, since they were tainted with the disreputable colors of the radical and utopian traditions.[12] By the interwar years women's communities faced public criticism, economic distress, and widespread disaffection. They were hardly in a position to consider alternative models of organization, even though the rhetoric of the Victorian family threatened to suffocate the residents. Since the leaders lacked an attractive alternative perspective, the communities became increasingly out of touch with the needs of a new generation of single women.

Educated working women had identified with their workplace and their profession, finding personal and work satisfactions in this immediate community. They had no tradition of trade unionism, another model that might have been a viable alternative to their family-based communities. Both the Labour party and the Trade Union Congress were actively recruiting nurses and teachers during the interwar years, encouraging the development of broader loyalties and a new kind of community through union activity. The union drive within nursing focused upon hours of work and pay, attracting many recruits from among those nurses who were not eligible for the professional organization, the College of Nursing. In spite of the shortage of nurses, the economic crisis of the voluntary hospitals, fears for the patients' situation, and divisions within the occupation itself prevented major gains from being won through trade unionism.[13] The teachers' union, dominated by men, accepted an egregiously lower pay scale for women as well as the passage by local councils of regulations banning married women from teaching.[14] Little effort was made to attract the elite of women's secondary-school teaching, but the women themselves usually felt no sympathy for trade unionism. Notions of professionalism dominated middle-class women's occupations, preventing the formation of one obvious alternative support community.

Nineteenth-century women seeking to improve their economic and social position had prized respectability and moral purity as cornerstones upon which to build change. If the larger society ex-

the sexes. The Men and Women's Club, founded by the eugenicist Karl Pearson, attracted women interested in discussing sexual relations in a value-free environment.[18] By the 1890s marriage, free love, frigidity, and venereal disease were openly discussed in women's fiction, the press, and educated circles.[19] These debates led the way to a different, radical feminist tradition that was then taken up with renewed energy during the years immediately before World War I. The brilliant young journalist Rebecca West and the editors of *The Freewoman* called for a sexual freedom that liberated both men and women from foolishly debilitating stereotypes.[20]

The sex radicals had been intensely idealistic in their concept of a new freedom between men and women. But they did not control the terms of the debate about sexuality, which moved into a consideration of the various theories of Freud and other Continental theorists. Outside the intelligentsia, sexual emancipation became transformed for middle-class consumption into an argument for "companionate marriage." As Christine Simmons has said in regard to a similar movement in the United States, the concept of a more equal marriage was an attempt to adapt to women's perceived new social and sexual power.[21] Sexual freedom became greater access to men on male terms, with the woman bearing the new responsibility of enjoying sex. In the process the discussion of the woman's position shifted from what role she should play in public to a consideration of her role in marriage. Individual psychology preempted social concerns, leaving the single woman a bystander, shorn of her carefully developed special mission. The sexual revolution placed new strains upon marriage and pushed the unmarried to question their state as sexually abnormal. Single women had no weapons with which to fight the labeling of their friendships as deviant because they had understood sexual activity as heterosexual. Without either a strong women's movement or a self-conscious homosexual subculture for support, middle-class women could only turn to friends—perhaps equally suspect—or religion for an alternative explanation.

Women's communities during the second half of the nineteenth century had been based upon the only available viable ideology for respectable single women, but they had failed to meet the changing demands of the interwar period and had become ideologically and conceptually obsolete. During the interwar years the major professional occupations for women—teaching, nursing, and social work—remained largely single-sex ghettos. But unmarried women who worked in these jobs had lost the richly nurturing women's subculture of the past without gaining access to an aggressively married and heterosexual world. Married women had been pushed back into a new, equally confining version of the domesticity that had dominated their lives before the suffrage movement and the war. Only a few women kept alive the visionary quality of the suffrage movement during these years, based now upon a new sex equality. The unmarried Winifred Holtby optimistically wrote in 1934,

> It seems possible that in a wiser world we should walk more delicately. We might, perhaps, consider individuals as individuals, not primarily as members of this or that race, sex and status. We might be content to love the individual, perceiving in him or her a spirit which is divine as well as human and which has little to do with the accident of the body. We might allow individual ability rather than social traditions to determine what vocation each member of our community should follow.
> And it is possible that in such a world we should find a variety of personality undreamed of to-day, a social solidarity to-day rendered unimaginable by prejudices, grievances, fears and repulsions, a radiance of adventure, of happiness and satisfaction now only hinted at by poets and prophets.
> At least we know definitely enough whither the other ideal leads us. "We want men who are men and women who are women," writes Sir Oswald Mosley. He can find them at their quintessence in the slave markets of Abyssinia, or in the winding alleys of a Chinese city. [22]

Single women have carried the utopian vision of a better world, of a more just and equal world for both women and men; but they have also been independent women, working today for that future world.

Appendix A:
Gross Population Figures

TABLE A.1
England and Wales, Total Population

Year	Total	Males	Females
1851	17,927,609	8,781,225	9,146,384
1861	20,066,224	9,776,259	10,289,965
1871	22,712,266	11,058,934	11,653,332
1881	25,974,439	12,639,902	13,334,537
1891	29,002,525	14,052,901	14,949,624
1901	32,527,843	15,728,613	16,799,230
1911	36,070,492	17,445,608	18,624,884
1921	37,886,699	18,075,239	19,811,460

TABLE A.2
England and Wales, Female Population, Aged Twenty Years and Upward

Year	20–44	45+
1851	3,350,806	1,748,778
1861	3,746,579	2,006,406
1871	4,144,056	2,319,589
1881	4,710,654	2,604,795
1891	5,405,513	2,957,978
1901	6,477,226	3,397,968
1911	7,307,019	4,116,311
1921	7,693,200[a]	5,127,900[a]

[a] Rounded to nearest hundred.

TABLE A.3
England and Wales, Female Population, Aged Twenty Years and Upward,
by Marital Status

	Unmarried		Married and Widowed	
Year	20–44	45+	20–44	45+
1851	1,239,906	204,650	2,110,900	1,544,128
1861	1,312,050	225,183	3,735,929	1,781,223
1871	1,410,421	260,404	2,733,635	2,059,185
1881	1,618,891	292,147	3,091,763	2,312,648
1891	2,009,489	342,072	3,396,024	2,615,906
1901	2,520,184	421,549	3,962,042	2,976,419
1911	2,869,416	579,026	4,437,603	3,537,285
1921	2,843,600[a]	788,800[a]	4,849,600[a]	4,339,100[a]

[a] Rounded to nearest hundred.

Appendix B: Model Housing and Clubs for Women

I am specifically concerned with communities of choice in this book, but an important, if minor, strand in the history of Victorian single women was the creation of subsidized housing and clubs for women who did not work in communities. So attractive did the model of community life become that in the late 1880s feminist journals vigorously advocated the establishment of "suitable house accommodation at reasonable rents to ladies of small incomes, where, while retaining their entire independence, they may live with greater comfort and economy than in lodging houses of the ordinary type."[1] In 1887 *Work and Leisure*, a magazine for working ladies, ran a competition calling for practical suggestions for the "Erection, Arrangement, and Management of a block of Associated Dwellings adapted to the needs of single women at 10–50 shillings per week."[2] Through such buildings, isolated working women in large cities would be able to form friendships and draw upon a community of like-minded individuals. Model houses would not be families, since the emphasis was upon freedom of movement, but they would be potential communities, offering protection, convenience, and opportunities for a fuller social life.

Soon after the *Work and Leisure* contest a "Ladies' Dwelling Company" was formed that built a large home on Lower Sloane Street. Several other successful schemes were initiated, enabling women to enjoy the privacy of a bed-sitting room with communal living and dining rooms at a reasonable cost. But like so many other Victorian philanthropic schemes, the model homes were rather more expensive than was originally intended and so helped only those who probably did not need them. Far more common were small boardinghouses taken over by a philanthropic organization, such as John Shrimpton's Society for Homes for Working Girls or the Young Women's Christian Association, run on a not-for-profit basis.[3] Most of these institutions catered to women under thirty, encouraging women to think of work as a temporary state before marriage. Both Shrimpton and the YWCA tried to create some kind of community through newsletters, parties, and group prayers, but many homes seem to have been dismal monuments to personal failure. Rachel McMillan in the 1880s took a job at £20 a year as a junior superintendent at a working girls' home in Bloomsbury. The atmosphere of the converted mansion was one of anxiety and adventure:

> It was a toss-up what became of any of us, and no amount of prudence and well-doing might avail. Many prudent, self-respecting and diligent failures were in this very home. The elder women sat in grim circles in the Sahara drawing-room, saying little of their dismal past and vanished hopes, but warming into life in discussing the royalties and the aristocracy. . . . The mere thought of them was like a fire lighted in a dim and draughty attic. All their criticism was for the frail and frivolous young creatures who came and went about them in this big, noisy house.[4]

Many homes were not able to strike the right balance between freedom and regulation; they held on to restrictive regulations for decades, making them increasingly unpopular in spite of their financial advantages. The morale of women in such "model homes" deteriorated further in the twentieth century, as women fought the stigma of living with other "failures."[5]

The more expensive homes, such as "Sloane Gardens," however, remained very popular with better-paid professional women. Unlike the cheaper homes, they offered self-contained flats and bed-sitting rooms, in addition to the more common dormitories with cubicles divided off by curtains. Since good housing in central London remained at a premium, well-managed model housing always had long waiting lists.[6] A major advantage of the housing schemes was the provision of a dining hall. Few working women had the time or energy to shop and cook properly for themselves, so an inexpensive meal with good companions was a real treat. M. V. Hughes speaks of the pleasures of living in a Ladies' Residential Chambers, sharing a flat with a good friend, where

> Meals gave us no trouble, for a good dinner was served in the common dining-room, lunch was either a picnic affair at home or else taken at a tea-shop, and our gas-ring was enough for breakfast requirements. . . . The evening dinner was al-

ways a pleasant interlude, for we met a variety of interesting
women, all of them at work of some kind—artists, authors,
political workers, and so on.[7]

Hughes was engaged, and so always went out weekends with her
fiancé, but other women found the Chambers improved their
social lives and gave them a place to invite friends to share a meal.

The physical mobility of single women was distinctly circumscribed in a city, in spite of the greater and greater freedom they
experienced during the last two decades of the century. A lady was
simply not supposed to be seen aimlessly wandering the streets in
the evening or eating alone; indeed, for many years she had nowhere to eat, since she could not enter a pub or chop house. Fortunately, in the early 1880s cafés and temperance restaurants,
both commercial and philanthropic, began to dot the central areas
of London and the major provincial cities. But this great boon did
not solve a problem that still plagues working women: how to
spend two or three hours after work but before a meeting or theater engagement. As a shorthand clerk explained,

> try all I can, I can't take more than an hour to dispose of [tea].
> Then if it is fine, I wander around; if it is wet, I lurk about
> railway stations, or any place with a roof. In fine weather it
> has its enjoyments, in wet it decidedly has not.[8]

This respectable clerk's plight simply would not have existed for
her mother or grandmother. Her greater freedom also brought
greater isolation. There were never enough clubs for the thousands of London women who needed a convenient place to go for a
brushup or to meet other women or simply to relax.

All the successful clubs, mostly founded in the 1890s and 1900s,
were subsidized by the founders, or admitted men at a higher rate,
or remained small, special-interest groups. Fortunately for the
clerk, in 1889 the Enterprise Club was founded, specifically to
meet the needs of City workers. At a subscription rate of ten shillings a year, it depended upon donations from interested friends.
A Miss Mabel Morgan of Hammersmith took on the club as her
specific charity, attending daily and supervising the meals and
various entertainments. She canvassed her friends and well-
wishers for donations of £1 per year to meet the cost of renting
rooms in the City. The Enterprise Club clearly met a felt need;
within a few years it had a membership of nearly three hundred. It

offered Saturday evening entertainment, cheap holiday information, a chess club, a hockey club, and courses in French conversation, wood carving, and shorthand practice. Open until eight in the evening every night, meals were offered at the "lowest prices compatible with refinement and good taste."[9]

Like so many other institutions for middle-class single women, clubs maintained clear class distinctions. The Enterprise Club and its imitators were intended for lower-middle-class women without professional skills or much social standing. The upper-middle-class clubs modeled themselves after the men's clubs of the day, offering rooms for short stays, better-than-average food, a smoking room, meeting rooms, and formal evening entertainment. One of the most popular of these clubs was the Pioneer Club, founded in 1892 by the wealthy and widowed Mrs. Massingberd. Limited to three hundred members, the Pioneers prided themselves on their feminism, temperance, and work for women. They attracted a good deal of positive publicity in the mid-nineties, but after the death of Mrs. Massingberd in 1897, the club broke into two opposing factions and seems to have lost its reputation for feminism.[10] The Lyceum Club, founded in 1904, provided a suitable meeting place for writers, artists, and other freelance workers who needed to meet male colleagues and agents without compromising themselves.[11] Although ostensibly organized to help the struggling artist, the entry fees and general requirements made the Lyceum Club accessible only to the well established. Indeed, the early membership lists read like a Who's Who of women's journalism, writing, and the arts. Probably the Women Writers' Club, which had a small office near Fleet Street with free typewriters for members' use, was a more valuable service for beginners.

Although women's clubs were never all that they could be—they never lost the stigma of being both feminine and feminist—they did meet a need for independent working women who lacked social contacts or did not work in an institution or needed an inexpensive pied-à-terre in London. The Cambridge classicist Jane Ellen Harrison regularly used the Sesame Club, praising in particular the services of the hall porter, who was "a kind of mother to me: finds me everything I lose, looks up trains and generally saves me when I am caught on the wheel of things."[12] But even she could not resist making self-conscious jokes about the club to her close friend Lady Mary Murray:

Also, like an idiot I forgot to show you our one high toned room, the Ruskin Room, that would have redeemed the club from ignominy—it is furnished with hard chairs and pens and maps and desks and every manner of austerity. I insisted upon Mr. Verrall going to see it, he stood desolate in the doorway and remarked—"Oh Lor!"[13]

Harrison seems to have half-regretted having to admit her need for a club to her well-connected and happily married friend.

Clubs never played a major role in the lives of the women members, as they did for upper-class men or trade unionists. Women themselves declared that they were not "clubbable," but preferred to create homes rather than clubs.[14] Possibly their rather limited success was more due to their being a combination of a men's club and a charity. The purely female institutions, such as schools or sisterhoods, were more fully shaped by women for their needs, even when they drew upon preexisting models. Clubs, moreover, were not intimate places; women's communities were habitually drawn from a rather narrow stratum of society, catering to shared interests, excluding those who did not fit. This snobbery was their strength and weakness, for it made it easier to unite together but more difficult to welcome outsiders. Clubs may have been too public, too filled with those who did not fit anywhere; women's space tended to be more private, more homelike, offering the accoutrements of the domestic even in such public spheres as a college or boarding school. Clubs did not fit readily into such a definition and suffered accordingly.

Notes

Introduction

1. Honnor Morten, *From a Nurse's Note-book* (London: Scientific Press, 1899), pp. 152–53.
2. Florence Nightingale, "Cassandra," reprinted in Ray Strachey, *The Cause* (London: Virago, 1978 [1852]), pp. 396 and 398.
3. Cecil Woodham-Smith, *Florence Nightingale, 1820–1910* (London: Constable, 1950), pp. 60–61.
4. See Kathryn Kish Sklar, *Catharine Beecher: A Study in American Domesticity* (New Haven: Yale University Press, 1973), pp. 155–67, 244–57; and Nancy F. Cott, *The Bonds of Womanhood: "Woman's Sphere" in New England, 1780–1835* (New Haven: Yale University Press, 1977), pp. 199–201, for a discussion of "woman's sphere" in America.
5. J. A. Banks, *Prosperity and Parenthood: A Study of Family Planning among the Victorian Middle Classes* (London: Routledge and Kegan Paul, 1954), pp. 36–47.
6. [Eliza Lynn Linton], "The Girl of the Period," *Saturday Review*, 14 March 1868, p. 340.
7. "Queen Bees or Working Bees?" Review of a paper read by Bessie Parkes to the Social Science Congress, *Saturday Review* (12 November 1859). Quoted in J. A. and Olive Banks, *Feminism and Family Planning in Victorian England* (Liverpool: Liverpool University Press, 1964), p. 43.
8. W. R. Greg, "Why Are Women Redundant?" *National Review* 15 (1862):436.
9. Greg, p. 451. Italics in the original.
10. See in particular Frances Power Cobbe, "'What Shall We Do with Our Old Maids?'" *Fraser's Magazine* 66 (1862):594–610, and Jessie Boucherett, "How to Provide for Superfluous Women," in *Woman's Work and Woman's Culture*, ed. Josephine E. Butler (London: Macmillan, 1869), pp. 27–48. See also the American Mary Ashton Livermore, *What Shall We Do with Our Daughters?* (Boston: Lee and Shepard, 1883), pp. 132–208.

11. For contemporary documentation of this point, see Clara E. Collet, "Prospects of Marriage for Women," in *Educated Working Women: Essays on the Economic Position of Women Workers in the Middle Classes* (London: P. S. King, 1902), pp. 48–55. See also Lee Holcombe, *Victorian Ladies at Work* (Hamden, Conn.: Archon Press, 1973), for an examination of the development of employment for middle-class women. Holcombe also makes the valuable point that the rate of increase for women employed as shop assistants, clerks, civil servants, and teachers was more rapid than that for men, but in no case did the absolute numbers of men decline. See p. 215.

12. Holcombe, p. 215.

13. B. L. Hutchins, *The Working Life of Women* (London: Fabian Society, 1911), p. 7. Hutchins's statistics are based on the 1901 census, the first to differentiate between single and widowed women. See also [Frances Power Cobbe], "Excess of Widows over Widowers," *Westminster Review* 131 (1889):501–5.

14. For a discussion of the ways women's culture is embedded in a larger, male-dominated culture, see Gerda Lerner, untitled response, in Ellen Dubois, Mari Jo Buhle, Temma Kaplan, Gerda Lerner, and Carroll Smith-Rosenberg, "Politics and Culture in Women's History: A Symposium," *Feminist Studies* 6 (1980):52–53.

15. American women's efforts, utopian and actual, to reorder and redesign their space are discussed by Dolores Hayden, *The Grand Domestic Revolution: A History of Feminist Designs for American Homes, Neighborhoods, and Cities* (Cambridge: MIT Press, 1981).

16. *Woman's Signal*, 29 November 1894. Quoted in Judith R. Walkowitz, *Prostitution and Victorian Society: Women, Class and the State* (Cambridge: Cambridge University Press, 1980), p. 255.

17. See Rosalind Rosenberg, *Beyond Separate Spheres: Intellectual Roots of Modern Feminism* (New Haven: Yale University Press, 1982), Nancy Chodorow, *The Reproduction of Mothering: Psychoanalysis and the Sociology of Gender* (Berkeley: University of California Press, 1978), and Carol Gilligan, *In a Different Voice: Psychological Theory and Women's Development* (Cambridge: Harvard University Press, 1982). This connection was first pointed out to me by Judith Walkowitz.

18. Mrs. Alexander Ireland, ed., *Selections from the Letters of Geraldine Endsor Jewsbury to Jane Welsh Carlyle* (London: Longmans, Green, 1892), pp. 347–48.

19. Ireland, p. 349.

Chapter One

1. Charlotte Yonge, *The Daisy Chain, or Aspirations* (New York: Garland, 1977 [1856]), part 2, chap. 27, p. 667.

2. Yonge, part 2, chap. 23, p. 620.

3. See Barbara Taylor, *Eve and the New Jerusalem: Socialism and Feminism in the Nineteenth Century* (London: Virago, 1983), for a study of the radical and utopian strands of feminism.

4. [Mrs. Ann Judith Penny], *The Afternoon of Unmarried Life* (London: Brown, Green, Longmans and Roberts, 1858), p. 142.

5. Ibid., pp. 144, 146.

6. C. B. Firth, *Constance Maynard: Mistress of Westfield College* (London: George Allen and Unwin, 1949), p. 54.

7. Dinah Mulock Craik, *A Woman's Thoughts about Women* (London: Hurst and Blackett, [1858]), pp. 347–48.

8. Mrs. [Anna] Jameson, *"Sisters of Charity" and "The Communion of Labour": Two Lectures on the Social Employment of Women* (London: Longman, Brown, Green, Longmans and Roberts, 1859), p. xxx (prefatory letter to Lord John Russell). The lectures were originally given in 1855 and 1856. At the time Jameson was writing it was by no means "generally acknowledged" that women had a part in the running of "all social institutions." Jameson had in mind workhouses, prisons, hospitals, orphanages, and other state or charitable institutions. In spite of her modesty, Jameson was indirectly questioning paternalism.

9. Frances Power Cobbe, "Social Science Congresses and Women's Part in Them," in *Essays on the Pursuits of Women* (London: Emily Faithfull, 1863), pp. 25–26. Italics in the original.

10. Cobbe lived at home quite happily until her father's death and then began her career. See her *Life*, 2 vols. (London: Richard Bentley, 1894). For a discussion of the conflicts felt by American single women who attempted to combine domestic duties and public (or creative) obligations, see Lee Chambers-Schiller, "The Single Woman: Family and Vocation Among Nineteenth-Century Reformers," in *Woman's Being, Woman's Place: Female Identity and Vocation in American History*, ed. Mary Kelley (Boston: G. K. Hall, 1979), pp. 334–50.

11. The most vigorous early exponent of intellectual and moral equality between men and women during the early years of the twentieth century was Rebecca West. See the essays in *The Young Rebecca: Writings of Rebecca West, 1911–1917*, selected and introduced by Jane Marcus (London: Virago, 1982).

12. See Gail Malmgreen, *Neither Bread nor Roses: Utopian Feminists and the English Working Class, 1800–1850* (Brighton: John L. Noyce, 1978), and Taylor, pp. 276–87.

13. Both Susan R. Gorsky and Nina Auerbach make this point in regard to women in fiction. See Gorsky, "Old Maids and New Women: Alternatives to Marriage in Englishwomen's Novels, 1847–1915," *Journal of Popular Culture* 7 (1973):68–85, and Auerbach, *Communities of Women: An Idea in Fiction* (Cambridge: Harvard University Press, 1978), p. 24.

14. Mary Taylor, *The First Duty of Women* (London: Emily Faithfull, 1870), p. 209.

15. Cobbe, "Celibacy vs. Marriage," in *Essays*, pp. 54–55.

16. For a discussion of the legal problems of married women, see Lee Holcombe, *Wives and Property: Reform of the Married Women's Property Law in Nineteenth-Century England* (Toronto: University of Toronto Press, 1982).

17. Mary Cadbury, unpub. letter, 17 December 1881, Nightingale Training School Archives, Greater London Record Office.

18. Cobbe, "Celibacy vs. Marriage," in *Essays*, pp. 52–53. Italics in the original.

19. The main arguments for and against providing viable alternatives to marriage are well summarized by J. A. and Olive Banks in *Feminism and Family Planning in Victorian England* (Liverpool: Liverpool University Press, 1964), pp. 42–44.

20. *Englishwoman's Review* 16 (15 April 1885): 160.

21. Quoted in Cecil Woodham-Smith, *Florence Nightingale, 1820–1910* (London: Constable, 1950), p. 77.

22. Constance Maynard, unpub. autobiography, section 33 (1878), p. 128, Westfield College Archives. Maynard transcribed large sections of her diary into her autobiography, including this comment. Italics in the original.

23. Nightingale's success in the Crimea has been questioned recently by two historians, F. B. Smith, *Florence Nightingale: Reputation and Power* (London: Croom Helm, 1982), pp. 25–71, and Anne Summers, "Pride and Prejudice: Ladies and Nurses in the Crimean War," *History Workshop Journal* 16 (Autumn 1983): 33–56. Despite latter-day reevaluations, contemporaries were convinced that Nightingale and her band of nurses were heroines who had saved countless lives.

24. Conservative commentators recommended emigration, since men were in the majority in Australia, Canada, and the western United States. But an extremely small number of middle-class women actually emigrated. See A. James Hammerton, *Emigrant Gentlewomen* (London: Croom Helm, 1979).

25. Emily Shirreff, *Intellectual Education and Its Influence on the Character and Happiness of Women* (London: John W. Parker, 1858), pp. 147–48. I am indebted to Janet Murray for this reference.

26. Taylor, p. 2. Taylor adopted the persona of a young woman in some essays in *The First Duty of Women.*

27. Josephine Kamm, *Hope Deferred: Girls' Education in English History* (London: Methuen, 1965), p. 181.

28. The debate on the intellectual capabilities of women versus their physiological limitations focused on higher education, though it was by no means limited to this level. The arguments are analyzed by Joan N. Burstyn in "Education and Sex: The Medical Case against Higher Education for Women in England, 1870–1900," *Proceedings of the American Philosophical Society* 117 (April 1973):79–89.

29. For a discussion of the impact of women on philanthropic work, see Anne Summers, "A Home from Home—Women's Philanthropic Work in the Nineteenth Century," in *Fit Work for Women,* ed. Sandra Berman (New York: St. Martin's Press, 1979), pp. 33–63.

30. Harriet Martineau, *Autobiography,* 3d ed. (London: Smith Elder, 1877), 1 : 141–42.

31. Ray Strachey, *The Cause* (London: Virago, 1978 [1928]), p. 60.

32. For a discussion of this first organized feminist group, see Strachey, pp. 89–98, and Hester Burton, *Barbara Bodichon, 1827–1891* (London: John Murray, 1949), pp. 97–114.

33. Jameson, p. 63.

34. Taylor, p. 203.

35. Lee Holcombe, *Victorian Ladies at Work: Middle-Class Working Women in England and Wales, 1850–1914* (Hamden, Conn.: Archon Press, 1973), passim, especially pp. 43, 57, 138–39, 151–52, 174–78, 184–85, and 191, for comparisons with men in the same fields of work. See also Clara E. Collet, "The Economic Position of Educated Working Women" and "The Expenditure of Middle Class Working Women," in *Educated Working Women: Essays on the Economic Position of Women Workers in the Middle Classes* (London: P. S. King, 1902), pp. 1–26 and 66–89. The essays were originally published in 1890 and 1898.

36. Ada Moore, "The 'Decayed' Gentlewoman: An Appeal to England's Chivalry," *Westminster Review* 162 (1904):457.

37. Collet, "The Expenditure of Middle Class Working Women," p. 77.

38. Frances H. Low, "How Poor Ladies Live," *Nineteenth Century* 41 (1897):411.

39. See Maud Pember Reeves, *Round about a Pound a Week* (London: Virago, 1979 [1913]), an account of Battersea families, and F. Mabel Robinson, "Our Working Women and Their Earnings," *Fortnightly Review* 48 (July 1887):50–63.

40. See Moore, and Low, "How Poor Ladies Live." See also Edith M.

Shaw, "How Poor Ladies Might Live: An Answer from the Workhouse" *Nineteenth Century* 41 (1897):620–27, and Low's rebuttal, "How Poor Ladies Live: A Rejoinder and a 'Jubilee' Suggestion," *Nineteenth Century* 42 (1897):161–68.

41. Banks and Banks, p. 45.

42. I am indebted to Rosemary Auchmuty for the formulation of these tables. See her "Victorian Spinsters," Ph.D. thesis, Australian National University, 1975, p. 40. The calculation of 15 percent of the population is based upon the census returns' classification of class 1 (upper professional) and class 2 (lower professional).

43. See D. V. Glass, "Marriage Frequency and Economic Fluctuations in England and Wales, 1851 to 1934," in *Political Arithmetic: A Symposium of Population Studies*, ed. Lancelot Hogben (London: Allen and Unwin, 1938).

44. The 1901 census is the first to differentiate between single, widowed, and married in employment figures.

45. For these figures, based upon table 2, see 1901 Census of England and Wales, Great Britain, House of Commons Sessional Papers 1903, 74:186–99; 1911 Census of England and Wales, 10, part 1:75–88, Great Britain, House of Commons Sessional Papers 1913, vol. 78.

46. *The Contemporary Review*, a religiously-oriented middle-of-the-road monthly, was generally in favor of women's education and scoffed at fears about women's health breaking down from overexertion. See, for example, the review of Emily Davies's *The Higher Education of Women* in *Contemporary Review* 4 (1867): 286–87. I am indebted to Donna Wessel Walker for this reference.

47. The best-known medical attack before the early twentieth century suffragette movement was Henry Maudsley's "Sex in Mind and in Education," *Fortnightly Review* 21 (1874):466–83, and Elizabeth Garrett Anderson's reply, "Sex in Mind and Education: A Reply," *Fortnightly Review* 21 (1874): 582–94. See also Burstyn.

48. This world has been most notably described for the United States by Carroll Smith-Rosenberg, "The Female World of Love and Ritual: Relations between Women in Nineteenth-Century America," *Signs* 1 (1975): 1–29. See also the forthcoming study of kinship and family networks, Leonore Davidoff and Catherine Hall, *The Domestic Enterprise: Men and Women in the English Provincial Middle Class, 1780 to 1850* (London: Hutchinson, 1985).

49. Elsie Bowerman, *Stands There a School: Memories of Dame Frances Dove* (Brighton: Wycombe Abbey School Seniors, [1966]), p. 25.

50.   Jo Manton, *Elizabeth Garrett Anderson* (London: Methuen, 1965), pp. 76–78.
51.   Quoted by Sir Edward Cook, *The Life of Florence Nightingale*, 2 vols. (London: Macmillan, 1913), 2:15.
52.   From Mrs. [Sarah Stickney] Ellis, *The Women of England: Their Social Duties and Domestic Habits* (New York: J. & H. G. Langley, 1843). Originally published in 1839. Quoted in Auerbach, pp. 17–18.
53.   Auerbach, p. 17.
54.   See Lillian Faderman, *Surpassing the Love of Men: Romantic Friendship and Love between Women from the Renaissance to the Present* (New York: William Morrow, 1981), pp. 85–102.
55.   Mrs. Alexander Ireland, ed., *Selections from the Letters of Geraldine Endsor Jewsbury to Jane Welsh Carlyle* (London: Longmans, Green, 1892), p. 57.
56.   Elizabeth M. Sewell, *Principles of Education, Drawn from Nature and Revelation, and Applied to Female Education in the Upper Classes* (New York: D. Appleton, 1871), p. 335. Originally published in 1865.
57.   Sewell, p. 330.
58.   Woodham-Smith, pp. 68–83, 100–101. Fanny Nightingale approved of Mrs. Bracebridge because she hoped that her wide circle of friends might yield a suitor for Florence.
59.   Firth, p. 70, and Constance Maynard, unpub. autobiography, section 2 (1868), p. 105, Westfield College Archives. Constance noted that her sister was stopped "from merely sentimental reasons, and not from fear of infection, and just in the last days when G[azy] was beginning to reap the fruit of her earnest prayers and labours [for his conversion]."
60.   Dinah Mulock Craik, *A Woman's Thoughts about Women* (London: Hurst and Blackett, [1858]), p. 174.
61.   For a discussion of these issues, see my articles, "'One Life to Stand beside Me': Emotional Conflicts of First-Generation College Women in England," *Feminist Studies* 8 (1982):603–28, and "Distance and Desire: English Boarding-School Friendships," *Signs* 9 (1984):600–22.
62.   See Appendix B for a discussion of the efforts in the 1880s and 1890s to provide communal arrangements for women who did not live in their workplaces.
63.   Caroline Emilia Stephen, *Light Arising: Thoughts on the Central Radiance* (Cambridge: Heffer, 1908), pp. 116–17. I am indebted to Jane Marcus for this reference.
64.   *The Englishwoman's Year Book*, ed. Louisa M. Hubbard (London: Labour News, 1875), p. 5.
65.   Cobbe, *Life*, 1:61.

66. Edward Garrett [Isabella Fyview Mayo], *By Still Waters*, quoted in *The Englishwoman's Year Book*, p. xxxix. My thanks to Margaret Maison for checking *By Still Waters* (London: S. King, 1874), pp. 82–83, and correcting Louisa Hubbard's errors in this quotation.

67. These views were espoused by Louisa Hubbard in her periodical *Work and Leisure* (1876–93); well-to-do herself, she spent a lifetime helping ladies find work suitable to their station in life. In spite of her insistence upon the respectability of paid work, at times Hubbard sounds as if a job were dreary penance.

68. For a sentimental treatment of this issue, see Moore and Low.

69. Constance Maynard, unpub. autobiography, section 43 (1882), p. 122, Westfield College Archives.

70. See, for example, Emily Davies, the founder of Girton College, who opposed all self-governance by the Girton tutors. Barbara Stephen, *Emily Davies and Girton College* (London: Constable, 1927), pp. 340–45. See also chapters 4 and 5 in this book.

71. Judith R. Walkowitz, *Prostitution and Victorian Society: Women, Class and the State* (Cambridge: Cambridge University Press, 1980), p. 122.

72. Lady Strachey to Constance Smedley, unpub. letter (25 May 1907). Autograph Collection, Fawcett Library, City of London Polytechnic.

73. Jo Manton, *Mary Carpenter and the Children of the Streets* (London: Heinemann, 1976), p. 147.

74. Manton, *Mary Carpenter*, p. 153.

75. See Firth, pp. 212–22, and the set of diaries about Effie, Westfield College Archives.

76. Andro Linklater, *An Unhusbanded Life: Charlotte Despard, Suffragette, Socialist, and Sinn Feiner* (London: Hutchinson, 1980), p. 146.

77. Linklater, p. 190. Matters were made more difficult by Despard's secretary's addiction to laudanum, which finally necessitated sending her to an asylum. Vere Hinton, the adopted daughter, seems to have been sent from pillar to post over the years and, like Maynard's Effie, used attention-getting devices that alienated adults. She never learned to read and write thoroughly, and was always "ill-mannered."

78. Firth, pp. 227–35.

79. Edith Simcox, "Ideals of Feminine Usefulness," *Fortnightly Review* 27 (May 1880):666 and 667.

80. Simcox, pp. 665–66.

Chapter Two

1. Mrs. [Anna] Jameson, *"Sisters of Charity" and "The Communion of Labour": Two Lectures on the Social Employment of Women* (London: Longman, Brown, Green, Longmans and Roberts, 1859), p. 13.
2. Jameson, p. 630.
3. A major issue was obedience to whom—local minister, bishop, or mother superior? For a full discussion of these distinctions, see Alan Deacon and Michael Hill, "The Problem of 'Surplus Women' in the Nineteenth Century: Secular and Religious Alternatives," *Sociological Yearbook of Religion in Britain* 5 (1972):87–102.
4. [J. S. Howson], "Deaconesses," *Quarterly Review* 108 (1860):384. Howson and other proponents did not speak of reviving a full—male and female—diaconate but wished to revive only deaconesses.
5. Rev. A. P. Forbes, *A Plea for Sisterhoods*, 2d ed. (London: Joseph Masters, 1850), p. 14.
6. Harriette J. Cooke, *Mildmay, or The Story of the First Deaconess Institution* (London: Elliot Stock, 1892), pp. 58–60.
7. See L. N. R. [Ellen Henrietta Raynard], *The Missing Link, or Bible-Women in the Homes of the London Poor* (London: James Nisbet, 1859). Later in the century the church organized a rival to the Salvation Army, the Church Army, largely composed of working-class women and men. See Graham Simpson, "A Sociological Study of the Church Army," Oxford D. Phil., 1979. I am indebted to Brian Heeney for this reference.
8. See F. K. Prochaska, *Women and Philanthropy in Nineteenth-Century England* (Oxford: Clarendon Press, 1980), for a discussion of the growth in volunteer philanthropic workers.
9. Henry Parry Liddon, *Life of Edward Bouverie Pusey* (London: Longmans, Green, 1894), 3:18–21. See also the unpublished correspondence of E. B. Pusey, Pusey House, Oxford. Lord John Manners chaired the committee, but Gladstone is generally credited with having written the proposal. For a full discussion of these early days, see Thomas Jay Williams and Allan Walter Campbell, *The Park Village Sisterhood* (London: SPCK, 1965), and Peter F. Anson and Allan Walter Campbell, *The Call of the Cloister*, rev. ed. (London: SPCK, 1964), pp. 220–40.
10. In 1861 the Reverend J. M. Neale, founder of the Society of St. Margaret, wrote to a friend that there were eighty-six sisters in seven orders, not including the Community of St. Mary Virgin at Wantage, with seven, and the Sellonites. See A. M. Allchin, *The*

Silent Rebellion: Anglican Religious Communities, 1845–1900 (London: SCM Press, 1958), p. 100. The estimate of two to three thousand sisters by 1900 is Allchin's (see p. 120). All figures for the number of sisters in orders throughout the chapter are drawn from Allchin or Anson and Campbell and exclude communities overseas. It is very difficult to obtain accurate figures on the number of women in religious life, as sisterhoods generally do not make the information available or count only professed sisters.

11. [Sisters of Bethany], *The Society of the Sisters of Bethany, 1866–1966* (Bournemouth, 1966), p. 5.

12. [Dinah Mulock Craik], *About Money and Other Things* (London: Macmillan, 1886), pp. 159–60.

13. Michael Hill, *The Religious Order: A Study of Virtuoso Religion and Its Legitimation in the Nineteenth-Century Church of England* (London: Heinemann, 1973), p. 39.

14. Jane Ellacombe to her father, Rev. M. T. Ellacombe, unpub. letters, 20 August 1843 and 13 May 1844, Pusey House, Oxford.

15. Margaret Goodman, *Sisterhoods in the Church of England* (London: Smith, Elder, 1863), p. 7. See also her *Experiences of an English Sister of Mercy* (London: Smith, Elder, 1862), which is largely an account of her experiences in the Crimea but does include some further information on her life as a sister under Lydia Sellon.

16. Sister Emmeline, "The Life of a Sister of the People," *Young Woman* 2 (1893–94):129.

17. [Mother Kate Warburton], *Memories of a Sister of St. Saviour's Priory* (London: A. R. Mowbray, 1903), pp. 3, 7–8.

18. [Mother Kate Warburton], *Old Soho Days* (London: A. R. Mowbray, 1906), p. 6.

19. Constance Maynard, unpub. autobiography, section 2 (1868), pp. 132–34, Westfield College Archives. The events are transcribed directly from Maynard's diary for 1867.

20. See Susan P. Casteras, "Virgin Vows: The Early Victorian Artists' Portrayal of Nuns and Novices," *Victorian Studies* 24 (Winter 1981):157–84.

21. See Mary F. Cusak, *The Story of My Life* (London: Hodder and Stoughton, 1891), p. 63.

22. Alice Horlock Bennett, *Through an Anglican Sisterhood to Rome* (London: Longmans, 1914), pp. 26–27.

23. *Our Work* 9 (January 1886):3. *Our Work* was the monthly newsletter of the Sisters of the Church.

24. For a detailed outline of each order's requirements and expenses, see *Directory of Religious Communities of Men and Women,*

and of Deaconesses (London: Faith Press, 1920). See also Allchin, passim, and Anson and Campbell, passim.

25. E. B. Pusey to Mother Bertha [Lydia Sellon's successor as mother superior of the Sisters of Mercy], unpub. letter, 12 April 1877, Pusey House, Oxford.

26. Allchin, p. 82.

27. For the most recent full discussions of sisterhoods, focusing largely upon Roman Catholic orders, see Marcelle Bernstein, *The Nuns* (New York: Bantam, 1979). See also Suzanne Campbell-Jones, *In Habit: An Anthropological Study of Working Nuns* (London: Faber and Faber, 1979), and Geoffrey Moorhouse, *Against All Reason* (London: Weidenfeld and Nicolson, 1969).

28. Personal conversation with the author, Community of St. John Baptist, Clewer (July 1980).

29. Anson and Campbell, p. 231, and unpub. correspondence of E. B. Pusey to William Dodsworth, Pusey House, Oxford.

30. The fullest description of Victorian convent life for interested laypeople was "Sisterhood Life," in *The Church and the World: Essays on Questions of the Day in 1867*, ed. Rev. Orby Shipley (London: Longmans, Green, Reader and Dyer, 1867), pp. 166–95.

31. See Janet Grierson, *The Deaconess* (London: Church Information Office, 1981). See also the history of the Deaconess Community of St. Andrew, the direct descendant of the LDDI, by Sister Joanna, "The Deaconess Community of St. Andrew," *Journal of Ecclesiastical History* 12 (1961):215–30. Sister Joanna points out that "even in its early days of expansion it numbered only 34" (p. 230).

32. No records of the Sisters of the People appear to have survived, although the activities of the Manchester branch are recorded in the annual reports of the Manchester and Salford Wesleyan Mission. See the brief accounts in Dorothea Price Hughes, *The Life of Hugh Price Hughes*, 4th ed. (London: Hodder and Stoughton, 1905), pp. 201–3, Emmeline Pethick-Lawrence, *My Part in a Changing World* (London: Victor Gollancz, 1938), pp. 71–88, 95–97, and "What It Means to Be a Sister of the People: A Talk with Sister Lily," *Young Woman* 10 (1901–2):406–8.

33. Charles Booth, ed., *Life and Labour of the People of London*, 3d ser., *Religious Influences* (London: Macmillan, 1903), 7:349–59.

34. Quoted in Cooke, pp. 48–49.

35. A. V. L., *The Ministry of Women and the London Poor*, edited and with an intro. by Mrs. Bayly (London: S. W. Partridge, 1870), pp. 27–28.

36. Cooke, p. 65.

37. Cooke, pp. 55–56, 60–61.

38. Pethick-Lawrence, p. 72.

39. The high Anglican poet Christina Rossetti worked for ten years (1860–70) at a House of Mercy, Highgate, run by the All Saints sisterhood. She was an associate of the order and regularly wore their special dress. In 1873 her sister Maria joined the order. See Georgina Battiscombe, *Christina Rossetti: A Divided Life* (London: Constable, 1981), pp. 94, 153–54.

40. A. V. L., pp. 17–18.

41. Pethick-Lawrence, p. 73.

42. *Our Work* 7 (December 1884):334.

43. Emily Janes, "On the Associated Work of Women in Religion and Philanthropy," in *Woman's Mission*, ed. Baroness [Angela] Burdett-Coutts (London: Sampson Low, Marston, 1893), pp. 144–45.

44. Mrs. Welland to H. P. Liddon, undated unpub. letter, Pusey House, Oxford.

45. Cooke, pp. 51–52.

46. Henry Daniel Nihill, *The Sisters of St. Mary at the Cross: Sisters of the Poor and Their Work* (London: Kegan Paul, 1887), p. 78.

47. Eleanor Towle, *John Mason Neale* (London: Longmans, Green, 1906), p. 304.

48. Liddon, 3:31, 187–91.

49. For a full account of these events, see *St. Margaret's Magazine* 4 (1894):109–25. See also Rev. J. Scobell, *The Rev. J. M. Neale and the Institute of St. Margaret's, East Grinstead* (London: Nisbet, 1857), and J. M. Neale, *The Lewes Riot, Its Causes and Consequences* (London, 1857).

50. *"Sisterhoods" Considered, with Remarks upon the Bishop of Brechin's "Plea for Sisterhoods"* (London, 1850), p. 7. See also William Morris Colles, *Sisters of Mercy, Sisters of Misery, or Miss Sellon in the Family* (London, 1852).

51. [Mrs. Anne Judith Penny], *The Afternoon of Unmarried Life* (London: Longman, Brown, Green, Longmans and Roberts, 1858), pp. 149–50.

52. [Community of St. John Baptist], *The Founders of Clewer* (London: A. R. Mowbray, 1952), p. 44.

53. Ibid. p. 70.

54. Ibid. p. 71.

55. Shipley, "Sisterhood Life," warns against following an admired friend into a sisterhood: "Not only are frivolous intimacies discouraged on principle, but, in point of fact, there is no time or opportunity for long private discourse; and the time-tables apportioning each Sister's daily and hourly life prevent her following the bent of her own wishes as to her associates not less than as to her manner of spending her time" (p. 176).

56. William Dodsworth to E. B. Pusey, unpub. letter, 9 September 1845, Pusey House, Oxford.
57. See Grace T. Kimmins, *Heritage Craft Schools and Hospitals, Chailey, 1903–1948* (London: Baynard Press, 1948), p. 25.
58. Pethick-Lawrence, p. 97.
59. Sister Emmeline, p. 131.
60. [Sisters of the Church], *A Valiant Victorian: The Life and Times of Mother Emily Ayckbowm (1836–1900)* (London: A. R. Mowbray, 1964), p. 42.
61. *Our Work* 7 (December 1884):346. The quotation comes from a fictionalized account of the founding of the Sisters of the Church.
62. Bennett, p. 12.
63. T. T. Carter, *The First Ten Years of the House of Mercy, Clewer* (London: Joseph Masters, 1861), p. 23.
64. Brian Heeney discusses the difficulties women faced in changing the church in "The Beginnings of Church Feminism: Women and the Councils of the Church of England, 1897–1919," *Journal of Ecclesiastical History* 33 (January 1982):89–109, and in "Women's Struggle for Professional Work and Status in the Church of England, 1900–1930," *Historical Journal* 26 (1983): 329–47.
65. Pethick-Lawrence, p. 72.
66. Mrs. Price Hughes at Pearse's death said, "dearest to his heart of all his work was the special work of the Sisterhood. He was especially attracted to their name; not from ecclesiastical reasons, but the idea of their being 'sisters of the people,' taking tender human sympathy into the homes of the people appealed to him. He entered into their work and encouraged them in disappointment and failure and rejoiced in their successes." Quoted by Frances M. Unwin and John Telford, *Mark Guy Pearse: Preacher, Author, Artist* (London: Epworth Press, 1930), p. 242.
67. F. Prescott to Louisa M. Hubbard, unpub. letter, 12 December 1874, Deaconess Community of St. Andrew.
68. See, for example, the letter sent to the archbishop of Canterbury, "Women Preachers," reprinted in *St. Margaret's Half-Yearly Chronicle* 5 (July, 1919): 125–30.
69. Thomas Jay Williams, in *Priscilla Lydia Sellon, the Restorer after Three Centuries of the Religious Life in the English Church* (London: SPCK, 1950), carefully avoids any general assessment of Sellon's leadership or character. But see Anson and Campbell, pp. 265–66, and Allchin, p. 68. Contemporaries ranged from Pusey's unquestioning confidence in Sellon to the virulent attacks of extremists.
70. See E. B. Pusey to Mother Bertha, unpub. correspondence in regard to Sister Lucy, 1876–1882, Pusey House, Oxford.

71. Commander [William R. B.] Sellon, R.N., *Miss Sellon and the Sisters of Mercy: A Contradiction of the Alleged Acts of Cruelty Exercised by Miss Sellon* . . . , 2d ed. (London: Joseph Masters, 1852).

72. *Report of the Inquiry Instituted by the Right Reverend the Lord Bishop of Exeter . . . February 10th, 1849* (Plymouth, 1849), p. 73.

73. The bishop of Exeter withdrew support in the face of a new series of allegations against Sellon. He especially criticized the difficulty women faced in leaving the order without loss of social and moral standing. See Henry, Lord Bishop of Exeter, *A Letter to Miss Sellon, Superior of the Society of Sisters of Mercy, at Plymouth* (London: John Murray, 1852). See also Goodman, *Sisterhoods*, p. 38.

74. Allchin, p. 89.

75. Anson and Campbell, p. 243.

76. Helen Folsom to Sister Jane [Haight], unpub. letter, 18 June 1866. I am indebted to the Community of St. Mary, Peekskill, N.Y., for permission to quote from this letter.

77. *A Valiant Victorian*, p. 220.

78. Ibid., p. 157.

79. Ibid., pp. 156–70.

80. Ibid., p. 164.

81. *Proceedings of the Church Congress held at York . . . 1866 . . .* (York: John Sampson, 1867), p. 194. Quoted in Hill, p. 283.

82. Bishop Ninde, "The Deaconess' Work," quoted in Cooke, p. 54.

83. M. A. M., *Agnes Grahame, Deaconess: A Story of Woman's Work for Christ and His Church* (London: William Hunt, 1879), p. 46.

84. Sister Lily, p. 408.

85. Booth, 7:356.

86. Booth felt that the Methodists were particularly guilty of an "economy of truth . . . and exaggeration in order to obtain money." Booth, 7:136.

87. See Prochaska, pp. 186–205.

88. Nihill, p. 6.

89. See, for example, Diana A. G. Campbell, "A Novice Lately Seceded," in *Miss Sellon and the Sisters of Mercy* (London: T. Hatchard, 1852).

90. Howson, "Deaconesses," p. 371.

91. This description of the penitents' lives is based upon accounts by T. T. Carter, *The First Five Years of the House of Mercy, Clewer* (London: Joseph Masters, 1855), idem, *Is It Well to Institute Sisterhoods in the Church of England for the Care of Fe-*

male Penitents? (Oxford: J. H. Parker, 1851); idem, *The First Ten Years*; [W. J. Butler], *Some Account of St. Mary's Home for Penitents, at Wantage, Berkshire* (Oxford: J. H. Palmer, 1852); Emma Smith [pseud.], *A Cornish Waif's Story* (London: Odhams Press, 1954); and Helen Folsom, unpub. letter.

92. Carter, *The First Ten Years*, p. 15.
93. Personal conversation with author, Community of St. John Baptist, Clewer (July, 1980).
94. See Emma Smith, pp. 140–41, describing the grief of this mother, and *A Valiant Victorian*, pp. 150–52. One of the attacks made upon Mother Emily and the Sisters of the Church was against their policy of accepting illegitimate children into their orphanages, because it was thought that this encouraged sexual freedom.
95. See Booth, 7:360–61.
96. Hill, pp. 292–93.
97. For a superficial discussion of this change, based largely upon literary sources, see Eric Trudgill, *Madonnas and Magdalens: The Origins and Development of Victorian Sexual Attitudes* (London: Heinemann, 1976), pp. 296–306. The sisters who ran the Houses of Refuge took no active part in the Contagious Diseases Acts agitation or in the various other social purity movements.
98. Sarah B. Wister, quoted in Henry C. Potter, *Sisterhoods and Deaconesses at Home and Abroad* (New York: E. P. Dutton, 1873), p. 281.
99. Information supplied by the sister secretary, Community of St. John Baptist, Clewer.
100. Pethick-Lawrence, p. 88.
101. See, for example, Bertha Lathbury, "Agnosticism and Women," *Nineteenth Century* 7 (1880):619–27.
102. *A Valiant Victorian*, p. 166.
103. *A Valiant Victorian*, pp. 165–70, and Allchin, pp. 211–14.
104. Hill argues that differentiation in all areas of modern society has also contributed to the changes in Anglican sisterhoods. See p. 293. Sister Gabriel, former mother superior of the Society of St. Margaret, explained that everything had changed "but the essentials" from the time she entered the order in the early 1930s until the present day (personal conversation, August 1979).
105. Sister Emmeline, p. 130. Internal evidence suggests that this essay was written by Emmeline Pethick-Lawrence; if so, this would be one of the earliest published statements of her faith in womankind. During her career as a suffragette leader she continually used religious metaphors to describe the struggle to win the vote. See chapter 7.

Chapter Three

1. See F. B. Smith, *Florence Nightingale: Reputation and Power* (London: Croom Helm, 1982) for a recent highly critical evaluation of Nightingale as a reformer. But see Eileen and David Spring, "The Real Florence Nightingale?" *Bulletin of the History of Medicine*, 57 (1983): 285–90.

2. Brian Abel-Smith, *A History of the Nursing Profession* (London: Heinemann, 1960), p. 6.

3. Mrs. [Anna] Jameson, *"Sisters of Charity" and "The Communion of Labour": Two Lectures on the Social Employment of Women* (London: Longman, Brown, Green, Longmans and Roberts, 1859), p. 58.

4. W. Farr, "Proposed Inquiry into the Occupations of the People: Medical Profession. Draft report," in *Census of England and Wales, 1861*, vol. 3 (appendix) (London: HMSO, 1863), p. 246. Quoted in Celia Davies, "Making Sense of the Census in Britain and the U.S.A.: The Changing Occupational Classification and the Position of Nurses," *Sociological Review*, n.s., 28, 3 (August 1980):607.

5. Both Florence Nightingale and Agnes Jones spent time at Kaiserswerth. Although later in life Nightingale was highly critical of her training there, her visit was clearly crucial in consolidating her plans for nursing reform in England. See Sir Edward Cook, *The Life of Florence Nightingale* (London: Macmillan, 1913), 1 : 104–5.

6. As quoted in *Englishwoman's Review* 1 (1869):54. The editors went on to comment tartly, "Mr. Cape's expressions, quoted above, all come to this. Women are weak and susceptible. They must have their parsons, their chasubles, their incense, their religious stimulants of all kinds, if you are to get work out of them, just as a navvy must have his beer. Give them what they want, and do not grumble at the order of nature. We have infinitely too much respect for women to take this view of their condition" (p. 56). I am indebted to Janet Murray for this reference.

7. Alfred Meadows, quoted approvingly by Maria Trench in "Sick-Nurses," *Macmillan's Magazine* 34 (September 1876):426. Trench's only concern was that not enough women would be willing to be religious sisters in order to nurse.

8. See M. Adelaide Nutting and Lavinia L. Dock, *A History of Nursing* (New York: G. P. Putnam's Sons, 1907), 2 : 172–206.

9. The phrase is Anna Jameson's, to describe the public reforms she wished women to participate in. See Jameson, p. li. Italics in the original.

Notes to Pages 90–95

317

10. Florence Nightingale, "Introduction," in *Memorials of Agnes Elizabeth Jones* by her sister (London: Strahan, 1871), p. xxi. Smith, pp. 172–77, argues that Jones was singularly unsuccessful at Liverpool and that Nightingale had held back from supporting her; only after her death did it become convenient to use her as modern nursing's martyr.

11. In a letter to Mrs. Pennefather, urging her to continue with the idea of a deaconess's home. Quoted in *Agnes Jones*, p. 312.

12. Nightingale, "Introduction," in *Agnes Jones*, pp. xiv–xv.

13. Cecil Woodham-Smith, *Florence Nightingale, 1820–1910* (London: Constable, 1950), pp. 347–48.

14. *Agnes Jones*, p. 252.

15. Sarah A. Tooley, *The History of Nursing in the British Empire* (London: S. H. Bousfield, 1906), pp. 99–101.

16. For a full discussion of this metaphor, see Charles E. Rosenberg, "Florence Nightingale on Contagion: The Hospital as Moral Universe," in *Healing and History*, ed. Charles E. Rosenberg (New York: Dawson, 1979), pp. 116–36.

17. H. C. O'Neill and Edith A. Barnett, *Our Nurses and the Work They Have to Do* (London: Ward, Lock, 1888), pp. 14–15.

18. Florence Nightingale, "Nursing the Sick," [1882], reprinted in *Selected Writings of Florence Nightingale*, compiled by Lucy Ridgely Seymer (New York: Macmillan, 1954), p. 336.

19. Rosenberg, pp. 125–27.

20. Eva Gamarnikow, "Sexual Division of Labour: The Case of Nursing," in *Feminism and Materialism: Women and Modes of Production*, ed. Annette Kuhn and AnnMarie Wolpe (London: Routledge and Kegan Paul, 1978), p. 120.

21. Gamarnikow, p. 119.

22. L. L. Dock, "The Relation of Training Schools to Hospitals," in *Nursing the Sick 1893*, ed. Isabel A. Hampton et al. (New York: McGraw-Hill, 1949), pp. 16–17.

23. Florence Nightingale, unpub. letter to Mary Jones, 8 January 1867. Nightingale Training School Papers, Greater London Council Record Office. Italics in the original.

24. Abel-Smith, pp. 28–29.

25. Mary Cadbury, unpub. letter to her family, 21 September 1892. Nightingale Training School Papers, Greater London Council Record Office.

26. H. C. Cameron, *Mr. Guy's Hospital, 1726–1948* (London: Longmans, Green, 1954), p. 208. Miss Burt insisted that the nurses purchase new uniforms that they could not afford; a sister lost her watch when she could not wear it on a chain after the edict against jewelry. See Abel-Smith, p. 26, notes 2 and 3.

27.   Cameron, p. 211.
28.   Margaret McEwan, with assistance from D. M. Landon, *Eva C. Lückes (Matron), the London Hospital, 1880–1919* (London: London Hospital League for Nurses, 1958), p. 39.
29.   Ethel Gordon [Manson] Fenwick, "How I Became Matron of St. Bartholomew's Hospital," *British Journal of Nursing*, 15 January 1910, pp. 48–49, and 5 February 1910, pp. 104–5.
30.   Winifred Hector, *The Work of Mrs. Bedford Fenwick and the Rise of Professional Nursing* (London: Royal College of Nursing and National Council of Nurses of the United Kingdom, 1973), pp. 34–45.
31.   Woodham-Smith, p. 477.
32.   Ibid.
33.   I am indebted to Christopher Maggs for this information.
34.   See Christopher Maggs, "Towards a Social History of Nursing 2," *Nursing Times Occasional Papers* 74, #15 (25 May 1978): 57–58, and Christopher Maggs, "Nurse Recruitment to Four Provincial Hospitals 1881–1921," in *Rewriting Nursing History*, ed. Celia Davies (London: Croom Helm, 1980), pp. 24–32.
35.   Woodham-Smith, p. 483. Italics in the original.
36.   Hector, pp. 25–26.
37.   See Mary Cadbury's unpub. letter to her family 24 June 1875 about how Sister Alice of St. Thomas' Hospital had to leave because she was caught drinking the patients' brandy. Nightingale Training School Papers, Greater London Council Record Office.
38.   Mary Cadbury, unpub. letter to her family, 18 April 1875, Nightingale Training School Papers, Greater London Council Record Office.
39.   Ibid.
40.   Margaret Lonsdale, "The Present Crisis at Guy's Hospital," *Nineteenth Century* 7 (April 1880):683. Lonsdale's attack brought a storm of replies. See William Gull, "On the Nursing Crisis at Guy's Hospital," *Nineteenth Century* 7 (May 1888):884–91; Octavius Sturges, Seymour J. Sharkey, and Margaret Lonsdale, "Doctors and Nurses," *Nineteenth Century* 7 (June 1880):1089–1108; and W. Moxon, "Miss Lonsdale on Guy's Hospital," *Contemporary Review* 37 (May 1880):872–92.
41.   Woodham-Smith, p. 484.
42.   This is hinted at by L. L. Dock, "The Relation of Training Schools to Hospitals," p. 28. I am indebted to Celia Davies for this suggestion.
43.   Laura Wilson, unpub. letter to Anne, 13 May 1876, Nightingale Training School Papers, Greater London Council Record Office.
44.   Mary Cadbury, unpub. letter to her mother, 27 September 1876,

Nightingale Training School Papers, Greater London Council Record Office.

45. In addition to the Cadbury letters, see also *Mary Christabel Cadbury: The Story of a Nightingale Nurse and Kindred Papers* (Headley: privately printed, [1939]).

46. For a discussion of American women reformers in a similar position, see Mary P. Ryan, *Cradle of the Middle Class* (Cambridge: Cambridge University Press, 1981), pp. 86–88. I am indebted to Christopher Maggs for this suggestion.

47. Mary Cadbury, unpub. letter to her mother, 26 November 1875, Nightingale Training School Papers, Greater London Council Record Office.

48. Gamarnikow, p. 120.

49. Florence Nightingale, unpub. letter to Catherine Marsh, 24 March 1892, Boston University Nursing Archives.

50. Lee Holcombe, *Victorian Ladies at Work: Middle-Class Working Women in England and Wales, 1850–1914* (Hamden, Conn.: Archon Press, 1973), pp. 204–5. See also Celia Davies, "Making Sense of the Census," for a consideration of the changing definition of the nurse, from the category of domestic service to that of professional occupation.

51. In the words of Charlotte Haddon, "Waiving the question of whether woman might or might not be made capable, with man's advantages, of doing man's work, it surely will not be denied that a sphere of action would be preferable in which she would not compete with him, but in which her own peculiar endowments would give her a special advantage. And here [in nursing] is an opportunity for showing how a woman's work may complement man's in the true order of nature. Where does the character of the 'help-meet' come out so strikingly as in the sick-room, where the quick eye, the soft hand, the light step, and the ready ear, second the wisdom of the physician and execute his behests better than he himself could have imagined?" See her "Nursing as a Profession for Ladies," *St. Paul's Magazine* 8 (August 1871):461.

52. Holcombe, p. 79; Abel-Smith, p. 55.

53. See, for example, Viscountess Emily Anne Strangford, *Hospital Training for Ladies: An Appeal to the Hospital Boards in England* (London: Harrison and Son, 1874), who argued that ladies would need to be in attendance only from nine or ten in the morning until three or four in the afternoon and could continue to live at home and perform their home duties. Such a plan would open up nursing to "hundreds and thousands of women of all classes who wish to work for their fellow-creatures and to spend their strength for their suffering neighbours, without entering

into Sisterhoods of any kind or sort; and who have no occasion for a Profession" (p. 15).

54.   Maggs, "Nurse Recruitment," pp. 36–37.

55.   Ibid., pp. 25–27. Maggs draws his evidence from four provincial hospitals, but given the pressure for cheap labor and "trained" nurses, there is no reason to doubt that his figures apply to other nonprestige hospitals. In his sample, the higher the status of the hospital, the larger the number of applicants and the higher the general age of admittance.

56.   See, for example, A. H. F. Barbour, *Under a Rowan Tree* (Edinburgh: privately printed, 1908), p. 7: "The discipline of home-life is the best preliminary training." This theme is repeated by all the leading matrons.

57.   Honnor Morten, *From a Nurse's Note-book* (London: Scientific Press, 1899), p. 8.

58.   Mary Cadbury, unpub. letter to her mother, 5 February 1874, Nightingale Training School Papers, Greater London Council Record Office.

59.   See, for example, Gladys M. Hardy, *Yes, Matron* (London: Edward O. Beck, 1954), p. 1, and C. M. Barker, *Call Me Matron* (London: Heinemann, 1980), p. 5.

60.   "Hours in a Hospital, by a Nurse," *Work and Leisure* 5 (January 1880):18.

61.   H. A. St. George Saunders, *The Middlesex Hospital, 1745–1948* (London: Max Parrish, 1949), p. 43. The lady probationers did not have to come on duty until 8:30 at the Middlesex and were then expected to wash only one patient and to make his or her bed. No matter how young or inexperienced, a lady pro took the place of an absent sister in the ward. See Saunders, p. 42.

62.   For a discussion of the failure to address the problem of formal education in nursing, see Celia Davies, "A Constant Casualty: Nurse Education in Britain and the USA to 1939," in *Rewriting Nursing History*, pp. 102–22.

63.   Eva Lückes, *Lectures*, p. 3.

64.   Mrs. Rebecca Strong, *Practical Ward Work* (Glasgow: Royal Infirmary, 1893), p. 6. See also the comments of Rachel Williams and Alice Fisher, *Hints for Hospital Nurses* (Edinburgh: MacLachan & Stuart, 1877), p. 10: "It is perhaps the first opportunity an educated woman has had of becoming perfectly acquainted with the moral and mental capabilities, and with the opinions and feelings of what is usually known as the 'working class.' Rightly used, the experience may be very valuable for her."

65.   Tooley, pp. 102–3. Tooley justifies the extreme discipline by arguing that "Thirty and forty years ago the lady probationers,

prompted by enthusiasm for the new calling, went straight from sheltered homes and a life of refined ease to face the routine of a hospital training-school with less preparation than does the modern girl. One can imagine the bewilderment of the mid-Victorian young lady, brought up at home in seclusion and refined ignorance, when her hospital studies suddenly plunged her into the heart of life's mysteries" (p. 103).

66. Nutting and Dock, 2 : 300–301.
67. *Hospital,* 28 April 1894, p. xxxv. Quoted by Gamarnikow, p. 110.
68. *Hospital,* 27 March 1897, p. 232. Quoted by Gamarnikow, p. 117.
69. E. J. R. Landale, "On Some Aims and Conditions of a Nurse's Life," *Nursing Record and Hospital World* 13 (7 July 1894):4.
70. C. Graves, *The Story of St. Thomas's, 1106–1947* (London: St. Thomas' Hospital, 1947), pp. 48–49.
71. Eva Lückes, *Hospital Sisters and Their Duties* (London: J. & A. Churchill, 1886), p. 62. See also Florence S. Lees, *A Handbook for Hospital Sisters,* ed. H. W. Acland (London: W. Isbister, 1874), pp. 22–23: "They [nurses] should regard her [their sister] as not only their Mistress, but their Mother, or rather Friend in the full sense of the word; as one to whom they could go in any trouble or doubt, being sure of finding sympathy, advice, and help, whether for themselves or others. . . . the sisters should regard their nurses as their pupils and children, for whom they are responsible, not only to the authorities of the hospital, but to God."
72. Ida Holford, *But the Nights Are Long* (London: Robert Hale, 1977), p. 78.
73. A. Beale, unpub. memoir, Nightingale Training School Papers, Greater London Council Record Office.
74. E. J. R. Landale, "A Few Hints to Sisters," *Nursing Record and Hospital World* 17 (4 July 1896):6.
75. See repeated comments in the unpublished letters of Mary Cadbury and Florence Nightingale, Nightingale Training School Papers, Greater London Council Record Office.
76. Miss E. Lees, unpub. letter to Lucy Seymer, May 1954, Nightingale Training School Papers, Greater London Record Office. Miss Lees completed her training in 1902. Her matron was L. M. Gordon.
77. C. M. Barker, p. 13.
78. "The Nightingale Special Lament," by Mrs. C. Boycott and Miss Le Mesurier, ca. 1900, Nightingale Training School Papers, Greater London Council Record Office.
79. Margaret Broadley, "It's Different Now—11: Crockery Day," *Nursing Times* 72 (8 April 1976):540–41. Broadley trained at the London Hospital.

80. Florence Nightingale, unpub. and undated letter to the editor of *Macmillan's Magazine*, Boston University Nursing Archives. Square brackets in the original. See Elizabeth Garrett, "Volunteer Hospital Nursing," *Macmillan's Magazine* 15 (April 1867):497.

81. Monica E. Baly, *Nursing and Social Change*, 2d ed. (London: Heinemann, 1980), p. 156. Bedford Fenwick had approximately the same rate of wastage when she introduced the three-year training program at St. Bartholomew's. See Hector, pp. 30–31. Maggs, "Nurse Recruitment," places the figure as high as 50 percent to 60 percent in the Southhampton Poor Law Infirmary, pp. 32–33, 36.

82. See Agnes Hunt, *This Is My Life* (London and Glasgow: Blackie, 1938), p. 77.

83. "Nurses and Nursing," *Westminster Review* 130 (1888):16. I am indebted to Janet Murray for this reference.

84. See M. F. Johnston, "The Case against Hospital Nurses," *Nineteenth Century* 51 (June 1902):966–71. See the defense of nurses, Isla Stewart, "The Case for Hospital Nurses," *Nineteenth Century* 51 (May 1902):780–84. See also Emma L. Q. Watson, "Some Remarks on Modern Nurses," *National Review* 28 (December 1896):567–72; Eliza Priestley, "Nurses á la Mode," *Nineteenth Century* 41 (January 1897):28–37, and the reply, Ethel Gordon Fenwick, "Nurses à la Mode: A Reply to Lady Priestley," *Nineteenth Century* 41 (February 1897):325–34.

85. Baly, p. 132.

86. Lucy M. Rae, "A Question of 'Class,'" *Nursing Record and Hospital World* 29 (28 June 1902):513–14.

87. Rae was answered a month later by Mary Gardner, "A Question of Character," *British Journal of Nursing* 29 (26 July 1902):71–72. Gardner argued "The 'society' which prides itself on being 'good' is not always gentle, whereas Nature's gentlewomen are to be found in every rank" (p. 71). Though more democratic, the terms of the debate were unchanged. (*The Nursing Record* had changed its name but remained under the same editor.) See also Mary Burr, "To What Extent Are the Matrons Responsible for the Want of Ethics in the Modern Nurse?" *Nursing Record and Hospital World* 28 (26 April 1902):335–36.

88. Baly, pp. 162–63. See also Abel-Smith, pp. 61–80, for the standard modern interpretation of the struggle; for a dissenting view, see Hector, pp. 34–45.

89. Abel-Smith, pp. 55–58.

90. Hunt, pp. 76–77.

91. See Miss Izod and Mrs. C. Boycott, unpub. memoirs, Nightin-

gale Training School Papers, Greater London Council Record Office.

92. See the supplement, "The London Hospital Scandals," *Nursing Record* 6 (1 January 1891):i–vii. See also the serial "Letters from Life," *Nursing Record* 7 (3 September 1891) through (31 December 1891).

93. McEwan, p. 10.

94. E. E. P. MacManus, *Matron of Guy's: An Autobiography* (London: Andrew Melrose, 1956), pp. 38–39.

95. Mrs. C. Boycott, unpub. memoir, Nightingale Training School Papers, Greater London Council Record Office.

96. Hunt, pp. 76–77.

97. Letter reprinted from *The Times* by Lucy Ashby, "Should Nurses Live Out?" *Nursing Times* 4 (1908):798.

98. C. C., "Living In," *Nursing Times* 4 (1908):818.

99. *Victoria Magazine* 27 (June 1876):181. I am indebted to Janet Murray for this reference.

100. Holcombe, p. 80.

101. E. J. R. Landale, "On Some Aims and Conditions of a Nurse's Life," *Nursing Record and Hospital World* 13 (7 July 1894):4.

102. Fanny Gilpin, *Scenes from Hospital Life: Being the Letters of a Probationer Nurse* (London: Drane's, 1923), pp. 25–27, 38–39. Gilpin also criticized the inadequate and poorly served food, the pall cast upon the nurses by the rigid and disapproving sisters and matron, and the generally poor treatment of probationers—all familiar criticisms of the previous forty years. Perhaps Sister E's love of cats over people explains Miss Thorold's relentless destruction of cats at the Middlesex Hospital. See Saunders, pp. 43–44.

103. Nursing leaders repeatedly blamed the women themselves for this situation. See, for example, the editorial, "Nurse Training Schools—I," *Nursing Record* 7 (24 September 1891):157–58: "It cannot be denied that there is a lamentable deficiency of *esprit de corps* among Nurses—due, perhaps, to the strange inability of women to work with other women to gain a common end. Whatever the reason be, it must be eradicated, and Nurses must become more devoted to their work, more devoted to their Training School, than the generality are at present, if the advancement of Nursing is to continue" (p. 158). Note the use of the imperative mood.

104. A. H. Stoney, *In the Days of Queen Victoria, Memories of a Hospital Nurse* (Bristol: Wright, 1931), p. 19. Originally published in 1910.

Chapter Four

1. Dorothy Sayers, *Gaudy Night* (London: Victor Gollancz, 1935), chap. 3.

2. Ibid.

3. Alice Zimmern, *The Renaissance of Girls' Education* (London: A. D. Innes, 1898), p. 103.

4. See Sheldon Rothblatt, *The Revolution of the Dons: Cambridge and Society in Victorian England* (London: Faber and Faber, 1968), for a full discussion of the organizational and intellectual changes at Cambridge during the second half of the nineteenth century. See also E. G. W. Bill, *University Reform in Nineteenth-Century Oxford: A Study of Henry Halford Vaughn, 1811–1885* (Oxford: Oxford University Press, 1973), and Christopher Harvie, *The Lights of Liberalism: University Liberals and the Challenge of Democracy 1860–86* (London: Allen Lane, 1976). Most of the coaches were married men who could therefore not be fellows; reforms in teaching progressed slowly and unevenly even after fellows could marry. See Rothblatt, pp. 227–35.

5. Rita McWilliams-Tullberg, *Women at Cambridge: A Men's University—Though of a Mixed Type* (London: Victor Gollancz, 1975), p. 16.

6. I am indebted to Gillian Sutherland for sending me her unpublished essay on the class backgrounds of the founders of the first four women's colleges. Her analysis reveals that most of the leaders came from a handful of reforming families with little money but much ambition and a willingness to work hard. See "The Social Location of the Movement for Women's Higher Education in England 1840–1880," presented at the George Eliot Centennial Conference (Rutgers University, 1980).

7. For a discussion of the move away from patronage and toward educational standards for the professions as it affected men, see W. J. Reader, *Professional Men: The Rise of the Professional Classes in Nineteenth-Century England* (New York: Basic Books, 1966), pp. 44–58.

8. Both Oxford and Cambridge had limited the number of women students in the 1920s, fearful of being overwhelmed by the success of the colleges. Various limitations have continued until the present. See Rita McWilliams-Tullberg, pp. 209–18, for a discussion of those at Cambridge.

9. Sutherland argues that the key years were 1869–80, but I have extended them to include the founding of Westfield College (1882) and Royal Holloway (1887). For an analysis of the founding of some sixty secondary schools for girls during these years, see

Sheila Fletcher, *Feminists and Bureaucrats: A Study in the Development of Girls' Education in the Nineteenth Century* (Cambridge: Cambridge University Press, 1980).

10. Barbara Stephen, *Emily Davies and Girton College* (London: Constable, 1927), pp. 103–5.

11. Stephen, pp. 148–79, 202–18.

12. A. J. Clough's various efforts on behalf of women's education are discussed by Blanche Athena Clough, *A Memoir of Anne Jemima Clough*, new ed. (London: Edward Arnold, 1903), pp. 37–40.

13. Stephen, pp. 188–201, McWilliams-Tullberg, pp. 46–47, 68–69.

14. For the full story of the effort to obtain degrees for women at Cambridge, see McWilliams-Tullberg. For an account of Oxford's struggle, see Annie Mary A. Henley Rogers, *Degrees by Degrees: The Story of the Admission of Oxford Women Students to Membership of the University* (London: Oxford University Press, 1938). For a discussion of the opposition to women's higher education, see Joan N. Burstyn, *Victorian Education and the Ideal of Womanhood* (London: Croom Helm, 1980), especially pp. 34–35, 52, and 122.

15. Mrs. Humphry Ward described these days: "My friends were all on fire for women's education, including women's medical education, and very emulous of Cambridge, where the movement was already far advanced. But hardly any of us were at all on fire for woman suffrage, wherein the Oxford educational movement differed greatly from the Cambridge movement." See her *A Writer's Recollections*, 2 vols. (New York: Harper, 1918), 1:203. See also Vera Brittain, *The Women at Oxford: A Fragment of History* (London: George G. Harrap, 1960), pp. 37–40.

16. Brittain, *The Women at Oxford*, pp. 66–68. The smell of the bakery seems to have gone down in LMH annals; see, for example, E. A. Pearson, "Memories of the Hall," *Brown Book*, 1928, p. 89.

17. C. S. Bremer, "Women in the British Universities," Appendix A of Mrs. Henry Sidgwick, *The Place of University Education in the Life of Women* (London: Transactions of the Women's Institute, 1897), pp. 34–52.

18. Stephen, p. 174.

19. Georgina Battiscombe, *Reluctant Pioneer: A Life of Elizabeth Wordsworth* (London: Constable, 1978), p. 68.

20. Battiscombe, pp. 68–69; Stephen, p. 206.

21. Newnham students were by no means always pleased to have Clough treating them like schoolchildren. See Mary Agnes Hamilton, *Newnham: An Informal Biography* (London: Faber and Faber, 1936), pp. 100–103, 132.

22. Louisa Innes Lumsden, *Yellow Leaves: Memories of a Long Life* (Edinburgh: William Blackwood, 1933), p. 47.

23. Alice Gardner, *A Short History of Newnham College Cambridge* (Cambridge: Bowes and Bowes, 1921), p. 28. The first hall, built in 1875, was designed to be transformed into two dwelling-houses, "if a hall for women students proved a failure."

24. Battiscombe, pp. 77–78.

25. Vera Farnell, *A Somervillian Looks Back* (Oxford: University Press, 1948), p. 16.

26. Battiscombe, p. 73. Italics in the original.

27. Undated unpub. letter, Newnham College archives. Courtesy of Ann Phillips.

28. M. A. Quiggin (1899), "'Students May Ride the Bicycle,'" in *A Newnham Anthology*, ed. Ann Phillips (Cambridge: University Press, 1979), p. 46.

29. Joan Evans, *Prelude and Fugue: An Autobiography* (London: Museum Press, 1964), p. 69.

30. Farnell, p. 11.

31. Anne de Villiers, Hazel Fox, and Pauline Adams, *Somerville College, Oxford, 1879–1979: A Century in Pictures* (Oxford: Somerville College, 1978), p. 40.

32. Brittain, *Women at Oxford*, pp. 88–89, 120–21, and Muriel St. Clare Byrne and Catherine Hope Mansfield, *Somerville College, 1879–1921* (Oxford: Oxford University Press, 1922), pp. 64–65.

33. Ethel Sargant, "The Inheritance of a University," *Girton Review*, n.s., 1 (1901):17.

34. Stephen, pp. 336–39.

35. Jane Ellen Harrison had already been invited back on another fellowship in 1898. See Gardner, pp. 92–94.

36. De Villiers, Fox, and Adams, p. 32.

37. See the unpublished correspondence between Barbara Bodichon and various students and committee members, Girton College Archives, and Constance Maynard, unpub. autobiography, section 26, "Evaluations of Girton Women," Westfield College Archives. Stephen, pp. 294–98, gives a brief account of Girton's early leadership problems.

38. This is the main argument for the difficulties of women and girls in gaining education in Sara Delamont, "The Contradictions in Ladies' Education," in *The Nineteenth-Century Woman: Her Cultural and Physical World*, ed. Sara Delamont and Lorna Duffin (London: Croom Helm, 1978), pp. 134–63.

39. These arguments are analyzed by Joan N. Burstyn in "Education and Sex: The Medical Case against Higher Education for Women in England, 1870–1900," *Proceedings of the American Philosophical Society* 117 (April 1973):78–89.

40. Paul Atkinson, "Fitness, Feminism and Schooling," in Delamont and Duffin, pp. 92–133, and Burstyn, "Education and Sex." The most important research published against the medical attack was Mrs. Henry Sidgwick's *Health Statistics of Women Students at Cambridge and Oxford and of Their Sisters* (Cambridge: University Press, 1890). This hundred-page treatise conclusively proved that women at Oxbridge were, if anything, healthier after attending college. See also Henry Maudsley's attack, "Sex in Mind and in Education," *Fortnightly Review*, 21 (1874):466–83, and Elizabeth Garrett Anderson's defense of women, "Sex in Mind and Education: A Reply," *Fortnightly Review*, 21 (1874):582–94. For Emily Davies's handling of this issue, see Stephen, pp. 290–94, and the unpublished correspondence of Emily Davies (and replies by various students to her inquiries), Girton College Archives.

41. Constance L. Maynard, "Girton's Earliest Years," in *Between College Terms* (London: James Nisbet, 1910), p. 189.

42. Margaret Murray, *My First Hundred Years* (London: William Kimber, 1963), pp. 158–60. These seemingly trivial slights were, as Murray points out, constant reminders to women staff that they were not equal colleagues with their male friends. See also, for example, the difficulties of day students at Manchester University, described in Mabel Tylecote, *The Education of Women at Manchester University, 1883–1933* (Manchester: University Press, 1941), pp. 28–38.

43. Emily E. C. Jones, *As I Remember: An Autobiographical Ramble* (London: A. & C. Black, 1922), p. 69.

44. Agnes Maitland, "The Student Life of Women in Halls of Residence," in *National Union of Women Workers Report for 1894* (London: National Union of Women Workers, [1894]), p. 100.

45. Victoria Glendinning, *A Suppressed Cry: Life and Death of a Quaker Daughter* (London: Routledge and Kegan Paul, 1969), p. 54.

46. When she was a guest speaker at the Girton Jubilee Celebration, Lumsden spoke of "a divine discontent" that made the limitations of her life at home intolerable. See the *Girton Review Jubilee Number*, n.s., 54 (1919): 26.

47. Marshall, p. 10.

48. Jane Ellen Harrison in her *Reminiscences of a Student's Life* (London: Hogarth Press, 1925) slides over some of her difficulties with her stepmother. See pp. 19–20, 27–28, and Jessie Stewart, *Jane Ellen Harrison: A Portrait from Letters* (London: Merlin Press, 1959), pp. 5–6.

49. Maynard, "Girton's Earliest Years," pp. 182–83, and Constance

Maynard, unpub. autobiography, sections 8–26 (1872–75), Westfield College Archives. See also C. B. Firth, *Constance Louisa
Maynard: Mistress of Westfield College* (London: George Allen
and Unwin, 1949), pp. 102–8.

50.   "Mary Lynda Dorothea Grier (1880–1967): A Memoir," *Brown
Book*, May, 1968, pp. 2–10, 23–25.

51.   Vera Brittain, *Testament of Youth: An Autobiographical Study
of the Years 1900–1925* (London: Victor Gollancz, 1933), pp.
67–74.

52.   Firth, p. 58.

53.   Edyth M. Lloyd, ed., *Anna Lloyd (1837–1925): A Memoir* (London: Cayme Press, 1928), p. 67.

54.   Glendinning, p. 94.

55.   Maitland, p. 100.

56.   Constance Maynard, "From Early Victorian Schoolroom to University: Some Personal Experiences," *Nineteenth Century* 76
(1914):1068.

57.   See Isabel Maddison, *Handbook of British, Continental and Canadian Universities, with Special Mention of the Courses Open
to Women*, 2d ed. (New York: Macmillan, 1899), pp. 87–112.
Fees remained at these levels from the founding days until World
War I. St. Hugh's was specifically founded by Elizabeth Wordsworth to help poorer (but still middle class) women, so its fees
were set as low as possible. See Battiscombe, pp. 119–26.

58.   Clara E. Collet, "The Economic Position of Educated Working
Women," in *Educated Working Women: Essays on the Economic Position of Women Workers in the Middle Classes* (London: P. S. King, 1902), pp. 6–8.

59.   Sara Burstall was one of Buss's early successes. Her father was
a builder, and she had been awarded a full scholarship to the
North London Collegiate on the basis of her mathematical skills
at a time when Buss was anxious to prove that girls could achieve
as good results in mathematics as boys. Under the tutelage of
Buss and her successor, Sophie Bryant, Burstall seems to have
had no trouble adapting to the higher cultural regions of the
middle class. See her *Retrospect and Prospect: Sixty Years of
Women's Education* (London: Longmans, Green, 1933). See
Constance Maynard, unpub. autobiography, section 25 (1875),
p. 712, Westfield College Archives, for the label of "Busters."
Maynard considered them "underbred and underfed."

60.   "An Old Newnham Student," "The Social Life of an Under-
graduate," *Girls' Realm* 5 (1902–3):411. See also Phillips, pp. 41,
66–68, 109, 111, 121, 128, 140, 177–79, 189–90.

61.   This schedule is described in virtually every memoir of the time.

During the early days at Hitchin, when the tutors had to come from Cambridge, lectures were scheduled according to the exigencies of the train schedule. But cocoa parties and afternoon walks or games established themselves very early. See Lloyd, p. 65, and Constance L. Maynard, "Girton's Earliest Years," pp. 177–98. The routine of plain living and high thinking was scarcely likely to appeal to any young woman interested in anything but self-improvement.

62. W. E. Delp, *Royal Holloway College, 1908–1914* (Egham: Royal Holloway, 1969), p. 10. A lecturer newly arrived from the more austere Girton commented to Delp that "our mode of dining was very civilized and civilizing" (p. 10).

63. For descriptions of "tray" by former students, see Olive Jocelyn Dunlop, *Leaves from a Cambridge Note-Book* (Cambridge: Heffer and Sons, 1907), pp. 43–47, and Emma B. E. List, *"Girton, My Friend" and Other Matter (in Prose and Verse)* (Cambridge: W. Heffer, 1908), p. 37.

64. C. Crowther (1896), "Women on Sufferance," in Phillips, p. 39.

65. See Constance Maynard, unpub. autobiography, sections 14, 20–25 (1873–75), Westfield College Archives. Louisa Lumsden felt that the special trip into Cambridge from Hitchin and the long wait for the examination papers the first day destroyed her equanimity, so that she ended with a third in classics. See *Yellow Leaves*, p. 54.

66. Maynard, "Girton's Earliest Years," p. 177.

67. Madeleine Shaw Lefevre, unpub. letter to Mary Lacy, 6 June 1886, Somerville College Archives.

68. "The Dream of Princess Ida," *Girl's Own Paper* (15 December 1883):171. Quoted by Deborah Gorham, *The Victorian Girl and the Feminine Ideal* (Bloomington: Indiana University Press, 1982), p. 114.

69. Constance Maynard, unpub. autobiography, section 50 (1886), p. 171, Westfield College Archives.

70. A scrapbook with pictures and dialogue survives in the Somerville College Archives.

71. Battiscombe, p. 117.

72. E. M. Riley (1916), "A Three Years' Fast," in Phillips, p. 109.

73. *Girton Review* 22 (April 1889):8–9.

74. Winifred Peck, *A Little Learning, or A Victorian Childhood* (London: Faber and Faber, 1952), pp. 154–57.

75. Quoted by McWilliams-Tullberg, p. 59.

76. Quoted by McWilliams-Tullberg, p. 66.

77. E. T. M., *An Interior View of Girton College, Cambridge* (London: London Association of Schoolmistresses, 1876), p. 8.

78. Quoted by McWilliams-Tullberg, p. 104.
79. A Newnham student of 1922 was shocked when B. A. Clough, the former principal, asked her at a reunion, "Did you fight much?" She then realized that "The pent-up energy and nervous irritation which found this curious form of expression in Miss Clough's generation was sweated out in my day on the lower river." See E. N. R. Russell-Smith (1922), "The Art of Theorising," in Phillips, p. 157. The Girton pillow fights are described in Constance Maynard, unpub. autobiography, section 15 (1874), p. 540, Westfield College Archives.
80. M. I. Corbett Ashby (1901), "A Revolutionary at Heart," in Phillips, p. 52.
81. E. M. Delf Smith, unpub. reminiscences of Westfield College, 1906–14, Westfield College Archives.
82. F. L. J. (1918), unpub. memoir, Newnham College Archives. Courtesy of Ann Phillips.
83. M. G. Wallas (1917), "A Restless Generation," in Phillips, p. 118.
84. Harrison, *Reminiscences*, p. 88.
85. Battiscombe, p. 146.
86. Stephens, pp. 294–95. Maynard gives a much fuller account in her unpub. autobiography, Westfield College Archives. See also the unpublished letters of Louisa Lumsden and Emily Davies, Girton College Archives. In later life Lumsden mellowed considerably and wrote of Davies, "I still hold that Miss Davies was right, heavy as was the cost to individuals—to none more than to myself." See *Yellow Leaves*, pp. 55–58.
87. Burstall, p. 67.
88. Gardner's disheveled appearance and dull teaching are mentioned by many students in reminiscences. See in particular Glendinning, pp. 73–74, 79, and F. M. Wilson (1906), "Friendships," in Phillips, p. 66.
89. Glendinning, p. 71.
90. E. E. H. Welsford (1911), "A Young Research Fellow," in Phillips, p. 153. Welsford had returned to Newnham as a research fellow with teaching responsibilities in 1921.
91. Delp, p. 11.
92. In her introduction to Jane Ellen Harrison's letters to Gilbert Murray, Jessie Stewart gives most of the known details about Harrison's life. See Stewart, pp. 1–12. See also Harry C. Payne's study "Edwardian Modern: Gordon Craig, Jane Harrison, Roger Fry." For a discussion of Harrison's role in the development of the ritualist critics, see Robert Ackerman, "Jane Ellen Harrison: The Early Work," *Greek, Roman and Byzantine Studies* 13 (1972): 209–30.

93. Harrison's views on the relation between sex and intellect are explained in her two essays "Homo Sum" and "Scientiae Sacra Fames" in *Alpha and Omega* (London: Sidgwick and Jackson, 1915), pp. 80–142. See also "Women and Knowledge," *Newnham College Roll*, 1913, pp. 22–25.
94. Ackerman, p. 217.
95. Stewart, pp. 89 and 114.
96. Stewart, p. 120. For a slightly different version, see "Scientiae Sacra Fames," in Harrison, *Alpha and Omega*, p. 160.
97. Stewart, pp. 33–35, 107.
98. Stewart, p. 38.
99. Robert Ackerman, "Some Letters of the Cambridge Ritualists," *Greek, Roman and Byzantine Studies* 12 (Spring 1971): 123. All emphases are in the original.
100. See unpub. letters, Jane Ellen Harrison and Jessie Stewart, Newnham College Archives. Hope Mirrlees appears to have been sexually attracted to Harrison, but it is unclear to what extent Harrison reciprocated. She was clearly more emotionally tied to Mirrlees than her friends thought appropriate.
101. E. M. Holland (1909), "The Suffrage March," in Phillips, pp. 86–87.
102. See her "Crabbed Age and Youth," in *Alpha and Omega*, pp. 1–26.
103. Letter from "V" (25 May 192?), Jane Ellen Harrison papers, Newnham College Archives.
104. Stewart, p. 88.
105. M. R. Levyns (1912), "Life in Peile Hall," in Phillips, p. 97.
106. *Reminiscences*, pp. 46–51, only mentions famous people and characters she knew.
107. Ackerman, "Some Letters," pp. 121–23.
108. See the obituaries in *Time and Tide*, *The Times*, and *The Scotsman* (all January 1935) in the Girton College Archives.
109. Firth gives a very full description of Maynard's religious vocation to middle-class young women. See pp. 81–186.
110. *The Godolphin School, 1726–1926*, ed. Mary Alice Douglas and C. R. Ash (London: Longmans, 1928), pp. 47–49.
111. See Constance Maynard, unpub. autobiography, unnumbered sections (1910–15), Westfield College Archives, and Firth, pp. 266–68. For the early days of Westfield, see Firth, and Eleanora Carus-Wilson, ed. *Westfield College, University of London, 1882–1932* (London: Favil Press, 1932), pp. 1–10, and Janet Sondheimer, *Castle Adamant in Hampstead* (London: Westfield College, 1983), pp. 10–47.
112. For a discussion of the connections between sexuality and spiri-

tual seeking, see chapter 5 and my "Distance and Desire: English Boarding-School Friendships," *Signs* 9 (1984):600–622.

113. Constance Maynard, unpub. autobiography, section 54 (1891), p. 281, Westfield College Archives.

114. For a fuller discussion of Maynard's difficulties with leadership and personal friendship in reference to Louisa Lumsden, see chapter 5 and my article "'One Life to Stand beside Me': Emotional Conflicts in First-Generation College Women in England," *Feminist Studies* 8 (Fall 1982), 603–28.

115. Quoted from a missing diary, Constance Maynard, unpub. autobiography, section 54 (1891), pp. 286–87, Westfield College Archives.

116. Constance Maynard in her unpub. autobiography, section 50 (1887), p. 172, Westfield College Archives, analyzed her unhappiness: "It is all very well to call [my] loneliness 'sex feeling,' but I can honestly say my thoughts never strayed to a man. I wanted to live thus with my flock in a happy community, but I wanted one life to stand beside me, one heart to pour its fullness into mine, and then I should be amply content."

117. Constance Maynard, unpub. diary, 30 April 1886, Westfield College Archives.

118. Constance Maynard, unpub. diary, 23 April 1886, Westfield College Archives.

119. Harrison, *Reminiscences*, p. 90.

120. Constance Maynard, unpub. autobiography, unnumbered section (1897–99), p. 450, Westfield College Archives.

121. Payne, "Edwardian Modern," p. 85.

122. Jane Ellen Harrison to Lady Mary Murray, 22 December 1913, Newnham College Archives.

123. Sargant, "The Inheritance of a University," p. 17.

Chapter Five

1. Quoted from "The Modern Girl," a talk given in 1907 to the Headmistresses' Association, in Anne Ridler, *Olive Willis and Downe House: An Adventure in Education* (London: John Murray, 1967), p. 72.

2. For a full discussion of the ways middle- and upper-class families collaborated in sending their sons to public schools that propagated values antithetical to the family, see J. R. de S. Honey, *Tom Brown's Universe: The Development of the English Public School in the Nineteenth Century* (New York: Quadrangle Books, 1977), pp. 151–53, 163–64.

3. Sara Burstall, *Retrospect and Prospect: Sixty Years of Women's Education* (London: Longmans, Green, 1933), pp. 91–93.

4.   For contemporary negative descriptions of boarding school life, see D. R. Fearon, "Girls' Grammar Schools," *Contemporary Review* 11 (1869):333–54, C. A. W., "Thoughts on Some of the Present Defects in Boarding Schools for Girls," *Victoria Magazine* 27 (1876):432–44, "An Enquiry into the State of Girls' Fashionable Schools," *Fraser's Magazine* 31 (1845):703–12, and the best-known account, Frances Power Cobbe, *Life* (London: Richard Bentley, 1894), 1:49–61, a description of her fashionable school in the 1830s. Historians have recently begun reassessing these early schools and have argued that many were quite good; certainly George Eliot received an outstanding education under the Misses Franklins of Coventry. See Gordon Haight, *George Eliot: A Biography* (New York: Oxford University Press, 1968), pp. 10–21. Eliot attended school in the mid-1830s, the same time as Frances Power Cobbe. For a discussion of nonconformist girls' education, see Clyde Binfield, *Belmont's Portias: Victorian Nonconformists and Middle-Class Education for Girls* (Leicester: Friends of Dr. Williams's Library, 1980).

5.   For an excellent discussion of these changes in regard to the Endowed Schools Act of 1869, see Sheila Fletcher, *Feminists and Bureaucrats: A Study in the Development of Girls' Education in the Nineteenth Century* (Cambridge: Cambridge University Press, 1980).

6.   Studies of secondary education at the time do not sufficiently differentiate between boys' and girls' schools. These figures are based upon the figures quoted by H. Bendell, "Secondary and Other Schools (ii) According to Recent Statistics," in *What Is Secondary Education? and Other Short Essays*, ed. R. P. Scott (London: Rivingtons, 1899), pp. 46–49. Bendell points out that the Report of the Royal Commission on Secondary Education (1894–95) had shown that no more than 1 percent of the population (some twenty-nine million) attended "secondary schools and other," and those under twelve were 40 percent of this figure. (Secondary schools refer to fee-paying schools for the middle class of all ages; elementary schools were state or religiously supported schools for the poor and working class, regardless of age.) Boys and girls over sixteen in school were fewer than 30,000, with girls slightly predominating. See also Barry Turner, *Equality for Some: The Story of Girls' Education* (London: Ward, Lock, 1974), p. 176, for an estimate, without mentioning specific ages, of 20,000 girls in secondary education. Only after the 1902 Education Act did the numbers enrolled climb rapidly; by 1920 185,000 girls attended recognized grammar schools. See Mary Cadogan and Patricia Craig, *You're a Brick, Angela!* (London: Victor Gollancz, 1976), p. 178. Cadogan and Craig give no docu-

mentation for their figures, but see G. A. N. Lowndes, *The Silent Social Revolution*, 2d ed. (London: Oxford University Press, 1969), pp. 78–105.

7. Alice Zimmern, *The Renaissance of Girls' Education in England: A Record of Fifty Years' Progress* (London: A. D. Innes, 1898), p. 237; Bendell, p. 47. Distinctions were not generally made between private preparatory and secondary schools, and it is also difficult to know exactly how many secondary schools existed for boys or girls. As Lowndes points out, pp. 39–46, the nine volumes of the Bryce Commission (Report of the Royal Commission on Secondary Education [1894–95]) give no figures for the number of schools or students. Lowndes estimates a total of 75,000 in endowed schools and 34,000 in proprietary schools, but he makes no distinctions between boys and girls. He also considers that only about 30,000 of the 75,000 received schooling at what could today be considered a sound secondary education level.

8. See Honey, and also Brian Heeney, *Mission to the Middle Classes: The Woodward Schools, 1848–1891* (London: SPCK, 1969).

9. Anna Stoddart, *Life and Letters of Hannah E. Pipe* (Edinburgh: William Blackwell, 1908), p. 62. Pipe's school was midway between the old-style seminary and the reformed schools. She continued a heavy emphasis upon training in the social graces, banned outside exams, and kept the school very small; but she also was committed to good academic standards and outside service.

10. Winifred Peck, *A Little Learning, or A Victorian Childhood* (London: Faber and Faber, 1952), p. 115.

11. Lynda Grier, *The Life of Winifred Mercier* (London: Oxford University Press, 1937), p. 74.

12. Dorothea Beale, "Intellectual Education: Introduction," in Dorothea Beale, Lucy H. M. Soulsby, and Jane Frances Dove, *Work and Play in Girls' Schools* (London: Longmans, Green, 1898), p. 5.

13. Dorothea Beale, "The Ladies' College at Cheltenham," *Transactions of the National Association for the Promotion of Social Science*, 1865, pp. 285–86.

14. Jonathan Gathorne-Hardy, in *The Public School Phenomenon, 597–1977* (London: Hodder and Stoughton, 1977), descends into easy clichés about the "dictator-headmistress tradition." See pp. 241–56. Joyce Senders Pedersen, "Some Victorian Headmistresses: A Conservative Tradition of Social Reform," *Victorian Studies* 24 (Summer 1981):463–88, offers an alternative sympathetic interpretation.

15. Elizabeth Raikes discusses the spiritual and emotional crisis

Dorothea Beale underwent in late middle age in her biography, *Dorothea Beale of Cheltenham*, new ed. (London: Constable, 1910), pp. 179–202.

16. Beale, "The Ladies College," p. 277, and also her *Home Life in Relation to Day Schools* (London: Civil Service Printing Company, 1879). She is even firmer in *Address to Parents* (London: George Bell, 1888).

17. Quoted by Pedersen, "Some Victorian Headmistresses," p. 487.

18. Elsie Bowerman, *Stands There a School: Memories of Dame Frances Dove, Founder of Wycombe Abbey School* (Brighton: Wycombe Abbey School Seniors, [1966]), p. 69.

19. For a fuller discussion of the concerns over professional status, see Joyce Senders Pedersen, "Schoolmistresses and Headmistresses: Elites and Education in Nineteenth-Century England," *Journal of British Studies* 15 (1975):135–62.

20. Raikes, pp. 275–80, and Florence Cecily Steadman, *In the Days of Miss Beale* (London: E. J. Burrow, 1931), pp. 139–49.

21. This was the pattern followed by M. V. Hughes, Margaret Nevinson, and Cecily Steadman, to name three who have left autobiographical accounts of their education. See M. Vivian Hughes, *A London Girl of the Eighties* (Oxford: Oxford University Press, 1978 [1936]), pp. 167–68; Margaret Wynne Nevinson, *Life's Fitful Fever: A Volume of Memories* (London: A. & C. Black, 1926), pp. 59–61; and Steadman, *In the Days of Miss Beale*, pp. 139–41.

22. Helena Deneke, *Grace Hadow* (London: Oxford University Press, 1946), p. 20. For the struggles of two poorer girls, see Dorothy Scannell, *Mother Knew Best* (London: Macmillan, 1974). Scannell was offered a pupil-teachership, but her father forced her to turn it down; she became her mother's chief helper until her marriage. See also the misery of Marianne Farningham after her mother's death, when as the eldest child she had to give up school and take care of her younger brothers and sisters; Marianne Farningham, *A Working Woman's Life* (London: James Clarke, 1907), pp. 43–50. She tried studying nights, and finally her father was able to let her go back to school, in return for her learning to mend shoes for him.

23. Constance Maynard, unpub. autobiography, section 30 (1876), p. 156, Westfield College Archives.

24. L. H. M. Soulsby, "The Religious Side of Secular Teaching," in *Stray Thoughts for Mothers and Teachers* (London: Longmans, Green, 1897), p. 2.

25. Quoted by Pedersen, "Some Victorian Headmistresses," pp. 478–79.

26.   *The Story of the Mary Datchelor School, 1877–1957* (London: Hodder and Stoughton, 1957), pp. 41–42.

27.   For a fuller discussion of the religious bent of the more conservative headmistresses, see Pedersen, "Some Victorian Headmistresses," pp. 474–83.

28.   Raikes, pp. 286–92.

29.   Grier, p. 62.

30.   Burstall, *Retrospect and Prospect*, p. 161.

31.   Amy Barlow, *Seventh Child: The Autobiography of a Schoolmistress* (London: Gerald Duckworth, 1969), pp. 53–60. With a London degree (taken at Aberystwyth) she earned £60 plus room and board per year at this school. Conditions might have been more cheerful but were just as cramped at some of the more renowned schools. Downe House paid a starting salary of £40 per year plus room and board when it opened in 1907.

32.   Barlow, p. 68.

33.   Pedersen, "Schoolmistresses and Headmistress," pp. 150–51, estimates the average salary of a headmistress as about £400 in 1894. She gives the average salaries for professional men in 1913–14 as: barristers, £478; solicitors, £568; general practitioners, £395; clergymen, £208. See below for salaries for assistant mistresses.

34.   In 1895 the Bryce Commission reported salary averages ranging from £84 for the lowest-paying schools to £147 nonresidential for the best-paying for assistant mistresses. Assistant masters ranged from £150 to £200. In 1911 average salaries at grant-earning secondary schools were £168 for men and £123 for women. See Lee Holcombe, *Victorian Ladies at Work* (Hamden, Conn.: Archon Press, 1973), pp. 56–57. Alfred W. Pollard recommended a minimum of £150 in his "The Salaries of Lady Teachers," *Murray's Magazine* 4 (1888):780–89. Beatrice Orange, "Teaching as a Profession," in *The Woman's Library*, ed. Ethel M. M. McKenna (London: Chapman and Hall, 1903), 1:65–66, gives beginning salaries as £100 to £110 for a fully trained secondary-school teacher, but she is probably on the optimistic side, as she dismisses the idea of teaching at inferior schools.

35.   Bowerman, pp. 25 and 45.

36.   Mary Price and Nonita Glenday, in *Reluctant Revolutionaries: A Century of Headmistresses, 1874–1974* (London: Pitman, 1974), describe the efforts of headmistresses to gain control over hiring and firing of their teachers and the establishment of a probationary period upon employment. See pp. 30–35. See also the memorandum of the Association of Head Mistresses (1906) reprinted as Appendix C in Sara Burstall, *English High Schools for*

337

Girls (London: Longmans, 1907), pp. 227–29. The Association of Head Mistresses began as early as 1876 to discuss the desirability of a pension fund for assistant mistresses. See Price and Glenday, p. 33. For a fuller discussion, see Holcombe, pp. 50–55.

37. Alice Gordon, "The After-Careers of University-Educated Women," *Nineteenth Century* 37 (1895):955–60.

38. *The Story of the Mary Datchelor School*, p. 28.

39. Ibid.

40. Mary E. James, *Alice Ottley: First Head-mistress of the Worcester High School for Girls, 1883–1912* (London: Longmans, 1914), p. 68.

41. See Constance Maynard, unpub. autobiography, section 30 (1876), Westfield College Archives.

42. Soulsby, "The Religious Side," pp. 4–5. See also her "The Moral Side of Education," in *Work and Play*, pp. 374–95.

43. Honey discusses the hold the classical curriculum had on the boys' schools of the period, pp. 126–41. See also Gathorne-Hardy, pp. 136–43 and passim. Some schools, of course, did encourage the classics, hoping to make up the "lost years" in which girls, unlike young boys, were not in preparatory schools studying the classics. St. Leonards offered two scholarships in classics to Girton, which were a powerful incentive to ambitious girls. They were rewarded in 1887 when Agnata Ramsey, daughter of a classics professor, was alone in division 1, class 1 of the Classics Tripos examination at Cambridge.

44. Nevinson, p. 24. See also Antonia White's "A Child of the Five Wounds," in *The Old School*, ed. Graham Greene (London: Jonathan Cape, 1934), pp. 229–46, and her first novel, *Frost in May* (London: Virago, 1978 [1933]), for an account of the severe religious rigors of a Roman Catholic boarding school.

45. Constance Maynard, unpub. autobiography, section 33 (1878), p. 297, Westfield College Archives.

46. Hughes, pp. 170 and 213.

47. See Peck, p. 140.

48. See, for example, Olive Willis, as described by Ridler, pp. 138–39.

49. Barlow, pp. 53–54.

50. Jane Frances Dove, "The Cultivation of the Body," in *Work and Play*, pp. 400–401.

51. Julia M. Grant, Katherine H. McCutcheon, and Ethel F. Sanders, eds., *St. Leonards School 1877–1927* (London: Oxford University Press, 1927), p. 79.

52. See Josephine Kamm, *How Different from Us: A Biography of Miss Buss and Miss Beale* (London: Bodley Head, 1958), pp. 175–82 and Raikes, pp. 170–74.

53. Grant, McCutcheon, and Sanders, p. 60.

54. [Margaret Haig Mackworth], Viscountess Rhondda, *This Was My World* (London: Macmillan, 1933), pp. 58–66.

55. Grant, McCutcheon, and Sanders, p. 60.

56. [Mackworth], p. 62.

57. See the unpublished anonymous manuscript diary, Cheltenham Ladies' College Library. I am indebted to the college for permission to quote from this manuscript.

58. Ibid.

59. Elizabeth M. Sewell, *Principles of Education, Drawn from Nature and Revelation, and Applied to Female Education in the Upper Classes* (New York: D. Appleton, 1871 [1865]), p. 392.

60. What documentation we have about middle-class attitudes toward masturbation tends to deal with extreme cases. See Mary S. Hartman, "Child-Abuse and Self-Abuse: Two Victorian Cases," *History of Childhood Quarterly* 2 (Fall, 1974):221–48, discussing two criminal cases involving the deaths of children.

61. Clara A. C. H. Jackson, *A Victorian Childhood* (London: Methuen, 1932), p. 146. She adds, "However there were plenty of clean, nice-minded girls as well, and one was very soon able to distinguish between them." She appears to have felt positively enough about Cheltenham to have sent one of her daughters there.

62. [Sisters of the Church], *A Valiant Victorian: The Life and Times of Mother Emily Ayckbowm, 1836–1900* (London: A. R. Mowbray, 1964), p. 152. At the time the sisters explained, "It was not a kind of evil which can be talked about; and therefore in sending away girls—whom it was imperatively necessary to remove for the sake of others—we have had to bear some misunderstanding from outsiders" (p. 152). Since bad language was openly lamented, the "immoral habits" were presumably masturbation.

63. Peck, pp. 116–17.

64. I am indebted to John Kucich, who shared his work with me and discussed the ideas in this paragraph.

65. Matilda Pullan, *Maternal Counsels to a Daughter* (1855), quoted in Deborah Gorham, *The Victorian Girl and the Feminine Ideal* (Bloomington: Indiana University Press, 1982), p. 113.

66. For a neo-Freudian analysis of this process, see Nancy Chodorow, *The Reproduction of Mothering* (Berkeley: University of California Press, 1978), pp. 136–40.

67. L. M. H. Soulsby, "Friendship and Love," in *Stray Thoughts for Girls* (London: Longmans, Green, 1910), p. 176. Originally published in 1893.

68. Ibid., p. 172.

69. Ibid., p. 176.
70. Burstall, *English High Schools for Girls*, pp. 160–61.
71. Mary Alice Douglas and C. R. Ash, eds. *The Godolphin School, 1726–1926* (London: Longmans, Green, 1928), p. 31.
72. Theodora Benson, "Hot-Water Bottle Love," in *The Old School*, p. 40.
73. See Dorothy Eva deZouche, *Roedean School, 1885–1955* (Brighton: privately printed, 1955), p. 37, and Rachel K. Davis, *Four Miss Pinkertons* (London: Williams and Norgate, 1936), p. 71. Davis does not reveal the name of her school, which she calls "Sutton Weald," but it is clearly Roedean.
74. Benson, "Hot-Water Bottle Love," p. 40.
75. [Dorothy Strachey Bussy], Olivia, *Olivia* (London: Hogarth Press, 1949), pp. 59–60. The events described occurred in the early 1880s, at "Les Ruches," Mlle Souvestre's school outside Paris. Soon after, Mlle Souvestre moved her school to Allenswood, near London. A close friend of the Stracheys, she hired Dorothy Strachey to teach Shakespeare and permitted her younger brother, Lytton Strachey, to attend informally. Marie Souvestre was renowned as a wit and conversationalist. See Michael Holroyd, *Lytton Strachey: A Critical Biography* (New York: Holt, Rinehart and Winston, 1967), 1:34–41. See also Eleanor Roosevelt's grateful appreciation of Mlle Souvestre in *The Autobiography of Eleanor Roosevelt* (New York: Harper and Brothers, 1958), pp. 29–32.
76. [Bussy], p. 82.
77. Davis, p. 62.
78. Ridler, p. 32.
79. Lilian Faithfull, *You and I: Saturday Talks at Cheltenham* (London: Chatto and Windus, 1927), p. 121. The chapter on friendships includes excerpts from letters Cheltenham students wrote to her after hearing her talks, most of which were originally given immediately after World War I.
80. Ridler, pp. 97–98.
81. Davis, p. 68.
82. A similar pattern of spiritual leadership and homoerotic emotions can be found in accounts of boys' public schools, although there was also much greater concern about masturbation. See David Newsome, *Godliness and Good Learning: Four Studies on a Victorian Ideal* (London: John Murray, 1961), pp. 79–91; Honey, pp. 167–96; and Gathorne-Hardy, pp. 156–80.
83. Constance Maynard, unpub. diary, 14 July 1878, Westfield College Archives.
84. Quoted by Constance Maynard, unpub. diary, 9 February 1879, Westfield College Archives.

85. Constance Maynard, unpub. diary, 12 April 1879, Westfield College Archives.
86. Ibid.
87. Ibid.
88. Similar emotions are described in regard to male homosexual love in a boys' public school by T. C. Worsley in *Flannelled Fool: A Slice of Life in the Thirties* (London: Alan Ross, 1967), pp. 122–24.
89. Constance Maynard, unpub. autobiography, section 44 (1882), pp. 19–20, Westfield College Archives. Maynard copied large sections of her diary into her autobiography.
90. Constance Maynard, unpub. autobiography, section 45 (1883), pp. 19–20, Westfield College Archives.
91. [Bussy], p. 102.
92. Bussy was a longtime friend and translator of the well-known homosexual André Gide; indeed, she was passionately in love with him and shared with him many of her thoughts and emotions. See *Selected Letters of André Gide and Dorothy Bussy*, ed. Richard Tedeschi, with an intro. by Jean Lambert (Oxford: Oxford University Press, 1983). Bussy originally wrote *Olivia* in 1933 when she was sixty four, recording events that took place when she was fifteen; Gide's rather neutral response to her manuscript appears to have discouraged her from seeking a publisher until after World War II, when both Rosamond Lehman (author of *Dusty Answer* [1927], which includes a lesbian romance at Girton College) and Leonard Woolf urged her to publish it with Hogarth Press. Gide was extremely enthusiastic and apologetic after he had read the published *Olivia*. See pp. 153, 155, 157, 277–90.
93. Deneke, p. 21.
94. Ibid., p. 17.
95. These issues are discussed at greater length in my article " 'One Life to Stand beside Me': Emotional Conflicts of First-Generation College Women in England," *Feminist Studies* 8 (Fall 1982): 602–28.
96. Constance Maynard, unpub. autobiography, section 30, (1876), pp. 161, 162, Westfield College Archives.
97. Constance Maynard, unpub. diary, 12 November 1876, Westfield College Archives. All emphases are in the original. At the time Louisa and Constance were at Cheltenham Ladies' College.
98. Constance Maynard, unpub. diary, 27 May 1877, Westfield College Archives.
99. Quoted in Constance Maynard, unpub. autobiography, section 33 (1878), p. 298, Westfield College Archives.

100. See deZouche, passim.

101. Ridler, pp. 106–17. After a detailed description of Nickel's eccentricities, Ridler comments, "Miss Nickel might have seemed a somewhat sinister figure to an outside observer, but Olive Willis was too strong a character to submit to any Rasputin-like influence" (p. 109).

102. Ridler, p. 105.

103. See, for example, Elizabeth Bowen's description of Downe House during World War I, "The Mulberry Tree," in The Old School, pp. 45–59.

104. In the late 1880s discussion of friendships between men and women were triggered by Alice Mona Caird's provocative series of articles on "the morality of marriage," and the many replies her articles elicited. See Alice Mona Caird, The Morality of Marriage and Other Essays on the Status and Destiny of Woman (London: G. Redway, 1897). See also Henry Quilter, ed., Is Marriage a Failure? (London: Swan Sonnenschein, 1888), which reprints a selection of letters on the subject received by the Daily Telegraph. Priscilla E. Moulder's "Friendship between the Sexes," Westminster Review 151 (1899):667–70, is typical of moderate pleas for increased opportunities for platonic friendships.

105. Grier, p. 30.

106. See the reevaluation of friendship among American women by Carroll Smith-Rosenberg, "The Female World of Love and Ritual: Relations between Women in Nineteenth-Century America," Signs 1 (1975):1–29; Blanche Wiesen Cook, "Female Support Networks and Political Activism: Lillian Wald, Crystal Eastman, Emma Goldman," Chrysalis, no. 3 (1977):43–61; Nancy Sahli, "Smashing: Women's Relationships before the Fall," Chrysalis, no. 8 (1979):17–27; Leila J. Rupp, "'Imagine My Surprise': Women's Relationships in Historical Perspective," Frontiers 5, no. 3 (Fall 1980):61–70; and Lillian Faderman, Surpassing the Love of Men: Romantic Friendship and Love between Women from the Renaissance to the Present (New York: William Morrow, 1981).

107. Grier, p. 34.

108. Ibid., p. 105.

109. Ethel Colquhoun, "Modern Feminism and Sex-Antagonism," Quarterly Review 219 (1913):155.

110. [Winifred Ashton], Clemence Dane, Regiment of Women (London: Heinemann, 1917), pp. 248–49. The ellipses are all in the original; Dane's style is fraught with dots and dashes.

111. See Carol Dyhouse, "Social Darwinistic Ideas and the Development of Women's Education in England, 1880–1920," History of Education 5 (1976):53–54.

112. Burstall, *English High Schools for Girls*, p. 210.
113. Carol Dyhouse, "Towards a 'Feminine' Curriculum for English Schoolgirls: The Demands of Ideology, 1870–1963," *Women's Studies International Quarterly* 1 (1978):305.
114. Downe School, founded in 1907, is a good example of a boarding school that attempted to apply more modern educational principles to girls' schools. But the headmistress found it difficult to talk to young people who did not respond to her moral teaching during World War II. See Ridler, pp. 165–66.
115. Judith Okely, "Privileged, Schooled and Finished: Boarding School Education for Girls," in *Defining Females: The Nature of Women in Society*, ed. Shirley Ardener (New York: John Wiley, 1978), pp. 109–39. Okely, p. 121, points out that by the 1950s teachers in girls' boarding schools came from a lower social class than their students—certainly a change from the nineteenth century.

Chapter 6

1. *In Statu Pupillari* (London: Swan Sonnenschein, 1907), p. 185.
2. For a full discussion of women's philanthropy, excluding settlements, see Frank K. Prochaska, *Women and Philanthropy in Nineteenth-Century England* (Oxford: Oxford University Press, 1980).
3. Louisa M. Hubbard, "Statistics of Women's Work," in *Women's Mission: A Series of Congress Papers on the Philanthropic Work of Women by Eminent Writers*, ed. Baroness [Angela] Burdett-Coutts (London: Sampson Low, Marston, 1893), p. 364. Hubbard frankly admits that statistics on volunteer work are hard to get and that her figures are only estimates. But in 1905 the London churches, chapels, missions, and charities were estimated to have 7,500 volunteers and 900 paid visitors. Between 1908 and 1914 the School Care Committees of the London County Council enrolled 10,000 volunteers. Since these figures refer only to select organizations in London, Hubbard's estimate is probably a reasonable one. See Anne Summers, "A Home from Home—Women's Philanthropic Work in the Nineteenth Century," in *Fit Work for Women*, ed. Sandra Burman (New York: St. Martin's, 1979), p. 34.
4. Anna Jameson, *"Sisters of Charity" and "The Communion of Labour": Two Lectures on the Social Employments of Women* (London: Longman, Brown, Green, Longmans and Roberts, 1859), p. 13.

5.   For a discussion of the roots of this change during the years 1780–1850, see Summers, pp. 35–38.

6.   For individual articles on each of these organizations, as well as many others, see Burdett-Coutts, *Woman's Mission*. The anthology gives a good sense of the scope of women's philanthropic work at the end of the nineteenth century.

7.   See F. K. Prochaska, "Women in English Philanthropy, 1790–1830," *International Review of Social History* 19 (1974):426–45, for a discussion of the relation between women's philanthropy and social control during and immediately following the Napoleonic Wars. See also Summers, pp. 36–41.

8.   For a call "to help to uplift the nation" by serving in local government, see J. M. E. Brownlow, *Women's Work in Local Government (England and Wales)* (London: David Nutt, 1911).

9.   Alice Stronach, *A Newnham Friendship* (London: Blackie and Son, 1901), pp. 215–16.

10.   For a modern analysis of Toynbee Hall's educational efforts, see Emily K. Abel, "Middle-Class Culture for the Urban Poor: The Educational Thought of Samuel Barnett," *Social Service Review* 52 (1978):596–620. See also J. A. R. Pimlott, *Toynbee Hall: Fifty Years of Social Progress (1884–1934)* (London: J. M. Dent, 1935).

11.   Samuel A. Barnett, "The Ways of 'Settlements' and of 'Missions,'" *Nineteenth Century* 42 (1897):977, and [Mary] Simmons, "Discussion [of] Social Settlements," in *Transactions of the Social Section of the International Congress of Women*, ed. Ishbel, Countess of Aberdeen (London: T. Fisher Unwin, 1900), 7:127.

12.   George Lansbury, *My Life* (London: Constable, 1928), p. 130. Among those who went on to distinguished government careers after a brief period at Toynbee Hall were C. R. Atlee, W. H. Beveridge, W. J. Braithwaite, A. M. Carr-Saunders, H. Llewellyn-Smith, R. H. Morant, J. A. Salter, J. A. Spender, and R. H. Tawney. See Emily K. Abel, "Toynbee Hall, 1884–1914," *Social Service Review* 53 (1979):606.

13.   The accusation was made by E. J. Urwick in 1903. Urwick was the first lecturer and tutor of the School of Sociology after it became independent of the Charity Organisation Society. He went on to become the first professor of sociology at the London School of Economics when it assimilated the School of Sociology in 1912. See Ronald G. Walton, *Women in Social Work* (London: Routledge and Kegan Paul, 1975), pp. 54, 61–62.

14.   Abel, "Toynbee Hall," pp. 609–10.

15.   Beatrice Webb, *My Apprenticeship* (London: Longmans, Green, 1926), pp. 212–13. When she visited Hull House, Jane Addams'

settlement in Chicago, she noted in her diary, "the residents consist, in the main, of strong-minded energetic women, bustling about their various enterprises and professions, interspersed with earnest-faced self-subordinating and mild-mannered men who slide from room to room apologetically." Quoted in Jill Conway, "Women Reformers and American Culture, 1870–1930," *Journal of Social History* 5 (1971–72):174.

16. Beatrice Webb worked briefly under Octavia Hill as a rent collector in 1885–86; she had little faith in the abilities of lady collectors to have more than a superficial impact upon the tenants of the model housing. See Webb, pp. 259–79.

17. For a modern evaluation of Octavia Hill's work, see A. S. Wohl, "Octavia Hill and the Homes of the London Poor," *Journal of British Studies* 10 (1971):105–31. See also C. Edmund Maurice, *Life of Octavia Hill as Told in Her Letters* (London: Macmillan, 1913).

18. For a full discussion of the COS and the development of its casework methods, see Charles Loch Mowat, *The Charity Organisation Society, 1869–1913: Its Ideas and Work* (London: Methuen, 1961). As social work became professionalized, middle-class women gradually replaced the working-class men who worked for the COS. See also Judith Fido, "The Charity Organization Society and Social Casework in London, 1869–1900," in *Social Control in Nineteenth-Century Britain*, ed. A. P. Donajgrodzki (London: Croom Helm, 1977), pp. 207–30.

19. Octavia Hill, "Trained Workers for the Poor," *Nineteenth Century* 33 (1893):37–38, and her "District Visiting," in *Our Common Land (and Other Short Essays)* (London: Macmillan, 1877), pp. 24–25.

20. Henrietta O. Barnett, *Canon Barnett: His Life, Work and Friends*, 2 vols. (Boston: Houghton Mifflin, 1919), 2:50–51. Mrs. Barnett justified her husband's position by pointing out that before the advent of Toynbee Hall philanthropy had been left to women and old men; Barnett was among the first to attract "young and brilliant men."

21. Werner Picht, *Toynbee Hall and the English Settlement Movement*, rev. ed., trans. Lilian A. Cowell (London: G. Bell, 1914), p. 102.

22. In 1895 Barnett broke publicly with the COS and called for a form of modified socialism, but he had been lukewarm toward many COS policies since the mid-eighties. See Barnett, 2:260–72, and Mowat, pp. 128–29.

23. Mary D. Stocks, *Eleanor Rathbone* (London: Victor Gollancz, 1949); Albert Mansbridge, *Margaret McMillan, Prophet and Pio-*

neer: Her Life and Work (London: J. M. Dent, 1932); and Muriel Lester, *It Occurred to Me: An Autobiography* (New York: Harper, 1937).

24. Margaret McMillan, *The Life of Rachel McMillan* (London: J. M. Dent, 1927), p. 199.

25. Alice Lucy Hodson, *Letters from a Settlement* (London: Edward Arnold, 1909), pp. 53–54.

26. See McMillan, pp. 194–95.

27. Octavia Hill, "A Few Words to Fresh Workers," *Nineteenth Century* 26 (1889):454.

28. See, for example, the novel *Polly: A Study of Girl Life* by Flora Lucy Freeman (Oxford: A. R. Mowbray, 1904). The orphaned Polly is befriended by a wealthy girl, who finds her a good position as a servant in the country in order to save her from her drunken mother and the temptations of the slum.

29. Ethel Hurlbatt, summary of a paper given at the Sixteenth Annual General Meeting of the Women's University Settlement, *Annual Report*, 1903, pp. 9–10.

30. The reports of the WUS are consistently longer in the *Newnham College Roll* than in the *Girton Review*, and the donations followed suit. In 1903, to take a typical year, WUS residents consisted of five Newnhamites, three from LMH, one each from Somerville and Royal Holloway College, and ten noncollege women. Out of fifteen resident visitors, one came from Girton and the remaining fourteen were noncollege. See *Annual Report* 1904, p. 27. A more detailed analysis of early settlements in the United States reveals the same breakdown in attitudes and colleges. See John P. Rousmaniere, "Cultural Hybrid in the Slums: The College Woman and the Settlement House, 1889–1894," *American Quarterly* 22 (1970):45–66.

31. Stronach, p. 102.

32. "The Hoxton Settlement," *Sunday at Home*, undated newspaper clipping, ca. 1900, Tower Hamlets Local History Library.

33. Honnor Morten, *From a Nurse's Note-book* (London: Scientific Press, 1899), pp. 127–28.

34. Alice Stronach, "Woman's Work in Social Settlements," *Windsor Magazine* 36 (1912):412.

35. Lucy Ashley Smith, "Guild of the Cheltenham Ladies' College," *Cheltenham Ladies' College Magazine* 10 (1884):244.

36. Lucy Ashley Smith, "Guild of the Cheltenham Ladies' College," *Cheltenham Ladies' College Magazine* 20 (1889):180–89.

37. For a brief history of the Cheltenham Ladies' College Settlement, see the unpublished and anonymous typescript in the Tower Hamlets Local History Library.

38. "Letter sent to the Headworker by certain members of the Committee," 11 December 1888, WUS Minutes, Blackfriars Settlement (the current name of the WUS settlement).

39. "Statement of the Head Worker in reply to letter received from certain members of the Committee," undated. WUS Minutes, Blackfriars Settlement. See also D. M. Brodie, *Women's University Settlement, 1887–1937* (London: WUS, 1937), p. 8.

40. WUS Subcommittee [to investigate complaints against Helen Gladstone, Warden] Minutes, 1903, Blackfriars Settlement. Ironically one of the blocks of flats next to the settlement is now named after Gladstone, while more effective and committed wardens are forgotten.

41. Winifred Peck, *A Little Learning, or A Victorian Childhood* (London: Faber and Faber, 1952), p. 138.

42. Irene Biss (Westfield, 1907–11), unpub. reminiscences, Westfield College Archives.

43. *Handbook of Settlements of Great Britain Affiliated to the British Association of Residential Settlements and the Educational Settlements Association* (London, 1927), p. 13. Paulinas paid £1.8.0 per week, outside residents doing full-time work £2.2.0, and visitors £3.3.0 to stay at the settlement.

44. M. McN. S[harpley], "Women's University Settlement, Southwark," *Newnham College Roll*, 1921, p. 40.

45. Hodson, p. 8.

46. Picht, p. 127.

47. WUS *Annual Report*, 1902, pp. 2–4, 26. Similar figures are given for residence and training costs at other settlements.

48. Hodson, pp. 52–53.

49. Reginald Kennedy-Cox, *An Autobiography* (London: Hodder and Stoughton, 1931), p. 78.

50. Hodson, p. 103.

51. "History of Blackfriars Settlement," unpub. essay, Blackfriars Settlement. "Not long ago I met in Bermondsey an elderly lady who had known the Settlement in that era [pre-World War I]. 'What' I asked her 'did she chiefly remember about Nelson Square?' 'Twelve grates before breakfast' she promptly replied."

52. *Hilda Cashmore (1876–1943)* (Gloucester: J. Bellows, [1944]), p. 34.

53. Ibid., p. 12: Violet Markham comments that Hilda Cashmore "was a little hard on the rich, a little over fastidious at times about her contacts with anyone above the poverty line. But leading a life of extreme discipline, the indiscipline which often goes with wealth and ease roused in her something akin to contempt."

54. Mary Simmons, "From St. George's House," *Bermondsey Settlement Magazine* 21 (May-June 1915):33. St. George's had been

called the George Public House before it was remodeled and
renamed.

55. Lester, p. 91.

56. "The Robert Browning Hall," *London*, 1 October 1896, p. 940.
Southwark Local History Library.

57. Abel, "Toynbee Hall," p. 620.

58. *Annual Report*, 1902, pp. 26–30.

59. It is exceptionally difficult to find out about settlements from
the community being served, although patronizing anecdotes
abound in the various annual reports. But see Lylie Valentine,
Two Sisters and the Cockney Kids (London: Club Row Press,
1978), an account of Kingsley Hall by an active member from its
earliest days until its demise. The author played at the Hall as a
child and teenager and met her husband there. She served on its
managing board as well as holding numerous unofficial jobs.
Picht, p. 131, comments that many settlers were simply met
with a "quiet refusal" by the respectable working class of the
friendship proffered, but he provides no further details.

60. Maude Stanley, *Clubs for Working Girls* (London: Macmillan,
1890), pp. 194–97.

61. F. Kirwan, "Some Mistakes of the Club Leader," *Girls' Club
Journal* 2, 4 (1910):11.

62. Emmeline Pethick, "Working Girls' Clubs," in *University and
Social Settlements*, ed. Will Reason (London: Methuen, 1898),
p. 104.

63. Pethick, pp. 107–9.

64. Lord F. W. Pethick-Lawrence, *Fate Has Been Kind* (London:
Hutchinson, 1942), p. 59.

65. Pethick, pp. 110–11.

66. For a discussion of the connections between imperialism, social
control, and attitudes toward working-class mothers, see Anna
Davin, "Imperialism and Motherhood," *History Workshop* 5
(Spring 1978):9–65.

67. Robert Browning Settlement, *Eighteen Years in the Central City
Swarm* (London: W. A. Hammond, [1913]), pp. 28–35, 115–16.
See also Lansbury, pp. 142–44.

68. The cooperative movement was always strongest in the North,
but a few stores and guilds succeeded in London. For a general
history of the Women's Co-operative Guild, see Catherine Webb,
*The Woman with the Basket: The History of the Women's Co-
operative Guild, 1883–1927* (Manchester: Co-operative Wholesale Society, 1927).

69. Janet Penrose Trevelyan, *The Life of Mrs. Humphry Ward* (London: Constable, 1923), pp. 129–41.

70. Mansbridge, pp. 87–111.

71.   Julia Cowan, "A Social Tonic," *Methodist Recorder*, 12 September 1901, p. 12. Newspaper clipping, Southwark Local History Library. See also E. J., "How to Deal with the Hooligan Girl: A Chat with Sister Grace," *Young Woman* 9 (1900–1901): 317–20.

72.   See Cowan, "A Social Tonic," and J. Scott Lidgett, *My Guided Life* (London: Methuen, 1936), pp. 126–27.

73.   See the commemorative volume, Grace T. Kimmins, *Heritage Craft Schools and Hospitals, Chailey, 1903–1948* (London: Baynard Press, 1948).

74.   For a full description of the CCHF, see Cyril Jackson, "The Children's Country Holiday's Fund and the Settlements," in *The Universities and the Social Problem: An Account of the University Settlements in East London*, ed. John Matthew Knapp (London: Rivington, Percival, 1895), pp. 87–105.

75.   Helen Barlow, transcript of interview, Women's University Settlement Papers, Blackfriars Settlement. Barlow was a long-term volunteer who worked especially closely with orphan boys.

76.   Valentine, pp. 7–8.

77.   WUS, *Annual Report*, 1902, p. 17.

78.   Clara Grant, *From 'Me' to 'We': Forty Years in Bow Common* (London: the author, [1939]), p. 28. The WUS obviously felt it beneath the dignity of trained social workers to sort and grade old clothes and miscellaneous gifts to be sold at a minimum cost, which was the basis of the Fern Street Settlement's work.

79.   Grant, p. 35. She does admit that Toynbee Hall "did not do all it hoped for the poor around" (p. 35).

80.   Maurice Bruce, *The Coming of the Welfare State*, 2d ed. (London: B. T. Batsford, 1965), p. 109. See also Walton, pp. 30–32.

81.   J. v. I. and B. S. W., "Women's University Settlement," *Newnham College Roll*, 1899, pp. 40–41. They did not, of course, consider that they might have been unwelcome intruders in the homes they visited.

82.   Constance Maynard, unpub. autobiography, section 43 (1882), p. 119, Westfield College Archives.

83.   McMillan, pp. 121, 127.

84.   Lester, p. 58.

85.   McMillan, p. 127.

86.   The Robert Browning Settlement argued that "the distinctive idea of the Browning Settlement . . . has been from the first that the aims of a Settlement are best carried out, not by a company of celibates, but by *Resident Households*" (*Annual Report*, 1900, p. 7). Nevertheless, aside from Herbert Stead and his wife and the subwarden and his wife, the bulk of Browning's workers were single men and women.

87. May Crask, "Girl Life in a Slum," *Economic Review* 18 (1908): 187–88.
88. Pethick, p. 102.
89. Flora Lucy Freeman, *Religious and Social Work amongst Girls* (London: Skeffington, 1901), p. 93.
90. Stanley, p. 48.
91. Cecile Matheson, Warden of the Birmingham University Settlement, quoted in Walton, p. 109.
92. *The Englishwoman's Year Book*, ed. Louisa M. Hubbard (London: F. Kirby, 1896), p. li.
93. See, for example, Mary Simmons's obituary of Laura A. Robinson, who spent eight years of her retirement with a close friend at the Bermondsey Settlement. She had been principal of the Halifax Girls' High School and of a high school in South Africa before donating her services to the Bermondsey Settlement. *Bermondsey Settlement Magazine*, February 1907, pp. 17–19. Hodson was rather scathing about the "delicate, nervous" elderly lady at her settlement. Hodson, pp. 45–46.
94. Reprinted in the WUS *Annual Report*, 1913, p. 23.
95. For a discussion of Booth's discovery of the depth and breadth of poverty in London, see Harold W. Pfautz, ed. and intro., *Charles Booth on the City: Physical Pattern and Social Structure* (Chicago: University of Chicago Press, 1967), pp. 21–35. The percentage of people living under the poverty line in East and South London was over 40 percent in most neighborhoods. See Pfautz, p. 56.
96. See Bruce, pp. 150–91, for an outline of the social reforms of 1905–14. The Robert Browning Settlement was active in sponsoring lectures by socialist leaders, including a regular series "The Labour Movement in Religion" during these years. The women's settlements tended to campaign for a single issue, such as school meals or schools for the handicapped. The WUS remained consistently pro-COS throughout the period; Octavia Hill was a supporter of the Poor Law Report of 1909, so vehemently attacked by the Webbs. The COS led the fight against government legislation, though it did favor some form of old-age pensions. See Mowat, pp. 154–66.
97. "Why Social Workers Want Women's Suffrage," *Common Cause* 8, 410 (16 February 1917):593.
98. See the Fabian Women's Group study on poverty, Maude Pember Reeves, *Round about a Pound a Week* (London: Virago, 1979 [1913]), and the more informal Women's Co-operative Guild publication, Margaret Llewellyn Davies, ed. and intro., *Maternity: Letters from Working Women* (London: G. Bell and Sons, 1915), as well as Pfautz.

99. Beatrice Webb, in spite of her negative impressions in regard to ladies' rent collecting, did maintain her contacts with friends such as Ella Pyecroft and Emma Cons. The latter opened a temperance music hall and a workingmen's college in the 1880s which became the Old Vic and Morley College. See Webb, pp. 251, 255–60, 263, 267–68, and Lilian Baylis and Cecily Hamilton, *The Old Vic* (London: Jonathan Cape, 1926).

100. See Mansbridge, pp. 80–89, for a description of her close work with the London County Council.

101. This point is also made by Barbara Corrado Pope, "Angels in the Devil's Workshop: Leisured and Charitable Women in Nineteenth-Century England and France," in *Becoming Visible: Women in European History*, ed. Renate Bridenthal and Claudia Koonz (Boston: Houghton-Mifflin, 1977), p. 321.

102. Picht, pp. 129–30.

103. See Mansbridge, pp. 21–52, and Stocks, pp. 59–71.

104. Kingsley Hall was named after the sisters' younger brother, who died in the summer of 1914. According to the *Handbook of Settlements* (1927), at least half of all settlements were started after 1914, despite the war and declining enthusiasm for the settlement idea. See *Adventures in Fellowship, 1915–1936* (London: Kingsley Hall, 1936) for a history of Kingsley Hall.

105. Lester, p. 91. Mary Hughes, daughter of Thomas Hughes, was also one of the Brethren. She was the only settlement worker George Lansbury approved of in his autobiography. See Lester, pp. 87–93, Lansbury, p. 131.

106. Lester, pp. 150–53. Beatrice B. Rogers, warden of the Manchester University Settlement in 1917–25, was equally saintly in her selfless work for the settlement, but she was much less successful in attracting allies and workers. According to Mary D. Stocks, no one would share the house with her after ineffectual efforts to improve the housekeeping and food. See her *Fifty Years in Every Street: The Story of the Manchester University Settlement*, 2d. ed. (Manchester: Manchester University Press, 1956), p. 57. She writes, "Miss Rogers herself occupied a room whose internal structure included a pipe which continually sneezed and gurgled on its way to and from an awkwardly placed attic lavatory. She appeared to be perfectly contented with it" (p. 57).

107. See in particular Valentine, passim.

Chapter Seven

1. See Clara E. Collet's detailed essays, *Educated Working Women: Essays on the Economic Position of Women Workers in the Mid-*

dle Classes (London: P. S. King, 1902). Although most of her essays were written in the 1890s, conditions had changed little in the early twentieth century.

2. For a detailed account of the suffrage movement up until militancy, see Helen Blackburn, *Women's Suffrage: A Record of the Women's Suffrage Movement in the British Isles, with Biographical Sketches of Miss Becker* (London: Williams and Norgate, 1902), and Millicent Garrett Fawcett, *What I Remember* (London: T. Fisher Unwin, 1924). A. E. Metcalfe includes a brief chapter on the days before militancy in *Woman's Effort: A Chronicle of British Women's Fifty Year Struggle for Citizenship (1865–1914)* (Oxford: B. H. Blackwell, 1917).

3. Such magazines as *Shafts* (1892–99), edited by Margaret Shurmer Sibthorp, kept alive suffrage, vegetarianism, birth control, and other avant-garde issues. See Dora B. Montefiore, *From a Victorian to a Modern* (London: E. Archer, 1927), pp. 42–83, for a discussion of militancy in its earliest days. See also Margaret Wynne Nevinson, *Life's Fitful Fever: A Volume of Memories* (London: A. & C. Black, 1926), pp. 66–67, on "the sentimentality and slave-spirit of women" before the days of militancy.

4. Andro Linklater, *An Unhusbanded Life: Charlotte Despard, Suffragette, Socialist, and Sinn Feiner* (London: Hutchinson, 1980), chaps. 4, 5, and 6.

5. Leslie Parker Hume, *The National Union of Women's Suffrage Societies, 1897–1914* (New York: Garland Press, 1982), pp. 11–13. Hume comments that "The profile of the NUWSS executive committee bears a striking resemblance to that of another feminist pressure group, the Ladies National Association for the Repeal of the Contagious Diseases Acts," and that "Approximately half of the committee [in 1897] had been actively working for women's suffrage for more than twenty years" (p. 12).

6. E. Sylvia Pankhurst, *The Suffragette Movement* (London: Longmans, Green, 1931), considered these to be the main reasons for the phenomenal growth of the Women's Social and Political Union, but similar motivations affected women who joined other groups. See pp. 226–27. See also Ray Strachey, *The Cause: A Short History of the Women's Movement in Great Britain* (London: Virago, 1978 [1928]), p. 304.

7. Mrs. Pethick-Lawrence, *The Faith That Is in Us* (London: Women's Press, [1908?]), p. 4

8. Julie Holledge, *Innocent Flowers: Women in the Edwardian Theatre* (London: Virago, 1981), pp. 59–72.

9. See Linklater, pp. 127–28, Nevinson, pp. 214–18.

10. Andrew Rosen, *Rise up, Women! The Militant Campaign of the*

Women's Social and Political Union, 1903–1914 (London: Routledge and Kegan Paul, 1974), p. 53.

11.   I have followed the practice of historians in referring to members of the militant WSPU as suffragettes and the nonmilitants as suffragists. At the time, however, WSPU members generally called themselves "militant suffragists," and only after Christabel Pankhurst adopted the sneering title "Suffragette" for her weekly paper in 1912 did the word come into use among militants themselves. I have also referred to the WSPU leaders by first or last names, according to the custom of the time.

12.   Betty Balfour, ed. and arranger, *Letters of Constance Lytton* (London: William Heinemann, 1925), p. 129. Lady Constance had suffered a debilitating stroke after undergoing forced feeding. See later in this chapter.

13.   Christabel Pankhurst converted to Second Adventism and became an active spokesperson for the Second Coming between the wars; see Rosen, pp. 196–97, 270, for a discussion of Christabel's millennial strain. Brian Harrison gives a judicious historian's view of the personal and organizational causes of militancy in "The Act of Militancy: Violence and the Suffragettes, 1904–1914," in *Peaceable Kingdom: Stability and Change in Modern Britain* (Oxford: Clarendon Press, 1982), pp. 26–81. See also Constance Rover, *Women's Suffrage and Party Politics in Britain, 1866–1914* (London: Routledge and Kegan Paul, 1967), pp. 74–76, 90–92, 99–101; Brian Harrison, *Separate Spheres: The Opposition to Women's Suffrage in Britain* (London: Croom Helm, 1978), pp. 153–54; and E. Sylvia Pankhurst, pp. 226–27.

14.   Christabel Pankhurst, *Unshackled: The Story of How We Won the Vote* (London: Hutchinson, 1959), p. 84.

15.   When the annual conference was dropped in September 1907, Charlotte Despard, Teresa Billington-Greig, and Edith How Martyn broke away to form the Woman's Freedom League. For criticisms, see Linklater, pp. 116–26, E. Sylvia Pankhurst, passim, and Teresa Billington-Greig, *The Militant Suffrage Movement: Emancipation in a Hurry* (London: Frank Palmer, 1912).

16.   [Margaret Haig Mackworth], Viscountess Rhondda, *This Was My World* (London: Macmillan, 1933), p. 124.

17.   Hannah Mitchell, *The Hard Way Up*, ed. Geoffrey Mitchell (London: Faber and Faber, 1968), p. 135.

18.   Emmeline Pethick-Lawrence, *My Part in a Changing World* (London: Victor Gollancz, 1938), pp. 213–14. See also Rosen, who gives all relevant financial figures for the WSPU each year of its public reports.

19.   See in particular E. Sylvia Pankhurst's detailed account of her

353

own life and that of other "mice" during these years, pp. 471–91, 578–80.

20. Elaine Kidd, *Materialism and the Militants* (Hampstead: Macdonald, n.d.), p. 1.

21. Quoted by Edith How-Martyn in a note dated 24 October 1937, Suffragette Fellowship Collection, the Museum of London.

22. Mrs. Pethick-Lawrence, *A Call to Women* 2d. ed. (London: National Women's Social and Political Union, n.d.), p. 1.

23. Emmeline Pethick-Lawrence, *My Part*, pp. 150–51.

24. Rosen, pp. 115, 210.

25. S. I. Stevenson, "No Other Way," unpub. autobiography, Suffragette Fellowship Collection, the Museum of London. See also Harrison, *Separate Spheres*, pp. 161–63, for a discussion of the price militants paid in regard to their families.

26. See the unpublished obituary of Aeta Lamb (1886–1928) by Vera Douie, Suffragette Fellowship Collection, the Museum of London. See also E. Sylvia Pankhurst, p. 224.

27. Zoe Procter, *Life and Yesterday* (London: Favil Press, 1960), p. 105.

28. Mary Nesbitt to Miss [May] Sinclair (1 May 1912), unpublished letter, Suffragette Fellowship Collection, the Museum of London.

29. Emmeline Pethick-Lawrence, *My Part*, p. 215.

30. Some members of the WSPU found the adoration of its leaders silly and schoolgirlish. See Nevinson, p. 196.

31. Billington-Greig, p. 197, quoted in Harrison, *Separate Spheres*, p. 176.

32. The most powerful attacks against the WSPU came from former members: Billington-Greig, passim, and E. Sylvia Pankhurst, pp. 220–22, 516–18.

33. Mary R. Richardson, *Laugh a Defiance* (London: George Weidenfeld & Nicolson, 1953), pp. 165–70.

34. Constance Lytton, *Prisons and Prisoners: Some Personal Experiences* (London: William Heinemann, 1914), p. 9.

35. Annie Kenney, *Memories of a Militant* (London: Edward Arnold, 1924), pp. 192–93.

36. Emmeline Pethick-Lawrence, *My Part*, p. 151.

37. B. M. Willmott Dobbie, *A Nest of Suffragettes in Somerset* (Bath: Batheaston Society, 1979), pp. 12–19. Annie Kenney particularly liked having Mary wash and massage her head at the end of a long day. See p. 19.

38. Elizabeth Robins, *In Defence of the Militants* (London: Women's Social and Political Union, [1912]). Reprinted from *The Times*, 7 March 1912.

39. For Despard's theosophy, see Linklater, pp. 156–59.

See also Despard's pamphlets, *Woman in the New Era* (London: Suffrage Shop, 1910), and *Theosophy and The Woman's Movement* (London: Theosophical Publishing Society, 1913). When Annie Kenney became interested in theosophy, Christabel forbade her to become involved, arguing that she could not divide her time between it and suffrage. Kenney, p. 127.

40. Undated correspondence between KM [Kitty Marion], MR [Mary Richardson], and RP [Rachel Peace], Suffragette Fellowship Collection, the Museum of London. Only Kitty Marion can be identified definitely by internal references to her theatrical career; however, Mary Richardson and Rachel Peace had been active together during the arson campaign, and all three were in prison during the years 1912–14, as they were among the most active supporters of the WSPU. See E. Sylvia Pankhurst, pp. 578–79.

41. Ibid.

42. For an examination of British and American posters, see Paula Hays Harper, "Votes for Women? A Graphic Episode in the Battle of the Sexes," in *Art and Architecture in the Service of Politics*, ed. Henry A. Millon and Linda Nochlin (Cambridge: MIT Press, 1978), pp. 150–61.

43. See, for example, A. M. Wright, *How I Became a Suffragette* (Chesham: Page and Thomas, [1960?]), pp. 3 and 6, and [Mackworth], pp. 120–23.

44. Emmeline Pankhurst, *Why We Are Militant* (London: Woman's Press, 1913), and Emmeline Pethick-Lawrence, *My Part*, p. 278.

45. *Suffragette*, 25 October 1912, p. 23.

46. Charlotte Marsh, in an interview with Lady Jessie Street, March 1960. Unpublished transcript, Suffragette Fellowship Collection, the Museum of London.

47. Lord F. W. Pethick-Lawrence, *Fate Has Been Kind* (London: Hutchinson, 1942), p. 101.

48. See, for example, the comic *A Suffragette's Love Letters* (London: Chatto and Windus, 1907).

49. The most notorious attack on suffrage was that made by Sir Almroth E. Wright, first in a letter to *The Times* and then in *The Unexpurgated Case against Woman Suffrage* (London: Constable, 1913). Mrs. Humphry Ward, the leading woman antisuffragist, was so horrified by his attack that she wrote *The Times* disavowing him. See Harrison, *Separate Spheres*, pp. 67–68.

50. Fawcett, pp. 215–16.

51. Walter Heape, *Sex Antagonism* (London: Constable, 1913), pp. 206–14.

52. Richardson, p. 12, Harrison, p. 189.

53. Cecily Hamilton, *Life Errant: Autobiographical Reminiscences* (London: J. M. Dent, 1935), pp. 75–76.

54. Dora Montefiore particularly protested against the WSPU's policy of fighting with the police, feeling that it would be easier and less destructive if women simply accepted being arrested when they trespassed. See Montefiore, p. 108. Both Rosen and Harrison describe the physical violence against women whenever they entered such male political preserves as Liberal meetings or outdoor Liberal party rallies and, of course, on Black Friday.
55. Dobbie, p. 30.
56. Harrison, *Separate Spheres*, p. 187.
57. Rosen, pp. 139–42.
58. Rosen, p. 142, and Harrison, *Separate Spheres*, p. 187.
59. Holledge, p. 71. Christabel considered Joan of Arc "the patron saint of Suffragettes." See E. Sylvia Pankhurst, p. 468. Mary Richardson, during a hunger strike, wrote Kitty Marion a note on lavatory paper, saying, "Certainly you get to know yourself physically and mentally in prison and I suppose if we were true philosophers we would be glad of this. I have been thinking of Joan of Arc to-day—How marvellous she was so alone, with vile men night and day so tormented." Suffragette Fellowship Collection, the Museum of London.
60. Rosen, pp. 103–4.
61. Nevinson, pp. 203–5.
62. Kenney, pp. 208–9.
63. Rosen, pp. 122–23.
64. The records of the WSPU were seized when the police raided its headquarters on 5 March 1912, so it is impossible to know exactly how many women went to prison. Estimates run as high as two thousand. When the Suffragette Fellowship set up a small fund for needy suffragettes during the interwar years, they had some difficulty checking applicants' credentials. See the note about a Miss Sprott who had not repaid money lent to her by the Fellowship. How-Martyn Correspondence, Suffragette Fellowship Collection, the Museum of London.
65. *Letters of Constance Lytton*, p. 129.
66. See Katherine Roberts's fictionalized account of her experience in prison, *Some Pioneers and a Prison* (n.p., 1913), p. 71.
67. Lytton, pp. 78–80.
68. Marion Wallace-Dunlop to the home secretary (5 December 1911), Suffragette Fellowship Collection, the Museum of London.
69. S. I. Stevenson, "No Other Way."
70. Helen Gordon [Liddle], *The Prison: A Sketch (An Experience of Forcible Feeding)* (Letchworth: Garden City Press, 1911), pp. 63–64.
71. Liddle, p. 64.

72. Evelyn Sharp, *Unfinished Adventure: Selected Reminiscences from an Englishwoman's Life* (London: John Lane, 1933), pp. 147–48.

73. Lytton, p. 283.

74. S. I. Stevenson described her gradual descent into illness as part of a pattern that affected many others: "Ever since the inauguration of our campaign combatants kept falling out from all ranks through overstrain. . . . there were legions who suffered in various and often fatal ways, and some in lesser but very inconveniencing directions. I had not been subjected to the ardours and truly terrible tortures of many of my brave comrades, nevertheless, into this van I was being rapidly drawn. Like the incoming tide creeping imperceptibly inch by inch, my malady steadily progressed." Her health became so poor that she was not able to do war work. See S. I. Stevenson, "No Other Way." Aeta Lamb was one of the most enthusiastic early members but was too high-strung to continue after being ridden down by mounted police and twice sentenced to Holloway. See Vera Douie, obituary.

75. Lilian Lenton, interview with Lady Jessie Stewart, March 1960. Unpublished transcript, Suffragette Fellowship Collection, the Museum of London. Suffragettes who regularly underwent forcible feeding and hunger striking feared most not death, but permanent injury. As Ethel Smyth wrote George Bernard Shaw, "Do you know it is a fact that these women dread becoming useless individuals far more than death. Think what it means, to these most active independent people,—the thought of being logs for life—many of them doomed to becoming a burden on poor relations!" Quoted by Harrison, *Separate Spheres*, p. 162. After being released under the "Cat and Mouse" Act Hugh Franklin, who was forcibly fed more than one hundred times, and his fiancée, Elsie Duval, fled to the Continent to avoid being rearrested. They married in 1915, but Duval's health never recovered, and she died in 1919. See the Hugh Franklin Papers, Fawcett Library, City of London Polytechnic. Numerous other examples of permanently broken health are mentioned in the Suffragette Fellowship Collection, the Museum of London.

76. Richardson, pp. 173–74. See her undated letter to Kitty Marion, "Gaye Bell has been here and shown me your last letter. I have thought of you each day since leaving [prison] and was relieved to hear you were safe (also our other friend) I should love to have seen you many times but this is of course impossible. It *is* a lonely life isn't it that we lead, but then it will not last *forever*. You probably suffer from depression after the fearful strain. I have been very dumpy too the last ten days always am after Holloway" (Suffragette Fellowship Collection, the Museum of London). See

also May Sinclair, *The Tree of Heaven* (London: Cassell, 1917), p. 197, where the heroine longs to return to her cell, to escape the celebratory breakfast held by the WSPU for the released prisoners: "The singing had threatened her when it began; so that she felt again her old terror of the collective soul. Its massed emotion threatened her. She longed for her white-washed prison-cell, for its hardness, its nakedness, its quiet, its visionary peace."

77. Rachel Peace, undated note, Suffragette Fellowship Collection, the Museum of London.

78. See Richardson, pp. 152–54, E. Sylvia Pankhurst, pp. 556–61.

79. Lytton, p. 187.

80. Olive Walton, unpublished diary (1912), Suffragette Fellowship Collection, the Museum of London. See also Margaret E. Thompson and Mary D. Thompson, *They Couldn't Stop Us! Experiences of Two (Usually Law-abiding) Women in the Years 1909–1913* (Ipswich: W. E. Harrison, 1957), pp. 44–51.

81. "Hammerers' Magazine," Winson Green Prison (Birmingham, 1912), Suffragette Fellowship Collection, the Museum of London.

82. E. Sylvia Pankhurst, p. 332.

83. *Letters of Constance Lytton*, p. 269.

84. These events are documented fully in Lytton's *Prisons and Prisoners*, as well as her correspondence and manuscript copy in the Suffragette Fellowship Collection, the Museum of London. It is interesting that the publisher, William Heinemann, felt called upon to disavow Lytton's ideas in a preface to her book.

85. *Letters of Constance Lytton*, p. 265.

86. Ibid., pp. 265–66.

87. Lytton, pp. 200–202.

88. Rosen, chapters 16 and 18, meticulously documents the month-by-month destruction caused by the arson campaign.

89. For a discussion of the antifeminism of the medical profession and feminists' distrust of doctors, see Brian Harrison, "Women's Health and the Women's Movement in Britain: 1840–1940," in *Biology, Medicine and Society*, ed. Charles Webster (Cambridge: Cambridge University Press, 1981), pp. 15–71. I am indebted to Judith R. Walkowitz for suggestions in regard to the connections between militant feminism and hatred of the medical profession.

90. Judith R. Walkowitz, *Prostitution and Victorian Society: Women, Class and the State* (Cambridge: Cambridge University Press, 1980), pp. 129–31.

91. Emily Wilding Davison, "The Price of Liberty," *Suffragette*, 5 June 1914, p. 10.

92. See Harrison, *Separate Spheres*, pp. 185–86, for a discussion of the failure of the suffragettes to distinguish between tactical violence and spontaneous mass violence. See also Millicent Faw-

cett's reply to the hunger strikers, "The objection which I feel to your voluntary starvation plan is that all the inconvenience and suffering it would cause would fall on suffragists and their families, and that it would not inconvenience the Government in the slightest degree. I can in my mind's eye see Mr. Asquith chuckling at the thought of the suffrage ranks being depleted by the suicide of whatever number of women decided to adopt your plan." Quoted in Ray Strachey, *Millicent Garrett Fawcett* (London: John Murray, 1931), p. 240.

93. Davison, p. 50. See also Rosen, pp. 198–200.

94. Davison, p. 50.

95. See Emmeline Pethick-Lawrence, "A Calendar of Saints," *Votes for Women*, n.s., 3 (5 November 1909):89, and numerous letters to released hunger strikers in the Suffragette Fellowship Collection, the Museum of London.

96. See her letters to Kitty Marion, Suffragette Fellowship Collection, the Museum of London, written in 1914.

97. See Rosen, p. 200, for a brief description of the funeral. G. Colmore in her memorial pamphlet, *The Life of Emily Davison* (London: Woman's Press, 1913), insisted that Davison "died that other women might find it possible to live truer, happier lives; who fought that other women might have freedom; who gave herself to the Women's Cause, without grudging and without fear, convinced, as every apostle of liberty has been convinced, that rebellion against tyranny is obedience to God, and never doubting that God will give the victory" (pp. 60–61).

98. Maud Arncliffe-Sennett, *The Child* (London: privately published, [1938?]), pp. 82–83.

99. Christabel Pankhurst, *The Great Scourge and How to End It* (London: E. Pankhurst, 1913), pp. 132–33.

100. Antonia Raeburn, *The Militant Suffragettes* (London: Michael Joseph, 1973), pp. 212–14, 223.

101. Rosen, pp. 247–48.

102. See E. Sylvia Pankhurst, pp. 593–94, Emmeline Pethick-Lawrence, *My Part*, pp. 307–17.

103. A statue in commemoration of Mrs. Pankhurst had been erected in 1930, with the names of all the known women who had gone to prison around the base.

104. Emmeline Pethick-Lawrence, undated letter to Elsa Gye [1934–35?], Suffragette Fellowship Collection, the Museum of London.

Conclusion

1. For example, the National Union of Women's Suffrage Societies in 1912 started an Election Fighting Fund to support candidates

in by-elections; they then actively sought Labour party support. These ties were an important step on the part of largely Liberal party middle-class women to extend their political allies and to attract working-class women to the cause. The outbreak of the war stopped the development of this potential alliance. See Leslie Parker Hume, *The National Union of Women's Suffrage Societies, 1897–1914* (New York: Garland, 1982), chap. 5.

2. Sandra Gilbert, "Soldier's Heart: Literary Men, Literary Women, and the Great War," *Signs* 8 (1983):425. In September 1916 the War Office declared that women had "shown themselves capable of replacing the stronger sex in practically every calling." Quoted by Andrew Rosen, *Rise up Women! The Militant Campaign of the Women's Social and Political Union, 1903–1914* (London: Routledge and Kegan Paul, 1974), p. 256.

3. In November 1917 the WSPU became "The Woman's Party," and Christabel Pankhurst published a political party platform that combined a xenophobic foreign policy with a radical domestic policy. After Christabel ran unsuccessfully for Parliament on an anti-Bolshevik platform in 1918, the Woman's party ceased to exist. Other militant leaders joined one of the many newly formed women's political organizations or the Women's Freedom League (Emmeline Pethick-Lawrence eventually became its president). But militancy as such was dead. See Rosen, pp. 266–69.

4. Quoted by Mary D. Stocks, *Eleanor Rathbone: A Biography* (London: Victor Gollancz, 1949), p. 116.

5. Stocks, pp. 116–18.

6. This dilemma is discussed in regard to present-day issues by Rosalind Pollack Petchesky, "Reproductive Freedom: Beyond 'A Woman's Right to Choose,'" *Signs* 5 (1980):661–85.

7. Jane Lewis, "Beyond Suffrage: English Feminism in the 1920s," *Maryland Historian* 6 (1975):11.

8. For a discussion of the medical model of homosexuality, see Jeffrey Weeks, *Coming Out: Homosexual Politics in Britain from the Nineteenth Century to the Present* (London: Quartet Books, 1977).

9. For the work of Labour party women, see Sheila Ferguson, "Labour Women and the Social Sciences," in *Women in the Labour Movement*, ed. Lucy Middleton (London: Croom Helm, 1977), pp. 38–56.

10. Celia Davies, "A Constant Casualty: Nurse Education in Britain and the USA to 1939," in *Rewriting Nursing History*, ed. Celia Davies (London: Croom Helm, 1980), p. 112.

11. Vera Brittain, "The Educational Veil: Women Teachers and Their Disadvantages," *Manchester Guardian*, 7 March, 1929, p. 8. I am indebted to Carol Dyhouse for this reference.

12. For a discussion of the participation of women in socialist communities before 1850, see Barbara Taylor, *Eve and the New Jerusalem: Socialism and Feminism in the Nineteenth Century* (London: Virago, 1983), chap. 8.

13. Brian Abel-Smith, *A History of the Nursing Profession* (London: Heinemann, 1960), pp. 130–37.

14. Asher Tropp, *The Schoolteachers: The Growth of the Teaching Profession in England and Wales from 1800 to the Present Day* (London: Heinemann, 1957), p. 216.

15. Jill Conway, "Women Reformers and American Culture, 1870–1930," *Journal of Social History* 5 (1971–72):164–77.

16. Constance Maynard, unpub. autobiography, section 50 (1887), p. 172, Westfield College Archives.

17. Emmeline Pethick-Lawrence, *My Part in a Changing World* (London: Victor Gollancz, 1938), p. 58.

18. Relations still remained unequal, and many women found it difficult to speak honestly. See Ruth First and Ann Scott, *Olive Schreiner: A Biography* (London: Andre Deutsch, 1980), pp. 145–57.

19. These developments are discussed in Gail Cunningham, *The New Woman and the Victorian Novel* (London: Macmillan, 1978), chap. 2, and Martha Vicinus, "Introduction" in George Egerton, *Keynotes* and *Discords* (London: Virago, 1983). Egerton's short stories were originally published in 1893 and 1894.

20. West's essays first appeared in 1911–13, when she was eighteen, in *The Freewoman* and its successor *The New Freewoman*, edited by Dora Marsden, a breakaway suffragette. The magazine was soon infamous for its open discussion of sexuality, avant-garde literature, and politics. See *The Young Rebecca: Writings of Rebecca West, 1911–1917*, selected and introduced by Jane Marcus (London: Virago, 1982), for a selection of West's essays, focusing upon her forthright feminism, socialism, and sexual libertarianism.

21. Christina Simmons, "Companionate Marriage and the Lesbian Threat," *Frontiers* 4, no.3 (1979):55.

22. Winifred Holtby, *Women and a Changing Civilization* (London: John Lane, 1934), pp. 192–93.

Appendix B

1. *Englishwoman's Review* 19 (15 March 1889):141, in a description of the Ladies' Dwellings Company's proposed "Sloane Gardens House."

2. *Work and Leisure* 12 (September 1887):231.

3. The papers and publications of both the YWCA's Housing Bu-

reau and John Shrimpton's Society are in the national head-quarters of the YWCA, London. Annual reports and newsletters document a slow rise in the standard of living for the largely lower-middle class residents of these homes. The YWCA was catapulted into providing housing for respectable working women when Florence Nightingale found that cheap, respectable lodgings could not be found for her nurses en route to the Crimea.

4. Margaret McMillan, *The Life of Rachel McMillan* (London: J. M. Dent, 1927), p. 35.

5. Jean Rhys's heroine in *Voyage in the Dark* (Harmondsworth: Penguin, 1969 [1934]) refuses to stay at the chorus-girls' hostel when she is unemployed "because they make you come down to prayers every morning before breakfast" (p. 18). The May of Teck Club "for the Pecuniary Convenience and Social Protection of Ladies of Slender Means below the age of Thirty Years" is treated with grim irony by Muriel Spark in *The Girls of Slender Means* (New York: Alfred Knopf, 1963), p. 6.

6. Both *Work and Leisure* and the *Englishwoman's Review* frequently comment on the need for more homes for working women of the middle class, and how those that exist always have a waiting list. See Evelyn March-Phillipps, "The Working Lady in London," *Fortnightly Review* 58 (1892):193–203, Gilbert Parker, "The Housing of Educated Working Women," in *Report of the Transactions of the International Council of Women* (London: T. Fisher Unwin, 1889), pp. 258–73, and Alice Zimmern, "Ladies Dwellings," *Contemporary Review* 77 (1900): 96–104.

7. M. V. Hughes, *A London Home in the Nineties* (Oxford: Oxford University Press, 1978 [1937]), p. 29.

8. Letter to the editor, *Golden Gates*, 28 November 1891, p. 51. I am indebted to Anna Davin for this reference.

9. See the *Writing Machine News* 6 (March/April 1901):23. I am indebted to Anna Davin for this reference.

10. See the report by B. S. Knollys, "Ladies' Clubs in London: No. 1: The Pioneer Club in Bruton Street," *Englishwoman* 1 (April 1895):120–25, "A Peep at the Pioneer Club," *Young Woman* 20 (1896):302–5, and the regular reports in the feminist journal *Shafts* (1892–98). The quarrel between the two factions is difficult to piece together from the guarded reports in *Shafts*, but it appears to have been over how radical the club should be on such issues as suffrage and temperance. The Grosvenor Crescent Club broke away and, under the leadership of Mrs. Phillipps, aligned itself with the new Women's Institute, while a rump group continued at Bruton Street as the Pioneer Club.

11. See Constance Smedley, *Crusaders: The Reminiscences of Con-*

362

stance *Smedley* (London: Duckworth, 1929), pp. 54–100. See also the correspondence between Constance Smedley, secretary, and Lady Strachey on appropriate members, Fawcett Library, City of London Polytechnic.

12.   Jessie Stewart, *Jane Ellen Harrison: A Portrait from Letters* (London: Merlin Press, 1959), p. 39. Harrison wrote in January 1902.

13.   Stewart, p. 40. Harrison wrote 2 January 1903. See also the comic treatment of a women's club in E. M. Delafield's *Diary of a Country Lady* (New York: Harper, 1930). Delafield's heroine leads a double life, finding in London the freedom and pleasures that are forbidden a respectable lady in the country.

14.   Eve Anstruther, "Ladies' Clubs," *Nineteenth Century* 45 (1899): 605, 611.

Selected Bibliography

Unpublished Sources

Autograph Collection. Fawcett Library, City of London Polytechnic, London.
Barbara Bodichon Papers. Girton College, Cambridge, England.
Blackfriars Settlement Archives, London.
Boston University Nursing Archives, Boston.
Cheltenham Ladies' College Archives, Cheltenham, England.
Constance Maynard Papers. Westfield College, London.
Community of St. John the Baptist Archives, Clewer, England.
Deaconess Community of St. Andrew Archives, London.
Edward Bouverie Pusey Papers. Pusey House, Oxford.
Emily Davies Papers. Girton College, Cambridge, England.
Florence Nightingale Papers. British Library, London.
Hugh Franklin Papers. Fawcett Library, City of London Polytechnic, London.
Girton College Archives, Cambridge, England.
Jane Ellen Harrison Papers, Newnham College, Cambridge, England.
Lady Margaret Hall Archives, Oxford.
Maud Arncliffe-Sennett Papers. British Library, London.
Newnham College Archives, Cambridge, England.
Nightingale Training School Archives. Greater London Record Office.
Society of St. Margaret's Archives, East Grinstead, England.
Somerville College Archives, Oxford.
Suffragette Fellowship Collection, The Museum of London, London.
Royal College of Nursing Archives, London.
Young Women's Christian Association Archives, London.

Parliamentary Papers

1901 Census of England and Wales, Great Britain. House of Commons Sessional Papers 1903, 74, 186–99.
1911 Census of England and Wales, Great Britain. House of Commons Sessional Papers 1913, 78.

364

Royal Commission on Secondary Education (Bryce). Parliamentary Papers 1895, 43–49.
Schools Inquiry Commission (Taunton). Parliamentary Papers 1867–68, 28 (1–17).

Annual Reports and Transactions

Bermondsey Settlement. *Annual Report.* 1905–14.
Central Bureau for the Employment of Women. *The Fingerpost: A Guide to Professions for Educated Women, with Information as to Necessary Training.* London, 1906.
Directory of Religious Communities of Men and Women, and of Deaconesses. London: Faith Press, 1920.
Handbook of Settlements of Great Britain Affiliated to the British Association of Residential Settlements and the Educational Settlements Association. London, 1927.
National Union of Women Workers of Great Britain and Ireland. *Annual Reports.* 1895–1911.
North of England Council for Promoting the Higher Education of Women. *Reports.* 1867–74.
Robert Browning Settlement. *Annual Reports.* 1896–1914.
Transactions of the International Congress of Women. 7 vols. 1900.
Transactions of the National Association for the Promotion of Social Science. 1859–84.
University Degrees for Women: Report of a Conference Convened by the Governors of the Royal Holloway College, Saturday, 4 December 1897. London: Spottiswoode, 1898.
Women's University Settlement. *Annual Reports.* 1887–1923.

Periodicals, Serials, and Newspapers

Bermondsey Settlement Magazine. 1895–1918.
The British Journal of Nursing. 1903–56.
Brown Book [of Lady Margaret Hall]. 1906–25.
Cheltenham Ladies' College Magazine. 1884–1921.
The Common Cause. 1909–14.
English Woman's Journal. 1858–65.
Englishwoman's Review. 1866–1906.
The Englishwoman's Year Book. 1881–1916.
The Freewoman. 1911–12.
Girls' Club Journal. 1909–20.
The Girls' Realm. 1898–1915.
Girton Review. 1882–1920.
Golden Gates. 1891–92.

New Freewoman. 1913–14.
Newnham College Roll. 1885–1925.
The Nursing Record and Hospital World. 1890–1902.
Nursing Times. 1905–20.
Our Work. 1892–1910.
St. Margaret's Magazine. 1887–1921.
Shafts. 1892–99.
The Suffragette. 1912–15.
Votes for Women. 1907–18.
Work and Leisure. 1876–79, 1880–93.
The Yearbook of Women's Work. 1875.
The Young Woman. 1892–1915.

Primary Sources: Books

Adderley, James. In Slums and Society: Reminiscences of Old Friends. London: T. Fisher Unwin, 1916.
Arncliffe-Sennett, Maud. The Child. London: privately published, [1938?].
[Ashton, Winifred]. Clemence Dane. Regiment of Women. London: Heinemann, 1917.
Balfour, Betty, ed. and arranger. Letters of Constance Lytton. London: William Heinemann, 1925.
Barbour, A. H. F. Under a Rowan Tree. Edinburgh: privately printed, 1908.
Barker, C. M. Call Me Matron. London: Heinemann, 1980.
Barlow, Amy. Seventh Child: The Autobiography of a Schoolmistress. London: Gerald Duckworth, 1969.
Bateson, Margaret. Professional Women upon Their Professions. London: Horace Cox, 1895.
Beale, Dorothea. Address to Parents. London: George Bell, 1888.
———. Home Life in Relation to Day Schools. London: Civil Service Printing Company, 1879.
Beale, Dorothea, Lucy H. M. Soulsby, and Jane Frances Dove. Work and Play in Girls' Schools. London: Longmans, Green, 1898.
Bennett, Alice Horlock. Through an Anglican Sisterhood to Rome. London: Longmans, 1914.
Billington-Greig, Teresa. The Militant Suffrage Movement: Emancipation in a Hurry. London: Frank Palmer, 1912.
Bird, M. Mostyn. Woman at Work: A Study of the Different Ways of Earning a Living Open to Women. London: Chapman and Hall, 1911.
Blackburn, Helen. Women's Suffrage: A Record of the Women's Suffrage Movement in the British Isles, with Biographical Sketches of Miss Becker. London: Williams and Norgate, 1902.

Bodichon, Barbara. *A Brief Summary in Plain Language of the Most Important Laws of England concerning Women.* 3d ed. rev. London: Trubner, 1869.

Booth, Charles, ed. *Life and Labour of the People of London.* 17 vols. London: Macmillan, 1892–1903.

Bosanquet, Helen Dendy. *Social Work in London, 1869–1912: A History of the C.O.S.* London: John Murray, 1914.

Bottome, Phyllis. *Search for a Soul.* London: Faber and Faber, 1947.

Boucherett, Jessie. *Hints on Self-Help: A Book for Young Women.* London: S. W. Partridge, 1863.

Bremner, C. S. *The Education of Girls and Women in Great Britain.* London: Swan Sonnenschein, 1897.

Brittain, Vera. *Testament of Youth: An Autobiographical Study of the Years 1900–1925.* London: Victor Gollancz, 1933.

Brodie, D. M. *Women's University Settlement, 1887–1937.* London: W.U.S., 1937.

Brownlow, J. M. E. *Women's Work in Local Government (England and Wales).* London: David Nutt, 1911.

Bulley, Agnes Amy, and Margaret Whitley. *Women's Work.* London: Methuen, 1894.

Burdett-Coutts, [Angela], Baroness, ed. *Woman's Mission: A Series of Congress Papers on the Philanthropic Work of Women by Eminent Writers.* London: Sampson Low, Marston, 1893.

Burstall, Sara. *English High Schools for Girls.* London: Longmans, 1907.

———. *Retrospect and Prospect: Sixty Years of Women's Education.* London: Longmans, Green, 1933.

[Bussy, Dorothy Strachey]. Olivia. *Olivia.* London: Hogarth Press, 1949.

Butler, Josephine E. *The Education and Employment of Women.* Liverpool: T. Brakell, 1868.

———, ed. *Woman's Work and Woman's Culture.* London: Macmillan, 1869.

[Butler, W. J.]. *Some Account of St. Mary's Home for Penitents, at Wantage, Berkshire.* Oxford: J. H. Palmer, 1852.

Caird, Alice Mona. *The Morality of Marriage and Other Essays on the Status and Destiny of Woman.* London: G. Redway, 1897.

Carter, T. T. *The First Five Years of the House of Mercy, Clewer.* London: Joseph Masters, 1855.

———. *The First Ten Years of the House of Mercy, Clewer.* London: Joseph Masters, 1861.

———. *Is It Well to Institute Sisterhoods in the Church of England for the Care of Female Penitents?* Oxford: J. H. Parker, 1851.

Cobbe, Frances Power. *Criminals, Idiots, Women and Minors: Is the Classification Sound?.* [Reprinted from *Fraser's Magazine,* December, 1868]. Manchester: A. Ireland, 1869.

———. *The Duties of Women: A Course of Lectures.* Boston: George Ellis, 1882.

———. *Essays on the Pursuits of Women.* London: Emily Faithfull, 1863.

———. *Life.* 2 vols. London: Richard Bentley, 1894.

Collet, Clara E. *Educated Working Women: Essays on the Economic Position of Women Workers in the Middle Classes.* London: P. S. King, 1902.

Colmore, G. [pseud.]. *The Life of Emily Davison.* London: Women's Press, 1913.

Cooke, Harriette J. *Mildmay, or The Story of the First Deaconess Institution.* London: Elliot Stock, 1892.

[Craik, Dinah Mulock]. *About Money and Other Things.* London: Macmillan, 1886.

Craik, Dinah Mulock. *A Woman's Thoughts about Women.* London: Hurst and Blackett, [1858].

Cusack, Mary F. *The Story of My Life.* London: Hodder and Stoughton, 1891.

Davies, Emily. *Thoughts on Some Questions relating to Women, 1860–1908.* New York: Kraus, 1971 [1910].

Davies, Margaret Llewellyn, ed. and intro. *Maternity: Letters from Working Women.* London: G. Bell and Sons, 1915.

Dunlop, Olive Jocelyn. *Leaves from a Cambridge Note-Book.* Cambridge: Heffer and Sons, 1907.

Ellis, Mrs. [Sarah Stickney]. *The Women of England: Their Social Duties and Domestic Habits.* New York: J. & H. G. Langley, 1843.

Evans, Joan. *Prelude and Fugue: An Autobiography.* London: Museum Press, 1964.

Eyles, Leonora. *The Ram Escapes: The Story of a Victorian Childhood.* London: Peter Nevill, 1953.

Faithfull, Emily. *How Shall I Educate My Daughter?* London: Victoria Press, 1863.

———. *On Some of the Drawbacks Connected with the Present Employment of Women.* London: Victoria Press, 1862.

Faithfull, Lilian. *In the House of My Pilgrimage.* London: Chatto and Windus, 1924.

———. *You and I: Saturday Talks at Cheltenham.* London: Chatto and Windus, 1927.

Farningham, Marianne. *A Working Woman's Life.* London: James Clarke, 1907.

Fawcett, Millicent Garrett. *What I Remember.* London: T. Fisher Unwin, 1924.

Forbes, Rev. A. P. *A Plea for Sisterhoods.* 2d ed. London: Joseph Masters, 1850.

Freeman, Flora Lucy. *Polly: A Study of Girl Life*. Oxford: A. R. Mowbray, 1904.

———. *Religious and Social Work Amongst Girls*. London: Skeffington, 1901.

Gilpin, Fanny. *Scenes from Hospital Life: Being the Letters of a Probationer Nurse*. London: Drane's, 1923.

Goodman, Margaret. *Experiences of an English Sister of Mercy*. London: Smith, Elder, 1862.

———. *Sisterhoods in the Church of England*. London: Smith, Elder, 1863.

Grant, Clara. *From 'Me' to 'We': Forty Years in Bow Common*. London: the author, [1939].

Gray, Frances Ralph. *And Gladly Wolde He Lerne and Gladly Teche*. London: Sampson, Low, 1931.

Greg, W. R. *Literary and Social Judgments*. London: Trubner, 1868.

Grey, Maria Georgina. *Old Maids: A Lecture*. London: Ridgeway, 1875.

Grey, Maria, and Emily Shirreff. *Thoughts on Self-Culture, Addressed to Women*. London: William Crosby and H. P. Nichols, 1850.

Hamilton, Cecily Mary. *Life Errant: Autobiographical Reminiscences*. London: J. M. Dent, 1935.

Hampton, Isabel A., et al. *Nursing of the Sick 1893*. New York: McGraw-Hill, 1949.

Hardy, Gladys M. *Yes, Matron*. London: Edward O. Beck, 1953.

Harrison, Jane Ellen. *Alpha and Omega*. London: Sidgwick and Jackson, 1915.

———. *Reminiscences of a Student's Life*. London: Hogarth Press, 1925.

Hays, Frances. *Women of the Day*. London: Chatto and Windus, 1885.

Heape, Walter. *Sex Antagonism*. London: Constable, 1913.

Hill, Octavia. *Our Common Land (and Other Short Essays)*. London: Macmillan, 1877.

Hodson, Alice Lucy. *Letters from a Settlement*. London: Edward Arnold, 1909.

Holford, Ida. *But the Nights Are Long*. London: Robert Hale, 1977.

Holland, Sydney. *In Black and White*. London: Edward Arnold, 1926.

Holyoake, George. *Bygones Worth Remembering*. 2 vols. London: T. Fisher Unwin, 1905.

———. *Sixty Years of an Agitator's Life*. London: T. Fisher Unwin, 1893.

Hughes, M. Vivian. *A London Girl of the Eighties*. Oxford: Oxford University Press, 1978 [1936].

———. *A London Home in the Nineties*. Oxford: Oxford University Press, 1978 [1937].

Hunt, Agnes. *This Is My Life*. London and Glasgow: Blackie, 1938.

Hutchins, B. L. *The Working Life of Women*. London: Fabian Society, 1911.

In Statu Pupillari. London: Swan Sonnenschein, 1907.

Ireland, Mrs. Alexander. *Selections from the Letters of Geraldine Endsor Jewsbury to Jane Welsh Carlyle*. London: Longman's, Green, 1892.

Jackson, Clara A. C. H. *A Victorian Childhood*. London: Methuen, 1932.

Jameson, Mrs. [Anna]. *"Sisters of Charity" and "The Communion of Labour": Two Lectures on the Social Employment of Women*. London: Longman, Brown, Green, Longmans and Roberts, 1859.

Jones, Emily E. C. *As I Remember: An Autobiographical Ramble*. London: A. & C. Black, 1922.

Kennedy-Cox, Reginald. *An Autobiography*. London: Hodder and Stoughton, 1931.

Kenney, Annie. *Memories of a Militant*. London: Edward Arnold, 1924.

Kidd, Elaine. *Materialism and the Militants*. Hampstead: Macdonald, n.d.

Kingsley Hall. *Adventures in Fellowship, 1915–1936*. London: Kingsley Hall, 1936.

Knapp, John Matthew, ed. *The Universities and the Social Problem: An Account of the University Settlements in East London*. London: Rivington, Percival, 1895.

L., A. V. *The Ministry of Women and the London Poor*. Edited and with an intro. by Mrs. Bayly. London: S. W. Partridge, 1870.

Lansbury, George. *My Life*. London: Constable, 1928.

Lees, Florence S. *Handbook for Hospital Sisters*, ed. H. W. Acland. London: W. Isbister, 1874.

Lester, Muriel. *It Occurred to Me: An Autobiography*. New York: Harper, 1937.

[Liddle], Helen Gordon. *The Prison: A Sketch (An Experience of Forcible Feeding)*. Letchworth: Garden City Press, 1911.

Lidgett, J. Scott. *My Guided Life*. London: Methuen, 1936.

List, Emma B. E. *"Girton, My Friend" and Other Matter (in Prose and Verse)*. Cambridge: W. Heffer, 1908.

Livermore, Mary Ashton. *What Shall We Do with Our Daughters?*. Boston: Lee and Shepard, 1883.

Lodge, Oliver, et al. *The Position of Woman: Actual and Ideal*. London: J. Nisbet, 1911.

Lückes, Eva. *Hospital Sisters and Their Duties*. London: J. & A. Churchill, 1886.

———. *Lectures on General Nursing*. London: Kegan Paul, Trench, Trübner, 1892.

Lumsden, Louisa Innes. *Yellow Leaves: Memories of a Long Life*. Edinburgh: William Blackwood, 1933.

Lytton, Constance. *Prison and Prisoners: Some Personal Experiences*. London: William Heinemann, 1914.

M., E. T. *An Interior View of Girton College, Cambridge*. London: London Association of Schoolmistresses, 1876.

M., M. A. *Agnes Grahame, Deaconess: A Story of Woman's Work for Christ and His Church*. London: William Hunt, 1879.

[Mackworth, Margaret Haig]. Viscountess Rhondda. *This Was My World*. London: Macmillan, 1933.

MacManus, E. E. P. *Matron of Guy's: An Autobiography*. London: Andrew Melrose, 1956.

McKenna, Ethel M. M., ed. *The Woman's Library*. London: Chapman and Hall, 1903.

Maddison, Isabel. *Handbook of British, Continental and Canadian Universities, with Special Mention of the Courses Open to Women*. 2d ed. New York: Macmillan, 1899.

Marcus, Jane, ed. *The Young Rebecca: Writings of Rebecca West, 1911–1917*. London: Virago, 1982.

Markham, Violet. *Return Passage: The Autobiography of Violet Markham, C.H.* Oxford: Oxford University Press, 1953.

Martineau, Harriet. *Autobiography*, ed. Maria Chapman. 2 vols. Boston: James R. Osgood, 1877.

Mary Christabel Cadbury: The Story of a Nightingale Nurse and Kindred Papers. Headley: privately printed, [1939].

Maynard, Constance. *Between College Terms*. London: James Nisbet, 1910.

Memorials of Agnes Elizabeth Jones. By her sister, with an introduction by Florence Nightingale. London: Strahan, 1871.

Metcalfe, A. E. *Woman's Effort: A Chronicle of British Women's Fifty Year Struggle for Citizenship (1865–1914)*. Oxford: B. H. Blackwell, 1917.

Mill, John Stuart. *The Subjection of Women*. Intro. Wendell Robert Carr. Cambridge: MIT Press, 1970 [1869].

Milne, John Duguid. *Industrial Employment of Women in the Middle and Lower Ranks*. Rev. ed. London: Longmans, Green, 1870 [1857].

Mitchell, Hannah. *The Hard Way Up*, ed. Geoffrey Mitchell. London: Faber and Faber, 1968.

Montefiore, Dora B. *From a Victorian to a Modern*. London: E. Archer, 1927.

Moor, Lucy W. *Girls of Yesterday and To-day: The Romance of the Y.W.C.A.* London: S. W. Partridge, [1911].

Morley, Edith J., ed. *Women Workers in Seven Professions: A Survey of Their Economic Conditions and Prospects*. London: G. Routledge and Sons, 1914.

Morten, Honnor. *From a Nurse's Note-book*. London: Scientific Press, 1899.

Murray, Margaret. *My First Hundred Years.* London: William Kimber, 1963.

Nevinson, Henry Woodd. *More Changes, More Chances.* London: J. Nisbet, 1925.

Nevinson, Margaret Wynne. *Life's Fitful Fever: A Volume of Memories.* London: A. & C. Black, 1926.

Nihill, Henry Daniel. *The Sisters of St. Mary at the Cross: Sisters of the Poor and Their Work.* London: Kegan Paul, 1887.

O'Neill, H. C., and Edith A. Barnett. *Our Nurses and the Work They Have to Do.* London: Ward, Lock, 1888.

Pankhurst, Christabel. *The Great Scourge and How to End It.* London: E. Pankhurst, 1913.

———. *Unshackled: The Story of How We Won the Vote.* London: Hutchinson, 1959.

Pankhurst, E. Sylvia. *The Suffragette Movement.* London: Longmans, Green, 1931.

Pankhurst, Emmeline. *My Own Story.* London: Eveleigh Nash, 1914.

———. *Why We Are Militant.* London: Woman's Press, 1913.

Peck, Winifred. *A Little Learning, or A Victorian Childhood.* London: Faber and Faber, 1952.

[Penny, Mrs. Anne Judith]. *The Afternoon of Unmarried Life.* London: Longman, Brown, Green, Longmans and Roberts, 1858.

Pethick-Lawrence, Emmeline. *The Faith That Is in Us.* London: Woman's Press, [1908?].

———. *My Part in a Changing World.* London: Victor Gollancz, 1938.

Pethick-Lawrence, Lord F. W. *Fate Has Been Kind.* London: Hutchinson, 1942.

[Phillipps, L. F. M.]. *An Old Maid. My Life and What Shall I Do with It?* London: Longman, Green, Longmans and Roberts, 1860.

Potter, Henry C. *Sisterhoods and Deaconesses at Home and Abroad.* New York: E. P. Dutton, 1873.

Pratt, Edwin A. *Pioneer Women in Victoria's Reign.* London: George Newnes, 1897.

Procter, Zoe. *Life and Yesterday.* London: Favil Press, 1960.

Quilter, Harry, ed. *Is Marriage a Failure?* London: Swan Sonnenschein, 1888.

R., L. N. [Ellen Henrietta Ranyard]. *The Missing Link, or Bible-Women in the Homes of the London Poor.* London: James Nisbet, 1859.

Reason, Will, ed. *University and Social Settlements.* London: Methuen, 1898.

Reeves, Maud Pember. *Round about a Pound a Week.* London: Virago, 1979 [1913].

Richardson, Mary R. *Laugh a Defiance.* London: George Weidenfeld and Nicolson, 1953.

Robert Browning Settlement. *Eighteen Years in the Central City Swarm.* London: W. A. Hammond, [1913].

Roberts, Katherine. *Some Pioneers and a Prison.* n.p., 1913.

Robins, Elizabeth. *Ancilla's Share.* London: Hutchinson, 1924.

———. *The Convert.* London: Women's Press, 1980 [1907].

———. *Way Stations.* London: Hodder and Stoughton, 1913.

Scharlieb, Mary. *The Bachelor Woman and Her Problems.* London: Williams and Norgate, 1929.

Scott, R. P., ed. *"What Is Secondary Education?" And Other Short Essays.* London: Rivingtons, 1899.

Sewell, Elizabeth M. *Principles of Education, Drawn from Nature and Revelation, and Applied to Female Education in the Upper Classes.* New York: D. Appleton, 1871 [1865].

Seymer, Lucy Ridgely, comp. *Writings of Florence Nightingale.* New York: Macmillan, 1954.

Sharp, Evelyn. *Unfinished Adventure: Selected Reminiscences from an Englishwoman's Life.* London: John Lane, 1933.

Shipley, Rev. Orby, ed. *The Church and the World: Essays on Questions of the Day in 1867.* London: Longmans, Green, Reader and Dyer, 1867.

Shirreff, Emily. *Intellectual Education and Its Influence on the Character and Happiness of Women.* London: John W. Parker, 1858.

Sidgwick, Mrs. Henry. *Health Statistics of Women Students at Cambridge and Oxford and of Their Sisters.* Cambridge: Cambridge University Press, 1890.

———. *The Place of University Education in the Life of Women.* London: Transactions of the Women's Institute, 1897.

Sinclair, May. *The Tree of Heaven.* London: Cassell, 1917.

Smedley, Constance. *Crusaders: The Reminiscences of Constance Smedley.* London: Duckworth, 1929.

Smith, Emma [pseud.]. *A Cornish Waif's Story.* London: Odhams Press, 1954.

Soulsby, L. H. M. *The Religious Side of Secular Teaching.* London: Longmans, Green, 1907.

———. *Stray Thoughts for Girls.* London: Longmans, Green, 1910.

———. *Stray Thoughts for Mothers and Teachers.* London: Longmans, Green, 1897.

Stanley, Maude. *Clubs for Working Girls.* London: Macmillan, 1890.

Stanton, Theodore, ed. *The Woman Question in Europe.* London: G. P. Putnam's Sons, 1884.

Stephen, Caroline Emelia. *Light Arising: Thoughts on the Central Radiance.* Cambridge: Heffer, 1908.

Stevens, Joan, ed. *Mary Taylor, Friend of Charlotte Brontë: Letters from New Zealand and Elsewhere.* Auckland: Auckland University Press, 1972.

Stocks, Mary D. *My Commonplace Book*. London: Peter Davies, 1970.
Stoney, A. H. *In the Days of Queen Victoria: Memories of a Hospital Nurse*. Bristol: Wright, 1931 [1910].
Strangford, Emily Anne, Viscountess. *Hospital Training for Ladies: An Appeal to the Hospital Boards in England*. London: Harrison and Sons, 1874.
Stronach, Alice. *A Newnham Friendship*. London: Blackie and Son, 1901.
Strong, Mrs. Rebecca. *Practical Ward Work*. Glasgow: Royal Infirmary, 1893.
A Suffragette's Love Letters. London: Chatto and Windus, 1907.
Swanwick, Helena M. *I Have Been Young*. London: Victor Gollancz, 1935.
Swiney, Frances. *The Awakening of Women*. London: G. Redway, 1899.
Taylor, Mary. *The First Duty of Women: A Series of Articles Reprinted from the Victoria Magazine, 1865–1870*. London: Emily Faithfull, 1870.
Thompson, Margaret E., and Mary D. Thompson. *They Couldn't Stop Us! Experiences of Two (Usually Law-Abiding) Women in the Years 1909–1913*. Ipswich: W. E. Harrison, 1957.
Thompson, William. *An Appeal to One-Half the Human Race*. London: Longman, Hurst, Rees, 1825.
Tooley, Sarah A. *The History of Nursing in the British Empire*. London: S. H. Bousfield, 1906.
Twining, Louisa. *Deaconesses for the Church of England*. London: Bell and Daldy, 1860.
———. *Recollections of Life and Work*. London: Edward Arnold, 1893.
———. *Workhouses and Pauperism and Women's Work in the Administration of the Poor Law*. London: Methuen, 1858.
Valentine, Lylie. *Two Sisters and the Cockney Kids*. London: Club Row Press, 1978.
[Warburton, Mother Kate]. *Memories of a Sister of St. Saviour's Priory*. London: A. R. Mowbray, 1903.
———. *Old Soho Days*. London: A. R. Mowbray, 1906.
Webb, Beatrice. *My Apprenticeship*. London: Longmans, Green, 1926.
White, Antonia. *Frost in May*. London: Virago, 1978 [1933].
Williams, Rachel, and Alice Fisher. *Hints for Hospital Nurses*. Edinburgh: MacLachan & Stuart, 1877.
Wright, A. M. *How I Became a Suffragette*. Chesham, Bucks: Page and Thomas, [1960?].
Wright, Sir Almroth E. *The Unexpurgated Case against Woman Suffrage*. London: Constable, 1913.
Yonge, Charlotte. *The Daisy Chain; or, Aspirations*. New York: Garland, 1977 [1856].

Primary Sources: Selected Articles

Anderson, Elizabeth Garrett. "Sex in Mind and Education: A Reply." *Fortnightly Review* 21 (1874):582–94.

Anstruther, Eve. "Ladies' Clubs." *Nineteenth Century* 45 (1899): 598–611.

Arling, Nat. "What Is the Role of the 'New Woman'?" *Westminster Review* 150 (1898):576–87.

Barnett, Samuel A. "The Ways of 'Settlements' and of 'Missions.'" *Nineteenth Century* 42 (1897):975–84.

Bright, Florence. "The True Inwardness of the Woman's Movement." *Fortnightly Review* 87 (1907):733–39.

Brittain, Vera. "The Educational Veil: Women Teachers and Their Disadvantages." *Manchester Guardian*, 7 March 1929.

[Cobbe, Frances Power]. "Excess of Widows over Widowers." *Westminster Review* 131 (1889)501–5.

Cobbe, Frances Power. "'What Shall We Do with Our Old Maids?'" *Fraser's Magazine* 66 (1862):594–610.

Colquhoun, Ethel. "Modern Feminism and Sex-Antagonism." *Quarterly Review* 219 (1913):143–66.

"Convent Boarding Schools for Young Ladies." *Fraser's Magazine* 9 (1874):770–86.

Crask, May. "Girl Life in a Slum." *Economic Review* 18 (1908):184–89.

Eastlake, Elizabeth Rigby. "*Vanity Fair* and *Jane Eyre*." *Quarterly Review* 83 (1848):153–85.

"An Enquiry into the State of Girls' Fashionable Schools." *Fraser's Magazine* 31 (1845):703–12.

Fearon, D. R. "Girls' Grammar Schools." *Contemporary Review* 11 (1869):333–54.

Fitch, J. G. "Women and the Universities." *Contemporary Review* 58 (1890):240–55.

"The Future of Single Women." *Westminster Review* 121 (1884):151–62.

Garrett, Elizabeth. "Volunteer Hospital Nursing." *Macmillan's Magazine* 15 (April 1867):494–99.

Gordon, Alice M. "The After-Careers of University-Educated Women." *Nineteenth Century* 37 (1895):955–60.

Greenwall, Dora. "Our Single Women." *North British Review* 36 (1862): 62–87.

Greg, W. R. "Why Are Women Redundant?" *National Review* 15 (1862): 434–60.

Haddon, Charlotte. "Nursing as a Profession for Ladies." *St. Paul's Magazine* 8 (1871):458–61.

[Hartley, May Laffen]. "Convent Boarding-Schools for Young Ladies." *Fraser's Magazine*, n.s., 9 (1874):770–86.

Hayllar, Florence. "The Superfluity of Women." *Westminster Review* 171 (1909):171–81.
———. "Women's Ideal of Womanhood." *Westminster Review* 171 (1909): 309–13.
Hill, Octavia. "A Few Words to Fresh Workers." *Nineteenth Century* 26 (1889):452–61.
———. "Trained Workers for the Poor." *Nineteenth Century* 33 (1893): 36–43.
Howard, Warrington. "Ladies and Hospital Nursing." *Contemporary Review* 34 (1878–79):490–503.
[Howson, J. S.]. "Deaconesses." *Quarterly Review* 108 (1860):342–87.
Lathbury, Bertha. "Agnosticism and Women." *Nineteenth Century* 7 (1880):619–27.
Low, Frances H. "How Poor Ladies Live." *Nineteenth Century* 41 (1897): 405–17.
———. "How Poor Ladies Live: A Rejoinder and a 'Jubilee' Suggestion." *Nineteenth Century* 42 (1897):161–68.
March-Phillipps, Evelyn. "The Working Lady in London." *Fortnightly Review* 58 (1892):193–203.
Maudsley, Henry. "*Sex in Mind and Education.*" *Fortnightly Review*, 21 (1874):466–83.
Maynard, Constance. "From Early Victorian Schoolroom to University: Some Personal Experiences." *Nineteenth Century* 76 (1914): 1060–73.
Moore, Ada. "The 'Decayed' Gentlewoman: An Appeal to England's Chivalry." *Westminster Review* 162 (1904):450–62.
Moulder, Priscilla E. "Friendship between the Sexes." *Westminster Review* 151 (1899):667–70.
Nightingale, Florence. "Cassandra." Reprinted in Ray Strachey, *The Cause*. London: Virago, 1978 [1852].
"Nurses and Nursing." *Westminster Review* 130 (1888):11–16.
Parker, Gilbert. "The Housing of Educated Working Women." In *Report of the Transactions of the International Council of Women*, pp. 258–73. London: T. Fisher Unwin, 1889.
Pearson, Karl. "Woman and Labour." *Fortnightly Review* 61 (1894): 561–77.
Pollard, Alfred W. "The Salaries of Lady Teachers." *Murray's Magazine* 4 (1888):780–89.
Robinson, F. Mabel. "Our Working Women and Their Earnings." *Fortnightly Review* 48 (1887):50–63.
Shaw, Edith M. "How Poor Ladies Might Live: An Answer from the Workhouse." *Nineteenth Century* 41 (1897):620–27.
Simcox, Edith. "The Capacity of Women." *Nineteenth Century* 22 (1887):391–402.

———. "Ideals of Feminine Usefulness." *Fortnightly Review* 33 (1880): 657–71.
Stutfield, Hugh E. M. "The Psychology of Feminism." *Blackwood's Magazine* 161 (1897):104–17.
Trench, Maria. "Sick-Nurses." *Macmillan's Magazine* 34 (September 1876):422–29.
W., A. S. "Thoughts on Some of the Present Defects in Boarding Schools." *Victoria Magazine* 27 (1876):432–44.
Zimmern, Alice. "Ladies Dwellings." *Contemporary Review* 77 (1900): 96–104.

Secondary Sources: Unpublished

Auchmuty, Rosemary. "Victorian Spinsters." Ph.D. thesis. Australian National University, 1975.
Deacon, Alan. "The Social Position of the Unmarried Woman in the Mid-Victorian period and Its Relation to the Development of Philanthropy." B. A. Honors thesis. University of London. 1967.
"History of St. Hilda's East, the Cheltenham Ladies' College Settlement." Untitled, anonymous manuscript. Tower Hamlets Local History Library.
McIlhiney, David Brown. "A Gentleman in Every Slum: Church of England Missions in East London, 1837–1914." Ph.D. thesis. Princeton University, 1977.
Payne, Harry C. "Edwardian Moderns: Gordon Craig, Jane Ellen Harrison, Roger Fry." Manuscript.
Simpson, Graham. "A Sociological Study of the Church Army." Oxford D. Phil., 1979.
Sutherland, Gillian. "The Social Location of the Movement for Women's Higher Education in England, 1840–1880." Essay presented at the George Eliot Centennial Conference (Rutgers University, 1980).

Secondary Sources: Books

Abel-Smith, Brian. *A History of the Nursing Profession*. London: Heinemann, 1960.
Adburgham, Alison. *Women in Print*. London: George Allen and Unwin, 1972.
Allchin, A. M. *The Silent Rebellion: Anglican Religious Communities, 1845–1900*. London: SCM Press, 1958.
Anson, Peter F., and Allan Walter Campbell. *The Call of the Cloister*. Rev. ed. London: SPCK, 1964.
Auerbach, Nina. *Communities of Women: An Idea in Fiction*. Cambridge: Harvard University Press, 1978.

————. *Woman and the Demon: The Life of a Victorian Myth.* Cambridge: Harvard University Press, 1982.

Baly, Monica E. *Nursing and Social Change.* 2d ed. London: Heinemann, 1980.

Banks, J. A. *Prosperity and Parenthood: A Study of Family Planning among the Victorian Middle Classes.* London: Routledge and Kegan Paul, 1954.

Banks, J. A., and Olive Banks. *Feminism and Family Planning in Victorian England.* Liverpool: Liverpool University Press, 1964.

Banks, Olive. *Faces of Feminism: A Study of Feminism as a Social Movement.* Oxford: Martin Robertson, 1981.

Barnett, Henrietta O. *Canon Barnett: His Life, Work and Friends.* 2 vols. Boston: Houghton Mifflin, 1919.

Battiscombe, Georgina. *Christina Rossetti: A Divided Life.* London: Constable, 1981.

————. *Reluctant Pioneer: A Life of Elizabeth Wordsworth.* London: Constable, 1978.

Berman, Sandra, ed. *Fit Work for Women.* New York: St. Martin's Press, 1979.

Bernstein, Marcelle. *The Nuns.* New York: Bantam, 1979.

Binfield, Clyde. *Belmont's Portias: Victorian Nonconformists and Middle-Class Education for Girls.* Leicester: Friends of Dr. Williams's Library, 1980.

Bowerman, Elsie. *Stands There a School: Memories of Dame Frances Dove, Founder of Wycombe Abbey School.* Brighton: Wycombe Abbey School Seniors, [1966].

Bradbrook, M. C. *"That Infidel Place": A Short History of Girton College, 1869–1969.* London: Chatto and Windus, 1969.

Brittain, Vera. *Lady into Woman.* New York: Macmillan, 1954.

————. *The Women at Oxford: A Fragment of History.* London: George G. Harrap, 1960.

Bruce, Maurice. *The Coming of the Welfare State.* 2d ed. London: B. T. Batsford, 1965.

Bryant, Margaret. *The Unexpected Revolution: A Study in the History of Education of Women and Girls in the Nineteenth Century.* London: University of London Institute of Education, 1979.

Burstyn, Joan N. *Victorian Education and the Ideal of Womanhood.* London: Croom Helm, 1980.

Burton, Hester. *Barbara Bodichon, 1827–1891.* London: John Murray, 1949.

Byrne, Muriel St. Clare, and Catherine Hope Mansfield. *Somerville College, 1879–1921.* Oxford: Oxford University Press, 1922.

Cadogan, Mary, and Patricia Craig. *You're a Brick, Angela!* London: Victor Gollancz, 1976.

Cameron, H. C. *Mr. Guy's Hospital, 1726–1948.* London: Longmans, Green, 1954.

Campbell-Jones, Suzanne. *In Habit: An Anthropological Study of Working Nuns.* London: Faber and Faber, 1979.

Carus-Wilson, Eleanora, ed. *Westfield College, University of London, 1882–1932.* London: Favil Press, 1932.

Clough, Blanche Athena. *A Memoir of Anne Jemima Clough.* New ed. London: Edward Arnold, 1903.

[Community of St. John Baptist]. *The Founders of Clewer.* London: A. R. Mowbray, 1952.

Cook, Sir Edward. *The Life of Florence Nightingale.* 2 vols. London: Macmillan, 1913.

Cott, Nancy F. *The Bonds of Womanhood: "Woman's Sphere" in New England, 1780–1835.* New Haven: Yale University Press, 1977.

Crow, Duncan. *The Victorian Woman.* London: Allen and Unwin, 1971.

Cunningham, Gail. *The New Woman and the Victorian Novel.* London: Macmillan, 1978.

Davies, Celia, ed. *Rewriting Nursing History.* London: Croom Helm, 1980.

Davis, Rachel K. *Four Miss Pinkertons.* London: Williams and Norgate, 1936.

Delamont, Sara, and Lorna Duffin, eds. *The Nineteenth-Century Woman: Her Cultural and Physical World.* London: Croom Helm, 1978.

Delp, W. E. *Royal Holloway College, 1908–1914.* Egham: Royal Holloway, 1969.

Deneke, Helena. *Grace Hadow.* London: Oxford University Press, 1946.

Dobbie, B. M. Willmott. *A Nest of Suffragettes in Somerset.* Bath: Batheaston Society, 1979.

Douglas, Mary Alice, and C. R. Ash, eds. *The Godolphin School, 1726–1926.* London: Longmans, Green, 1928.

Dunbar, Janet. *The Early Victorian Woman.* London: Harrap, 1953.

Dyhouse, Carol. *Girls Growing up in Late Victorian and Edwardian England.* London: Routledge and Kegan Paul, 1981.

Ellsworth, Edward W. *Liberators of the Female Mind: The Shirreff Sisters, Educational Reform and the Women's Movement.* Westport, Conn.: Greenwood Press, 1979.

Evans, Richard J. *The Feminists: Women's Emancipation Movements in Europe, America, and Australasia, 1840–1920.* London: Croom Helm, 1977.

Faderman, Lillian. *Surpassing the Love of Men: Romantic Friendship and Love between Women from the Renaissance to the Present.* New York: William Morrow, 1981.

Farnell, Vera. *A Somervillian Looks Back*. Oxford: Oxford University Press, 1948.

First, Ruth, and Ann Scott. *Olive Schreiner: A Biography*. London: Andre Deutsch, 1980.

Firth, C. B. *Constance Louisa Maynard: Mistress of Westfield College*. London: George Allen and Unwin, 1949.

Fletcher, Sheila. *Feminists and Bureaucrats: A Study in the Development of Girls' Education in the Nineteenth Century*. Cambridge: Cambridge University Press, 1980.

Freeman, Gillian. *The Schoolgirl Ethic: The Life and Works of Angela Brazil*. London: Allen Lane, 1976.

Fulford, Peter. *Votes for Women*. London: Faber and Faber, 1957.

Gardner, Alice. *A Short History of Newnham College Cambridge*. Cambridge: Bowes and Bowes, 1921.

Gathorne-Hardy, Jonathan. *The Public School Phenomenon, 597-1977*. London: Hodder and Stoughton, 1977.

Glendinning, Victoria. *A Suppressed Cry: Life and Death of a Quaker Daughter*. London: Routledge and Kegan Paul, 1969.

Gorham, Deborah. *The Victorian Girl and the Feminine Ideal*. Bloomington: Indiana University Press, 1982.

Grant, Julia M., Katherine H. McCutcheon, and Ethel F. Sanders. *St. Leonards School, 1877–1927*. London: Oxford University Press, 1927.

Graves, Charles. *The Story of St. Thomas's, 1106–1947*. London: St. Thomas' Hospital, 1947.

Greene, Graham, ed. *The Old School*. London: Jonathan Cape, 1934.

Grier, Lynda. *The Life of Winifred Mercier*. London: Oxford University Press, 1937.

Grierson, Janet. *The Deaconess*. London: Church Information Office, 1981.

Haight, Gordon S. *George Eliot: A Biography*. Oxford: Oxford University Press, 1968.

Hamilton, Mary. *Newnham: An Informal Biography*. London: Faber and Faber, 1936.

Hammerton, A. James. *Emigrant Gentlewomen: Genteel Poverty and Female Emigration, 1830–1919*. London: Croom Helm, 1979.

Harrison, Brian. *Separate Spheres: The Opposition to Women's Suffrage in Britain*. London: Croom Helm, 1978.

Harvie, Christopher. *The Lights of Liberalism: University Liberals and the Challenge of Democracy, 1860–86*. London: Allen Lane, 1976.

Hayden, Dolores. *The Grand Domestic Revolution: A History of Feminist Designs for American Homes, Neighborhoods, and Cities*. Cambridge: MIT Press, 1981.

Selected Bibliography

Hector, Winifred. *The Work of Mrs. Bedford Fenwick and the Rise of Professional Nursing.* London: Royal College of Nursing and National Council of Nurses of the United Kingdom, 1973.

Heeney, Brian. *Mission to the Middle Classes: The Woodward Schools, 1848–1891.* London: SPCK, 1969.

Hilda Cashmore (1876–1943). Gloucester: J. Bellows, [1944].

Hill, Michael. *The Religious Order: A Study of Virtuoso Religion and Its Legitimation in the Nineteenth-Century Church of England.* London: Heinemann, 1973.

Holcombe, Lee. *Victorian Ladies at Work: Middle-Class Working Women in England and Wales, 1850–1914.* Hamden, Conn.: Archon Press, 1973.

———. *Wives and Property: Reform of the Married Women's Property Law in Nineteenth-Century England.* Toronto: University of Toronto Press, 1982.

Holledge, Julie. *Innocent Flowers: Women in the Edwardian Theatre.* London: Virago, 1981.

Holtby, Winifred. *Women, and a Changing Civilisation.* London: John Lane, 1934.

Honey, J. R. de S. *Tom Brown's Universe: The Development of the English Public School in the Nineteenth Century.* New York: Quadrangle Books, 1977.

Hughes, Dorothea Price. *The Life of Hugh Price Hughes.* 4th ed. London: Hodder and Stoughton, 1905.

Hume, Leslie Parker. *The National Union of Women's Suffrage Societies, 1897–1914.* New York: Garland, 1982.

James, Mary E. *Alice Ottley: First Head-Mistress of the Worcester High School for Girls, 1883–1912.* London: Longmans, 1914.

Jones, Peter d'A. *The Christian Socialist Revival, 1877–1914: Religion, Class and Social Conscience in Late Victorian England.* Princeton: Princeton University Press, 1968.

Kamm, Josephine. *Hope Deferred: Girls' Education in English History.* London: Methuen, 1965.

———. *How Different from Us: A Biography of Miss Buss and Miss Beale.* London: Bodley Head, 1958.

———. *Rapiers and Battleaxes.* London: Allen and Unwin, 1966.

Kimmins, Grace T. *Heritage Craft Schools and Hospitals, Chailey, 1903–1948.* London: Baynard Press, 1948.

Liddon, Henry Perry. *The Life of Edward Bouverie Pusey.* 3 vols. London: Longmans, Green, 1894.

Linklater, Andro. *An Unhusbanded Life: Charlotte Despard, Suffragette, Socialist, and Sinn Feiner.* London: Hutchinson, 1980.

Lloyd, Edyth M., ed. *Anna Lloyd (1837–1925): A Memoir.* London: Cayme Press, 1928.

Lowndes, G. A. N. *The Silent Social Revolution.* 2d ed. London: Oxford University Press, 1969.

McEwan, Margaret, with assistance from D. M. Landon. *Eva C. Lückes (Matron), the London Hospital, 1880–1919.* London: London Hospital League for Nurses, 1958.

McMillan, Margaret. *The Life of Rachel McMillan.* London: J. M. Dent, 1927.

McWilliams-Tullberg, Rita. *Women at Cambridge: A Men's University—Though of a Mixed Type.* London: Victor Gollancz, 1975.

Malmgreen, Gail. *Neither Bread nor Roses: Utopian Feminists and the English Working Class, 1800–1850.* Brighton: John Noyce, 1978

Mansbridge, Albert. *Margaret McMillan, Prophet and Pioneer: Her Life and Work.* London: J. M. Dent, 1932.

Manton, Jo. *Elizabeth Garrett Anderson.* London: Methuen, 1965.

———. *Mary Carpenter and the Children of the Streets.* London: Heinemann, 1976.

Martindale, Hilda. *Women Servants of the State: A History of Women in the Civil Service.* London: Allen and Unwin, 1938.

Maurice, C. Edmund. *Life of Octavia Hill as Told in Her Letters.* London: Macmillan, 1913.

Middleton, Lucy, ed. *Women in the Labour Movement.* London: Croom Helm, 1977.

Mowat, Charles Loch. *The Charity Organisation Society, 1869–1913: Its Ideas and Work.* London: Methuen, 1961.

Murray, Janet, ed. *Strong-Minded Women and Other Lost Voices from Nineteenth-Century England.* New York: Pantheon, 1982.

Newsome, David. *Godliness and Good Learning: Four Studies on a Victorian Ideal.* London: John Murray, 1961.

Nutting, M. Adelaide, and Lavinia L. Dock. *A History of Nursing: The Evolution of Nursing Systems from the Earliest Times to the Foundation of the First English and American Training Schools for Nurses.* 4 vols. New York: G. P. Putnam's Sons, 1907–12.

Pfautz, Harold W., ed. and intro. *Charles Booth on the City: Physical Pattern and Social Structure.* Chicago: University of Chicago Press, 1967.

Phillips, Ann, ed. *A Newnham Anthology.* Cambridge: Cambridge University Press, 1979.

Picht, Werner. *Toynbee Hall and the English Settlement Movement.* Rev. ed., trans. Lilian A. Cowell. London: G. Bell, 1914.

Pimlott, J. A. R. *Toynbee Hall: Fifty Years of Social Progress (1884–1934).* London: J. M. Dent, 1935.

Price, Mary, and Nonita Glenday. *Reluctant Revolutionaries: A Century of Headmistresses, 1874–1974.* London: Pitman, 1974.

Prochaska, Frank K. *Women and Philanthropy in Nineteenth-Century England.* Oxford: Clarendon Press, 1980.

Raeburn, Antonia. *The Militant Suffragettes.* London: Michael Joseph, 1973.

Raikes, Elizabeth. *Dorothea Beale of Cheltenham.* New ed. London: Constable, 1910.

Reader, W. J. *Professional Men: The Rise of the Professional Classes in Nineteenth-Century England.* New York: Basic Books, 1966.

Rice, Anna .V. *A History of the World's Young Women's Christian Association.* New York: Woman's Press, 1947.

Ridler, Anne. *Olive Willis and Downe House: An Adventure in Education.* London: John Murray, 1967.

Rogers, Annie Mary A. Henley. *Degrees by Degrees: The Story of the Admission of Oxford Women Students to Membership of the University.* London: Oxford University Press, 1938.

Rosen, Andrew. *Rise up Women! The Militant Campaign of the Women's Social and Political Union, 1903–1914.* London: Routledge and Kegan Paul, 1974.

Rothblatt, Sheldon. *The Revolution of the Dons: Cambridge and Society in Victorian England.* London: Faber and Faber, 1968.

Rover, Constance. *Women's Suffrage and Party Politics in Britain, 1866–1914.* London: Routledge and Kegan Paul, 1967.

Saunders, H. A. St. George. *The Middlesex Hospital, 1745–1948.* London: Max Parrish, 1949.

Sayers, Dorothy. *Gaudy Night.* London: Victor Gollancz, 1935.

[Sisters of Bethany]. *The Society of the Sisters of Bethany, 1866–1966.* Bournemouth, 1966.

[Sisters of the Church]. *A Valiant Victorian: The Life and Times of Mother Emily Ayckbowm (1836–1900).* London: A. R. Mowbray, 1964.

Sklar, Kathryn Kish. *Catharine Beecher: A Study in American Domesticity.* New Haven: Yale University Press, 1973.

Smith, F. B. *Florence Nightingale: Reputation and Power.* London: Croom Helm, 1982.

Sondheimer, Janet. *Castle Adament in Hampstead.* London: Westfield College, 1983.

Steadman, Florence Cecily. *In the Days of Miss Beale.* London: E. J. Burrow, 1931.

Stephen, Barbara. *Emily Davies and Girton College.* London: Constable, 1927.

———. *Girton College, 1869–1932.* Cambridge: Cambridge University Press, 1932.

Stewart, Jessie. *Jane Ellen Harrison: A Portrait from Letters.* London: Merlin Press, 1959.

Stocks, Mary D. *Eleanor Rathbone: A Biography.* London: Victor Gollancz, 1949.

———. *Fifty Years in Every Street: The Story of the Manchester University Settlement.* 2d ed. Manchester: Manchester University Press, 1956.

Stoddart, Anna. *Life and Letters of Hannah E. Pipe.* Edinburgh: William Blackwell, 1908.

The Story of the Mary Datchelor School, 1877–1957. London: Hodder and Stoughton, 1957.

Strachey, Ray. *The Cause: A Short History of the Women's Movement in Great Britain.* London: Virago, 1978 [1928].

———. *Millicent Garrett Fawcett.* London: John Murray, 1931.

Taylor, Barbara. *Eve and the New Jerusalem: Socialism and Feminism in the Nineteenth Century.* London: Virago, 1983.

Thomas, Clara. *Love and Work Enough: The Life of Anna Jameson.* Toronto: University of Toronto Press, 1967.

Tilly, Louise A., and Joan W. Scott. *Women, Work and Family.* New York: Holt, Rinehart and Winston, 1978.

Towle, Eleanor. *John Mason Neale.* London: Longmans, Green, 1906.

Trevelyan, Janet Penrose. *The Life of Mrs. Humphry Ward.* London: Constable, 1923.

Tropp, Asher. *The Schoolteachers: The Growth of the Teaching Profession in England and Wales from 1800 to the Present Day.* London: Heinemann, 1957.

Trudgill, Eric. *Madonnas and Magdalens: The Origins and Development of Victorian Sexual Attitudes.* London: Heinemann, 1976.

Tuke, Margaret J. *A History of Bedford College for Women, 1849–1937.* London: Oxford University Press, 1939.

Turner, Barry. *Equality for Some: The Story of Girls' Education.* London: Ward, Lock, 1974.

Tylecote, Mabel. *The Education of Women at Manchester University, 1883–1933.* Manchester: Manchester University Press, 1941.

Unwin, Frances M., and John Telford. *Mark Guy Pearse: Preacher, Author, Artist.* London: Epworth Press, 1930.

Vicinus, Martha, ed. *Suffer and Be Still: Women in the Victorian Age.* Bloomington: Indiana University Press, 1972.

———. *A Widening Sphere: Changing Roles of Victorian Women.* Bloomington: Indiana University Press, 1977.

de Villiers, Anne, Lady, Hazel Fox, and Pauline Adams. *Somerville College, Oxford, 1879–1979: A Century in Pictures.* Oxford: Somerville College, 1978.

Walkowitz, Judith R. *Prostitution and Victorian Society: Women, Class and the State.* Cambridge: Cambridge University Press, 1980.

Walton, Ronald G. *Women in Social Work*. London: Routledge and Kegan Paul, 1975.

Ward, Mrs. Humphry. *A Writer's Recollections*. 2 vols. New York: Harper, 1918.

Webb, Catherine. *The Woman with the Basket: The History of the Women's Co-operative Guild, 1883–1927*. Manchester: Co-operative Wholesale Society, 1927.

Weeks, Jeffrey. *Coming Out: Homosexual Politics in Britain from the Nineteenth Century to the Present*. London: Quartet Books, 1977.

White, Cynthia Leslie. *Women's Magazines, 1693–1968*. London: Joseph, 1970.

Widdowson, Frances. *Going up into the Next Class: Women and Elementary Teacher Training, 1840–1914*. London: Women's Research and Resources Centre Publications, 1980.

Williams, Thomas Jay. *Priscilla Lydia Sellon, the Restorer after Three Centuries of the Religious Life in the English Church*. London: SPCK, 1950.

Williams, Thomas Jay, and Allan Walter Campbell. *The Park Village Sisterhood*. London: SPCK, 1965.

Woodham-Smith, Cecil. *Florence Nightingale, 1820–1910*. London: Constable, 1950.

Worsley, T. C. *Flannelled Fool: A Slice of Life in the Thirties*. London: Alan Ross, 1967.

Zimmern, Alice. *The Renaissance of Girls' Education in England: A Record of Fifty Years' Progress*. London: A. D. Innes, 1898.

deZouche, Dorothy Eva. *Roedean School, 1885–1955*. Brighton: privately printed, 1955.

Secondary Sources: Articles

Abel, Emily K. "Middle-Class Culture for the Urban Poor: The Educational Thought of Samuel Barnett." *Social Service Review* 52 (1978):596–620.

———. "Toynbee Hall, 1884–1914." *Social Service Review*. 53 (1979): 606–32.

Ackerman, Robert. "Jane Ellen Harrison: The Early Work." *Greek, Roman and Byzantine Studies* 13 (1972):209–30.

———. "Some Letters of the Cambridge Ritualists." *Greek, Roman and Byzantine Studies* 12 (1971):113–36.

Antler, Joyce. "'After College, What?' New Graduates and the Family Claim." *American Quarterly* 32 (1980):409–34.

Ashley, Percy. "University Settlements in Great Britain." *Harvard Theological Review* 4 (1911):175–203.

Burstyn, Joan N. "Education and Sex: The Medical Case against Higher Education for Women in England, 1870–1900." *Proceedings of the American Philosophical Society* 117 (April 1973):79–89.

Casteras, Susan P. "Virgin Vows: The Early Victorian Artists' Portrayal of Nuns and Novices." *Victorian Studies* 24 (Winter 1981):157–84.

Chambers-Schiller, Lee. "The Single Woman: Family and Vocation among Nineteenth-Century Reformers." In *Woman's Being, Woman's Place: Female Identity and Vocation in American History*, ed. Mary Kelley, pp. 334–50. Boston: G. K. Hall, 1979.

Conway, Jill. "Women Reformers and American Culture, 1870–1930." *Journal of Social History* 5 (1971–72):164–77.

Cook, Blanche Wiesen. "Female Support Networks and Political Activism: Lillian Wald, Crystal Eastman, Emma Goldman." *Chrysalis*, no. 3 (1977):43–71.

Davies, Celia. "Making Sense of the Census in Britain and the USA: The Changing Occupational Classification and the Position of Nurses." *Sociological Review*, n.s., 28, 3 (August 1980):581–609.

Davin, Anna. "Imperialism and Motherhood." *History Workshop* 5 (Spring 1978):9–65.

Deacon, Alan, and Michael Hill. "The Problem of 'Surplus Women' in the Nineteenth Century: Secular and Religious Alternatives." *Sociological Year Book of Religion in Britain* 5 (1972):87–102.

Dyhouse, Carol. "Social Darwinistic Ideas and the Development of Women's Education in England, 1880–1920." *History of Education* 5 (1976):41–58.

———. "Towards a 'Feminine' Curriculum for English Schoolgirls: The Demands of Ideology, 1870–1963." *Women's Studies International Quarterly* 1 (1978):297–311.

Fido, Judith. "The Charity Organisation Society and Social Casework in London 1869–1900." In *Social Control in Nineteenth-Century Britain*, ed. A. P. Donajgrodzki, pp. 207–30. London: Croom Helm, 1977.

Freedman, Estelle. "Separatism as Strategy: Female Institution Building, 1870–1930." *Feminist Studies* 5 (1979):512–29.

Gamarnikow, Eva. "Sexual Division of Labour: The Case of Nursing." In *Feminism and Materialism: Women and Modes of Production*, ed. Annette Kuhn and AnnMarie Wolpe, pp. 96–123. London: Routledge and Kegan Paul, 1978.

Gilbert, Sandra. "Soldier's Heart: Literary Men, Literary Women, and the Great War." *Signs* 8 (1983):422–50.

Glass, D. V. "Marriage Frequency and Economic Fluctuations in England and Wales, 1851 to 1934." In *Political Arithmetic: A Symposium of Population Studies*, ed. Lancelot Hogben, pp. 251–82. London: Allen and Unwin, 1938.

Gorsky, Susan R. "Old Maids and New Women: Alternatives to Marriage in Englishwomen's Novels, 1847–1915." *Journal of Popular Culture* 7 (1973):68–85.

Harper, Paula Hays. "Votes for Women? A Graphic Episode in the Battle of the Sexes." In *Art and Architecture in the Service of Politics*, ed. Henry A. Millon and Linda Nochlin, pp. 150–61. Cambridge: MIT Press, 1978.

Harrison, Brian. "The Act of Militancy: Violence and the Suffragettes, 1904–1914." In *Peaceable Kingdom: Stability and Change in Modern Britain*, pp. 26–81. Oxford: Clarendon Press, 1982.

———. "Women's Health and the Women's Movement in Britain: 1840–1940". In *Biology, Medicine and Society*, ed. Charles Webster, pp. 15–71. Cambridge: Cambridge University Press, 1981.

Hartman, Mary S. "Child-Abuse and Self-Abuse: Two Victorian Cases." *History of Childhood Quarterly* 2 (Fall 1974):221–48.

Heeney, Brian. "The Beginnings of Church Feminism: Women and the Councils of the Church of England, 1897–1919." *Journal of Ecclesiastical History* 33 (1982):86–109.

———. "Women's Struggle for Professional Work and Status in the Church of England, 1900–1930." *Historical Journal* 26 (1983):329–47.

Joanna, Sister. "The Deaconess Community of St. Andrew." *Journal of Ecclesiastical History* 12 (1961):215–30.

Lewis, Jane. "Beyond Suffrage: English Feminism in the 1920s." *Maryland Historian* 6 (1975):1–17.

Moore, Michael J. "Social Work and Social Welfare: The Organization of Philanthropic Resources in Britain, 1900–1914." *Journal of British Studies* 16 (1977):85–104.

Okely, Judith. "Privileged, Schooled and Finished: Boarding School Education for Girls." In *Defining Females: The Nature of Women in Society*, ed. Shirley Ardener, pp. 109–39. New York: John Wiley, 1978.

Pedersen, Joyce Senders. "The Reform of Women's Secondary and Higher Education: Institutional Change and Social Values in Mid and Late Victorian England." *History of Education Quarterly* 19 (1979):61–91.

———. "Schoolmistresses and Headmistresses: Elites and Education in Nineteenth-Century England." *Journal of British Studies* 15 (1975):135–62.

———. "Some Victorian Headmistresses: A Conservative Tradition of Social Reform." *Victorian Studies* 24 (Summer 1981):463–88.

Pope, Barbara Corrado. "Angels in the Devil's Workshop: Leisured and Charitable Women in Nineteenth-Century England and France." In *Becoming Visible: Women in European History*, ed. Renate Bridenthal and Claudia Koonz, pp. 296–324. (Boston: Houghton-Mifflin, 1977).

Prochaska, F. K. "Women in English Philanthropy, 1790–1830." *International Review of Social History* 19 (1974):426–45.

Rosenberg, Charles E. "Florence Nightingale on Contagion: The Hospital as Moral Universe." In *Healing and History*, ed. Charles E. Rosenberg, pp. 116–136. New York: Dawson, 1979.

Rousmaniere, John P. "Cultural Hybrid in the Slums: The College Woman and the Settlement House, 1889–1894." *American Quarterly* 22 (1970):45–66.

Rupp, Leila J. "'Imagine My Surprise': Women's Relationships in Historical Perspective." *Frontiers* 5, no. 3 (1980):61–70.

Sahli, Nancy. "Smashing: Women's Relationships before the Fall." *Chrysalis*, no. 8 (1979):17–27.

Simmons, Christina. "Companionate Marriage and the Lesbian Threat." *Frontiers* 4, no. 3 (1979):54–59.

Smith-Rosenberg, Carroll. "The Female World of Love and Ritual: Relations between Women in Nineteenth-Century America." *Signs* 1 (1975):1–29.

Summers, Anne. "Pride and Prejudice: Ladies and Nurses in the Crimean War." *History Workshop Journal* 16 (Autumn 1983):33–56.

Vicinus, Martha. "Distance and Desire: English Boarding-School Friendships." *Signs* 9 (1984): 600–622.

———. "Introduction." In George Egerton, *Keynotes* and *Discords*. London: Virago, 1983.

———. "'One Life to Stand beside Me': Emotional Conflicts of First-Generation College Women in England." *Feminist Studies* 8 (Fall 1982):603–28.

Wohl, A. S. "Octavia Hill and the Homes of the London Poor." *Journal of British Studies* 10 (1971):105–31.

Index

Abel, Emily K., 216
Actresses' Franchise League, 249
Addams, Jane, 20, 215, 279, 289
Afternoon of Unmarried Life, The, 13
Aging, 40
Agnes Grahame, Deaconess, 74–75
Agnosticism, 42, 82, 157
Alexandra College (Dublin), 177
Amazons, 31
Anderson, Elizabeth Garrett, 33, 111
Anglican sisterhoods, 42, 94, 128; history of, 46–90; nursing by, 11, 46, 58, 77, 88–89; teaching by, 46, 58, 81, 181, 186
Apple of Discord, The (play), 144
Arncliffe-Sennett, Maud, 278
Arnold, Clare, 173, 200
Arson, by suffragettes, 253–54, 261, 279
Ashby, Lucy, 117
Asquith, H. H., 254, 267
Association for the Education of Women (AEW), 126, 132
Austen, Jane, 37
Ayckbowm, Emily, 72–74, 82–83, 134

Baly, Monica, 115
Barlow, Amy, 176, 177
Barnett, Canon Samuel, 214–18, 241
Barnett, Mrs. Samuel, 214–16, 221
Beale, Dorothea, 134, 200, 224,

287; and Cheltenham Ladies' College, 167–74, 180, 184–86; teachers college of, 172
Bedford College, 123, 127, 221, 222, 223
Benson, Archbishop, 73
Benson, Theodora, 190
Bermondsey Settlement, 230, 235
Bernard, A. F., 134
Bible women, 48
Billington-Greig, Teresa, 258
Birmingham Women's Settlement, 243
Black Friday, 253, 265
Blathwayt, Mary, 259, 264–65
Boarding schools, 34–35, 38, 286; history of reformed, 163–210
Bodichon, Barbara Leigh Smith, 7, 24, 146
Booth, Charles, 58, 75, 242–43
Borland, J. K., 204–6
Boucherett, Jessie, 24
Bracebridge, Selina, 35
Brethren of the Common Table, 245
Bristol settlement, 230
Brittain, Vera, 137–38, 287
Brönte, Charlotte, 35
Brönte sisters, 23
Browning Settlement, 231, 234
Bruce, Marion, 224
Burdett, Henry, 118
Burstall, Sara, 150, 175, 189, 209
Burt, Miss, 94–95, 98, 101
Buss, Frances Mary, 140, 168
Bussy, Dorothy Strachey: her *Olivia*, 191–92, 198–99